DATE DUE	RETURNED

STUDIES IN AMERICAN POPULAR HISTORY AND CULTURE

Edited by
Jerome Nadelhaft
University of Maine

A ROUTLEDGE SERIES

Studies in American Popular History and Culture

Jerome Nadelhaft, *General Editor*

Labor and Laborers of the Loom

Mechanization and Handloom Weavers, 1780–1840

Gail Fowler Mohanty

Routledge
New York & London

Portions of this book have previously been published in:
Gail Fowler Mohanty, "Outwork and Outwork Weavers in Rural Rhode Island 1810–1821." *American Studies* 30 (1989): 41–68. (Reprinted with permission of *American Studies*)
Gail Fowler Mohanty, "Experimentation in Textile Technology." *Technology and Culture* 29 (1989): 1–30. Copyright Society for the History of Technology (Reprinted with permission of Johns Hopkins University Press)
Gail Fowler Mohanty, "All Other Inventions were Thrown into the Shade: The Power Loom in Rhode Island 1810–1830." *Working in the Blackstone River Valley: Exploring the Heritage of Industrialization.* Douglas Reynolds and Marjory Myers, eds. Blackstone River Valley National Heritage Corridor Commission in conjunction with the University of Rhode Island's Labor Research Center, 1990: 69–89. (Reprinted with permission of the Rhode Island Labor History Society)
Gail Fowler Mohanty, "Putting Up with Putting-Out: Power-Loom Diffusion and Outwork for Rhode Island Mills, 1821–1829." *Journal of the History of the Early American Republic* 9 (1989): 191–216. (Reprinted with permission of University of Pennsylvania Press)

Routledge
Taylor & Francis Group
270 Madison Avenue
New York, NY 10016

Routledge
Taylor & Francis Group
2 Park Square
Milton Park, Abingdon
Oxon OX14 4RN

© 2006 by Taylor & Francis Group, LLC
Routledge is an imprint of Taylor & Francis Group, an Informa business

Printed in the United States of America on acid-free paper
10 9 8 7 6 5 4 3 2 1

International Standard Book Number-10: 0-415-97902-1 (Hardcover)
International Standard Book Number-13: 978-0-415-97902-3 (Hardcover)

Library of Congress Cataloging-in-Publication Data

Mohanty, Gail Fowler.
    Labor and laborers of the loom : mechanization and handloom weavers, 1780-1840 / Gail Fowler Mohanty.
        p. cm. -- (Studies in American popular history and culture)
    Includes bibliographical references and index.
    ISBN 0-415-97902-1
    1. Handloom industry--Rhode Island--History. 2. Weavers--Rhode Island--History. 3. Industrialization--Rhode Island--History. I. Title. II. Series: American popular history and culture (Routledge (Firm)

HD9857.R46M64 2006
331.7′6770282420974509034--dc22   2006008528

Visit the Taylor & Francis Web site at
http://www.taylorandfrancis.com

and the Routledge Web site at
http://www.routledge-ny.com

To Dad,
for tramping through the cemeteries and old mill sites with me,
and Udayan.

Table of Contents

Introduction

The following narrative explores the effects of changing textile technology on handloom weavers and weaving. The discussion centers primarily on weavers and weaving in Rhode Island, and in particular the experiences of Rhode Island's handloom artisans but looks at Massachusetts, Connecticut and New Hampshire outworkers weaving for Rhode Island firms. The New England and Middle Atlantic states experienced the great industrial transformation wrought by textile manufacturing during the late 18th and early 19th centuries. Although the industries developed in different ways, the rise and decline of handloom weaving occurred universally. Handloom weavers in all the industrializing textile regions shared the experiences of artisan and outworker.

The title of this work indicates that the study discusses the period between 1780 and 1840, but I found that the economic, social and technological contexts throughout the 17th, 18th and 19th centuries played vital roles in understanding the historical era. Historical continuity could not otherwise be established without grasping the significance of handloom weaving or domestic production prior to the introduction of waterpowered spinning. The first chapter looks at Rhode Island's population, geography and economy during the waning years of the 18th century. By skewing the viewpoint toward textile manufacture and importation from the very outset, and the information revealed by looking at what came before 1780 proved extremely enlightening and an important component, which put weaving in perspective. The inclusion of the segments on woolen manufacture seeks to demonstrate that outwork continued in the state beyond the introduction of the cotton power loom but also to show that the development of the industry and the consequent rise and decline of outwork weaving mirrored that of cotton manufactures.

The volume develops several interdependent themes important to the understanding of technological change and industrialization. While scholarship has touched these themes, their application to extra-factory, and in most cases extra-artisanal workers, makes the study different. The study centers on handloom weavers including both commercial independent craftsmen fabricating a wide variety of cloth for upper and middle class populations and outwork weavers producing simple utilitarian goods for spinning mills. The rapid and wide ranging increase of the outwork weaving population in direct response to the introduction of waterpowered spinning in about 1790 is significant. An investigation of the population of handloom weavers determined what factors contributed to their participation in outwork, what kind of training they received that enabled them to undertake factory outwork, or what led some craftsmen to resist the change and continue working in independent workshop enterprises. These factors point to reasons why the outwork weaving population mobilized quickly. The rapid increase in demand for weavers of simply constructed fabrics is examined from the viewpoints of mechanics, technological limitations, characteristics of weaving, skills, income and cost.[1] When originally embarking on this research, the vocal British handloom weavers described in the works of Duncan Bythell and Norman Murray were striking. As a result, the question of displacement loomed large, and the silence of American handloom weavers in the wake of increased mechanization was deafening. As my understanding increased, the questions changed to center not on displacement but on survival. What steps if any did hand weavers take to avoid the plight of British handloom weavers? How did American handloom weavers survive in an ever-decreasing market for hand-woven goods? The absence of a guild system in America is not the only factor delineating differences between American and English hand weavers and weaving. When confronted by industrialization, commercial handloom weavers reacted, as had British handloom weavers despite the absence of a guild system. This theme is both significant and closely tied to technological change. The contrasts between independent commercial artisans and outwork weavers are striking. Painful displacement occurred among artisans devoting their time to workshop weaving in independent enterprises. Outwork weavers adapted readily to changing markets and took on different kinds of weaving or shifted to more lucrative forms of outwork.[2]

Technological change and innovations to machinery relate to the types of fabrics produced and to the use of hand as opposed to mechanized fabric production. Preliminary findings encouraged an analysis of how specific technological improvements related to the work available to hand weavers and how mechanical innovations eliminated the demand for certain hand-woven fabrics while the call for others remained constant or increased. Though the design and development of spinning and weaving devices are stressed, the emphasis did not result in technological determinism because the roles of economic conditions, management organization, size of firms, political implications and social factors are also examined for their contributions to the impact of technological change.

Technological descriptions emphasize the work of Rhode Island mechanics and experimentation in machine shops in southeastern Massachusetts and eastern Connecticut. Inventors who developed machinery incorporated into Rhode Island mills, but worked outside the state received attention. The roles of economics and politics are also integrated into the study because of their impact on the industry and therefore on the workforce employed by the textile firms. Textile manufacture was and continues to be a volatile industry. Economic depressions of both industrial and national scopes affected the market for handloom weavers and the introduction of new technologies. Although technological developments continued despite economic conditions, the adoption of new technologies was inhibited or promoted by profit margins, available capital, and success of the firm and the significance of the innovation. Political influences on the textile industry relate to those that resulted in the use of bounties or tariffs to protect specific manufactures. These factors are incorporated into the study as they relate to the rate of technological change, the ability of firms to adopt mechanical or organizational improvements, how they effect the use of outwork weavers and in turn what impact it has on commercial independent enterprises.

The work was born out of research supported in part by a William F. Sullivan Fellowship from the American Textile History Museum. The passage of time and subsequent grant awards has led to a reevaluation of the material and expansion of scope, a strengthening of arguments and a maturation of thought. An Essex Institute Research Fellowship enabled me to initiate research on commercial handloom weavers and weaving prior to industrialization. This study in particular guided the expansion of scope to 17th and 18th century pre-industrial handloom weaving. An individual award from the National Science Foundation enabled me to devote myself to this work entirely for three to four month periods at a time, to finish statistical study, to pursue additional avenues of research, to write the text and to revise according to reader's suggestions without interruption. The award has been a great treasure.[3]

As with any long-term project like this, it was neither researched nor written in a vacuum. Over the course of the past years, I have encountered kindred spirits, discussed the work with many and benefited greatly from talking, and thinking about their comments and their review of what I have written. As they told me then (and I did not believe them), this work is only distantly related to its original form but their suggestions and comments are indelibly reflected in this work. Anthony F.C. Wallace, Judith Mc Gaw and Robert Schyler all saw this study in its earliest incarnation. Subsequently the work has benefited from discussions with Thomas Dublin, James Conrad, Gary Kulik, Adrienne Hood, Merritt Roe Smith, Beverly Lemire, Thierry Ruddel, Kris Inwood, Michael Folsom, Laurel Thatcher Ulrich, Linda Welters, Margaret Ordoñez, Steven Lubar, Gail Putnam, Susan Smulyan and Kris Van Den Bossche. I thank Bruce Sinclair for his encouragement. The manuscript curators of the numerous repositories I visited throughout Rhode Island and New England receive an intuitive standing ovation from me. Most particularly I appreciate the extra effort and interest expressed in my project by Harold Kemble and Cynthia Bendroth both of the Rhode Island Historical Society. I thank the Old Slater Mill Association and former Director of Slater Mill Historic Site, Holly Begley for granting me several leaves while I revised and prepared the manuscript for publication. As with any list of thank yous, I fear I may have forgotten someone but I do sincerely thank those of you who have read, and commented on this work in such a way as to make me think, question and analyze just that much more. Each thought provoking comment has contributed in some way to the resulting manuscript.

Chapter One
Of Oil, Seed, and Flock

Giovanni da Verrazano captured the first European images of Rhode Island's coastline in a letter written in 1526. The document reported discoveries made during a 1524 voyage. Over two hundred fifty years before the earliest efforts to industrialize, Verrazano noted key elements that made this region attractive to early industrialists. The explorer identified Rhode Island's aesthetic and natural attractions stating:

> The harbor mouth, which we call Refugio, on account of its beauty, faces south and is half a league wide from its entrance. It extends for 12 leagues in a northeasterly direction and widens out to form a bay of about 20 leagues in circumference. In this bay are five small very fertile islands and full of tall spreading trees and any large fleet could ride safely among them without fear of tempest or other dangers. Then going southward to the entrance of the harbor, there are very pleasant hills on either side with many streams of clear water flowing from the highland to the sea.[1]

In a little over a century following Verrazano's report, these features drew a varied population of colonists to pioneer the region. Fertile coastal soils led colonizing Rhode Islanders to settle on the coastal strips and to graze animals on the many islands in Narragansett Bay. The "safe harbors" promoted the development of inter-colonial trade from many small ports along Rhode Island's coast including among others Newport, Providence, Warwick, East Greenwich, and Warren. Ultimately Newport and Providence entered into international commerce. At first the 'many clear flowing rivers' powered water wheels. The water wheels turned grinding stones and pushed saws in small single purpose mills. Each of the towns erected mills to support the manufacture of simple necessities such as flour and lumber.

Later man-made dams created additional mill privileges on the same rivers. By capturing more energy the dams provided water wheels with the motive force behind all sorts of mechanical devices including spinning throstles, carders, and power looms in mills and workshops. Though useful, Verrazano's description reflects impressions garnered during a few days' explorations while anchored off Newport. He and his comrades ventured five to six leagues (15–18 miles) into the interior and offered no descriptions of more distant geography. Verrazano was unaware of the nature of lands lying much beyond the coastal plains and islands of Narragansett Bay.[2]

Massachusetts and Connecticut settlers garnered more detailed impressions prior to Rhode Island's founding in 1636. Before their expulsion from Massachusetts, Roger Williams and other colonists had ventured southward to Rhode Island to assess economic opportunities and to trade with Native Americans. The Narragansetts were so fond of Roger Williams that they awarded him land in exchange for a token payment. Both Williams and Anne Hutchinson pioneered small groups of exiles to Rhode Island over land. Others among Rhode Island's original settlers transported their families and goods to the new colony aboard small vessels. The same transport ships established inter-colonial trade from the outset. Though religious belief nurtured their spirits, the safe harbors and fertile lands offered the pioneers more corporal sustenance.[3]

Seventeenth century accounts by Rhode Islanders lack basic geographic description. They recount how colonists initiated agricultural enterprises by introducing domesticated animals to an undescribed landscape. The accounts are silent concerning efforts to reclaim swampland for pasturage, or the limited fertile soil, or rock and boulder strewn landscape requiring extreme effort to reveal tillable soil.[4]

Seventeenth century Massachusetts and Connecticut residents described Rhode Island and Providence Plantations shortly after its establishment but from their perspective of looking in from the outside. What was called a "Lively Experiment" in Rhode Island's royal charter of 1663 was viewed less enthusiastically as "Rogue's Island," "the island of error," "Saint's errant," and "a receptacle for people of several sorts and opinions."[5]

Though outsiders commonly characterized the population in this fashion, the subjective evaluations of the nature of the colony's European inhabitants portrayed a two-dimensional caricature of Rhode Island and provided little information about natural resources or of the economic basis of the colony. The descriptions contrast Rhode Island and the other New England colonies but over emphasize disparities that did not greatly effect interactions between the colonies and Rhode Island on the long term.

Though repulsed by Rhode Islanders' social and political leanings, the colony's natural resources enthralled 17th century settlers in Connecticut and Massachusetts. Avarice rather than divine inspiration drove Massachusetts and Connecticut settlers to reform or correct the heretical bent of Rhode Island's population. Certainly the observations of some colonists centered on economic opportunities rather than religious or political diatribes. Dr. Robert Child described "Rhoade Ile" in 1645 stating: "this place abounds with corne and cattle especially sheep, there being nigh a 1000 on the Isle."[6] Edward Winslow observed "Rhode Island is very fruitful and plentifully abounding with all manner of food the country affordeth and hath two towns, besides many great farms well stocked with same."[7] Rhode Island offered seventeenth century European settlers with excellent agricultural opportunities that enabled them to develop an economic base admired by their colonial neighbors. So well regarded were Rhode Island's fruit and bounty, that Connecticut and Massachusetts colonies schemed to absorb their neighbor. Judging from boundary disputes with Connecticut and Massachusetts that endured into the nineteenth century, neighboring colonies and early settlers recognized and were not repulsed by Rhode Island's economic potential.[8]

Once the three colonies resolved their boundary disputes, Rhode Island's area encompassed forty-eight miles north to south and thirty-seven miles east and west. In large part, Rhode Island offered its residents a mixed setting as its fertile coasts and rough terrain fell away to a rocky interior of limited land mass. The state currently consists of 1497 square miles, two hundred of which are Narragansett Bay (Refugio). The bay extends 28 miles inland from the sea. It separates Aquidneck Island (Rhode Island) from the remainder of the state (Providence Plantations). Two hundred forty-six miles of bay- and Atlantic-facing coastlines offer numerous port or harboring opportunities in many of the cities and towns. Three main topographical divisions correspond to geological formations: (1) sandy plain lowlands adjacent to the ocean and Narragansett Bay; (2) rolling lands composed of sandstone and conglomerate in the upper bay region; (3) higher topography beginning west of Providence rising from 200 feet to 812 feet maximum at

The colony offered fertile farmland and ample pasturage for 17th century inhabitants, yet the landmass; the soil quality and the brief growing season ultimately resulted in a varied and speculative economic system. Geographic features, however, were not the sole driving forces behind the growth of commerce and pre-industrial manufacturing. The political, religious and economic character of the population contributed to the colony's growth by separating church concerns from economic, political and social ones. Unlike Massachusetts and Connecticut, Rhode Island's settlers had no utopian or communal ideals. Their desires met in economic solvency and in an organized but less structured society. As a result of the more flexible society, the population formulated a much less restrictive government that fostered the population's entrepreneurial focus. The population's unique nature, government and society illustrates some patterns in economic progression and industrialization that influenced Connecticut, Southeastern Massachusetts and some regions of New England at a later date. Rhode Island's population may have initiated the settlement in a unique and uncharacteristic fashion but in time Rhode Island became a small yet homogeneous sample of the rest of the region.[10]

SEVENTEENTH AND EIGHTEENTH CENTURY SHEEP AND WOOL ECONOMY

The driving forces behind initial emigration to the colony and the geographic factors that greeted the pioneering population are perhaps distant and distinct from the mid-eighteenth century Rhode Islander, yet they are related. As the pioneering populations confronted obstacles and opportunities, resolved problems and took advantage of fortuitous conditions, they shaped the future. During the seventeenth century, Rhode Island and Providence Plantations consisted of several independent and separate communities tied to one another by a charter issued by Charles II in 1663. The towns included Providence (1636), Portsmouth (1638), Newport (1639), Warwick (Shawomet 1643), Narragansett (Cocumscussuc 1637), Pawtuxet (1638), and Conanicut (1657). Until 1663, their colonial status was under question and John Clarke worked with Roger Williams to garner a charter that would justify their claims and their rights to property in Rhode Island. Providence and Newport became the leading settlements in population, in locus of government and in economic advantage. By the end of the seventeenth century over 4,000 people populated the colony in eight towns. Over 3,000 people resided in Providence and Newport.[11]

Commercial and subsistence agriculture and commerce with some limited manufacturing as ancillary enterprises supported the region. Agricultural technology adopted by early settlers enabled them to clear lands rapidly and put the soil to immediate use. Trees were girdled and allowed to die while crops were planted in small hills containing corn, bean, pea and pumpkin seeds. This method of farming demonstrated to residents by Native Americans initiated the subsistence agriculture that supported the local population. Within a decade after settlement residents readopted a plowed field form of farming similar to what they had known in England. In addition to corn, peas, beans and pumpkins, Rhode Islanders added barley, rye, wheat, flax, oats and apples. Husbandry was also important though large-scale husbandry was limited to those of substance and means. Sheep, raised in large quantities, could be pastured on some of the smaller islands in Narragansett Bay to prevent wolf attack and required little maintenance.[12]

During the 1640s, British domestic concerns effectively deterred trade with the colonies. Rhode Island's port cities focused on inter-colonial trade rather than supplying the Mother Country with raw materials. As a result by mid-century after only four years of existence, the population relied on domestic resources and the surpluses of nearby colonies for survival. Communities encouraged the raising of sheep to offset the lack of imported cloth. Husbandry proved to be appropriate for the climate and for the developing economy of the region. The sheep flourished and while they did not produce the long staple fleece of merino wool, their staple was ample for the manufacture of woolen fabrics domestically. Rhode Islanders exported wool or used it to supplement meager merino wool imports that made good fabric when mixed with domestic wool. By 1661 there were over 100,000 sheep in Rhode Island grown for both meat and fleece. The colony produced enough wool to outfit its entire population; and they also produced ample surplus for export. The colony received acclaim for the amount of wool produced and made available to other colonies. In 1685, Thomas Budd wrote a brief work regarding settlement in New Jersey and Pennsylvania. He suggested what settlers to the colony should bring with them and described available domestic production:

> But it may be queried, where shall Wool Be gotten to carry the woolen Manufacture until we have our own raising? I answer; in Road Island and some other adjacent Islands and places, wool may be bought at six pence a pound, and considerable quantities may be there had which will supply until we can raise enough of our own.[13]

So important was sheep husbandry to the economy of Newport that the town fathers used an image of a sheep on Newport's seal.

In his study of early Rhode Island, Carl Bridenbaugh suggested that weavers fashioned flax and wool into fabric and farmers raised the fibers to support the exportation of raw materials to foreign markets by way of England.[14] Contemporary accounts confirm his assertion. In 1656 Dutch New Yorker, Adriaen Van der Donck, observed that sheep husbandry was great in New England "where the weaving business is driven and much attention is paid to sheep."[15] During the 1640s Rhode Island and other colonies needed to fabricate their own textiles due to domestic problems abroad, which prevented Britain from sending vessels to trade with the colonies. Over 1,000 sheep raised to support the provisions' trade also grew thick woolly coats with at least a seven-inch staple whether used or not. Each spring farmers sheared their sheep. The wool gathered from Rhode Island's sheep by the mid-17th century offered ample wool for coastal trade and to supply the local population with sufficient material for flock beds, felt hats, stockings and fabric. The super-abundance of woolen fiber is evident. Budd suggested that Rhode Islanders raised sufficient wool to export quantities to other colonies. By 1675, William Harris of Providence Rhode Island wrote that the amount of wool available enabled Rhode Islanders to export wool to France in return for linens, Spain and Portugal for wines.[16]

As trade normalized after the resolution of civil unrest in England, the British regarded the colonial wool trade as a threat to their own economic wellbeing. By 1699 England passed the Wool Act. The act forbade the exportation of wool from American colonies. With the act Britain attempted to curtail any competition rising from Rhode Island's or any other colony's developing wool trade. The Woolen Act restricted the sale of wool outside the borders of the colony to prohibit inter-colonial trade as well.[17]

Despite the passage of laws in England, British efforts to control or eliminate wool manufacture did little. Wool production continued and is manifested by the increased number of fulling mills and continued and expanded sheep farming. Fulling mills show not only that wool was used, but also it was woven in such quantity for fabrics that it required a mechanized finishing procedure in the form of single process fulling mills.

The fulling process consists of soaking, shrinking and beating fabric with heavy hammers to felt and soften woolen cloth. Additional finishing techniques including napping and shearing might further improve the fabric. Waterpowered mills need not perform the fulling process. On the domestic level hand fulling consisted of soaking, shrinking and beating fabric with sticks. Some sources describe the process as a social activity similar to a husking bee or scutching party. These social events added an element of festivity to what otherwise might be time consuming, uninspiring and arduous. If the fulling were to be performed by many for fun, the cloth would be beaten by foot in time to music rather than by mallet.[18]

The finishing procedures that might follow required skill and experience and were rarely performed at home but more frequently put out to a skilled artisan. Individuals also brought their cloth to the mill to be fulled by a simple waterpowered mechanism and to subject the material to final finishing processes. Exporters sold already fulled and finished fabrics such as broadcloth, shalloon, taminy and bombazines. The names of each fabric denote both weaving patterns and finishing processes necessary to create a particular look and feel. Broadcloth, for instance, is a wide fabric woven in plain weave, fulled and then napped in one direction. For a salesperson to call a fabric by a particular name, it had to have been finished properly or not be the product advertised. The imported fabrics arrived in port ready for cutting and sewing into garments and did not require subsequent finishing for use.

Fulling mills on Rhode Island's landscape during the late 17th and early 18th century suggests that Rhode Islanders produced woolen fabrics at a level that made hand fulling or fulling bees unsatisfactory means of finishing fabric. As of 1700 at least five fulling mills in the towns of Warwick, Providence, S. Kingstown and East Providence operated. The colony consisted of 9 cities and towns by that date. Whereas this figure does not match the one per community figure suggested by Bishop or the one per 200 to 300 families by Cochran, the tendency to use one waterpower site for more than one kind of mill operation masks the number of fulling mills in each community.[19] Additionally the use of the generic term "mill" to refer to a variety of operations in civil records also clouds the actual numbers of fulling operations extant at any one time.

Towns often provided land, housing and help to a miller establishing a grist or sawmill. Providence encouraged John Smith to build a gristmill in 1646 and as you will note the purpose of the mill is unclear. "It is agreed at the monthly court meeting that he should have the valley wherein his house stands in case he set up a mill as also excepting insufficient highways. The town agreed to permit no other mill to be erected."[20] He operated a gristmill until about 1648 when he died. His son John inherited the mill and ran it until he died in 1682. Between 1648 and 1682 Captain Richard Arnold established a second mill further outside the town. Despite Smith's loss of the sole gristing proprietorship in Providence, the town supported Smith by erecting a wind powered saw mill on ten additional acres of property contiguous to his grist mill site located on the Woonasquatucket River in the center of Providence near where it meets the Moshassuck River in 1678. Half ownership of the mill was given to his son John and half to his widow.[21]

By the time John the third died in 1737, the property at Wenscutt included a saw, grist and fulling mill. Sometime earlier Smith added a fulling mill to the site. John the third's son John was called John the fuller and he died in 1719. Smith probably erected the fulling mill to support John's effort to establish himself in a trade and to encourage John to remain on the family's land. Finally Smith sought to increase the profitability and use of the mill privilege once again. Someone must have trained John to full cloth, and it is not clear from whom or how John learned the trade. In 1660, Providence granted land on the east side of the Moshassuck River to Thomas

Olney, Jr., weaver, for a mill. The records do not state what purpose the mill served. The mill probably fulled fabric given the grantee's profession. Olney's probate in 1722 does not mention a millwright but his son Thomas III's inventory in 1718 values half interest in a corn and saw mill. If this is the same mill then the town once again supported the processing of necessities. Smith probably erected his mill prior to the turn of the century. Given the location of Olney's and Smith's mills, perhaps Smith acquired Olney's mill in return for giving half interest in the saw and gristmill to Olney's son. The records are silent on this point. Since John Smith IV of Providence predeceased his father, Phillip Smith inherited full ownership of the saw, grist and fulling mills in 1737. Civil records other than a will including deeds, council records and other sources fail to mention the fulling mill.[22]

From 1700 to 1730, Daniel Williams and William Hawkings owned a fulling mill on Hawkings' land on Mill Dam Pond in Providence. The notice of this mill's establishment in Providence town records occurred because the partners disagreed about the operation of the mill and the town interceded to arbitrate between the two parties. In December of 1700, the city required Hawkings to turn over ownership and operation of the mill to Daniel Williams for a period of thirty years as long as he continued to use it for fulling. If he discontinued use of the site, the land and the building would revert to William Hawkings.[23]

Although Providence's demand for fulled fabric might support two or maybe three fulling mills and several corn and saw mills by 1696, it could and would not support an additional fulling mill. That John Micarter, fuller of Providence, turned to Warwick for assistance in establishing a fulling mill, suggests that Olney, Smith and Williams all offered Providence the service of fuller prior to 1700.[24] In addition, it indicates that fabric manufacture must have increased just prior to the end of the seventeenth century making necessary the initiation of several fulling enterprises in a short span of time. Micarter requested Warwick's aid to establish a fulling mill on June 6, 1696.

> These presents declare and testify that John Micarter of the Town of Providence in the colony of Rhode Island and Providence Plantations, having made application by way of a petition to this town of Warwick desiring leave and liberty for the building and setting up of a fulling mill upon a small river at the place called and known by the name Aponake, also some convenient accommodations for the abode and residence of himself and family.[25]

The town of Warwick consented and Micarter established a mill there, which operated until 1815.

Although generally erected as single process mills, many water-powered operations ultimately combined grist, lumber, oil, shingle, tar or additional functions due to the seasonality of grain grinding and lumber cutting. As a result of this tendency, more fulling mills existed than those clearly identified in the record. Contrary to the success of James Micarter, few Rhode Island towns offered bounties or lands and buildings for the establishment of fulling enterprises. Instead cities and towns encouraged the institution of staple production such as grist or lumber. If each town had at least one fulling mill to support woolen textile production, then there should have been at least nine or ten mills in the state by 1700.

By 1750 there were approximately 15 fulling mills in Rhode Island located in Warwick (1), Hopkinton (1), Pawtucket Village (2), S. Kingstown (8), Providence (1), Westerly (1), and East Providence (1). Pawtucket and East Providence were then part of Massachusetts. The number of grist and sawmills far exceeds this calculation approaching several per town and maybe one or two per village within the political division. The state consisted of 20 cities and towns by 1750. By 1800, the state had approximately 8 fulling mills and 28 cities and towns. Apparently Rhode Island's population created and finished woolen fabrics starting probably by the mid-17th century.[26]

The limited number of fulling mills in Rhode Island prior to the end of the seventeenth century does not necessarily indicate that individuals were not processing fibers into fabric. Bridenbaugh suggests that people initiated textile manufacture in the 1640s out of necessity and continued throughout the century. The ability to hand full the textiles or not to full woolen fabrics at all and still use the textile made fulling mills not a necessity but a convenience. The use of waterpower to operate small manufacturing enterprises and draw processes out of the home is the first phase of mechanization. During this developmental period individuals performed work in different buildings erected for a special purposes located near a power source and not necessarily near the home. This early mechanization did nothing to change the flow of life or society but integrated easily into the traditional community network system already established to support survival in the New World.

SEVENTEENTH AND EIGHTEENTH CENTURY FLAX PRODUCTION

In addition to wool production, Rhode Islanders raised flax after the initial settlement of agricultural regions and the institution of plowed acreage. Seventeenth century weaver's account books for the region are not available but evidence from Massachusetts suggests that flax and wool were produced to fabricate utilitarian cloth during the seventeenth century. Many historians attribute the development of flax culture to the rise of domestic yarn spinning for stockings or fabric. Evidence of the flax cultivation in Rhode Island though not clearly evident during the seventeenth century became important during the eighteenth century for commerce rather than domestic textile manufacture.[27]

By 1730, a growing population in the coastal areas pushed westward and northward to less fertile agricultural lands. Providence divided its large sparsely populated acreage into three additional towns. To subsist on less fertile tracts in northwestern Rhode Island, farmers diversified their income producing efforts developing skills in crafts and trades or in small manufacturing establishments. Merchants and farmers both initiated small pre-industrial manufacturing enterprises. The by-professions supplemented agricultural pursuits while contributing goods for commerce. In 1731, Britain's House of Commons required the Board of Trade to report on colonial manufactures. The House of Commons request for a report suggests that manufacturing and agriculture initiated by the mid-17th century continued and grew.

> In New England, New York, Connecticut, Rhode Island, Pennsylvania and the county of Somerset in Maryland, they have fallen into the manufacture of woolen cloth and linen cloth for the use of their own families only, for the product of these colonies being chiefly cattle and grain. The estates of the inhabitants depended wholly on farming which could not be managed without a certain quantity of sheep; and their wool would be entirely lost were not their servants employed during the winter in manufacturing it for the use of families.
>
> Flax and hemp being likewise easily raised, the inhabitants manufacture them into a coarse sort of cloth bags, traces and halters for their horses, which they found did more service than those they had from any part of Europe.[28]

While the report identified the link between the production of fibers as a byproduct of commercial and subsistence agriculture the report fails to recognize fabric and labor as a commodity whereby linen could be exchanged from one family to another for goods needed or to a storeowner like cash. As a result, Britain determined that the meager agricultural resources of the New England colonies necessitated the supplement of domestic manufacturing, yet the Mother Country decided to encourage the colonists in the area of lumber and naval stores rather than in areas that competed directly with Britain.

Rhode Islanders raised flax chiefly for seed or oil export. Ireland imported flaxseed because they harvested their flax while the seeds were green. In this way the linen produced was softer and finer. Farmers, raising flaxseed for exportation, harvested the seeds and the fiber as the seeds ripened. By the time the seeds matured, the fibers had become coarse and less suitable for fabric production. Pennsylvania, Connecticut, and, Maryland produced a major percentage of the flaxseed sold to Irish linen farmers. However, other colonies also produced and exported it in quantity[29]

Truxes' study of 18th century flaxseed export from Connecticut suggests that Rhode Island was the site of exportation rather than growth. Examples of Connecticut and Rhode Island interaction indicate that Connecticut traders bought flaxseed from Rhode Island to supplement their local production. Rhode Island did not grow flaxseed in the quantity grown in Connecticut but their involvement in seed production is evident in various accounts. Christopher Champlin of Newport is only one of Rhode Island's merchants to launch flaxseed exportation. The purpose of the commerce was to generate cash resources in British pounds. Merchants used British currency to defray debts incurred by importing British goods to Rhode Island. As early as 1768, Champlin considered participating in the flaxseed trade. He did not gather seeds and sell the commodity abroad until 1775.[30] Withey's work indicates that flaxseed exported from Rhode Island to Ireland between 1768 and 1772 totaled £699 for the four years.[31] This suggests that while some seed found its way to Ireland through Rhode Island merchants the trade did not boom until later. Champlin procured flaxseed largely from farmers in East Greenwich Rhode Island. For Champlin, flaxseed commerce peaked in the mid-1780s and, continued through 1792. Although the trade continued, low prices reduced profits. Champlin discontinued his involvement in flaxseed commerce by the end of 1792. In 1792, Newry merchants Russ Thompson and Sons reported that they sold 6,000 hogsheads of flaxseeds at 52.10 per hogshead. During his most profitable year Champlin exported 880 hogsheads and tended to export under 200 hogsheads during average years. Champlin raised £13,963.05.10 in Irish currency between 1784 and 1790.[32]

Although Rhode Island's flaxseed export was certainly not as significant as Connecticut's, Rhode Island's production probably contributed and supported Connecticut's trade as overland transportation brought western Rhode Island farm goods to Connecticut ports. In 1838, Timothy Pitkin mentioned that flaxseed was one of the more common agricultural products exported from the United States. Merchants exported flaxseed from the middle of the 18th century. Federal documents record transactions beginning in 1791. Documented annual export varied ranging from 200–400 bushels annually. The accounts are not very accurate since Champlin alone exported 169 bushels in 1789.[33]

Rhode Island merchants also exported linseed oil. The value of oil commerce recorded for the year 1827 was valued at $20,704. The number of oil mills erected in Rhode Island during the 17th and 18th century and primary materials indicate that flax was harvested when optimal for seed processing and export not when appropriate for fiber processing. Flax's primary agricultural function was to be an exported commodity. Despite the flaxseed and linseed oil production, the flax straw did not remain untouched after harvesting the seeds. People could process the straw to create linen and duck fabrics.[34]

The presence of linseed oil mills on Rhode Island's landscape indicates only that farmers raised flax and processed seeds into oil used in making paint for houses or sailing vessels. The presence and location of oil mills through time on Rhode Island's landscape offer an interesting picture. Unlike corn and sawmills, oil mills do not mark Rhode Island's landscape until the 18th century. The earliest oil mills were located in Hopkinton and S. Kingstown. These two communities differ in population and economy. S. Kingstown was the location of the large plantations and an economy centered on raising sheep, flax and horses for trade. South Kingstown may have been an excellent source of flaxseed for exportation to Ireland and this focus may have limited but not eliminated the demand for linseed oil mills. Hopkinton, never densely populated, had about 200 people at the turn of the 17th to 18th century, yet they had fulling, carding and oil mills suggesting that manufacturing focused on the byproducts of farming and raising commercial products as well as subsistence. Hopkinton's location away from the coast or port seems puzzling initially but the oil mill was located close to Westerly's border and no distance in Rhode Island is too far from the coast.[35]

In Pawtucket, Hugh Kennedy, an Irish immigrant, founded an oil mill at the falls where numerous iron foundries and forges cast anchors in support of the shipbuilding trade. This oil mill continued operation until the freshet of 1807 washed away the building in the rising waters along with two clothier's shops. Like the fulling mill, oil mills were often linked to other kinds of manufacture such as grist and saw mills. The mills in Pawtucket and one in South Kingstown were single process mills but others fulling mills may have operated alongside grist, and saw mills those cited in records by name. In other instances the purpose is assumed to be grist or saw mills when accounts identified structures by the generic term. The actual number of oil mills may have exceeded those identified here. Clearly these mills were not as plentiful as the fulling mills; however, flaxseed export provided competition for the use of seeds in making linseed oil.[36]

In 1783, Nailer Thomas Hazard planted flax in his yard in May. It is important to note that Hazard ordinarily planted his yard with subsistence crops such as corn, bean and pea. The flax remained in the ground until July 29 when he began to pull it. The harvesting of the flax took about one week. The flax was allowed to dry for about a month and then he began to ripple the flax or remove the seed and spread out the flax for retting. A month later the flax was removed from the field where it was dew retted and in October Hazard brought the seed to Newport aboard a ferry. The seeds become part of the export from the colonies to England, Ireland, southern Europe, the West Indies or Africa. Hazard's neighbors processed the remaining flax in return for his service as a nailer and metalworker. Local weaver Joseph Oatley wove the flax into fabric. Elsewhere the diary notes that Hazard took another crop of seeds to a mill to extract the oil.[37]

As the population spread to the central and western portions of the colony, the food produced by farmers could no longer feed the population. Inter-colonial trade with Massachusetts and Connecticut was required to feed Rhode Islanders. The population of the state was finally reaching its natural limits. A varied economy had developed to accommodate the inability to feed the growing population and to create goods for trade. The economy continued to combine agriculture, horticulture, and commerce. Some small industries developed on mainland Rhode Island supported by Providence merchants and assisted by artisan farmers including rum distilling, lime, potash, spermaceti candles, oil, tar, turpentine, iron, and rope making. Already overland commerce and inter-bay trading in small vessels bound the not so distant hinterlands to the cities. Providence was able to take best advantage of commodities available from Rhode Island's mainland communities and those in nearby northeastern Connecticut. Overland trade developed between Connecticut's land-locked eastern population and Providence their closest port. Providence traders encouraged manufacturing to develop goods for inter-colonial and foreign trade by investing in or instituting the manufacture of iron, lime, potash and candles. By-professional farmers supported manufacturing goods to supplement farming and thereby encouraged both overland and coastal trading. Some of the by-professional agricultural craftsmen combined as small investors in vessels for maritime ventures.[38]

From the very beginnings of settlement, water surrounded and confronted Rhode Islanders. Whether farmer, merchant or craftsmen, the geography of the region united the populace with the sea and the bay. This natural resource shaped the initial economy of the state. It is also the speculative nature of Rhode Island's trade and the population's ties with commerce that led to the changes that took place in Rhode Island's economy during the late eighteenth and early nineteenth century. Water, wind, tide and animals powered grist, fulling, oil and saw mills during the seventeenth century.

OF ARTISANS, INDUSTRIOUS FAMILIES, FARMERS AND TRADE

Providence benefited from two general trends in Rhode Island's economy and demography. The population base began to shift northward with population spreading throughout the northern parts of the colony into less fertile agricultural regions. The increased dependency on by-professions led to the increased importance of small manufacturing establishments. This growth of manufacturing increased the goods available to Providence merchants for trade and made these additional commodities less available to Newport as most of the manufacturing was performed on the mainland. Aquidneck Island and the Islands in the bay remained predominantly agricultural.

In addition, Providence mercantile community was less diverse than Newport's. A single family dominated Providence's merchants. The family made a concerted effort to control sources of exports, and used political skills to manipulate decisions. Their experimentation in manufacturing also contributed to the growing dominance of Providence. Newport's mercantile community was much more diverse consisting of Baptists, Jews from Portugal, and Huguenots from France. Newport's population was not as diverse as New York's or Philadelphia's but Newport's population lacked the unity of the single dominant family.

During the 1760 to 1770 period, Rhode Island's varied exports included whale oil, potash, iron, naval stores, lumber, cotton from the southern colonies, rum produced in America and the West Indies, fish, livestock, rice, beeswax, flaxseed, beef, pork, spermaceti candles, bread and flour, wine, wheat, and Indian corn. Not all the goods were grown or manufactured in the colony. Some were part of a re-export trade as noted above. The slave trade was also very active during this period among both Providence and Newport merchants. During the Revolution, trade became even more risky. Initially, the Declaration of Independence served to open trade to regions closed to merchants due to British restrictions. As the war progressed, a blockade of Narragansett Bay and British occupation of Newport inhibited trade from both major ports. Newport traders were forced to move their center of operations to continue trade or to decide to discontinue commerce activity. Providence merchants could move or explore overland transportation to resolve wartime trade restriction. After the war, Providence was able to recover from dislocation and the blockade within five years but trade was irrevocably changed due to Rhode Island's transformation from colony to state. Newport, however, suffered more severe problems as many of their merchants relocated forever. There was a significant loyalist population in Newport that left after the Revolution. In addition, some relocated merchants remained at their new site never to return to the island.[39]

The occupational structure of the colony also began to vary in response to limited land resources and the less fertile land being occupied in the northwestern portions of the state. Many farmers combined agricultural pursuits with a trade or craft. Between 1760 and 1775, Withey identified over 900 occupations represented in Rhode Island's population. These included basic subdivisions of merchant, shopkeeper, mariners, inn holders, farmers, laborers, the shipbuilding, food, clothing, building, metal, and leather trades. Although the clothing trades represented a small number in her survey, there were approximately 100 textile artisans occupied in the trade in Providence and Newport between 1768 and 1770 including tailors, clothiers, fullers, dyers, finishers and seamstresses who do not fabricate materials as well as weavers and spinners but the number suggests that some cloth manufacture continued.[40]

Between 1675 and 1700, Providence supported at least 6 weavers and had two or three fulling mills finishing woolen fabrics for the weavers and the community. In 1704, the need for weaving services was great enough that Providence awarded William Smith a 40 foot square piece of land on which to build and to establish a weaver's shop. The town granted land based on the terms that Smith would build upon the land within one year of receipt. Smith was not the only weaver during this period. Thomas Olney, Joseph Smith, John Angell, John Warner, and Thomas Barnes also wove.[41]

The maximum population during this period was 1,179 or about 175 families. In addition, families performed some portion of textile manufacturing including carding, flax processing, spinning, knitting and weaving in the home. If we are to judge the activity based on probate inventories of the 1675 to 1720 period, many households pursued some aspect of textile processing within the home. Thirteen inventories listed some kinds of fiber preparatory equipment but few other than the homes of weavers identified looms. Spinning was evidently often carried on within the home as was carding or combing wool and worsted. Twenty-three spinning wheels were listed in the inventories and 9 pair of cards. Flax, cotton, yarn, wool and homemade cloth were also identified among the belongings of the deceased. The small number of spinning wheels relates largely to the fact that deceased people represent a small proportion of the population. The living would have had a similar percentage of spinning wheels and cards as well as other kinds of fiber processing equipment.[42]

In Newport the story is different. As early as the 1640s, weavers operated shops in Newport. Both Thomas Applegate and John Swallow wove in Newport between 1640 and 1650. From that point onward each decade or so at least one weaver worked in Newport producing textiles in competition with imports brought in by the very people who hired the weaver's services. No Newport probate from the period evidences looms, spinning wheels or other equipment used in making fabric.[43]

Other more agricultural communities such as Portsmouth, and East Greenwich, however, evidence that families processed fibers in the home. The Carder family of Warwick Rhode Island maintained an account book dramatically documenting a complex exchange network spanning three generations of Carders. The earliest records document exchanges made during the late seventeenth century and include the weaving of worsted cloth with additional charges added to the price for "half fulling" some of the yardage. The weaver may have brought the yardage to the Warwick fulling mill erected by Micarter in about 1720. Providence and Newport weavers may have subsisted primarily on their weaving. In less urban areas such as Warwick, weavers like John Carder combined the weaving task with farm related activities. In 1689, the Carder family produced stockings and spun worsted for neighbors nearby. The account book identifies additional work relationships with family and community members as well. Several men and women in the family performed spinning. Edith and Mary Carder received credit for spinning yarn in 1756. John Carder spun knitting yarn the same year. The family also exchanged day labor for farm goods while occasionally producing textiles for the community members.[44]

Between 1772 and 1781, Oliver Gardner of North Kingstown wove 1,855 yards of linen, kersey, flannel sagathsee, tow, drugget, and broadcloth for 21 customers including 10 relatives. He also produced rag rugs, coverlets and handkerchiefs. In addition to weaving, Gardner raised pigs and his account book contains some farm accounts as well as records of fabric production. In a single year Gardner might weave as much as 400 yards of mixed fabrics but this amounts to only about 8 yards of fabric a week which does not denote full time devotion to the craft. The yardages ranged in value from 4 pence to 29 pence per yard. Gardner charged 1£10s for coverlets and 3£ for rag rugs. At his level of productivity he would have earned under £100 per year from weaving. While weaving provided substantial supplementary earnings for him, it would not suffice as a sole means or even predominant means of producing income. Gardner was unmarried and therefore did not have family members to spin yarn for him as he wove for his neighbors and relatives. His weaving supplemented the pig farming and the goods received from customers for weaving contributed to his sustenance and support.[45]

Throughout the seventeenth and eighteenth century there is ample evidence to support that colonists actively manufactured fabrics for community trade and for use. A minimum of fifty individuals called "weaver" pursued the trade in nine towns between 1680 and 1780. This does not account for the individuals that wove and were not noted in civil records. Household accounts and store records vividly demonstrate the prevalence of domestic textile manufacture. Catherine Greene, wife of Governor William Greene, maintained a record of fabric produced for the family at Potawomut (part of Warwick) in 1776. Mrs. Greene did not perform the weaving task herself but hired a series of men and women to produce the fabric including several blacks. The fabric was diverse including worsted, linen, linen/woolen blends like coverlets and tow. There is no evidence that cotton was woven into any of the fabrics. Flannel, kersey, worsted, tow, checks, handkerchiefs, coverlets, blankets, bed tick and diaper were fabricated in their home from 1776 through 1780.[46]

Nailer Thomas B. Hazard left us an enticing record of a network of exchanges in South Kingstown Rhode Island. His diary incorporates social notations, and a record of accounts spanning 1778 to 1840. During that time, Hazard employed several weavers and spinners to transform fiber grown on his property into fabric for personal use. One of the artisans trained Hazard's daughter to weave. As with many households teetering on the brink of the industrial revolution, the mechanization of textile manufacture touched Hazard's family. His son wove on a water loom in a relative's textile mill during the nineteenth century. The diary entries detail the growth of the fiber, its processing, its weaving, fulling and tailoring and as such not only links the work to exchanges but clearly shows how the work was performed. Hazard condenses daily information into a few terse sentences. A typical entry might be "went to meeting. And went to Rodmans to borrow brass kittle. Joseph Oately brought home the Cloth he wove for me." The next month, Nailer Tom brought the cloth to Henry Knowles's house for dyeing and pressing. Once Hazard had raised the fiber, whether on sheep or as flax, it entered the exchange network. Someone might shear the sheep for Nailer Tom in trade for horse shoeing. Selar Rodman hackled the flax for him in 1790. Hazard borrowed the hackles used to process the flax from Robert Browning. Joseph Knowles carried the hackles to Browning for Hazard. By the time the dross was removed from the exterior of the flax, Thomas Hazard owed Selar Rodman, Robert Browning and Joseph Knowles. Hazard settled with weaver Joseph Oately, repaying him four

crane eyes two months later. Shortly after he borrowed the hackle from
Robert Browning, Hazard sold him a cow for eight dollars and a note for
14 bushels of corn. This may have been discounted based on the donation
of the hackle. The series of exchanges paid for textile manufacture instead
of cash. The complexity of the transactions as noted above is mind-bog-
gling. Yet, Thomas Hazard maintained accurate records of the accounts in
his diary.[47]

Various people wove for Thomas Hazard both by taking the makings
of the cloth to their own property and after 1795 weaving occasionally
at the Hazards. Weaving at the Hazards must not have been easy as no
weaver wove more than once at their house before returning to the habit
of taking webs home with them. Shortly after Nailer Tom had the loom
erected, he notes that they took the loom down. The weavers included
Affabe Exchange (1794–5), Pattee Brown (1795), John Holloway (1795,)
James Gardiner (1793), Joseph Oately (1793–5). Neighbors also spun for
Hazard in his home including Selar Rodman, Anna Champlin (1795) Molly
Fowler (1795) Robe Congdon (1795) Jonathon Locke's wife (1794), and
Hannah Jack (1790). Many times Hazard hired spinsters to work in his
home. For instance, Anna Champlin came to the house on July third and
stayed until the fifth spinning for the family.[48]

It is unclear what specific kinds of fabrics that weavers wove for family use. The fabrics included both linen and wool. Sheep produced enough
wool in the area that in 1719 Thomas Hazard's father gave Thomas Cul-
verwell land for a fulling mill. In large part Nailer Tom described, coating,
tow and cloth made in order to make clothes for the children. Apparently
the fabric produced at home was used and not saved as something special.
Hazard was not ashamed to be seen in homespun nor did his use of the
domestic manufacture indicate that he was a person of low economic status. Hazard's economic importance is apparent from his wide-ranging deal-
ings with people and investments. The fabric was useful and utilitarian and
not representative of poverty or insignificance.[49]

Also revealing are store accounts of the late eighteenth century, which
evidence the use of textiles for trade. Daniel Mowry of Smithfield and
Rowse Babcock of Westerly operated stores between 1790 and 1796. In
each case, the owners became commission agents for textile outwork networks during the nineteenth century. The store accounts establish a link
between textile manufacture for domestic consumption and outwork weaving for income supplementation.[50]

Between 1794 and 1796, Mowry exchanged store goods for spinning,
weaving, swiggling and making webs for the loom. Individuals identified
as "weaver" in civil records were largely male. A mixed male and female

work force produced textile goods and exchanged them for merchandise at country stores. In large part male store accounts are credited with fabric brought in to trade but notes within the record such as "wife had a slay 28 biers" "Abel Mowry's wife buys a 36 bier slay" or "Joab Man wife 1 shuttle." These entries clearly identify who performed the weaving. The kinds of fabric produced by the over 31 families were simple including home cloth, tow, diaper, and stockings.[55] Between 1790 and 1792, Rowse Babcock accepted tow and flannel in exchange for store goods.[56] His work-force was similar to Daniel Mowry's in that both men and women wove and the notes within the male accounts acknowledged female workmanship in creating the fabric. The relationship established between Rowse Babcock and the Westerly community in 1790 continued through his involvement in the H.N. Campbell Company in the 1840s and his death. The families that exchanged fabric at his store later made fabric on an outwork basis for a textile firm using him as a commission agent. Over 120 families exchanged fabrics for goods at Babcock's store.[51]

These accounts whether domestic or commercial evidence an intense level of activity in textile production that matches the level of fiber production associated with the provision's trade, oil production and flaxseed exportation. It far exceeds previous interpretive analysis of textile manufacture during the colonial period that suggests that there was an upswing from 1750 onward. Rather than purport that there was an increase in textile manufacturing from a very small base of early textile manufacture, clearly textile production continued to grow without abatement from the 1640s onward. The consistent increase in the number of fulling mills, sheep, weavers, evidence in probate inventories, and in diaries, and accounts clearly demonstrate the growth of textile manufacture. While the significance of dissatisfaction with British rule to increasing the focus on domestic manufacture can not be denied, clearly the significance of textile manufacture from 1640 through at least 1760 can not be denied either.

PRE-REVOLUTIONARY SPINNING

As with other colonies, Rhode Islanders developed a self-consciousness about domestic textile manufacture by 1768. British restrictions on importation of equipment to and exports of manufactures from America rankled the colonial population. A social movement grew out of these resentments that encouraged individuals to make and wear their own clothes. Rhode Island newspapers recorded amounts spun at spinning bees; and the state offered bounties on the growth of flax, hemp and sheep. According to one account published in May 1768:

What a glorious example Newport has set us. Rouse O, my country-
men! We are well informed that one married lady and her daughter
of about sixteen, have spun full sixty yards of good fine linen cloth,
nearly a yard wide since the first of March, besides taking care of a
large family. The linen manufacture is promoted and carried on with
so much spirit and assiduity, among all ranks that we are assured there
is scarcely enough flax to be had in town to supply the continued Consumption of that Article.[52]

In 1769, the graduating class at Rhode Island College (now Brown University) dressed completely in fabrics of American manufacture for their
commencement. The ratio of looms to spinning wheels also increased suggesting that individuals produced more fabric and that a broader spectrum
of the population wove. Nailer Thomas B. Hazard's diary for this period
also denotes increased textile manufacture in his home and that women as
well as men made fabric for his family.[53] The *Providence Gazette* assessed
the industriousness of Rhode Island's population as follows:

From divers parts of the colony we learn that considerable quantities of cloth have been and continue to be manufactured by the inhabitants and that people, in general, seem heartily disposed to yield every
discouragement to the present excellent scheme for promoting industry and economy from a conviction that the happy effects which must
naturally result therefrom can alone avert the ruin which for sometime
past has threatened British America.[54]

The availability of raw materials and concern over textile production
appeared even more boldly in advertisements. Nicholas Brown and Company promoted spinning by offering local spinsters cotton to make into
yarn. By 1787, even poetry extolled the benefits of home manufacture and
urged domestic production as the following suggests: "From me let men
and women too. The Homespun Lesson learn, Not mind what other people
do but eat the Bread they earn"[55]

During riots against the British colonial government in Newport during
the 1760s, the state was required to reimburse losses sustained by British sup-
porters. The losses were inventoried and even among the loyalists homespun
fabrics were noted along side-imported cloth. For instance Augustus Johnson's
inventory cites "At least two dozen homespun towels valued at £2,08,00."[56]
Although the social movement sought to encourage the domestic manufacture
of cloth, the colony could not manufacture sufficient cloth by hand processes
to cloth the state as well as Rhode Island's revolutionary soldiers.

During the Revolutionary war, Rhode Islanders provided blankets, stockings, overalls, suits, knapsacks, shoes and tents for their soldiers. Initially advertisements, placed in the local newspapers, announced the need for certain commodities. For instance in September of 1776 the committee of safety advertised the army's need for 1500 pair of yarn stockings and 1500 pair of double soled shoes. Later that month Congress attempted to organize the acquisition of materials in a more orderly fashion and required each colony to appoint an agent clothier who would procure "a sufficient number of blankets and woolens fit for soldiers' clothes; and that they take the most effectual and speedy methods for getting such woolens made up and distributed among the regular Continental army in such proportion as will best promote the public service . . . "[57] By December 1776 Jonathan Hazard Esq. had acquired enough clothing for two battalions and Metcalfe Bowler had bought and paid for wool and flannel to make clothing for more. The state hired Daniel Rodman to oversee the making of uniforms out of that fabric.

During the same session, legislators passed an act preventing "monopolies and oppression by excessive and unreasonable prices for many of the necessaries and conveniences of life. . . . "[58] The law regulated prices on various commodities including wheat, rye, Indian corn, wool, pork, swine, beef, hides, salt, sugar, rum molasses, butter, peas, beans, potatoes, stockings, shoes, salted pork, cotton, oats, flax, coffee, tallow, tow-cloth and flannels. The prices of stockings were limited to 6s. per pair because the army required substantial numbers of stockings. The prices of flannels, also needed for the army, were set at 3s; 6d for good yard-wide striped flannel.[59] The description that followed the price limitations on flannel indicates that flannel was in large part imported.

In April of 1777, John Reynolds of East Greenwich had become agent clothier; the state empowered him to purchase blankets and cloth sufficient for making a thousand suits of clothing for the troops. In May of 1777, the state taxed each town for commodities needed in barrels, blankets and iron. Each town provided the amounts listed within ten days of the vote. The state required stocking apportioned as well in October 1777. Providence provided 136 pair, S. Kingstown 108 pair, Charlestown 28 pair and so on until 1,000 pair were allocated. In December of the same year 2,000 pair of stockings were apportioned as a tax against the towns. In September of 1778 legislators divided 3,000 pair of stockings as taxes for towns.[60]

On several occasions the state received word that their soldiers suffered due to lack of shoes, blankets and even firearms. It is obvious that the state struggled to provision the armed forces. Equally, Rhode Island was not the only colony to suffer this difficulty. To show that the state had trouble providing woolens or stockings for their army, whether imported or not, does not necessarily suggest that little weaving and little textile manufacture was pursued. It does indicate that there were insufficient supplies to clothe both the army and the residents of the state. One also suspects that conditions of war enhanced and aggravated the wear and tear on clothing, blankets, knapsacks and stockings placing additional strain on normal domestic production. Families could ordinarily provide for their needs at home. The wear and tear on the clothing of those same individuals while at war placed greater demands on family manufacture. Those who had woven and spun to fulfill family needs, in wartime had to perform all their usual tasks along with the tasks of those who were in the army and not at home helping. Catherine Greene hired several women to weave and perform other services for her. Those who, like the Hazards, engaged in complex exchanges suffered as many of their resources went off to war leaving the rest of the community in want of their services.[61]

TEXTILE TRADE AND DOMESTIC MANUFACTURE

Textile manufacture by weavers in their shops and the productivity of domestic craftsmen indicated in family papers and in store records evidences that colonists and artisans spent considerable time, effort and resources on fabricating cloth from fibers available. Inventory records and studies of trade and export offer counter examples. Bernard Bailyn noted that the proportion of textiles produced by a single productive weaver did not compare favorably with amounts imported. "An idea of the proportion of native and foreign textiles in use is suggested by the fact that during 9 years between 1673 and 1682 the most productive weaver in Rowley which at that time contained not more than forty families, processed at Pearson's mill [fulling] considerably less cloth than one Boston merchant imported in one shipload in 1650."[62] The Rowley weaver's productivity may not be accurately gauged based on his use of a single fulling mill. Pearson's mill was the first fulling mill erected in Rowley in 1643. By 1673, there were undoubtedly more mills. In addition, use of the fulling mill only accounts for some woolen fabrics woven by the weaver and assumes that the weaver's customer asked him to have the cloth fulled for them. In the case of Thomas Hazard's relationship with weavers, Hazard only paid for the fabric to be woven. If the cloth required fulling, then he or a neighbor took the resulting woolen fabrics to Rodman's mill in South Kingstown. It is unlikely that the Essex County weaver took on the additional responsibility of overseeing the fulling unless paid extra for that service by his customers. Bailyn's proportional analysis also implies that the weaver only produced fabrics, which required fulling. Not all fabrics need to be shrunk and beaten and this weaver may have produced linens, and blend fabrics in addition to woolen, which would not have required the finishing, process. As a result the comparison cannot be made based on the information Bailyn had at his disposal.[63]

The primary sources currently available regarding Rhode Island handloom weavers prior to industrialization do little to shed light on their productivity. An estimate of the proficiency of Rhode Island's professional handloom weavers might be drawn from analogous weaver's account books generated contemporaneously in other colonies. Essex County Massachusetts' weavers weaving prior to 1790 produced between 250 and 750 yards of fabric per year. Although the yardages do not suggest full time devotion to the craft, the yardages are significant and numerous weavers and domestic production combined with those figures suggests that large amounts of fabric were produced locally. In addition to the quantities produced by handloom are the even larger quantities produced domestically by a mixed population of male and female weavers fabricating cloth in addition to farming during the 17th and 18th centuries. Catherine Greene's records evidence that weavers wove 524.75 yards of tow, kersey, flannel, checks and linen as well as 27 handkerchiefs and five coverlets in 1776.[75] Store accounts clearly demonstrate that individuals produced ample cloth for their own usage and retained some yardage for trade at the local store. Often cloth was traded for imported cloth or ribbons but also for goods such as molasses or other staples. It is the interaction between the dry goods retailer and local family that established the place of imported goods in family life at least in the cases here of rural family life. Daniel Mowry's account indicates a growing significance of weaving by the exchanges of goods for supplementary weaving tools such as shuttles, quill wheel, loom, and various sized slays.[64]

In 1729, Joshua Gee, an Englishman, wrote an essay describing how New England's commerce operated.

> New England takes from us all sorts of woolen manufacture, linen, sail cloth, cordage for rigging their vessels, haberdashery etc. To raise money to pay for what they take of us they are forced to visit the Spanish Coast where they pick up any commodity they can trade for. They carry lumber and provisions to Sugar Plantations, exchange provisions for Logwood with Logwood cutters at Campeachey. They send pipe and barrel staves and fish to Spain, Portugal and the Streights. They send Pitch, tar and turpentine to England with some skins. But all those commodities fall very short of purchasing their cloathing in England.[65]

In light of Gee's description of New England's market for import goods, it astonishes the role vanity and fashion played in the market place. Baumgarten points out that merchants encountered resistance to fabrics imported if sleazy, not the appropriate color and not in style. The response of buyers suggests that imported cloth was not purchased with the idea of warmth and shelter from the elements. Where imported fabrics were concerned, style and design were of the utmost consideration. In Massachusetts color came in to play because the population dressed in "sad colors" and did not desire bright hues such as red. The merchants could not sell out of fashion or inappropriate colors and therefore constantly requested precisely what goods would be saleable. Aesthetic taste rather than desperation marked colonial fabric choice despite Gee's remark:

> New England and the Northern Colonies have not commodities and products enough to send us in Returns for purchasing their necessary cloathing etc. but are under very great Difficulties and therefore any ordinary sort sells with them and when they are grown out of fashion with us, they are new fashioned enough there; and therefore those places are the great markets we have to dispose of such goods, which are generally sent at the Risque of the shopkeepers and traders of England, who are the great exporters, and not the inhabitants of the colonies, as some have imagined.[66]

Although it is difficult to resolve the conflicting statements of British exporters and the availability of domestic manufactures, colonial merchants clarify the importance of fashion and color to their ability to sell imported textiles. John Hull as quoted in Baumgarten's study suggested that the British imports were "both the worse goods and the dearest that I have had from any." His remark refers in part to damage incurred during shipment "ye role of taffatas was greatly discoulord some of them & very unvendible."[67] Color and fashion were important and the risk of increased indebtedness to British exporters threatened bankruptcy. "Pray send me noe more than the balance for I will note be in debt in England any more if I can help it & indead you know my orders had they bine observed I had not bine in yor debt."[68] Although Rhode Island and other colonies did not manufacture sufficient fabrics to meet all their needs, ample utilitarian goods produced effectively reduced demand and enabled colonists to look toward fashion rather than necessity when considering purchases.

Equally it is difficult to assess the percentage of domestic or imported fabrics used by colonists based on inventories, advertisements or accounts for various reasons. First, probate inventories are taken of goods in a household and the terminology used to describe them is based on the knowledge of the surveyor not on actual fact. Occasionally, inventories indicate domestic production by using the terms "home cloth" or "homespun cloth." While the use of these terms indicates domestic manufacture they do little to identify if the cloth was fabricated in a weaver's shop or in a home. Occasionally inventories cite "piece at weaver's" or "piece of cloth at fulling mill," which also serves to place the fabric somewhere among domestic manufactures but such citations are rare. Rather fabric is ordinarily cited by its type if left uncut and on the bolt or as woolen, linen clothing or sheeting. The ticking surrounding flock beds or feather beds is undescribed as are toweling and handkerchiefs because they are bunched with other evaluations. Among fabrics cited in inventories in Providence between 1680 and 1726 are blanketing, kersey, home spun cloth, bagging, linen and woolen cloth, coverlet, serge, dowlas, oznaburgs, Irish Linen, flannel, stockings, and tow. Some of the fabrics are most likely imports but evidently if items were not available through import such as French goods between 1678 and 1685 and 1689 and 1696 when importation was prohibited, the names of other items were changed to imply a French source during the interim.[69] Joshua Gee wrote "Altho' we have the Manufactures made as good, if not better than the French, yet they are forced to be called by; the Name of French to make them sell."[70]

The kinds of fabrics traded to retailers and identified in family accounts also shed light on the place of domestic manufacture in clothing and fitting out the colonial home. Hazard purchased coating, blanketing, curtain material and linen. Greene produced tow, linen, coverlets, plain worsted, handkerchiefs, blanketing, kersey, flannel, bed ticks and checks. Mowry and Babcock store accounts record receipt of tow, drugget, diaper, stockings, and home cloth.[85] These fabrics do not compare to the silks, mohair, penistone, nail dowlas, oznaburgs, shalloon, satins and baronette imported and recorded in Baumgarten's and Montgomery's studies. The imported goods are the fine, special, rich and highly prized goods described by Hull. Domestic manufactures provided individuals with blankets, coverlets, work shirts, toweling, diapers for the baby, coarse sheets, and other everyday fabrics used throughout the house and until turned into rags to be sold to the local paper manufacturer. They filled a distinct need but were not dear as the imports, which required not only the initial exchanges to make a product to trade but also that last negotiated trade to acquire what could not be produced at home.[71]

Chapter Two
Of the Weaver's Art, and Organization of Labor

With the exception of carding and fulling, the technological aspects of the weaving craft and the associated fiber processing and finishing procedures prior to 1788 combined a complex of skills and techniques performed by hand. Textile production involved many steps that differed according to kind of fiber and availability of the skill to perform the process. From the late seventeenth century onward to acquire cotton through inter-colonial trade to port cities required capital. Climate and geography precluded cotton raising in Rhode Island. Farmers did not produce cotton as a by-product of some other income earning endeavor or necessity. Readily available flax and wool fibers were harvested during other fruitful activities and farm families processed them as part of the community cooperative network system. Cotton's introduction into the exchange system occurred by the mid-17th century but until mechanization, cotton use was not as extensive as flax and woolen culture.

The organization of hand textile production bears analysis because of both its complexity and its apparent lack of planning. Despite intricate series of trades, exchanges and bartering, the procedures led to the production of ample yardage to meet the fabric necessities. The following views textile production prior to 1788 in terms of both domestic and artisanal manufacture. The discussion centers on the relationship between the various processes and the artisans executing the procedures that transformed fiber into finished product. Comparisons of pre-and post-industrial work consider how mechanization requires the fracturing of activities into many procedures. Where pre-industrial textile processing entails picking, carding, and spinning, industrial work organization included picking, carding, drawing, roving and spinning. Industrial operations seem complex because of the number of times the same material ran through machinery. The same or even more complexity entered into domestic production as the same material passed through various hands and traveled to different locations for processing while individuals forged compensatory agreements for each transaction. The procedures, the location of the work, the people performing the task and the result are all part of work formulation. The machines and equipment used, and skills associated with the technology all combine to create an image of pre-industrial textile manufacture.[1]

ORGANIZATION OF FIBER PROCESSING

The skills needed to ret, break, swiggle, or hackle flax or process tow, to scour, pick and card wool did not require intensive or lengthy training. Probate inventories' evidence tools to make processing possible in the home. The frequencies of appearance in inventories as a whole and the identification of wide ranges of textile equipment in probate suggest extensive textile manufacture took place and indicate who may have performed the work during the period prior to industrialization. Approximately 82% of Providence Rhode Island probate inventories between 1636 and 1790 had one or more spinning wheels identified in the record. Most of the accounts had more than one wheel and distinguished between walking or woolen wheels and foot or linen wheels. Thirty-five percent of the probate inventories listed cards or combs for woolen processing and only 18% included looms. Evidence of finishing or dyeing, however, rarely appeared in the records. A few accounts included clothier's or tailor's shears that the family may have used to clip the nap evenly once the material had been fulled. These tasks and later, carding were put out to skilled artisans or millwrights as described earlier.[2]

Flax processing involved retting, breaking, scutching or swiggling, hackling and spinning. These procedures resulted in extracting the long fibers from the plant and leaving the shorter fibers or the tow behind. A comb extracted and disentangled tow or the remaining shorter fibers. The farmer or a neighbor or both harvested ripened flax by removing the entire plant from the soil in bundles. The bundles dried in the fields and rippling removed the flaxseeds. Nailer Tom built a special hackle to assist his brother Robert in rippling the flaxseeds from the stalks. By spreading out flax bundles over a field, or submerging them in a pond or river, flax retted. During the course of a few weeks dew or the water partially rotted the plant. In 1702 a Providence deed between William Randall and son William transmitted the right to ret flax in Toppamispauge pond—a pond shared with another property owner.[3] Nailer Tom began pulling his flax on

July 29th 1783. Once he pulled the crop, he wrote "brought my flax from the yard and put it in the N. Meadow."[4] Hazard dew retted his crop of flax rather than water retting, as did the Randalls. Hence, Rhode Islanders used both techniques in partially rotting their flax crops. Before storing the plant or leaving the plant to process during the quieter winter months, the retting process should be completed. Contemporary accounts suggest that if not retted the resulting fiber could be harsh or coarse.[5]

Flax retting took some skill and patience so as not to destroy the fiber by over rotting. The process softened the stalk enabling the exterior coating to be broken by a flax break and scutched (remove the outer sheath from the fiber). The long fibers would not separate from the outer portion of the plant unless retting had taken place. Neighbors, local artisans, or friends at a scutching bee or social event performed the scutching or swiggling that scraped off the flax stalk revealing the fiber. Over the course of several days, hired workers accomplished the dull yet arduous task. In Essex County Massachusetts, weavers John Gould and David Tilton carried out this task as a side profession.[6] David Mowry's eighteenth century store account also indicates that men completed the scutching process to supplement their family's income. Mowry records scutching credits for Isaac Thing, and Stephen Latham.[7] Flax hackling removed the remaining bast and further organized and straightened the long fibers or line. A neighbor of Nailer Tom's came to do Hazard's hackling and Hazard borrowed another neighbor's hackles to tool the task.[8] The dross or left over pieces of sheath may be gathered and used for stuffing mattresses or upholstery. The shorter fibers are also collected to process into tow cloth for toweling and work shirts.

A member of the family, probably a young woman, might spin. The task was carried out on a foot wheel or linen wheel. Two hundred twenty-five out of 279 inventories in Providence Rhode Island between 1636 and 1790 listed one or more spinning wheels as part of the moveable estate. Often families owned enough mechanisms for each of the women in the family to operate. In 1734, Benjamin Wait clearly left each of his daughters a wheel in his will linking this activity to the women of his family.[9] Nailer Tom's account recorded six women and no men who helped with the household spinning. Catherine Greene hired Betty Quaco in 1780 to spin and do "a little weaving" for her household. Mercy Curtis, Alpha Inman, Silva Bundy, and Elizabeth Mitchell all spun at home for David Mowry between 1794 and 1808.[10] Once spun, dyers might color the yarn at this point or weavers might be hired to fashion the yarn into fabric.

Woolen fibers are processed similarly. Each spring farmers sheared their sheep. One third of a single fleece's weight might be grease or suint.

The suint may be extracted by scouring the fleece in urine or lye. In 1812 Nailer Tom washed his sheep prior to shearing. In this way Hazard would reduce the amount of work necessary to process his wool. Sheep shearing required skill in order to cut the hair away without cutting the sheep, which struggled during the operation. Hazard hired Jeremiah Knowles for 4s/6d to cut the wool off. The Hazard's sheep produced 53 pounds of wool without the suint and filth that William Knowles had washed off two weeks before. The dirtiest parts of the fleece may be cut away or skirted. The then-cleaned coarse material is used for flock beds. Some fleece might be used to create felt. The cleanest, softest and longest staple (length of hair) portions of the fleece would be used for making yarn.[11]

A sorter categorized the woolen fibers according to staple or length before spinning. The task required skill and ability to feel the change in length and texture. The youngest and oldest members of the family picked any remaining twigs, leaves or other debris from the fleece after sorting. The longest staple wool would be combed as worsted. Wool combing required more skill than carding and the tool consisted of long sharp iron teeth placed close together on a wooden handle to comb through the longer staple woolen fibers. Although Nailer Tom records making combs for his neighbors as part of his business, it is unclear whether he hired anyone to comb or card for him.[12] Trained men combed the wool by dragging it through a heated worsted comb that was attached to a post. A second comb drawn through the wool straightened and aligned fibers. Essex County, Massachusetts weaver John Hovey combed worsted wool of various colors as almost fifty percent of his income producing activity.[13]

Younger members of the family could perform carding. Carding required little skill and dexterity but taught patience. The carders would place a small amount of wool on the surface of a card that consisted of a rectangle of leather pierced by curved wire needles. To add rigidity to the structure the leather was affixed to a wooden board with a handle. To card wool the carder must take a utensil in each hand and drag the wool-less card across the surface of a wool covered card. The movement of the two devices aligns the fibers. By dragging the cards across each other in the opposite direction the carder may remove the wool from the wire teeth in a roll called a rolag.

Families and artisans could procure both hand cards and combs locally but many were imported. An early 18th century account indicates that 155 dozen cards were imported to New England between 1705 and 1706 just after the Woolen Act of 1699. Blacksmiths, nailers and others able to produce wire could manufacture combs and cards. Carding manufacture developed as a separate small industry in Rhode Island prior to industrialization. During the Revolutionary War, Daniel Anthony of Providence Rhode Island manufactured hand cards. Jeremiah Wilkinson of Cumberland Rhode Island, a blacksmith, developed a new procedure for cutting the wires. R. Mathewson of East Greenwich used horsepower to manufacture cards. Before the end of the 18th century, cards were fashioned on an outwork basis in a very tedious fashion.[14] "The wire for the teeth was secured at the nearest store. Even after the invention of machinery for cutting the teeth and piercing the backs, the women and children spent many hours around the open fire setting the wire teeth in leather backs."[15] Carpenters, cabinet makers, turners, beam makers, harness makers, timber sawyers constructed and repaired looms and fashioned harnesses, shuttles, quills, reeds and other wooden accessories. Harness and reed making sometimes constituted specialized occupations, as indicated in the following advertisement. "Wanted to Hire. A journeyman for making weaver's slays."[16] Thomas Champlin owed Nailer Tom for services and paid him in goods including two weaver's shuttles. Nailer Tom made all sorts of metal goods including worsted combs and hackles for his neighbors.[17]

Both young and old women spun carded rolags on great wheels or walking wheels. Probate inventories often distinguish woolen or walking wheels from foot or linen wheels. Henry Brown's will of 1702 promised his wife Hannah should retain ownership of the items she brought into the marriage with her.[18] Among the goods she brought with her were one woolen wheel and one linen wheel. Nailer Tom noted several women who came to his house to spin for his family. The women at the Hazard household did not spin but relied on neighbors to produce the yarn in exchange for other goods and services.[19] Unlike Chester County, Pennsylvania or Essex County, Massachusetts's weavers, who relied on the assistance of many family members to spin, Rhode Island weavers received yarn and wove cloth ordered from yarn provided by the customer.[20] The spinners were not trained craft people who had served apprenticeships under masters but were handy domestically trained artisans who offered their skills to neighbors in exchange for goods and services.

The domestic fiber processors tended to be family members of the customer and not the weaver and they produced the materials seasonally or as the need arose. The processing could be started and stopped largely as needs required with certain exceptions. Farmers scoured the wool to prevent infestation prior to storing. In addition farmers saw to retting flax prior to storing to elicit finer, softer results. Fiber processing incorporated well into the general flow of farming life. Several travelers to the United States at the end of the eighteenth century noted how citizens could easily integrate the various stages of textile production into their general daily routine. Henry Wansey stated, "Every housewife keeps a quantity of these cards by her to employ in the evenings when they have nothing to do out of doors." [21]

WEAVING: ORGANIZATION, AND SKILLS

The complex relationship of weavers to textile production, equipment used and location of the work signifies their adaptation to new circumstances and the absence of guild oversight and regulation. The level of competence attained by textile craftsmen varied depending on the market for their product. With the assistance of supportive crafts such as clothiers, dyers, and dressers, the need for proficiency in the trade might diminish to tossing the shuttle across the warp and beating the fiber back and treadling to a very simple pattern. In its most complex state weaving entailed calculating yarn necessary to make fabric, choosing the correct fiber for the cloth winding the appropriate amount of yarn to make a fabric of a specific length and width, winding the weft into quills, threading warp onto the loom according to a specific draft, treadling as needed to create a pattern and removing the cloth from a loom.[22]

A weaver required some education. He needed to read, to consult graphs that calculated the amount and weight of warp and filling used to make a certain yardage of cloth and decipher a pattern book. Weaving demanded basic arithmetic. The textile artisan determined the proper reed size by wrapping warp threads around a ruler, and counting how many threads fit into one inch. The resulting ends per inch suggested the correct bier or reed to use. Although somewhat flexible, if the warp contained too few threads, the resulting fabric became weak, gauzy or sleazy. To compute the necessary amount of warp and determine the quantity of yarn to wind about the warping bars, the weaver multiplied the number of threads per inch by the desired width of the cloth and that total by the length of the piece plus waste. Loom wastage or unused warp occurred because the warp tied to the two beams and the area between the warp beam and the beater consumed one yard of unusable yarn in floor looms, and 24 inches in a ribbon, tape or table loom. If the weaver wished to incorporate more than one color into the cloth as in checks, plaids or stripes, he divided the warp to insure consistent stripes and an even number of color repeats across the width of the fabric.

The pattern books utilize a variety of notational styles. Each graphic formulation provided weavers with the recipe for a specific kind of fabric.[23] To make matters more complex, a good weaver planned the width of the fabric or number of threads in the warp to allow for selvages, and a balanced weave. Textile craftsmen balanced weaves by planning warps that contained an even number of complete repetitions. Denser threads per inch and threading plain weave through the harnesses created selvages.[24] A textile artisan also transcribed designs into his personal draft book from swatches. The craftsman required only one pattern repetition and paper on which to note where weft looped over or under the warp to obtain an accurate copy. The initial draft created a draw down similar to the design of the fabric only in two dimensions. From that graph, the weaver transcribed the pattern into one of the many shorthand notational styles.[25]

The complete weaver needed all the aforementioned skills before putting any of the warps onto the loom. This explains why some home manufacturers had a professional artisan apply the yarn to the loom and properly pull the threads through the heddles. The domestic craftsman then wove the cloth according to the treadling pattern. As with any task, weavers put warp onto looms in a variety of ways. The following is only one example. After winding an even number of bouts or small bunches of threads of the correct length onto the warping bars, the warper attached the yarn to either beam (in this case the warp beam). Lease sticks placed on the loom maintained the criss-cross formed while winding the yarn onto the bars properly. The weaver then rolled all but about a yard of the warp onto the beam. The remaining fibers, distributed evenly across the raddle in the center of the loom, awaited threading through the heddles, and finally the reed. Once accomplished, the artisan retied the yarn into small groups for attachment into the cloth beam. Establishing uniform tension throughout the warp made the final task more difficult. To produce even stripes or smooth fabric demanded consistent stress placed on each strand of warp. The craftsman secured equal tautness through feel and experience. Fastening the yarn to the cloth beam was one aspect of warping that was not mechanical.[26]

In addition, weavers knew the individual characteristics of vegetable and animal fibers. Problematic to weave, wool shredded and broke due to friction between the thread and reed. To limit abrasion, craftsmen sized the woolen warp with water-soluble glue before weaving. Since wool stretched under stress, difficulties arose in maintaining constant tension. Cotton and flax, the more stable fibers made easier weaving materials. Flax tended to be a more rigid less elastic material and therefore was less forgiving of inconsistencies of weave.

Other skills necessary for weaving included even beating of the weft into the body of the cloth, maintenance of consistent width and selvage throughout and finishing off the raw edges after taking the completed piece off the loom. Once woven, the weaver might hem or fringe the cloth before removing it from the loom. Otherwise the simple knotting of warp threads

sufficed to prevent raveling after removal. Additional fringe or other orna-
mentation might complete the item or the textile artisan might tie off
threads in a decorative fashion.

Cloth production from fibers produced as a by-product of other
enterprises and the limited availability of clothiers and finishing may have
restricted the kinds of fabrics produced by handloom weavers and governed
in part the market for imported goods. The fibers used in Rhode Island and
other locations differed in quality and staple from those exported to the
colonies as fine fabrics from Britain. Handloom weaving relied on flax harvested for seed export rather than earlier in its maturation when appropriate for linen production. Once pulled, the flax was retted by farmers who
had other pressing concerns that may have pulled them away from examin-
ing the flax to determine if had rotted enough to free the inner fibers from
the outer bast. In Essex County, the hand weavers often criticized the quality of flax fibers calling them 'rotten' suggesting that the material had retted
excessively or was stored in a damp place prior to weaving.[27] Although
contemporary accounts suggest that the woolen staple of sheep raised in
Rhode Island enabled the exportation of the material to France and Portugal, the unexported product may not have been the highest quality since
farmers probably sold the best quality to export traders.[28] In addition,
wool is subjected to a process called scouring to remove the grease or suint
that may comprise 30% of the initial weight of the fleece. Farmers may
scour the wool in various ways but if the wool remains in the base solution longer than necessary to rid the wool of the grease or if the tempera-
ture of the water changes rapidly or the material is agitated then damage
occurs to the fiber. Many weavers complained of the condition of woolen
fibers and charged more for work that involved rotten or sleazy materials.[29]
Textiles commonly produced from domestically grown fibers were simple
utilitarian cloth such as coating, sheeting, tow, and handkerchiefs. Some
store accounts indicate that individuals exchanged domestic manufacture
directly for imported fine materials such as ribbons or shalloons. Although
home spun cloth created the medium of exchange for some fine and fancy
imported materials, domestic handloom weavers also fabricated some complex materials including coverlets and blanketing. The availability and quality of fibers as well as the organization of the work that required customers
to bring the yarn necessary to fabricate the cloth to the weaver determined
the kinds of fabrics produced by the handloom weavers.[30]

The absence of a regulatory organization promoted changes in craft
classification already in progress in England during the eighteenth century
and accelerated in new surroundings. That is, the relationships among
craft workers were not as sharp as those that had existed among artisans

in England during the sixteenth and seventeenth centuries. During the initial emigration to the United States colonies in the seventeenth century, the labels "master," "journeyman," and "apprentice" survived, but their meanings had shifted in response both to the economic needs in the colonies and to the absence of guild oversight there. There is ample evidence in the published records of the town of Providence spanning 1636–1712, that apprenticeships persisted. Contracts recorded in civil documents indicate that apprenticeships negotiated without guild oversight changed. The quality of the apprenticeship and the skills required to advance to the status of journeyman were not fixed. As a result, it is possible that individuals of varying skills called themselves journeyman. Without the guild oversight and evaluation, it would have been impossible to advance to the master level of the craft.[31]

Further modifications to the craft subclasses accompanied the emigration of British artisans during the 18th century. By this time the British guild system had lost much of its control over craftsmen as a result of the mechanization and industrialization of the British cotton textile industry.[32] Therefore, immigrant textile artisans brought an altered view of the trade and craft stratification with them. Even so, the subclasses of apprentice, journeyman, and master continued to have meaning in the crafts. The classifications marked relative amounts of training, experience and levels of expertise, even if they no longer indicated specific periods of training and particular methods of evaluating expertise.

Initially, the British guild had controlled the number of apprentices with whom a master could contract. The organization limited the master to one student for every two journeyman hired. This limitation generated positions for the more expensive journeymen. The guild also specified the duration of the apprenticeships. Until 1814, the Statute of Artificers required the training period to be a minimum of seven years; however, by the 18th century the law no longer applied or else the craft no longer enforced it.[33]

In a study of apprenticeship in the United States, Paul Douglas determined that instructional periods for weavers averaged three years.[34] No governing body determined how many apprentices or journeymen a single craftsman could hire in Rhode Island. Neither in England nor in Rhode Island did the craft define the content of the training. Weaving apprentices sometimes received academic as well as trade instruction. In Rhode Island and in England the formally apprenticed artisan lived with the master and was dependent upon him for care and education. One exception to this rule was the British custom of outdoor apprentices but there is little evidence to suggest a widespread use of this system in the United States. By the end of the 18th century, weaving apprenticeships were no longer commonplace in either Rhode Island or England.[35]

The differences between the journeyman and master subclasses blurred over time and with the loosening of guild regulation. In England, the guild had formerly required that weavers attain a level of experience, pay entrance fees and weave a masterpiece before using the title "master." By the mid-18th century, British master craftsmen had lost much of their independent status by contracting work from spinning mills and relying on the factories for orders. The masters still retained control over the intensity and pace of the workweek and in this way, maintained independence from factory labor. In addition, they continued to sell goods and not their time. The term "journeyman" signified a wage-earning artisan who had attained the intermediate stage between completing an apprenticeship and finding capital to set up his shop.[36]

In Rhode Island, the handloom artisans probably adopted the master distinction either after a suitable period had elapsed between termination of a formal apprenticeship and title assumption or else as their level of expertise increased with experience. A letter written by Isaac Peckham in 1789 suggests that he had adopted the master subclass rather than receive the title as an award for the attainment of a level of expertise. He wrote: " . . . [I] think myself a master of the business."[37] Attainment of the title "master" required proficiency in weaving, capital to initiate an independent enterprise and a staff of less experienced co-workers to weave under supervision. Public opinion may also have contributed to the weaver's status. Instead of advertising themselves as members of a particular subclass, weavers listed their achievements. One such notice claimed skill in fabricating twelve varieties of cloth and several finishing techniques.[38]

In turn the break down of the guild system enabled individuals to pursue the craft without formal or with limited training. A less structured organization developed and worked side by side the formally trained group of individuals. The unnoticed portion of the weaving population consisted largely of women. Store accounts record immense amounts of simply constructed fabric woven by women especially towards the end of the eighteenth century. Store accounts indicate that women not men produced the fabric that was used to pay for store accounts by asides and marginal notations. For instance Daniel Mowry's account cites that Abel Mowry's wife bought a 36 bier slay, and Phoebe Mowry, David's wife bought a 28 bier slay. Hannah Holden and Deborah received credits for weaving diaper and Ananias Mowry's widow wove druggett.[39] Weavers often transmitted their tools to others at their death and although many weavers received tools from the master under whom they learned the skill such as Nicholas Whitford of Portsmouth received a loom from his master in 1748 and Joseph Johnson of Westerly who inherited a loom from his father in 1731, women also inherited looms from their fathers. Elnathan and Mary Harris each received one loom and half the tackling associated with it at the decease of their father, Thomas in Providence in 1710.[40]

The problem of distinguishing between those, who wove following a lengthy apprenticeship under a master, and those that did not, stems from the gradual and continual leveling of the system. The two groups of weavers received recompense in the same way as a series of exchanges. Both populations produced fabric from materials provided to them by their customers and either wove in their own homes or wove in the home of the customer. The fabrics produced also represent similar qualities and varieties so that it becomes more and more difficult to differentiate except based on gender that does not relate to the outcome or the product.

PRE-INDUSTRIAL TEXTILE TECHNOLOGY

Handloom weavers commonly used either the counterbalanced or countermarche loom in cloth manufacture prior to the 19th century. A large rigid superstructure that formed a rectangle over the weaver's head extending from the front to the back of the loom characterized the loom design. The structure allows for the formation of the shed by depressing warp yarns rather than raising them or forming a sinking shed. The joints, formed largely of mortise and tenon, facilitated the dismantling of the structure when necessary. The majority of contemporary pattern books depict countermarche tie-ups suggesting that most weavers used looms of that design.

Once erected the countermarche loom probably remained stationary because of its rigid structure and heavy timbers. Some authors maintain that the loom construction copied the mortise and tenon joints of architecture simplifying assembly and disassembly of the seven foot by five-foot structures. Mortise and tenon joints appear in both buildings and furniture for the strength of the construction not for assembly and disassembly purposes. The loom's size and length of use suggest that the loom remained in position until not needed for extended periods.[41]

Probate inventories indicated four common locations for the loom including shops, bedchambers, kitchens and attics. Looms stayed in these locations unless unused, then the jumble of wood mixed with lumber appeared in barn and corn crib inventories. Other evidence for loom location appears in family papers and court cases. Reuben Smith Jr. filed for divorce from his wife in 1816. Several collaborating witnesses filed statements with the court describing the wife's behavior toward her husband. One by Job Smith of Warwick revealed where the work took place and under what conditions Smith wove.

I was going by the house about 3 weeks past and I heard a noise and
I went into the cellar where Mr. Reuben Smith Jr. was to work on
weaving and I found Mr. Smith bracing up the floor. I heard noise
overhead which Mr. Smith said was Mrs. Smith trying to stave the
floor through and I heard her call to him for the victuals that he had
brought down for his supper and he said there was a plenty upstairs
and then she said if he did not bring it up she would be the death of
him before night. After that she came to the door with a log of wood
to stave the door down and he got me to help brace that and she said
she wished she could see him brought in dead and wished someone
would poison him.[42]

Although Smith's working conditions were complicated by marital difficulties, the cellar most likely had egress to the outside independent of the interior access and an entry at ground level admitting light through exterior
openings. Though damp, the conditions were not necessarily lightless or
airless but sufficient to make fabric. Jonathan Knowles's probate inventory
listed a total of five looms and all equipment to work them housed in a
small workshop. Knowles's use and furnishing of the loom shed suggest the
shop of an artisan devoting most of his energies to weaving rather than to
farming, weaving and other tasks.[43]

The countermarche's large size and superstructure raises questions
about its use by itinerant weavers. Once erected these looms remained
in situ. Nailer Tom had a loom erected in his home. The loom remained
in location until it became obvious that local weavers would rather take
yarn home to work it into fabric there than to work in Hazard's house.
When Hazard's daughter learned to weave, Hazard had the loom reassem-
bled again to enable her to learn the work at home from a trained weaver.
Bowles maintains that itinerants brought their looms with them.[44] "Often
these wandering craftsmen loaded their cumbersome looms on oxcarts
and traveled about with them from hamlet to hamlet and farm to farm or
came to thread looms for housewives wishing to do their own weaving."[45]
Because of the heavy beams used to frame the counterbalanced loom and
the necessity of putting it together and taking it apart to transport, it is
highly unlikely that the weavers brought their own looms with them. More
likely they used looms available in the locality or collected yarn to bring
back to their own shops for weaving. Probate inventories between 1636–
1790 indicated that approximately 27% of inventories evidencing any textile equipment had looms. A smaller percentage recorded more than one
loom with a handful recording three or more indicating a high level of textile fabrication and perhaps a weaving workshop.[46]

Four harness looms produced many of the fabrics later manufactured by the textile mills of the nineteenth century including more complex weaves such as velvet, plaid or baronette. These simple mechanisms more than satisfied the needs of the average home weaver. Four harness looms wove all types of utilitarian fabrics such as diaper, sheeting, shirting, plaid, stripe, bed tick and could produce some figured designs such as honeysuckle and summer and winter used in coverlets. An inventory citing an eight-harness machine indicated a high level of proficiency and knowledge of very complex patterns.

Late in the eighteenth century, some weavers began using the fly shuttle in Rhode Island. Invented by John Kay of England in 1733 and improved by his son Robert in 1760, no record of the fly shuttles used in Rhode Island exists until about 1788. According to Rivard, Rhode Island weavers first employed the fly shuttle in 1789 to weave cotton goods. Bagnall suggested that Joseph Alexander and James McKerris; two Scottish weavers demonstrated its value in weaving corduroy in Providence in 1788 and thus introduced fly shuttle technology to the United States.[47] Other accounts suggest otherwise. In 1788, David Buffum operated a small weave shed in Newport Rhode Island using fly shuttle looms. He developed a drop box system for shuttles, which enabled the weaver to produce checks with ease.[48] His son, Darius, recalled: "My father invented an improvement on the loom by introducing a sliding box at each end of the lathe for weaving checks; the box so fixed as to raise and fall first throwing one shuttle and weaving a stripe and then the other."[49] The drop box mechanism is an improvement of the fly shuttle suggesting that fly shuttles were known and used in Rhode Island prior to 1788.

In addition to Buffum's unpatented improvement were those of Amos Wittemore and David Greive of Massachusetts. According to the *Repertory of Arts, Manufactures and Agriculture*, in 1806 Sieur Despeau registered a patent, which made the shuttle work more or less automatically. Despeau's loom used the treadle to separate the warp and to actuate two springs on either side of the warp. The springs forced the shuttle across the loom's expanse once the shed was opened to its most extreme point. The attachment reduced fatigue, allowing the weaver to produce more cloth per day. The device was affordable for the artisans costing only 48 francs. Originally invented to assist in the manufacture of broadcloth (a woolen fabric) the fly shuttle increased the weaver's production level when applied to narrower cloth. Composed of two boxes containing horizontal posts a shuttle designed to rest on each post alternately and a cord, which acted as a track along which the shuttle could pass, the mechanism attached onto any existing loom. The weaver yanked the cord from side to side to propel the shuttle from one selvage to the other.[50]

Aside from the fly shuttle the only other improvement to the basic handloom in the late eighteenth century was to the heddles. A wood frame with yarn heddles constituted harnesses before 1780. The fiber heddles caused problems by breaking or sticking to the warp. By the nineteenth century, metal or wire heddles began to replace threads.

With the exception of weaver's tools, the other textile processes could be performed with limited materials. The utensils in question were smaller in size and could be shared between households. Flax breaks, scutches, hackles, cards and combs are not listed in the majority of probate inventories. These smaller implements were either missed during the inventory or shared by neighbors. Spinning wheels are more often identified and distinguished from one another indicating the kinds of fiber processing taking place within the home. These instruments are larger than the other equipment and therefore are less likely to be shared even though one family might spin for another. The spinning wheel consists of a circular spoked wheel on an axle. The wheel is linked to another pulley on which a spindle is attached. Spinning consists of drawing out an even length or a rolag or fibers as the spinner turns the great wheel slowly the spindle turns. The fibers are placed in such a way as to allow the roving or rolag to slip off the spindle to impart a twist to the fibers. Once the rolag has been twisted enough the resulting fiber is wound onto the spindle and the process begins again. The flax wheel operates somewhat differently because of the differing characteristics of the fibers. The long fibers or line are attached to the flyer and dampened. As a foot treadle moves the wheel, the wheel imparts a twist to the fibers as they are drawn out. Once sufficient twist is added the fibers are allowed to wind onto the cop. The spinning process requires knowledge of the characteristics of the fiber and dexterity to produce an evenly spun yarn. While the skill does not take years to acquire and is not as complex as weaving, spinning does require some skill and experience for success. Once yarn is spun, it might be plied to other yarns to make a stronger or larger diameter yarn for weaving. Otherwise yarn might be used in sewing, knitting, tatting, lace making or darning.

FULLING, CARDING AND CLOTHIER'S MILLS

Grist, saw, fulling, oil, carding and clothiers mill technology enabled millwrights to draw some operations out of the domestic environment into a separate facility. These small operations provided services to the community without appreciably altering the flow of work and activities. The mills introduced mechanisms powered by water, wind or animal rather than hand and thus foreshadowed industrialization without the radical social changes that followed.

Although waterpowered grist, saw and fulling mills drew on the same power source, as did the later spinning, drawing, and weaving mechanisms the method of translating the kinetic energy of the water to the mechanisms differed and for the latter processes, the methodology was less direct and more complex. As a result technological development had to occur both in power generation technology and textile mechanization prior to the development of the textile industry.

The distinction between industrial mills and pre-industrial mills may not be restricted entirely to technology. Power generation advancement and change focused on the means of translating the circular motion of the wheel to multiple mechanisms and governing the consistency of power flow. These changes are minimal in light of the tremendous advances made in mechanization and its impact on work organization and society.

Fulling and gristmills drew power from a breast, undershot or overshot designed water wheel. The wheel designs get their name from where the water first strikes the wheel and for the design of the wheel pit area. The positioning of the wheel in relation to the water determined where the water struck the water wheel. Once the water moved the wheel a crown gear or a lantern gear redirected the kinetic energy or the motion of the wheel to a shaft at a right angle to the water wheel, which in turn translated the motion to grinding stones, or saw or heavy hammers. The series of gears placed at right angles to each other altered the direction of the circular motion. When the wheel turned rapidly because the speed of the water was great the grinding stones and hammers also moved more rapidly. If drought lowered the water to a level too low to operate the wheel then work stopped. Sometimes millwrights stored water collected behind the dam in millponds. Millponds lessened the impact of low water and enabled millwrights to maintain operations between rainfalls.

The application of waterpower to the mechanisms was direct and very simple in orientation requiring some knowledge of the process and some training to understand and to produce a good result. Some of these skills were present in the earliest of Rhode Island's populations. The establishment of gristmills early on in settlement and the encouragement of their erection by the community demonstrated the need and necessity as well as the availability of the skill. Fulling mills founded later required no less knowledge of waterpower generation and were often associated with other processes on the same site indicating in part that knowledge of how to tap the power source was at least as important as knowledge of the process.

Nailer Tom's diary and probate inventories describe the organization of work at a mill site and suggest its incorporation into fabric manufacture. First several of Providence's 18th century probate inventories value fabric retained at the fulling mill. The linkage of the fabric to the owner and not to the weaver indicates that Nailer Tom as other individuals brought fabric to the fuller for finishing.[51] The person, who raised the fiber from the time the lamb grew it or the seed planted until the clothing wore out, owned the fabric. Spinners, weavers and fullers sold their services and not the product, as the customer owned the product in the raw state. None of the artisans sold their time by the hour or day but by the result. For instance in 1776 Jeffrey Watson Junior bought 39 yards of weaving from Oliver Gardiner of North Kingstown for £19-10-0. Jeffrey Watson owned the yarn from which Gardiner wove the fabric and therefore Watson paid for the weaving process by the yard produced not by the time it took to weave it.[52] This distinction proved important when textile mills and weaving workshops united to produce fabrics from machine spun yarn.[53]

During the late eighteenth and early nineteenth century carding mills joined fulling, saw, grist and oil mills on the landscape. Although the mill sites incorporated an element of the newer textile technology they retained the work organization of the earlier mills. Individuals brought the woolen fiber to the mill for carding thus relieving younger family members of the task of aligning the fibers and making rolags for spinning. As with other textile mechanisms, British mechanics developed woolen carding machines prior to colonial mechanics. By the mid-eighteenth century Britain had mechanized wool-carding machines in operation. In New England carding machine technology was developed in the late 1780s. By that time millwrights had begun to incorporate carding technology into single process mill environments. As with combing and carding by hand, machine carding straightens and aligns the fibers in preparation for further processing. Rather than flat sheets of card clothing, the mechanical carders use a series of rollers covered with card clothing. The rollers revolve at various speeds in opposing directions to comb and straighten fibers while removing some debris and mixing the varying qualities of fibers for a smooth and consistent lap or sheet of cotton or wool at the end. Almost simultaneously with the first cotton-spinning mill, carding mills began to appear on the landscape first in Hopkinton, then Pawtucket, South Kingstown, Warwick and Westerly. The organization of work was similar to that established for fulling, and gristmills whereby individuals would bring picked and scoured fleece to the mill for carding. Although textile mills began to dot Rhode Island's geography during the early 19th century, carding mills persisted through the first quarter of the 19th century in rural and some urban environments.[54]

The persistence of the carding mill is not idiosyncratic to Rhode Island as Zeloda Barret of New Hartford Connecticut continued to bring carding to the local mill into the 1820s when she wrote "I went to the carding machine got twenty pounds of wool carded returned very tired."[55] Barret spun yarns to support her sister, Samantha's weaving business. In addition to this individual example carding mills persisted through the first half of the 19th century when this road not taken by entrepreneurs died out.[56]

Pre-industrial organization of work focused on the performance of tasks in exchange for goods and services. The tasks viewed as "skilled" received payment valued in monetary terms based on the amount of material processed and not on time spent performing the task. Spinners might spin a certain number of knots of yarn for pay rather than work seven days being paid a certain amount a day or by the hour. Tasks viewed as requiring less skill such as carting or day labor received pay based on the amount of time spent completing the job requirements. Textile artisans received recompense based on the amount of work put in or by the quantity of spinning, carding, weaving or picking performed. Individuals providing the skills of spinning, carding, hackling, scutching, braking, and picking were either family members who received no recompense for their efforts or neighbors who largely received payment in services or goods. Various members of the community performed weaving. Many textile artisans wove to supplement income from farming, others operated weaving workshops, or were itinerant artisans. A female workforce closely linked to the exchange network, also produced fabric and participated in the textile-processing network. During the last half of the eighteenth century growing numbers of women wove simple utilitarian fabrics in their homes or the homes of neighbors in exchange for goods and services. Some of the fabric was used as payment for goods acquired in the local store. As time progressed the differences between the two traditions blurred. Weaving artisans trained by the vestigial apprenticeship system continued but diminished while the population of women weaving simple utilitarian fabrics grew. [57]

Textile technology though not stagnant during the seventeenth and eighteenth century did experience the rapid changes and advancements seen at the end of the eighteenth and the nineteenth centuries. The kinds of changes that took place enabled individuals to incorporate machinery into their own homes and simplify their means of processing fibers. Water-powered mills also assimilated well into the rural landscape providing a service that neither changed life nor introduced new social stratification or influenced urban growth. Waterpowered mills provided a service, which reduced the tedium of performing the task within the home by hand and for minimal cost, or exchange enabled individuals to simplify the number and range of tasks to be completed at home. Although the introduction of waterpowered textile mechanisms hearkened the awakening of the soon to be industrialized world, the use of waterpower to operate textile machines did not have to alter the way work was organized and fibers fashioned into fabrics but demonstrated that technology could be introduced without radically altering the known world.

Chapter Three

"I am well acquainted with working a spring shuttle and think myself a master of the business": Beginnings and Experimentation 1787–1790[1]

The American Revolution ended with the treaty of Paris in 1783. Subsequently statesmen formulated a new national government rising out of the ashes of a bankrupted one and, with entrepreneurs, sought ways to fortify and to stabilize both economic and political independence from England. Napoleon's quest for territory and Britain's efforts to limit French control disrupted European trade during the last decade of the 18th century. The United States remained neutral trying to take advantage of new markets available to them during the interim. Efforts to capture the new country's support and to limit its inroads into European markets led both France and England to seize vessels, goods and personnel or to sink foreign trade ships entering into their territory. Trade, which had always been a risky venture, had become even riskier. Merchants sought new trade markets and less risky land-based enterprises for investment diversification. Many merchants turned to manufacturing goods and some initiated textile manufacture. In Hartford; Worcester, and Beverly, Massachusetts; New York, Baltimore, Maryland; Philadelphia, Pennsylvania; and Providence, Rhode Island investors established textile manufacturing operations during the last two decades of the eighteenth century. The investors endeavored to take advantage of known fiber processing and spinning technology. Jenny workshops, founded during this era, initiated changes in the organization of work and the use of labor foreshadowing the more dramatic, social, economic and technological changes, which took place with the rise of water, powered textile manufacture during the last decade of the 18th century and the 19th century.[2]

Providence Rhode Island was one of the handful of American cities to develop commercial domestic textile manufacture during the late 18th century. By 1780 at least six weaving workshops operated there, each of which probably housed between two and four looms manufacturing fabrics from locally grown and processed fibers. Providence's economic climate differed little from the situations present in the other early textile manufacturing towns. In Hartford Connecticut Worcester, and Beverly Massachusetts, New York, Baltimore Maryland, and Philadelphia Pennsylvania similar craftsmen established weave sheds and produced fabrics for their communities. The ready supply of artisans soon found increased kinds of yarns available from different sources.[3]

As demonstrated earlier individual commercial weavers operated enterprises throughout the state prior to the end of the 18th century. A census of weavers indicates that over sixty weavers operated enterprises in the state between 1700 and 1788. By 1791, five additional weavers had instituted businesses in Providence.[4] Two more, one in Newport and the other in East Greenwich also increased the number of commercial weaving enterprises. The weaver's workshops instituted rapidly after 1787 responded to the increased availability of raw materials for fabric making and a greatly increased supply of cotton. Master owned and managed weave sheds grew and flourished in response to jenny spinning workshops, which had been initiated in Providence Rhode Island by the 1780s. One of the firms, Brown and Almy has left a considerable body of business records documenting the birth and rise of the just pre-industrial textile manufacturing business.[5]

Brown and Almy's business constituted the largest of the yarn and cloth making enterprises in Rhode Island during this period. Between 1788 and 1790, the total number of weavers employed by Brown and Almy comprised only three master weavers, four to six journeymen, about eight apprentices, and a few weavers working outside of the factory-owned weave shed. Although the partners employed few craftsmen, they hired many more handloom artisans than the average number working in local independent weaving operations. Thus, although the number of artisans examined here is limited, the pattern of behavior they exhibited is striking. Moreover, the small weaving population allows for a detailed analysis of workshop organization and labor practices in all of the known weave sheds in Providence.

In addition to Brown and Almy's early efforts, there were comparable entrepreneur-owned jenny workshops and weaving sheds elsewhere in Rhode Island and also in Worcester, Beverly, Hartford, Norwich, New

York City, Baltimore and Philadelphia. The management and organization of work and labor in these enterprises offers a counterpoint to Brown and Almy's factory system. In addition many of the early workshops shared the limited labor force. Individuals working for Brown and Almy left to work for others of the firms, and one or more of the other jenny workshop enterprises hired many of Brown and Almy's original workers.[6]

The jenny workshops were organized in similar ways. A single entrepreneur, a few partners or a society for the development of industry formed to establish workshops operated out of buildings. Not artisans but entrepreneurs, or merchant investors, who knew little about the manufacturing of cloth, founded the jenny workshop system. These individuals relied on the skills and experience of their workers to realize a profit through manufacture. In addition few of the investors understood the technology or would recognize operable or inoperable systems. Many sought the aid of foreign immigrants to assist in the development of mechanical devices that would answer to their needs. In Hartford, the woolen factory hired chiefly soldiers who had either deserted the British Army or had been taken prisoner. The financial, and managerial aspects of the businesses as well as the introduction of technological devices differed from previous textile operations and impacted upon those that worked in and outside of the workshop environment.[7]

The introduction of spinning, roving, carding mechanisms and fly shuttle looms in the late 18th century served as a catalyst for changes in workshop management and in the status of artisans. From 1788 to April 1790 there were three types of machinery available to Rhode Island entrepreneurs, merchants, and master weavers: Hugh Orr's "state model" designs,[7] equipment used by factories in Beverly, Hartford, and Worcester, and imitations or improvements to existing mechanisms by Rhode Island mechanics. In sum, the experimental machinery consisted of only a few kinds of equipment; their strengths and weaknesses provide some of the impetus behind changes to weaving and hand spinning.

Most accounts credit Daniel Anthony, Andrew Dexter and Lewis Peck as the earliest group of Rhode Island merchants to invest in mechanizing fiber-preparing processes, in 1788. Rather than re-invent machinery already in use in nearby Massachusetts, Anthony, a mechanic, constructed a thirty-eight spindle hand-powered jenny from drawings of the "state models" in Bridgewater. In addition, the three partners hired Joshua Lindley, a Providence mechanic, to build a roller-type carder designed after machinery in use in Beverly. Peck, Dexter, and Anthony used the equipment to produce yarn for their "homespun cloth" business in Providence—but only briefly. By May 18, 1789, they had decided to dissolve the partnership and sell their machines, which by then included two spinning jennies of sixty spindles each, a thirty-eight-spindle frame, a carder, and a slubbing billy.[8]

John Reynolds, a master weaver of East Greenwich, also oversaw the construction of both carding and spinning machinery. Unfortunately, Reynolds's experimentation in textile technology failed because the machines did not function efficiently enough to operate at a profit. Reynolds sold some of his equipment to Moses Brown, a retired merchant of Providence. Brown purchased Reynolds's spinning frame, which was a full-sized Arkwright model consisting of six sets of four spindles, but he refused the carding machinery. Reynolds decided that greater financial security rested along more conventional lines and returned to weaving woolen cloth in his East Greenwich shop.[9]

In addition to Reynolds's experimental equipment, Moses Brown purchased the machinery previously owned by Anthony, Dexter, and Peck; two clockwork-geared spinning devices from John Bailey, a clockmaker of Hanover, Massachusetts; looms from Josiah Westcott, a Cranston weaver; more handlooms from Steven Arnold; and an additional carder from Joseph Congdon, a mechanic of Providence. With these acquisitions, Brown had obtained almost all the promising spinning, carding and roving equipment available in Rhode Island. By 1789, he housed in the Market Building in Providence at least three spinning frames totaling 190 spindles, two carding machines, and roving equipment. Despite the advances represented by the early equipment, the machinery functioned far from satisfactorily.[10]

Fiber preparation incorporated both hand and mechanical processing. Cotton picking or willowing removed debris from the raw uncarded cotton. The tedious hand process required little skill and offered outwork to the very young and old local people. Other jenny workshops pursued the same organizational avenue. The Hartford Woolen Company, for instance, put out wool to families for willowing and spinning.[11] Scouring and finishing processes were performed at a local fulling mill after artisans wove the fabric at the factory. As a result the investors oversaw work in several locations and the process required that raw materials travel to different buildings and significant distances away from the workshop.[12]

The hand cranked spinning jennies created yarns of insufficient strength to withstand the tension of warping. Moses Brown, and his son-in-law, William Almy, used the product as weft in the cloth woven in their weave shed and sold it as weft to local weavers. Brown and Almy and other textile firms relied on hand-spun cotton, woolen or linen warp.[13] Brown and Almy were not the only late 18th century jenny workshops owners to operate their equipment by hand power, it is clear that few if any of these early mechanized spinning establishments anywhere used waterpower to operate the equipment. Brown and Almy located their operation initially in the Market Building in Providence, which is at the head of the bay in Providence at sea level. The location of the Beverly factory was also inappropriate for the use of a water wheel. Neither the Hartford Woolen Company, The New York Manufactory, nor the Baltimore Cotton Manufactory used waterpower prior to 1790. The only one of the early jenny workshops to be credited with early waterpower usage is the Worcester Cotton Manufacturing Company based solely on the name of the dam located nearby—the "Corduroy Factory Dam." Clearly one technological leap not successfully attained prior to the use of a spinning throstle was the application of power to the equipment used in the jenny workshops. [14]

The jennies did not create yarn strong enough for warp and mechanical spinning devices carrying more than twelve spindles required substantial strength to operate. Hence, a dual system developed among the spinners.[15] In Providence as well as in each of the other jenny workshop towns, the demand for hand-spun warp increased with the emergence of several weave sheds and jenny workshops. Each of the weaving workshops was dependent on hand spinners at least for their warps. As suggested by advertisements appearing in Providence newspapers, entrepreneurs put out fibers or purchased the completed yarn from workers who spun at home.[16] The sale of yarn in this system was the same as it was before 1787, except spinners sold their warps to different buyers. Rather than receiving most of their orders from handloom craftsmen, spinners sold their goods to entrepreneurs. Yet even this was not without precedent, Nicholas Brown and other local merchants had procured flax yarn from local spinners before the 1780s.[17]

The resulting outwork system was similar to that described by Cynthia Shelton in her study of Philadelphia's textile factory in 1787. However, unlike Philadelphia's hand spinners, Providence's outwork spinners did not display their dissatisfaction with mechanical encroachment on their livelihood during this period. In Philadelphia, the factory originally housed small jennies of a dozen or fewer spindles that could be operated by women as well as men. Once the Philadelphia factory increased the number of spindles carried by the spinning machinery, however, immigrant male or local male labor displaced the female operatives, who were not strong enough to move the carriage. As a consequence, Philadelphia's hand spinners were dissatisfied with the new factory and expressed their discontent by not celebrating its existence in the Grand Federal Procession of July 4, 1788. By contrast, Philadelphia's handloom weavers had experienced an increased demand for their labor and they marched behind floats bearing textile machinery throughout the city.[18]

Rhode Island hand spinners were neither displaced by machinery nor incorporated into the mill system until later. As a result, in the 1780s they did not encounter the same unsettling experiences as their Philadelphian counterparts. Between 1788 and 1790, the Providence jenny workshops hired both local and immigrant men to operate the spinning mechanisms in the factory or in buildings near their weave sheds. For instance, Brown and Almy hired William McClure, William Buffum, and Thomas Kenworthy, among others, to operate their equipment in cellars or in the Market Building in Providence. Either evidence of the spinners' distaste for factory work did not survive or shifts in the work environment and routine did not create dissatisfaction among the spinners. Kenworthy both spun and wove for the partners and left after his initial yearlong contract expired. William McClure spun and cut webs for Brown and Almy through 1789 and 1790.[19] McClure complained of the work environment rather than of the organization of the shop or control of his time and work by managers. Moreover, despite ill health that he attributed to spinning in cellars, McClure did not threaten to leave the firm. He wrote: "Likewise my confinement in that cellar seeming to agree so little with my constitution has caused me to think of giving you some proposals."[20] In the same letter to Moses Brown, he expressed concern that he might have offended his employer by requesting an improved work setting.

Brown and Almy's accounts contain much less correspondence relative to the hiring of spinning operatives than to the employment of weavers between 1788 and 1790. What does remain indicates much less dissatisfaction among the spinners than among the weavers. In part, the reasons for this difference reflect the absence of a craft tradition among the spinners and the mobilization of a male spinning labor force that had neither existed previously nor competed directly with a local work force in Providence. In addition, Brown and Almy did not impose craft sub-classifications on the spinners they hired between 1788 and 1790. After Slater's arrival, however, the firm did employ apprentices to learn spinning.

The experiences of spinners in Providence differed from those of hand spinners in Philadelphia in several ways. The Philadelphia factory originally housed small jennies that could be operated by women and only later introduced larger eighty-spindle jennies. Therefore, the labor force first hired by the Pennsylvania Society for the Encouragement of Manufactures and the Useful Arts was rapidly displaced by more efficient machinery and by the male workers needed to run it. In contrast, from the outset in Providence, the jenny workshops used mechanisms carrying many more than a dozen spindles. Therefore, in Rhode Island the introduction of mechanized spinning increased the demand for hand spinners' services rather than reducing or eliminating it.

Both immigrant and native-born male laborers attended the mechanical spinning devices in Providence from the earliest stages. For their part, local female spinners retained their independence by selling their product from their traditional home setting, not by selling their time inside factory walls. Therefore, changes in the workplace and in rhythms of life affecting factory labor had little effect on Rhode Island outwork spinners. In addition, fewer immigrants came to the New England area than to Philadelphia, and, as a consequence, foreign spinners did not threaten to displace or usurp employment from local laborers.

The use of mechanized spinning, roving and carding equipment had a greater effect on the handloom weavers than on the spinners. Because the machine-generated yarn was unsuitable for warp, commercial cotton cloth production was limited to just a few kinds of fabrics such as linen/cotton or woolen/cotton blends. Brown and Almy's workshop produced double jean back corduroy[21] and materials that incorporated flax warp with cotton weft such as velvet and velveteen.[22] As suggested by a contemporary Brown and Almy advertisement, the Providence firm as well as factories in Beverly and Worcester chose to produce fabrics combining linen warp with cotton weft.[23]

To make fabrics for early cloth manufacturers, weavers needed only rudimentary knowledge of their craft. For instance, the velvets manufactured by Brown and Almy required that the weavers know tabby or plain weave and that they know how to create floats or the loops of thread that later became the pile. Tabby is the simplest pattern and the first one that a weaver would learn. It is a two- or four- harness design, consisting of interlacing weft under or over every other warp thread. Double jean back corduroy, a four-harness design using the twill pattern, is only slightly more complicated than tabby. Both velvet and double jean back corduroy required greater proficiency than other fabrics, which are coarse in construction and in texture such as sheeting, muslin or calico (also tabby-weave fabrics). Corduroy and velvet require that floats or loops be made consistently and evenly, and they require expert shearing of the fabric surface. Clothiers and cloth finishers clipped the loops, but if the weaver had not done his utmost to maintain floats of a consistent size, the cloth would not be suitable for commercial sale.[24] Even so, the level of skill required of the workshop weavers was no more than a craftsman might acquire during the first year of an apprenticeship.

Rhode Island weavers were willing to use machine-spun cotton yarn because the development of experimental fiber processing and of spinning machinery encouraged the organization of both independently operated and merchant-owned weaving workshops. Several craftsmen and entrepreneurs joined Brown and Almy in producing fabric from early machine-spun weft.[25] One such craftsman was John Reynolds. Aside from his efforts to develop textile machinery, Reynolds recommended artisans to Brown and Almy, purchased yarn from the partners to weave into cloth in his own workshop, and invested in Brown and Almy's jenny workshop and weave shed.[26] Although he suggested weavers for the Providence enterprise, Reynolds neither oversaw work nor wove in Brown and Almy's shed. However, accounts of yarn sold by Brown and Almy to independent artisans indicate that Reynolds bought large quantities of weft and later warp and weft from Almy and Brown after 1791.[27]

John Reynolds also contracted with Almy and Brown to manufacture fabrics for the firm from their warps and filling.[28] Reynolds's decisions to continue manufacturing woolen cloth, contract to manufacture cotton fabrics for the firm in his own shop, and buy webs from Almy and Brown to make fabrics to sell directly from his East Greenwich business emphasize his intention to remain autonomous in weaving. He willingly provided suggestions for, and invested in, Brown and Almy but kept a certain professional distance. Reynolds's reaction to technological change typifies that of other professional weavers in Rhode Island. He embraced the products manufactured by the equipment, but he rejected the managerial organization of millwork.

Another master weaver, David Buffum, also pursued independent professional weaving in Rhode Island during this era. David and his brother, George, had been born in Smithfield, Rhode Island, but moved to Newport, a more densely populated region of the state to set up their weaving business. Between 1782 and 1783, David and George Buffum opened a workshop in the basement of Newport's courthouse. About 1788, David Buffum entered into a partnership with Joseph Anthony and Nathan Spencer. The partners procured several pieces of textile equipment including spinning jennies, fly shuttle looms, a carder from the East Indies, and a horse-powered calender.

Buffum's sons, George and Darius, wove in the weave shed beside their father, and George became "very dexterous" on the fly shuttle loom. In addition to employing family members, Buffum probably hired other local laborers to operate the jennies, carder and other textile equipment. The company produced a variety of fabrics, including velvet and flannel. The flannel was composed of woolen weft spun by Thomas Bush of Newport by agreement and of cotton warps provided by Almy, Brown and Slater after 1790. Between 1795 and 1796, Buffum's weavers supplied Almy and Brown with nankeen, velvet and weaverette. By 1796, Nathan Spencer acted as an agent for Almy and Brown, selling their yarn, "suitable for weaving and knitting" in Newport. David Buffum sold most of his machinery to Almy and Brown by 1795 when they brought the mechanisms to Pawtucket. The Providence partners supplied Buffum with both warp and weft until 1810, when he closed his shop to become a sheep farmer.[29]

Other professional weavers purchased warps from Brown and Almy and Almy and Brown including James and William Wheaton, Peter and Jonathan Stowell and Jonathan Whiting. James and William Wheaton operated a workshop producing girth-width material as early as 1779. Peter and Jonathan Stowell had worked for the Worcester Cotton and Woolen Manufacturing Company from June 1789 to July 1790 when they opened an independent weave shop and began purchasing their yarn from Almy and Brown of Providence. Between 1792 and 1795 both the Wheatons and the Stowells bought warp and weft from Almy and Brown. [30]

In addition to buying machine-spun yarn, merchants procured weft to manufacture cloths on contract and for their own sale. Among the merchants were Lewis Peck, William Potter, and Andrew Dexter. Like Peck and Dexter, Potter invested capital in his textile venture and hired craftsmen laborers to operate the equipment. These three men were not themselves textile craftsmen but rather were investors, albeit on a smaller scale than Moses Brown and William Almy. William Potter initiated his textile business in 1789 by manufacturing both wool- and cotton-blend mixed goods. He obtained cotton yarn from Brown and Almy. Local hand spinners spun his woolen warps. Both Peck and Dexter established their own weave sheds after dissolving their partnership with Daniel Anthony. In 1790, Dexter's workshop produced 2,164 yards of cotton cloth, and Peck's workers wove 2,500 yards of material that same year. In 1791, Lewis Peck agreed to produce 1,000 yards of jean for Almy and Brown.[31]

On the surface, the entrepreneur-owned weave sheds that developed in this environment of experiment and change were organized and operated similarly to those owned by master craftsmen. In fact, however, their management differed from customary weave shop management in important ways.[32] The differences reflected the shift in ownership and management of the weaving business from master craftsmen to entrepreneurs. One important consequence of that shift was a decrease in the importance of distinctions among craftsmen according to expertise. Master artisans no longer owned their own equipment or rented or owned the shop in which they worked. Rather, merchant entrepreneurs employed master artisans as wage earners to oversee journeymen and apprentices according to the owners' wishes. As a consequence, the importance of the master to the shop diminished and interactions among masters, journeymen and apprentices changed. The proprietor, not the master craftsman, determined the flow of work, defined jobs to be performed by his employees, and demanded a structured work environment. The master craftsman was reduced from merchant capitalist to wage-earning laborer.

To a great extent, the entrepreneur-managed enterprises accelerated the redefinition of the craft that was already in progress among weavers and other artisans in England during the 16th and 17th centuries. Between 1788 and 1790, the relationship between Rhode Island handloom weavers and jenny workshops shifted to resemble that characteristic of participants in the British system of contracted outwork. Like their British counterparts, professional or full-time Rhode Island weavers resisted placements under the oversight of weave shed managers by taking large orders to weave for textile enterprises within their shops.[33] As entrepreneurs began employing primarily foreign-born and trained artisans in the factory workshops in Worcester, Beverly, Hartford, Norwich, and Philadelphia, conflicts arose between them and the factory owners. The conflicts reflected different concepts of craftsmanship and of each of the subclasses of the craft held by the foreign- and native-born artisans.

Between 1788 and 1790, those Rhode Island handloom craftsmen who were employed in entrepreneur-owned sheds wove under conditions similar to those described by Herbert Gutman, E.P. Thompson and others.[34] Although these merchant-owned weave sheds operated during an earlier period than the mills discussed by most labor historians their proprietors required similar changes in work habits. The weave shed itself was not located near or in the master's home. Instead, entrepreneurs housed looms in the jenny shop building, in cellars or in rented rooms nearby. In order to work in the shops, artisans had to leave their homes, journey to Providence and board in local taverns or houses. As a result, the location and atmosphere of workers' residences changed. Rather than living with the master's family, they lived in rented housing. This, in turn, eliminated the possibility of master craftsmen combining their weaving work with supplementary income-earning activities. Master weavers could no longer farm their own acreage or perform day labor on nearby farms as had been customary among handloom craftsmen. The weave shed operated on a schedule that gave the artisans ample time to weave the required daily yardage, but it also required consistent attendance and punctuality.[35]

The entrepreneurs used these restrictions to encourage efficiency and prevent idleness. As Sidney Pollard suggested, the change in the employment schedule imposed a new rhythm of work on life. It required the employees to give up the customs and pace of one way of living for another, more controlled life.[36] Whereas the pre-industrial cadence was governed by the seasons, by the rising and setting of the sun, by traditions and family or community activities, suddenly it was tied to specific minutes and hours of the day and to the proprietor's demands for consistent output.[37] In short, shop owners attempted to regulate the behavior of artisans and to establish an efficient profit-making work setting long before the advent of the modern-style factory.

Through contracts and correspondence, manufacturers have left a description of the artisan's role, responsibilities, production rates and other conditions of employment. Brown and Almy's agreements and correspondence pertaining to the hire and employment of their weavers reveal some of the practices of an entrepreneur-owned workshop. On May 27, 1789, Joseph Alexander, a Scottish weaver, left his job at the Worcester Cotton and Woolen Manufacturing Company where he had woven for two months and contracted with Brown and Almy for three months. His agreement with Brown and Almy depended on the engagement of a spinner from Boston, the provision of board and fifteen pounds. Alexander promised to weave a total of 390 yards of double jean back corduroy at the rate of 5 yards per diem. If his production rate fell short, Brown and Almy would charge Alexander the value of 5 yards for every day overtime required to satisfy the contract. In addition, Alexander agreed to warp his own loom and wind his own quills.[38]

This single contract, along with correspondence and accounts of Alexander's employment in the entrepreneur-owned weave shed, manifests a variety of changes in organization from that of artisan-owned workshops. Alexander had attained the level of journeyman weaver by the time he was hired by Brown and Almy.[39] Ordinarily, a master weaver would have evaluated the quality of his cloth and determined the pace and flow of his work. Alexander would have woven a variety of fabrics rather than a single kind of cloth for the duration of his employ.[40] In contrast, in the company-owned shop, Moses Brown and William Almy or their agents, none of them trained weavers, determined the quality, quantity and type of cloth woven. Although evaluation by those not instructed in the craft may have allowed Alexander more leeway in quality and quantity control it may also have rankled because he had been trained in weaving and knew his craft better than his valuators.

Though the contract did not make it obvious, the conditions of Alexander's hire must have differed from those characteristics of traditional weaving employment. Alexander worked in a company-owned workshop on mill-owned machinery, whereas, in the past, a weaver obtained or retained autonomy by owning his own loom and working at home or in master-owned weave sheds. The importance of equipment ownership to professional Rhode Island weavers is evident in a letter from Isaac Peckham of Newport requesting information regarding employment with Brown and Almy. He described his status and capabilities as follows: "I am well acquainted with working a spring shuttle and think myself a master of the business. I have four looms and if we can agree, I should be glad to bring them with me."[41]

Brown and Almy were not attracted by Peckham's offer of looms and labor, for they neither hired the artisan nor purchased or rented his equipment. By 1789, they had acquired more looms than they could keep active. In any case without his looms, Peckham evidently wanted no part of Brown and Almy's workshop either; he did not respond to the partners' letter. For Alexander, using company-owned tools rather than his own implements reduced his future employment options. Either the next proprietor would have to provide the equipment or Alexander himself would have to save enough capital to open an independent shop. In contrast to Brown and Almy, Christopher Leffingwell, an early 18th century master weaver of Connecticut, assisted his journeyman weaver in attaining the master status by offering him means to procure capital beyond his annual earnings. Any yardage woven above the agreed daily amount Leffingwell gave to his employee so that the journeyman might sell the goods to his own profit.[42] Brown and Almy's compact showed no concern for encouraging Alexander to improve his lot.

In addition to furnishing the looms, quills, warp and weft, Brown and Almy supplied Alexander with a fly shuttle mechanism. Originally, British inventors had developed the shuttle to enable a single artisan to span the width of a broadloom. The mechanism also increased production rates when applied to narrower cloth. In 1788, Joseph Alexander and James McKerris demonstrated its value to cloth manufacturers in Providence.[43] Between September 1789 and August 1790, Brown and Almy hired Cyril Dodge to wire and box shuttles and wire temples for their workshop looms.[44] Brown and Almy undoubtedly offered Alexander and their other weavers the fly or spring shuttle to use in the workshop. Using the mechanism to fabricate double jean back corduroy increased production rates over hand-thrown shuttle weaving.

In comparison to the eight-yard limit required of Christopher Leffingwell's journeyman weaver to manufacture coverlets, linen, calico, tow and blanketing in a period before the invention of the fly shuttle, Brown and Almy had diminished aspirations for their artisans. Although we have not precise indication of the acceptable daily weaving rate for double jean back corduroy during this time, John Reynolds suggested that the partners might increase the yardage they required of their workers in 1789. The master craftsman wrote: "Consider if we don't give too much when the weaver does Thursday's work in half a day."[45] This suggests that the firm did not require as much as it could of its workers. In addition, it is probably even more indicative of the firm's inability to provide sufficient supplies because of mismanagement of the jenny workshop, inefficient fiber-processing machinery and the inability to obtain adequate amounts of high-quality cotton.[46]

Both Alexander and Brown and Almy found the contract difficult to fulfill. Alexander began his work May 27, 1789. He finished the first piece of corduroy in eighteen days. It contained 29.5 yards, which amounted to 1.6 yards each day. These statistics are deceptive, however, since Alexander devoted the first days to setting up the loom, winding the wrap and quills, putting the yarn on the loom, tying the treadles, and then weaving. A week later, he completed a second 29.5 yards of corduroy.[47] Thus, his weaving rate did approach 5 yards a day in view of the fact that he had to rewarp the loom. By the end of the contract period, he had manufactured a total of 316.5 yards of fabric, an average of 4.05 yards a day. Although he was 73.5 yards short of the agreed yardage, Alexander received the fifteen pounds originally stipulated, because the yardage shortfall was the fault of Brown and Almy, not of Alexander. In July, he lacked quills with which to weave. Because of that and other problems, including Brown and Almy's failure to provide him with weaving supplies, Alexander lost a total of fifteen days' work. Therefore, the weaver turned Brown and Almy's contracted penalty against them and charged the partners for lost time at the rate of five yards a day. By adding the resulting 75 yards to the actual yardage produced, Alexander more than satisfied the requirements of the contract. His total earnings for the three-month period, however, just equaled assorted debts incurred to individuals, to Brown and Almy for sundries and to Richard Olney, the tavern-keeper.[48] Consequently, without additional earnings or incentives, employment by Brown and Almy offered Alexander little hope for advancement from journeyman to master of the craft. Unless he could complete his work, support himself, and retain a profit by the end of his contract period, an independent workshop of his own would forever be out of his reach.

Another immigrant weaver, John Bradburn, billed Brown and Almy twenty-one shillings for periods "kept idle/odd hours" and for "three days altogether idle warping a piece." Evidently, the partners felt these additional costs unwarranted as Bradburn suggested that the firm choose arbitrators if they wanted to challenge the charges. In addition, in a letter urging William Almy to keep all of the mill employees busy, Moses Brown made references to increased fees charged against Brown and Almy for lost time.[49] Mismanagement of the factory, balky equipment, and the problem of paying for idle periods plagued Brown and Almy through 1790.

As early as May 1789, Alexander had written John Cabot of Beverly offering his services as a journeyman once his contract expired.[50] Within the first month of his employ at Brown and Almy's workshop, he knew he would leave the firm on completing his contract. In September 1789, Alexander did leave to find employment elsewhere. He may have been an itinerant artisan; indeed Alexander may have planned to leave Brown and Almy the day he signed the three-month contract. He had worked for the Worcester Cotton and Woolen Manufacturing Company for at least two months before arriving in Providence, he contracted with Brown and Almy for only three months, and then he contacted the Beverly Manufacturing Company about possible employment there after his contract expired with Brown and Almy. His willingness to work for several entrepreneur-owned establishments for short terms does not signify dissatisfaction with the factories themselves.

In addition to experience attained by pursuing short-term weaving positions, however, Alexander may have wanted to find employment that would provide him with the opportunity to save capital and advance in the craft. Since he did not reap a profit from his employment in Providence, he might have sought higher wages elsewhere.

Shortly after hiring Alexander, Brown and Almy signed a contract with Thomas Kenworthy, a spinner and master weaver. The compact described Kenworthy as "formerly of England late of Boston," indicating that he was the spinner mentioned in Alexander's agreement. Brown and Almy stipulated that Kenworthy "weave, spin or perform any other service the said Brown and Almy shall require of him which he is capable of performing."[51] In particular, the firm wanted Kenworthy to produce 60 yards of double jean back corduroy every twelve days or other goods of the same weight and filling. For completing the work outlined by the document, Kenworthy received $120 and board and lodging for the year. The agreement also defined Kenworthy's deportment for the period, stating: "He covenants to execute the same with honesty, integrity and in a manner to the best of his abilities" and "to conduct himself in a sober and orderly manner."[52] These requisites may evidence Brown and Almy's attempts to control behavior, dictate productivity, and possibly limit visits to Richard Olney's tavern. The restrictions might also indicate that Brown and Almy attempted to issue similar contracts to masters, journeymen, and apprentices in the trade. Apprenticeship papers often outlined the appropriate moral and ethical behavior of the signer for the duration of the term. Few journeymen's contracts remain, and even fewer contain similar phrases. Leffingwell dictated the daily yardage to be produced by his weaver and listed holidays but did not stipulate behavior. During the early 19th century, many of the contracts between textile-factory laborers and their employers contained phrases that referred to company rules but did not identify proper deportment within the agreement itself.[53] Master weavers had not contracted to weave in workshops prior to the advent of entrepreneur-owned enterprises; instead, the master craftsmen had initiated their own enterprises. By creating contracted master positions in the weave shed, Brown and Almy instituted a new relationship among the craftsmen and probably based the wording of their master and journeyman agreements on apprenticeship papers.

Brown and Almy specified Kenworthy's production rate for the simple fabric at the same level as Alexander's. The contract provided Kenworthy with a longer term of employment than did Alexander's but also expected more services. Moses Brown and William Almy asked him to weave and spin and to train apprentices. Kenworthy was a master craftsman and the conditions of his contract served to reduce his status by having him work under a proprietor rather than in his own shop. The entrepreneurs procured his apprentices and determined what instruction the young weavers would receive and how Kenworthy would best serve the shop.[54]

Remuneration had also changed from compensation for goods manufactured. One hundred twenty dollars and the provision of board covered the term of employment. The weaver received pay for his time rather than for the product only, as had been customary.[55] This sort of agreement has some precedents in New England for journeymen weavers but not for master craftsmen. In 1698 Christopher Leffingwell hired John Burchard to weave 8 yards a day for one year. Burchard received fifteen pounds for the work and additional profits if he produced more than the prescribed yardage per diem.[56] Rule suggests that, during this period in England, the journeymen weavers were in fact wage laborers rather than sellers of goods.[57] However, Brown and Almy applied this system of remuneration to Thomas Kenworthy and other master weavers. Working for wages diminished the master status to a greater degree than did manager oversight and regulation. Indeed, it reduced the master sub-classification to almost the same level as journeyman. Kenworthy remained with Brown and Almy for the year but no longer. Like Alexander, he left Providence; eventually he found employment in Newburyport, Massachusetts.

Thomas Somers, a weaver and expert on cotton manufacture from England, and James Leonard, also a technical engineer and British immigrant both managed the Beverly Cotton Manufacturing Company for the Cabots and the firm's other investors. On May 15, 1789, the two men wrote to Brown and Almy to suggest another weaver: "We recommend the bearer, Mr. Maguire, an honest industrious good workman who will not mislead you by pretending to more knowledge than he really possesses. He has more general knowledge of the business than any person in Worcester or Greenwich."[58] With this enthusiastic report in hand, Brown and Almy set Maguire, an Irish immigrant, to work in the weave shop.

Either the partners failed to write an agreement, or Maguire's short-term contract expired before a new one was drafted. In any case, by September 1789 Maguire sent Brown and Almy an ultimatum concerning the terms of his employment. "It is eleven days since I requested that you would please to fix upon certain rules for the regulation of my future as well as my past work. Your reasons for not complying, you are the best judge of. My thoughts on the matter are not perhaps true as I sometimes think them to be. I don't wish to trouble you any more upon the subject than this now conveys to you. If it is not done by Tuesday let what will be the consequence."[59] Brown and Almy must have met Maguire's request as he appeared in company rolls as both their employee and an independent contracting weaver until 1796. On May 7, 1790, Maguire severed his weaving-shop connections with the partners and received a profit of over sixty-one pounds for his services above board and lodging for one year. The account constituted a release since Brown and Almy and Maguire agreed that all debts and demands were met by the exchange of money and receipt. The wording of the paper suggests that either a spoken or written yearlong contract had existed between the two parties.[60]

By February 1791, John Maguire was able to organize an independent weaving shop on Lewis Peck's wharf in Providence with his savings. The change in employment elevated Maguire to master craftsman. According to an advertisement, he wove "corduroy, velvets, thicksets, honeycomb, twilled, figured or plain, 1/2 wide jean, fustians, collonade from 1/4 yard to 1/2 yard width. Federal ribs stockinets or any other goods filled with cotton."[61] Maguire offered a much wider variety of fabrics, although not much more complex ones, than those produced by Brown and Almy's workshop. All the fabrics manufactured by Maguire consisted of four-harness weave patterns using primarily tabby and twill but also some figured designs. His autonomous undertaking allowed him to demonstrate his weaving skills to a greater extent than did weaving large quantities of corduroy for Brown and Almy. His choice of fabrics for manufacture probably reflected public demand and market for domestic products rather than any limits to his expertise.

Maguire and his employees wove almost 9,000 yards of jean for Almy and Brown from their cotton yarn in 1795.[62] Maguire probably purchased his filling or weft from local mills and most probably from Almy, Brown and Slater since all the materials produced at his workshop consisted of cotton weft. In this respect he still relied on factory products for his livelihood from 1791 onward, while he retained control over the pace and flow of work within his shop. Maguire encouraged outside orders by advertising in Providence newspapers. Purchases made by the local citizens, in addition to company weaving, gave Maguire the best of commercial hand weaving without overlooking machine-spun materials.

In contrast to the short term he worked for Brown and Almy, Maguire's lengthy involvement in the shop on Peck's wharf suggests a certain reluctance to comply with all the requirements of entrepreneur-owned weave shed work. In a company workshop, weavers received detailed instructions concerning each piece woven. The firm determined fabric types, colors, density of warp, how to warp, poundage of yarn required and size of the resulting piece. Although no actual weaving accounts exist for the period in question, Kenworthy's and Alexander's contracts were explicit. In addition to double jean back corduroy, Alexander was to "weave any kind that he is wanted to do which he can do."[63] An independent master rented or owned a shop and equipment. He hired journeymen and apprentices and sought orders for his work as well as producing fabrics for commercial sale. Master craftsmen determined many of the cloth making procedures regulated by proprietors of mill-owned shops.

Weavers, especially immigrants, brought with them an ideal of independence and sense of craft. The examples both of British weavers who contracted to weave cloth for spinning workshops and of Maguire indicate that weavers opted to retain control over time, pace of work and profits available to them. The Rhode Island weavers wanted "encouragement"[64] to weave a variety of plain and fancy fabrics on equipment they owned. The weavers wanted to have some say in how and what they produced and especially when or how much yardage they manufactured.

Working conditions and the desire to advance in the craft led four of Brown and Almy's six journeymen and master weavers to leave the firm and establish their own businesses. The tendency of those who experienced weaving with factory oversight to leave in favor of self-management suggests that most weavers wanted to work outside the entrepreneur-owned workshop system. As mentioned earlier, John Maguire worked for Brown and Almy between 1789 and 1790. He left their employ to found his own weaving company. Brown and Almy hired James McKerris, a Scottish immigrant, son-in-law of John Reynolds, and friend of Joseph Alexander, in July 1789.[65] By 1790, however, McKerris had established himself in a shed in Providence. During that year he produced 700 yards of cotton goods. McKerris probably did not hire other weavers to assist in increasing the level of manufacture. Similarly he must have operated his shop for part of the year or part-time; otherwise his annual yardage would have been far greater. McKerris did earn enough from his independent endeavor to invest in the Warwick Spinning Mill in 1791. By 1799, when he sold his shares in the mill, McKerris had left the state.[66]

Ichabod Tabor also worked for Brown and Almy but left the firm to enter into his own weaving business. Tabor, formerly a resident of Tiverton, Rhode Island had attained a high level of skill before joining the entrepreneur-owned weave shed. He is listed variously in civil records as a cotton spinner, weaver and tailor. He and his sons wove in the Almy and Brown workshop from November 1789 until 1795. From 1795 to 1797 Tabor provided the company with large quantities of fabric amounting to over 15,000 yards of nankeen, rib, jean, thickset, ticking, fustian and plain cloth manufactured within an independent operation. Since Tabor's workshop sold over 8,000 yards of material to Almy and Brown in 1795 alone, he probably employed many artisans in addition to two of his sons.[67] Like the cloths manufactured by Maguire, Tabor's fabrics consisted of simple weave structure and utilitarian materials requiring little skill. The fourth craftsman hired by the partners who left to initiate an autonomous textile business was John Fulham. In October 1788, Reynolds suggested that Brown hire the Irish stocking producer as he was "an industrious a person as any I saw."[68] Fulham agreed to weave stockings and oversee apprentices for four years, receiving $100 per annum. Fulham's attendance at the stocking frames suggests that he may have supplemented his earnings with extra-factory employment and that the firm did not attempt to control his productivity with penalties, as in Alexander's case. By May 1791, Fulham left the shop to establish a stocking knitting shop in Providence. In 1795, he returned to Almy and Brown's employ, remaining until his death in 1797.[69] Each of the four trained artisans chose alternate ways of utilizing machine-spun warps to their advantage. After spending some months or years in the employ of the mill, these craftsmen opted for increased profit, flexibility of manufacture, and control over the pace and flow of their work.

The master weaver's distaste for factory work is further affirmed by the number of Rhode Island weavers who remained outside of the entrepreneur-owned sheds and contracted to weave for the jenny workshops independently. These weavers included Jonathan Whiting, David Buffum, and John Reynolds. Since few Rhode Island weavers participated in Brown and Almy's initial weave shed experiment, and the firm's correspondence indicates that few Rhode Island weavers wrote requesting employment, the artisans were evidently not attracted to the entrepreneur-owned weave shed employment. In addition, few professionally trained weavers participated in the putting-out system that developed later on a web-by-web basis, as the firms did not contract out large amounts of weaving except to cloth agents. The small amounts offered to individuals attracted part-time semi-skilled weavers rather than professional craftsmen.

Since no apprentice indentures from the workshop exist, little is known of the conditions of their employment or terms of agreements. Information pertaining to the kinds of fabric manufactured, living arrangements, kinship and percentage of apprentices to trained labor allows for some inferences. The status of apprenticeship changed with the organization and management of the company-owned shop in that the partners controlled some responsibilities previously given to master weavers. Whereas traditional American apprenticeship compacts consisted of a private agreement between master and student in the 1780s the entrepreneur reached an agreement with the apprentice's guardian as to the length and quality of the training.[70] When Fulham left Almy and Brown in 1791, he was not required to ensure the proper education of his apprentices. Almy and Brown wrote to Barnabas Allen, Joseph Allen's father to determine the course of Joseph's apprenticeship. The partners offered the choice of learning spinning or dyeing at the company mill. Joseph Allen or his father chose to have Joseph work under Samuel Slater in the Pawtucket spinning mill, and he did so until 1810.[71]

Owners also arranged for living accommodations for the entire weaving staff.[72] Consequently, apprentices did not necessarily board with their master, and many of the ties customarily established between master and student deteriorated. According to Seybolt, the master had previously developed an almost parental relationship with the young apprentice as he governed education, supplied lodging and food, offered clothing and shoes, and oversaw the moral life of his contractual son.[73] In contrast among company-owned workshop apprentices it was the entrepreneur who provided lodging and governed the training of the worker. Joseph and Lawton Tabor retained the traditional bonds between master and apprentice only because their father was their master weaver and they lived at home. Joseph Allen boarded with Smith Brown for seventy weeks and four days between 1789 and 1790. In so doing, the apprentice resided with his contractual agent, not his master. The firm limited the master's role in apprenticeship to craft instruction. Brown and Almy also oversaw the schooling received by some of their apprentices—sending for example, Joseph Allen to night school for two quarters in 1790.[74]

The content and duration of apprenticeships rarely prepared young artisans for independent enterprise. Of Brown and Almy's early apprentices only Joseph Tabor wove at the shop for over six years. Both Thomas and Joseph Allen found other employment after 1791 when Fulham left the firm and Lawton Tabor departed in 1793. The simple fabrics taught to these young men left them severely under skilled for independent work. As mentioned earlier, velvet and corduroy required knowledge of twill and tabby patterns. The apprentices' workshop training would have allowed them to take in jean, sheeting, stripe and other simple fabric weaving from mills after 1790, but only one Brown and Almy apprentice did this. The remainder of the student weavers found employment as machine spinners, mariners, mill agents, hucksters, boardinghouse keepers, night watchmen, and factory agents.

By the end of 1789, four weavers, a weaver/spinner, a stocking weaver, and a few apprentices composed the staff of the Brown and Almy weaving workshop, working in basements throughout Providence.[75] None of the trained craftsmen employed at weaving was a native of Providence. Brown and Almy brought a single Rhode Islander to Providence from Tiverton. This plus Reynolds's statement cautioning the partners to hire James McKerris because "good hands are not everyday found"[76] suggests that Brown and Almy encountered difficulty in attracting weavers to work in a company shop. Correspondence between Moses Brown and merchants in Philadelphia, East Greenwich, and Hartford also indicates that professional artisans did not flock to Brown and Almy's shop.[77] For instance, John Walsh of Philadelphia failed to procure weavers for the firm despite the recent displacement of artisans by the destruction of Philadelphia's manufactory in 1790. This indicates an unwillingness to participate in the Providence workshop.

Professional weavers worked at their own looms in Providence during the era but understandably expressed no enthusiasm for factory weaving. A number of master-owned shops functioned in the state before the advent of mechanized spinning. John Reynolds, David Buffum, James and William Wheaton, Christopher Fowler produced fabrics there before 1788. Brown's inability to lure any of the local professional weavers into his workshop stemmed from the master artisan's unwillingness to change the conditions under which they worked and to limit their profits to wage earning. The master weavers had much to gain or retain by keeping themselves separate from merchant-owned weave sheds. In addition master craftsmen who joined the entrepreneur-owned enterprises lost status, independence and a share of the profits. Most of the weavers preferred to combine traditional workshop weaving with jenny workshop cloth contracts. In their own shops, they might take in orders from the general public to increase profits while continuing to govern the flow and pace of work for themselves.

Brown and Almy based their workshop organization on traditional craft sheds, yet they attempted to mold the work habits of the handloom weavers to conform to new ideals. The partners sought to impose schedules, alter standards of remuneration and redefine craft subclasses. Even so, Brown and Almy did not change the work behavior of their artisans significantly. Their weavers maintained habits similar to those described as natural or traditional by E.P. Thompson.[78] The work pattern consisted by alternate bouts of intense weaving and nonattendance. Since accounts do not record the artisan's activities outside the mill, it is unclear whether they wove independently during off-hours while in the employ of Brown and Almy.

Two factors contributed to Brown and Almy's inability to shape their workers' behavior. First, demand for workshop weavers exceeded the number of artisans willing to contract with the firm. Few weavers needed to participate in this sort of labor since the community at large required their services to produce fabrics for home use out of native grown flax and wool. Second, the early factory workshop system presented too confining and demeaning an atmosphere to satisfy traditionally trained artisans. As a consequence, between 1790 and 1800, Almy and Brown altered hiring practices by employing a greater number of apprentices and journeymen proportionate to masters. In addition, the firm began to employ a predominantly American work force rather than foreign-born and trained weavers in an attempt to alleviate some of their personnel problems. With balky and unsatisfactory spinning and fiber preparing machinery combined with problems engendered by the entrepreneur-owned weave shed organization, Brown and Almy sought to improve both the technology and to reduce their reliance on hand production.

Chapter Four

Giving Out the Psalm:[1] Samuel Slater and the Arkwright System of Manufacture 1790–1800

Spinning jenny workshops associated with entrepreneur-owned weave sheds combined many great technological advances. The organization of business and the formulation of labor within the working space also changed. These modifications marked the early murmurings of the immense technological, social, and economic transformations of 19th century industrialization. If the inadequate machinery, the awkwardness of labor organization or the limited product line had combined to create profitable jenny workshops then entrepreneurs would not have eagerly and ardently sought ways to better the system. Dissatisfied spinning shed owners coveted British technology and the English mill owners' understanding of mechanized textile manufacture.

Each of the major jenny workshops throughout the colonies cataloged the problems faced by mechanized textile manufacturers prior to 1790. The Hartford Woolen Company found the establishment of their business less problematic than some. They acquired a substantial supply of their workers from a population of abandoned and deserted British Revolutionary war soldiers. Despite an experienced and trained labor force, the firm struggled to establish itself due to "the Ignorance, the Knavery or the Fickleness of the workmen"[2] as well as the cost of material. Tools were not readily available to make repairs or adjustments. Despite the problems, the Hartford factory produced over 20,000 pounds of woolen goods. Elisha Colt reported that the manufacturers had encountered many stumbling blocks to production. They could not obtain sufficient supplies of quality wool to keep their machines in motion. The equipment compared inadequately to contemporary British technology. The scarcity of experienced machine operators also impeded the firm.[3]

George Cabot acknowledged that the Beverly Cotton Company failed for many of the same reasons cited by Elisha Colt:

> Almost 4 years have expired since a number of Gentlemen in this place associated for the purpose of establishing a manufactory of cotton Goods of the kinds usually imported from Manchester for men's wear—the various parts of this complex manufacture are performed by machines, some of which are very intricate and others delicate—a want of skill in constructing the machinery and of dexterity in using it, added to our want of a general knowledge of the business we had undertaken, have proved the principal impediments to its success . . . [4]

In 1790 when writing to John Dexter regarding the manufactures of Rhode Island, Moses Brown stated that as of 1789 his textile machines were unacceptable but that he and his partners had made various attempts to alter the equipment to meet their needs.

> These mashines made here not answering the purpose and expectations of the proprietors and I being desireous of perfecting them if possible . . . The fraim with One Other on nearly the same construction Made from the same Moddle and Tryed without success in East Greenwich, which I allso purchased, I attempted to set to work by Water and made a Little Yarn so as to Answer for the Warps, but being so Imperfect both as to the quality and Quantity of the yarn that their progress was suspended til I could procure a person who had Wrought or seen them wrought in Europe . . . [5]

The similarity of manufacturers' comments shows that the early industrialists recognized the limitations of the system, the technology and their own knowledge of the business. Each sought ways to improve their own companies to be the first to establish successful and profitable enterprises on a long-term basis. Moses Brown with William Almy and Smith Brown at his side were at the forefront of the quest for better machinery, and a suitable labor force managed by an experienced mill overseer. As Brown endeavored to improve his equipment, he also solicited someone with recent British textile mill experience to turn their failure into success.[6]

Jenny workshop equipment included carding machines, willows, slubbing billies, drawing frames, roving machines and spinning jennies. All these mechanisms prepared the fiber for spinning and spun yarn. Both cotton and wool manufacturers used carding machinery. Woolen manufacturers used scribbling machines to perform the first stage of carding. A rotary carding engine would then complete the woolen carding process. Woolen manufacture required different technology even during the earliest phases of industrialization. The spinning jennies spun cotton yarns suitable for weft. Most of the woolen manufacturers did not use jennies to produce yarns but as in the case of the Hartford Woolen Company, put out rovings to local hand spinners. The hand spinning of yarn by outworkers was expensive and made it difficult for woolen manufacturers to compete with the more mechanized British woolen industry.[7] In Philadelphia, the same was true and manufacturers looked for outwork spinners willing to produce yarns both near and far from the factory.

> To the good women of this province. As the spinning of yarn is a great part of the business in cloth manufacture in those countries where they are carried on extensively and to the best advantage, the women of the whole country are employed as much as possible. The managers of the American Manufactory in this city being desirous to extend the circle of this part of their business wish to employ every good spinner that can apply, however remote from the factory, and as many women in the country may supply themselves with materials there, and may have leisure to spin considerable quantities, they are hereby informed that ready money will be given at the factory up Market street, for any parcel, either great or small of hemp, flax or woolen yarn.[8]

As with picking, scouring and other processes that occurred on an outwork basis, transportation away from the facility, lack of oversight and limited productivity inhibited workflow within the factory. Immediate subsequent technological changes centered on the processing of cotton rather than wool or flax. Domestic manufacture of woolen and flaxen yarns continued unabated and actually increased for two more decades beyond water-powered cotton spinning. Rhode Islander Thomas Robinson Hazard recalled putting out wool rolls for local South Kingstown women to spin as late as the second quarter of the 19th century. According to his recollection, the spinners received 4 ¢ a skein enabling them to earn about 12 ¢ per day. Hazard made his deliveries on horseback and after outworkers spun the yarn he would take the product to outside contractors for scouring and then again for dyeing. He wrote: "How many thousands of miles I have ridden in that way with bundles of rolls and yarn on each side and before me through sunshine rain and snow, storm over bogs, stone walls, rocks, swamps and the Devil knows what—it would be hard to tell."[9] The Beverly

Cotton Manufactory, Almy and Brown, Hartford Woolen Company and the Philadelphia Cotton Manufactory all required hand spinners to produce warp for the fabrication of cloth. Many of the firms also used outside contractors to accomplish specialized processing such as dyeing and finishing.[10] Reliance on hand spinners and other outside contractors extended the time it took to turn raw material into finished product.

The rise of jenny workshops removed some textile processing labor out of the domestic setting. Work moved away from craftsman-owned and operated workshops and weave sheds, which distinguished it from the community network system. Spinning and carding businesses relied on work performed outside the factory. Almy and Brown completed the processes of picking, scouring, spinning warp, and weaving either in Providence cellars or in the Market Building workshop in Providence. A dual system developed with mechanized work procedures being performed in entrepreneur-owned facilities and hand processes being carried out as they had been traditionally in domestic or artisan-owned workshops. For a span of about twenty years the mechanization of spinning strengthened the community network system by expanding a source of supplementary income for families in ways that allowed individuals to continue working within the domestic sphere. The development of the two labor systems included hand weaving and picking. Both hand and mechanical manufacture continued side-by-side until about 1830 in cotton and later in wool and flax.

The lack of, transience of or inadequate training of labor impeded the development of commercial textile manufacturing. Hartford, Beverly, and Providence manufacturers complained about the quality, quantity, honesty and dependability of workers. Moses Brown wrote:

> Altho I had found the Undertaking much more Arduous than I expected both as to the Attention Necessary and the Expence being Necessitated to Employ Workmen of the most Transient kind and on whom Little Dependence could be placed and Collect Materials to Compleat the Various Mashines from Distant parts of the Continent . . .[11]

As a result, the pool of labor available to work in the jenny shop was limited by experience willingness to work in the factory environment. The limited work force prevented the development and profitability of the jenny workshops.

Available textile machinery functioned far from satisfactorily. The motive force was largely human. Some mills applied waterpower to carding machinery, or horsepower to calendaring. Hand crank devices performed other fiber processing and spinning operations. Human musculature required both nourishment and rest during a long day at the factory. The discontinuous impetus resulted in something less than perpetual operation. Moreover, the machines themselves sometimes broke, required more raw material than that available, or for some other reason failed to operate. In 1789, Moses Brown wrote an enlightening letter to William Almy describing both personnel and mechanical problems:

> Understanding, since I came home, that MacLure and Daniel are both waiting, one for roving and the other for the head of the cylinder to season. On inquiring, finding but one roper of worth nor a probability of the other girls going at it this week induces me to think attention is more wanting to thy object. You will hereafter have machines out of loss time.[12]

Machine breakdowns, and inadequate personnel to affect repair on damaged or incomplete machines led many jenny workshop owners to seek more advanced reliable mechanisms to operate under the supervision of an experienced mill superintendent. The use of spinning jennies did not eliminate the need for outwork spinning; it merely increased the necessity of hiring outworkers to produce stronger, harder warp yarns. The finite cotton supply of the 1780s led early cotton manufacturing entrepreneurs to put out wool or flax, which restricted their product lines to blend fabrics. Therefore the jennies produced inadequate materials with limited application to the making of fabric.

To feed mechanized textile manufacture, cotton supplies had to become more easily accessible and more plentiful. The needs of early cotton manufacturers met with the interests of founding politicians eager to strengthen the economic stance of the new country. Statesmen, such as Jefferson, Hamilton, and Coxe debated the appropriate avenues for the economic development of the New Republic. Several schools of political and economic thought converged in the rise of cotton manufacture. Initially, the arguments centered on agriculture as an appropriate economic base for a democratic republic. Others like Alexander Hamilton proposed government sponsorship of manufacture. He saw manufacture as a way to secure the new country's economic independence. By 1786, Tench Coxe developed a policy that married both agricultural and manufacturing ideals. For Coxe, agriculture was the foundation upon which to build manufacturing. His viewpoint centered on the growth of a crop that manufacturers had not used commercially on a grand scale and cotton was just such a staple.[13]

By 1787, Tench Coxe wrote an address to read before Philadelphia's Society for the Encouragement of Manufactures and the Useful Arts. His thesis linked the rise of commercial cotton growth in the southern states to the success of textile manufacturing elsewhere. "It is much to be desired that the southern planters would adopt the cultivation of an article from which the best informed manufacturers calculate the greatest profits, and on which some established factories depend."[14] Jefferson also promoted expanding domestic agricultural scale to a commercial or cash crop level. Farmers had already accomplished this feat in the southern states with such commodities as tobacco, rice and indigo. In 1788, Jefferson wrote: "If any manufactures can succeed there, it will be that of cotton. I must observe for his information that this plant grows nowhere in the United States North-ward of the Potowmack and not in quantity until you get Southward as far as York and James Rivers."[15] Both Coxe and Hamilton worked tirelessly to encourage the rise of manufacture in the United States at large and the development of cotton cultivation in the southern states. Investors, planta-tion owners and mechanics followed the prominent rhetorical arguments.

Cotton fibers most easily adapted to the spinning jenny and to sub-sequent technological developments. Woolen and flax technology tended to lag behind or even to progress based on successful cotton machinery. According to Alexander Hamilton in 1790, the fiber characteristics made cotton more suitable for textile mechanization.[16] It is unclear whether this was the case, or whether the implementation of such mechanisms in Eng-land prior to 1790 made technological piracy and the development of the industry in the United States more fortuitous. The combined developments of commercial cotton culture in the southern states, the cotton gin and the transmission of British textile technology to the United States all contrib-uted to the use of cotton in mechanized mills.

Domestic and commercial weavers wove cotton and cotton blend fab-rics from the mid-17th century onward. Cotton arrived in New England in small quantities and in varied states of processing. In large part the cotton did not come from the southern colonies until the late eighteenth century. Most of the limited supply came in trade from the Indies. Statesmen and political rhetoric encouraged the southern states to embark on commercial cotton agriculture but it took several years for quantities of domestically grown cotton to begin arriving in New England.[17] Thomas Robinson Haz-ard, who was born in 1797, recalls that cotton grown in South Carolina came to South Kingstown's Peacedale Mill in various conditions. Some-times it arrived as warps in small packages called "pockets" or still in the seed.[18] Seventeenth and 18th century weaver's accounts do not clarify this matter except to indicate that weavers received the cotton as yarn. The weaver's accounts do not necessarily suggest in what condition the cotton arrived in ports.[19]

One key technological development was the introduction of the cotton gin. Before the end of the 18th century, removal of the cottonseeds from the fiber inhibited the commercial marketing of the cotton in the United States and abroad. Cotton fibers are attached to the seeds in a pod called a boll. Each boll has four sections. Individual sections may contain anywhere from six to twenty seeds, which must be removed from the fiber before yarn may be produced. Labor costs and time considerations of seed removal made cotton unprofitable with the exception of long staple cotton that could only be grown on the seacoast.[20]

The cotton gin was not introduced until about 1793. The cotton, used in the early jenny workshops, was of limited supply, in varying states of preparedness, and differing qualities. As late as 1790, Massachusetts' manufacturers did not generally use domestically grown cotton. The Beverly Cotton Manufacturing Company preferred supplies from Cayenne and Surinam because of the quality and staple length. Their jennies worked best with the longer staple fibers.[21] Although Almy and Brown of Providence supported southern cotton growers, they soon discovered that domestic cotton arrived in market in a mixed state improperly cleaned, retaining seeds and pod fragments making their picking or cleaning process more arduous than if they were to import cotton. In addition cotton arrived stained, unripe, rotten and dirty which added to the loss inherent in having to spend more time picking or cleaning the fibers by having some fibers arrive already damaged to destruction. Hence Moses Brown suggested that the government should award bounties to encourage the improvement of the raw material and lift the imposts on imported cotton until the domestic raw materials were available.[22] Certainly Brown sought to acquire the least expensive raw material and support domestic production, but not at the expense of the success of his business.

If the manufacturers had been able to operate profitably despite technological and work organizational problems, then they might not have had to be as concerned for the marketability of their limited selection of textiles. Firms developed product lines suitable for the technology and skills of workers. This does not suggest that fashion or necessity in product selection did not concern mill owners. Almy and Brown produced a variety of both plain and fine fabrics such as velvet, flannel, nankeen, weaverette, jean, and fustian between 1790 and 1797. The cloth tended to be cotton and wool or cotton and linen blends because of the technology and skill of hand weavers available.

Correspondence between Almy and Brown and their customers is edifying because it shows how demand and price shaped product lines. In 1794, the firm received correspondence from Jackson and Nightingale of Savannah, Georgia. Almy and Brown had sent the firm fabric samples. They wanted Jackson and Nightingale to trade fabric for bales of cotton for the Providence firm. Jackson and Nightingale offered Almy and Brown guidance about what kinds of fabrics would be salable to their customers.

> We believe this to be the first sale of home manufactured cottons which has been made in this town. The country, therefore are ignorant of the comparative worth to between home and foreign manufacture of this article. This information is only to be acquired by experience, which we are assured by some of our northern friends and prove the superior excellence of home manufacturing. Should it prove so the consumption of this country would favor any considerably quant. of light cotton goods of every description particularly jeanettes and fustians . . . The dark olive is the best color for the jeanettes and fustians and other fashionable colors for which the striped nankeen and white for Dimities, muslinettes etc. The prices of the articles will be regulated by the price at which the foreign articles of equal quality can be imported.[23]

While complementary of the kinds of cottons sent to them, the firm guided Almy and Brown in color selection and fabric type. The letter mentions neither weaverette nor velvet among the cloths suggested for sale. The remainder are also durable everyday fabrics, such as fustians, dimity and jean, which would directly compete with non-spinning mill associated fabric manufacture but not necessarily with imports.[24]

In 1797 Catherine Haines of New York also provided Almy and Brown with insights into what they ought to be sending her for sale. She states:

> The coarsest whitened cotton was very sailable and perhaps when our citizens return the fine may prove so too, but the unwhitened remains unsold neither do I think it will sell at all. . . . if it is not too much trouble MS mentioned your having good homespun linen. I have had very good from New England. I mean tow cloth, if you have any, I shall be obliged by putting in same box with cotton from 30–40 yards of good whitened tow linen sheeting width. I don't know the price but I have had the brown for 16 to 18p per yd tho' I expect the whitened will come higher if you have none bleached send 20 to 30 yds of brown.[25]

Comparative British and American textile prices determined the profitability of manufacturing specific fabric types, and therefore, contributed to domestic product selection. Initially, Brown and Almy selected goods that competed with imported textiles by manufacturing velvets, baronettes, caronettes and other piled weaves but the cost of fabrication overshot the profit margin and prevented the sale of the material. In a letter to Alexander Hamilton in 1790 describing the state of Manufactures in Rhode Island, Moses Brown suggested that the legislature should encourage domestic manufactures by protecting them from the flood of imported goods. In addition he suggested that the best quality of cotton grown in the South be sold to New England Manufacturers before exportation to England. In this way Northern manufacturers would receive fine quality and staple cotton.[26]

The jenny workshops faced insurmountable problems during the 1780s and 1790s. Available technology did not bring the fiber processing out of the domestic environment but paired workshop with outwork in a time consuming system resulting in loss and low productivity. The labor force relied on the hiring of some British immigrants to educate owners and manufacturers about profitable textile manufacturing and management. Immigrant and native workers duped manufacturers. Their workers' transience and lack of training caused workshop owners' losses. The quality of the cotton and the quantity available also led the manufacturers to combine mechanized production with outwork. Extra-workshop labor disrupted the flow of work and the completion of the product. In general the system developed was awkward and resulted in profitable business in only a few cases. Manufacturers like Almy and Brown searched for ways to improve their machines, work organization, raw materials and knowledge of the industry.

SAMUEL SLATER AND THE FIRM OF ALMY BROWN AND SLATER

Since the jenny workshops could not produce yarn suitable for warp and since the lack of technological information inhibited the incorporation of more processes into the mill before 1790, jenny workshop owners needed to acquire waterpower sites and to find a person knowledgeable in applying waterpower to multiple mechanisms performing various tasks. The application of waterpower to several mechanisms required spanning a technological hurdle that local artisans could not vault. The inexpertly designed machinery, operated out of the workshop, was not on the forefront of British technology. Yet each partnership had devoted time and money procuring imperfect machinery and wanted to adapt these mechanisms to profitable manufacture prior to investing in additional equipment.[27]

In December of 1789, Moses Brown received an unsolicited letter from twenty-one year old British immigrant Samuel Slater. This letter led to the financial and technological breakthrough that Almy and Brown required and caused radical changes in textile manufacturing and industrialization as a whole. Young Samuel Slater wrote:

> Sir—a few days ago, I was informed that you wanted a manager of cotton spinning, etc. in which business I flatter myself that I can give the greatest satisfaction in making machinery, making good yarn either for stockings or twist as any made in England; as I have had an opportunity and an oversight of Richard Arkwright's works and in Mr. Strutt's mill upwards of eight years. If you are not provided for, I should be glad to serve you; though I am in the New York Manufactory and have been for three weeks since I arrived from England. We have but one card, two machines, two spinning jennies which I think not worth using. My encouragement is pretty good but should rather have the care of the perpetual carding and spinning. My intention is to erect a perpetual card and spinning (meaning the Arkwright's Patents). [28]

After traveling from England to the United States with the idea of finding his fortune in industrialized textile manufacture, Slater found himself employed in a jenny workshop overseeing the operation of five hand-cranked machines. Although his pay for supervising was acceptable, the encouragement he wanted to receive to develop technologically advanced machinery was not forthcoming. Discouraged after only three weeks of employment, Slater sought different forward-looking circumstances. Brown's initial response was cautious. He anxiously sought a skilled mill superintendent knowledgeable in British textile technology. Brown hesitated over expending sums hiring an emigrant that he knew little about on the off chance that it would improve the business. The result was a letter that cautiously invited Slater to come to Providence if Slater knew what he claimed or to send an associate knowledgeable in textile manufacture.[29]

Slater's qualifications were exemplary. He had served a seven-year apprenticeship in England at Strutt's mill in Derbyshire. In 1782 at the age of 14 he began his studies under Jedediah Strutt, the inventor of the Derby ribbed stocking machine, was Richard Arkwright's partner for many years. Initially Slater worked as a clerk at the mill in Milford England. For the last four years of his indenture, Samuel Slater acted as a general overseer in that factory. His responsibilities included supervising the building and repair of textile machinery. Once his apprenticeship drew to a close he looked for a suitable permanent position. Slater observed an advertisement in an American paper, which offered a reward for developing a mechanical spinning frame that could produce cotton yarn suitable for weaving. He left England in September 1789 and arrived in New York in November.[30]

Undeterred by Brown's epistle, Slater traveled to Providence in January 1790 to view the machines at work in the Market Building in Providence. The carding, slubbing and spinning machinery left Slater unimpressed as the machinery, and organization of work differed slightly from the New York business. According to Smith Wilkinson many years later, "Mr. Samuel Slater came to Pawtucket early in January 1790, in company with Moses Brown, William Almy, Obadiah Brown and Smith Brown who did a small business in Providence at manufacturing on billies and jennies driven by men as also were the carding machines."[31] Slater informed the partners that the machines could not be made into efficient waterpowered machinery without extensive improvements. Moses Brown, who had spent large sums obtaining the equipment and time and effort in making them work, found the prospect of scrapping the machinery at the word of a man who had not yet proved his abilities unacceptable. The partnership of Almy and Brown, however, formulated a contract, which gave Slater the opportunity to demonstrate his qualifications.

> Almy and Brown on their part are to turn in the machinery which they have already purchased at the price they cost them and to furnish materials for the building of two carding machines, viz., a breaker and finisher, a drawing and roving frame and to extend the spinning mills or frames to 100 spindles. And the said Samuel on his part covenants and engages to devote his whole time and service and to exert his skill according to the best of his abilities and have the same effected in a workmanlike manner similar to those used in England, for the like purposes.[32]

The contract required Slater to demonstrate his skills by ameliorating existing machinery prior to developing improved equipment from new materials. Once concrete evidence of his abilities existed, he renegotiated his contract to include payment for his services and percentages of the profits.[33]

Almy, and Brown required Slater to make fiber preparing and spinning devices. Almy and Brown received their raw cotton in bales from the southern states and some through importation. The cotton had already had many of the seeds removed but sticks, dirt, and pieces of pod often remained. Outworkers and sometimes factory workers performed the task of removing the debris, called picking by hand. The pickers placed the raw but almost seedless cotton on a screen made from criss-cross reeds or rope. Workmen beat the cotton with sticks to knock the debris out of the fibers and onto the floor. The process was time consuming, expensive because labor intensive and was not mechanized for three more decades.

Once workers had substantially removed the debris from the cotton, it was then carded. A hand cranked device, called a carding machine or lapper, consisted of a large drum covered with leather that had been pierced by curved wires. Smaller similarly constructed drums rubbed against the large drum in the opposite direction at different speeds. The action combed and aligned cotton fibers. The results of carding were laps or sheets of combed cotton that were then made into sliver or long thin rolls of cotton. The slubbing billies or drawing frames drew out and combined two or more slivers thereby ensuring consistency of texture. The result was a sliver of even consistency that could be made into roving. Roving machines drew out the sliver and added a slight twist imparting additional strength. A spinning jenny or throstle then, made rovings into yarn.[34]

Slater's goal as stated in the contract was to improve the jenny workshop machinery and adapt it to operate by waterpower or perpetually. Slater initially worked to develop spinning machinery and achieved success in duplicating the Arkwright patents early on in the contract. To feed the machines and test their abilities, Slater had to reconstruct fiber-processing equipment including a carding machine, slubbing billy or drawing frame and a roving machine. Slater's carding machine, "a flat top," presented him with the most difficulties. The experimental hand run equipment used in the early mill was a roller-type carding machine developed by Joshua Lindley and which had already been in use in Beverly. In addition to Lindley's carders, Oziel Wilkinson built some of Brown's machinery designed similarly to Lindley's roller-type model. Slater's machine rolled the cotton up on the top of the cards instead of passing the cotton through on top of the large cylinder. The problem centered on fixing the wires firmly in the card clothing or leather base and giving them sufficient curve to comb the fibers. Pliney Earle provided Slater with a resolution. Earle was perhaps the only hand card maker in New England in about 1814. Earle maintained a shop in Leicester Massachusetts.[35] Earle noted that the hand set wires were not fixed firmly into the leather. To remedy this problem the wires were beaten to provide a greater crook and fix them in place.

No accounts or physical remains of either Slater's billy or roving machine exist; however, the spinning frames represent his greatest accomplishment. As Rivard suggests: "Very likely it was built neither entirely from memory nor entirely from scratch but rather a modification of one of the machines Slater found when he arrived, probably David Anthony's frame of 24 spindles."[36] According to Smith Wilkinson the spinning frames allowed Slater to produce both warp and filling.[37] This meant that the frames produced yarn hard enough to withstand the tension of warp without breaking. The mill no longer required hand spinners to provide cotton warps in order to make fabric from their product. The throstles could also produce yarns that could be adapted to a variety of purposes including sewing thread. Water powered throstles relinquished Slater from size restrictions based on human strength. Slater increased the efficiency of the frame from twenty-four to forty-eight spindles. By the end of 1790, he added twenty-four more spindles to the machine.

By April of 1790, Slater had completed the requirements of his contract. Satisfied with the outcome, William Almy and Smith Brown[37] entered into a partnership with Slater. "Under this agreement, Almy and Brown furnished the capital, and Slater in return for constructing the machinery and spinning the cotton was to have one half the profits and one half the machinery."[38] The partnership of Almy, Brown and Slater operated a spinning mill but Almy and Brown ran a general merchandising operation, which also marketed the yarn and oversaw a weaving workshop.

Almy and Brown established Slater and the machinery in Ezekiel Carpenter's clothier's shop in Pawtucket. Slater's responsibilities entailed the day to day running of the mill. Almy and Brown endeavored to dispose of the mill's product by direct sale through their shop on South Main Street in Providence, consignment to agents and weaving the yarn into fabric. Local artisans' children aged between 6 and 11 years comprised Slater's first labor force. The first four weeks of operation the work force consisted of four boys. Afterward an additional four children including some girls supplemented his original workers. The machines set up in Ezekiel Carpenter's clothier's shop at the falls in Pawtucket made suitable work for the children of artisans whose shops lined both the river and the channel called Sargeant's Trench. The trench, which had originally been a natural channel off the Blackstone River, ran parallel to the river for some distance. With use, artisans had widened and dammed the trench to power artisanal shops. Slater's laborers performed all the tasks necessary to keep the small spinning mill in operation. The children monitored the carding machine, the slubbing billies, the roving devices and throstles. Adults supervised the workers and repaired damaged machines. The oversight of the equipment required little training but attentiveness and a willingness to take some risk. The artisans' children included one son of Oziel Wilkinson with whom Slater resided and who later became Slater's father-in-law. The socio-economic level of the workers' parents and the ease with which Slater was able to secure their employment suggests that the millwork was viewed as appropriate training for the children and not as hazardous or injurious in any way. Smith Wilkinson recalled his work for Samuel Slater some years later.

> I was then in my tenth year and went to work with him and began
> attending the breaker. The mode of laying the cotton was by hand, tak-
> ing up a handful and pulling it apart with both hands shifting all into
> the right hand to get the staple of the cotton straight and fix the hand-
> ful so as to hold it firm and in turn applying it to the surface of the
> breaker moving the hand horizontally across the card to and fro until
> the cotton was prepared.[39]

Wilkinson's description of the work conditions incorporates none of the
danger, discomfort, boredom or health risks usually linked to industrial
environments. Wilkinson's machine was probably operating at the time he
was applying the fibers to the surface of the roller. Obviously the danger to
his limbs and hands was serious. Today, mechanical feeders provide carding machines with sustenance and thereby reduce the human risks to an
acceptable level. Smith had to perform the same task over and over again
throughout the workday and without catching his clothing, hair or body
in the machine. The air in the former clothier's shop filled with noise, and
lint from processing a short staple fiber. The machinery including the water
wheel vibrated the building. One wonders how much the environment differed from that at the anchor forge where Smith Wilkinson's father worked
or the machine shop where his brother worked.[40]

Without viewing the working conditions as too arduous or hazardous, the children continued to work in the mill. The workforce, machinery used, and yarn produced continued to expand. Slater's improvement of
the machinery, use of an unskilled labor force, application of waterpower
developed a productive and profitable cotton spinning enterprise for the
partners. The success of the machinery brought additional commodities to
market in increased amounts.

Increased yarn production created some problems for Almy and Brown.
The firm had to procure sufficient bales of adequate staple cotton to supply
the mill. The cotton arrived by ocean sometimes water stained or otherwise
damaged much to Slater's clearly stated disappointment. Slater's complaints
centered on three problems, including quantity available, rotten or stained
fibers and imperfect seed removal. He viewed these problems as Almy and
Brown's failures. Slater's comments pinpointed the problems faced by northern manufacturers endeavoring to increase the amount of cotton available
while awaiting the expanding cotton production of southern farmers. At this
point in time the cotton gin was not yet available to southern farmers and
as a result debris including pods and seeds were removed from the raw cotton by hand and often imperfectly to reduce the cost. To improve the quality of the raw cotton sent through the mill, the firm incorporated a second

picking process after the commodity arrived in the Port of Providence. The picking procedure removed rotten or stained fibers as well as remaining plant debris. This difference required some rethinking of procedures that no amount of haggling at the docks would remedy.[41]

The firm of Almy, Brown and Slater produced cotton yarn, which could be used for sewing, knitting, lace, fabric and sale to weavers. The firm of Almy and Brown chose to market the yarn in as many forms and for as many purposes as possible. An advertisement provides us with a good idea of the range of materials produced by Almy and Brown in the interest of marketing the mill's production:

> Almy and Brown at their store opposite the Baptist meeting house by wholesale and retail.
>
> A variety of cotton goods manufactured in this town among which are cords of various sorts, ribs, plain, thickset, stockinet rib and plain, Denim, Jeans, Jeanets, Fustians etc. Also cotton yarn of various sizes spun by water suitable for warps or stockings, superior in quality to any spun by hand or on jennys.[42]

Almy and Brown marketed most of the yarn as yarn in cities near and far. Almy and Brown worked hard to develop interest in their product among shopkeepers and domestic manufacturers who had traditionally sold flax, wool, and only a small amount of cotton. The two partners placed advertisements in newspapers and wrote to friends in Pennsylvania, Massachusetts, Connecticut and other states to interest buyers in their yarn and cloth. Almy and Brown issued form letters to various stores throughout the country trying to increase yarn sales. The letter, issued in 1796, stated: "We have taken the liberty to send thee 25 pounds of our cotton stocking yarn spun by water. As we spin more of this article than can be vended here away, we were recommended to thee to introduce the sale of it in Salem."[43] The two partners also enlarged their geographical sales area by selling some of the thread and yarn on consignment at their own risk to retailers. In 1798, they advertised their product sold at stores in Albany. They published newspaper notices forty-eight times that year in an effort to increase their sales.

Their efforts met with mixed results. The pricing of the yarns had to be competitive and the buyers had to be willing to market them. By 1796, Nathan Spencer of Newport opposite the state house advertised the sale of their yarns suitable for weaving and knitting cheaper and better than those spun by hand. "The prices are the same as it is sold for at the factory in Providence."[44] Germantown stocking weavers resisted the change, and forced a merchant to write back that the sale of yarn "met with great discouragements, the weavers there being all poor men and principally engaged in worsted."[45] In other localities, however, the cotton yarn met such success that supplies could not always keep up with demand. The terms of the sale were either consignment to shops, goods needed by the firm, cash or notes payable within four months.[46]

Almy and Brown took account of cotton yarn production at the spinning mill after about one year of operation. The company manufactured a total of 2,715.75 pounds of yarn numbers ten through twenty-four.[47] Almy and Brown sold or used all of numbers 10, 21, 22 and 23 but a total of 1,020 pounds remained of yarn numbers 12 through 20. Clearly surpluses taught Almy and Brown about markets and demand. The firm had either to develop demand for their full range of yarns or to discontinue or to reduce manufacture of yarns with limited demand. Understandably yarns falling into the middle range of texture proved most popular.

The immediate impact of yarns sold to general stores and to merchandisers on handloom weavers was limited. Almy and Brown sold their yarn to many small and large merchants all over the country in small amounts. The firm sometimes traded yarn to southern merchants in exchange for cotton bales rather than cash. Yet even the small amounts of cotton yarn available to merchandisers made cotton yarn less rare than it had been and introduced cotton to a wider and wider group of customers. Cotton yarn became more readily available to domestic manufacturers for making blend fabrics but was still a difficult commodity to acquire because it was not produced as a by-product of agricultural activities and required exchange or purchase for acquisition. Almy, Brown and Slater was perhaps the only mill producing cotton yarn by waterpower for approximately three years. The firm could not produce enough alone to eliminate hand spinning or create a tremendously greater demand for hand weavers. The demand for hand weavers did increase in the immediate area of Providence as merchants purchased Almy, Brown and Slater's product and began to fashion goods out of it in the same ways as they had during the jenny workshop era. Almy and Brown worked to develop a more efficient, more productive environment in their weaving workshops and began to contract with independent master weavers unwilling to work within the entrepreneur-owned weave shed.

ALMY AND BROWN'S WEAVING WORKSHOP 1791–1793

Despite the change in spinning and fiber processing machinery and mill management organization, the weaving workshop established by Almy and Brown to produce fabrics from cotton weft and linen warp continued without pause after 1790. Product lines changed reflecting the production of cotton yarn suitable for warp. The improved technology did not altogether eliminate the manufacture of blends.[48]The firm produced fustian, a fabric made of both linen and cotton both before and after the introduction of waterpowered spinning. The partners continued to put out linen for spinning during this phase of the operation and as a result outwork spinning did not diminish but thrived between 1791 and 1793.

Workshop records for the 1791 to 1793 period reflect increased productivity of both apprentices and more skilled weaver employees. Weaving rates rose from about 3 yards a day to well over 5 yards a day by the end of the period suggesting that the firm used fly shuttle looms to increase weaving proficiency and capacity. Apprentices, who had now worked for the firm for several years increased in proficiency and could produce more varieties of fabric more quickly with skill. In addition the firm began to contract with independent master weavers including Ichabod Tabor, David Buffum, Thomas Robinson, John Maguire, and Lewis Peck, to produce fabrics in independent shops. As indicated earlier, Almy and Brown contracted to produce large amounts of fabric with some of these workshops, thus simplifying and diversifying their weaving organization. Although the contractual relationships took work oversight away from the entrepreneurs, it reduced the risk and perhaps increased productivity and profit. The firm did not have to pay for the oversight and only paid the weavers for yardages produced. In many ways the contractual arrangement created a more attractive organizational structure for the firm that persisted through the 1800s. Almy and Brown's weaving contracts with independent shops encouraged the establishment of independent weaver-owned shops dependent upon machine-spun yarns for manufacturing fabrics to be marketed through retail and wholesale firms like but not limited to Almy and Brown. Although the impact of the procedure on handloom weaving, as a whole was slight, it marked the beginnings of an increased demand that ballooned with widespread industrialization.

In 1791 workshop weavers used 765.25 pounds of 12 to 17 grade yarns to fabricate thickset, corduroy, dimity, jean and fustian. Fine grade yarns produced finer dimities in Almy and Brown's attempts to produce and market fine quality fabrics at a profit. The firm employed nine weavers, masters, journeymen and apprentices, manufacturing a total of 1,182.75 yards of material. The yardage produced by each weaver averaged 131.42 yards for the month. Most apprentices wove about half as much as the journeymen because of the apprentices' needs to learn the trade. In addition, skilled weavers wove at a rate greater than or consistent with the 5 yards daily minimum dictate required by the early contracts. The weavers in training also worked only one or two fabric types. Alexander T. Shaw, a journeyman, produced the greatest amount of cloth totaling 295 yards of corduroy and fustian—a rate of almost 12 yards a day suggesting that he, at least, used a fly shuttle loom. Although not indicated in the records, it may be that work organization changed during period. Initially, workshop weavers had to wind their own quills and dress their own looms. These responsibilities diminished productivity as winding a warp and dressing looms in even simple patterns was time consuming and would reduce monthly yardage production significantly. Perhaps the partners hired individuals to dress unattended looms while weavers fabricated cloth on looms already dressed.

The 1791 weaving record refers to only one month's production, consequently the account may not provide a complete roster of employees and October's level of manufacture may not be consistent with other months. A published record of fabric woven between January and October 1791 indicates that Almy and Brown textile production consisted of 325 pieces of velvet (660 yards), thickset (745 yards), corduroy (1001 yards), fancy rib (664 yards), denim (1284 yards), jean (1769 yards) and fustian (1691 yards) totaling 7823 yards of fabric. The account presents a more accurate idea of the year's manufacture rate. During October, the weaver's production level rose above the other months.

By the end of 1792, Almy and Brown supported a staff of eighteen weavers. It is unlikely that the company suddenly doubled their staff in three months time. The yearly total amounted to 11,978.25 yards far less than if October's account had illustrated an average month for the same number of artisans. A year of 1791s would have led to the manufacture of over 14,000 yards of cloth by eight craftsmen.[49] During 1792 the workshop fabricated an even wider selection of goods including baronette, nankeen, plain cloth, sheeting and cotton satin, which had not appeared in earlier records. The consistent inclusion of fancy fabrics such as velvet and corduroy, and the wide variety of cloth types evidence Almy and Brown's experimentation with marketing domestic goods, 6,323.75 yards of jean composed the dominant product for 1793.[50] Jean, a utilitarian fabric provided competition for home manufacturers and independent craftsmen. Large quantities of corduroy (2613.25 yards) and velvet (920.75) designed to compete with the import market offered little competition due to its high price. The average yearly production for each weaver amounted to 665.46 yards. The amounts woven by individuals, however, fluctuated widely. Joseph Tabor fabricated the largest quantity totaling 1,240.25 yards. Ruth Anthony, who appeared in only one weaving account, wove a mere 47.5 yards.[51]

Almy and Brown employed thirteen workshop weavers between January and October 1793. On the average each craftsman wove 807.62 yards during the ten-month period manufacturing a total of 10,499 yards. A rate of about 3.2 yards per day and the weavers maintained a consistent rate of production. Alexander T. Shaw provided Almy and Brown with 1,550.25 yards the greatest amount produced by a single weaver in 1793. Thomas Robinson, a British master weaver hired the previous year, either worked part time for the firm out of his weaving workshop. In 1792, he wove 427.5 yards; a year later he produced only 221 yards. Apprentices who had worked for the company for several years and attained a certain level of skill, manufactured cloth at a rate comparable to journeymen and masters by 1793. As in 1792, jean comprised over fifty percent of the total yardage woven for Almy and Brown. Corduroy and thickset continued to be woven in quantity. [52]

THE CONSTRUCTION OF A BUILDING TO MANUFACTURE COTTON YARN

In 1791, Oziel Wilkinson, Moses Brown and Thomas Arnold purchased a plot of land including a mill privilege from Cynthia Jenks of Pawtucket. The property was located just above the clothier's shop being used by Samuel Slater to produce cotton yarn. The property was divided into three sections with Almy, Brown and Slater gaining control of 3/8ths of the land and 3/16th of the mill privilege. In August of 1792, Oziel Wilkinson, part owner of the plot, oversaw the erection of a dam above the natural falls. In February of 1793, they broke ground to build a textile mill and construct a raceway taking water off the river and allowing it to flow into Sargeants Trench. The textile mill measured 43' X 29' with two stories and an attic. Local artisans erected the building using post and beam construction. The simple clapboard structure was not distinguished by a clerestory in the roof or by its large scale, as were later mill structures. The many windows and narrow width of the building allowed natural light to illuminate the largely unpartitioned space. The walls received a coat of plaster and the Benjamin Kingsley's plastering bill provides us with the best description of the early structure since no contemporary prints or plans remain. The plaster was applied to the walls to allow for whitewashing and further light reflection.[53]

By March of 1793, Slater discontinued spinning operations at the clothier's shop and sent his workers home so that he could oversee the mill construction. Almy and Brown evidently retained yarn stores in order to maintain their weaving workshop throughout the construction period. The remaining yarn stock supplied faithful customers. As soon as Almy and Brown had sold all leftover yarn, their correspondence with customers assured the resumption of the operations by May. Unfortunately the firm could not manufacture yarn by the end of May in 1793. It was not until July 1793 that the firm began to test machinery and by August of 1793 the firm manufactured cotton yarns on a commercial scale at the new mill.[54]

By the time mill operations resumed, the children of artisans were no longer available to work for Samuel Slater. Initially Slater sought to hire orphans, the poor or other willing youths as apprentices to operate mill machinery. Slater advertised for workers in the *Providence Gazette* in 1794 "Wanted, Four or five active lads about 15 years of age to serve as Apprentices in the Cotton Factory."[55] The advertisement generated responses from private citizens and from regional cities and towns cognizant of those poor or orphaned individuals requiring some training in order to support themselves. Initially, Slater was able to hire sufficient numbers of pauper and orphan apprentices to meet his needs but the system failed for various reasons. Apprenticeship brings with it certain responsibilities on the part of the master that proved expensive to the extreme for the firm to uphold. Masters had to provide their students with some academic education so Slater established a Sunday School. Masters had to train their workers in the craft, art or trade sufficiently to enable them to find employment in the field elsewhere after their apprenticeship ended. As one of Slater's runaway apprentices stated

> If Mr. Slater had taught me to work . . . all the different branches I should have ben with you now but instead . . . he ceepe me always at one thing and I might have stade there until this time and never new nothing. I don't think it probable that I shall return . . . for the business I follow now I think is much more bennefisheal to my interest.[56]

Health care, boarding, clothing and other expenses contributed to making apprentice mill workers an inappropriate means of filling the mill with operatives.

As the apprenticeship system failed Slater, he returned to hiring children to work within the new mill building under contract. This work system also had its problems and Slater turned to hiring families in order to prevent transience, discipline problems, and expense. A growing landless population contributed to this system of mill workers. They came to Pawtucket from northwestern Rhode Island, southern Rhode Island and other sectors where inheritance factors and soil fertility contributed to the rise of a population of individuals who did not own land but wandered from job to job. The system of work that developed within the 1793 mill provided the organizational prototype for the mills that arose afterwards. In 1799 a second Almy and Brown supported mill enterprise was initiated in Warwick Rhode

Island. Soon other mills followed. In capitalization, machinery, work organization and labor force they were modeled after Almy, Brown and Slater.

For Slater, the new mill offered him the opportunity to establish water-powered spinning in a building erected specifically for the purpose of processing fibers, and spinning yarn. There he could expand, which he did beginning in 1801; organize the work along his own idealized lines; hire a new workforce; improve the technology used; and if necessary enhance waterpower production. Slater no longer made do with a structure and a situation originally developed for another purpose. At the new mill, Slater was able to create the prototypical spinning mill for others to follow. Here Slater "gave out the psalm" for cotton manufacturers to sing to afterwards.

THE ALMY AND BROWN WEAVING WORKSHOP 1794–96

The development of the spinning mill and increased spinning productivity provided Almy and Brown with additional yarns to market. The impact of the spinning mill was not discernable in 1793 because the mill only began production in August of that year. By 1794, the twelve weavers working at Almy and Brown wove 14,401 yards of nankeen, corduroy, jean, velvet, tick, fustian and thickset. Nankeen overtook jean in importance to the company yet, Almy and Brown continued to order large amounts of jean, velvet, and corduroy. Individual craftsmen produced on the average of 1,200.1 yards of fabric during the year. This level of manufacture amounts to about 4 yards of cloth per weaver per day.

By 1795, however, workshop weaving production peaked. This is not necessarily because of increased yarn production but may be due to a concentration on workshop weaving and making that system of fabric production profitable. Almy and Brown's sixteen artisans wove 48,401 yards of over eleven varieties of cloth during 1795. Fabrics included nankeen (29,469.5), corduroy (4291.5 yards), jean (10,063.25 yards), satin (412.25 yards), velvet (569 yards), weaverette (1033.5 yards), fustian (1051.25 yards) thickset (595.5 yards) baronette (116.25 yards), plain (284 yards), and small amounts of unspecified types. Nankeen comprised 61.3 percent of the total but as always jean amounted to a large portion of the total manufacture.[57] By this time both John Maguire and Ichabod Tabor supplied Almy and Brown from independent shops. Maguire sold the company 9,526 yards of fabric and Tabor 10,055.5 yards. The yardages indicate that many more than one weaver was working at these independent shops. Aside from Tabor's and Maguire's work, individual weavers averaged 1,674.1 yards for the year. (This amounts to about a six yard a day production level, which does not take into account rewarping or winding quills.)

From 1797 to 1800 weaving declined. According to Kulik:

> Almy and Brown had come to the conclusion only later confidently
> articulated that 'no company can carry on the business of weaving or
> spinning to the same profit as individuals may' and the reason had
> much to do with the scarcity of weavers and skilled finishers. William
> Almy complained that the weavers were so scarce that he frequently
> had 'three looms idle for want of workmen.[58]

By 1797, only eight weavers worked at Almy and Brown including Patrick McCann who had emigrated from Ireland that year.[59] Total production
for 1797 decreased to 9873.25.[60] The weavers fabricated all common cloth
types such as ticking, nankeen, shirting, fustian, plain cloth jean and muslin. Between 1798 and 1800 only Alexander T. Shaw and Ichabod Tabor
continued to weave for the company.[61]

Production levels and fabrics manufactured provide only the barest
idea of how Almy and Brown organized the workshop, who they hired, why
they could not keep the shop staffed and why the business proved unprofitable. Ideally William Almy and Smith Brown desired to employ about twelve
weavers. Although a maximum of eighteen weavers worked for the company,
many only wove for portions of the year. At the rate established in the early
Brown and Almy contracts each weaver should have produced about 1,200
yards per year or a total of 14,400 yards of cloth if the company employed
twelve artisans. The early years of the shop, individual performance proved
far from satisfactory. By 1794, however, Almy and Brown weavers attained
an adequate rate of manufacture. In 1795, the partners greatly increased their
yardage by contracting weaving to other workshops. This alleviated some of
their problems by shifting many of the responsibilities to other shoulders.

In the years that followed Slater's partnership with William Almy and
Smith Brown, the character of their weavers changed. Between 1788 and
1789 immigrant artisans predominated the weaving roster. After 1789,
however, with the exception of Patrick McCann, Thomas Healy, Thomas
Robinson, John Byrnes, James McKerris and John Maguire, weavers were
native to America and many Rhode Island born. In addition Robinson,
McKerris and Maguire all operated independent shops contracting with
Almy and Brown suggesting that immigrant workers preferred establishing
their own weave sheds rather than working for the entrepreneurs. Predominantly male, their ages at employment averaged 28 years.[62] Apprentices
ranged in age between nine and nineteen. Oliver Shaw was the eldest student weaver. Alexander T. Shaw, his brother, was the youngest journeyman
or trained weaver aged 22.

Since the Rhode Island mill system tended to hire family units, strong marital, sibling and parent child ties occurred among the company artisans. Nineteen weavers worked beside sibling at the looms including the Shaws, Tabors, Spencers, and Brownells. As stated earlier, McKerris and Reynolds were related by marriage after 1792; and the Tabor brothers and Stephen Hopkins wove supervised by their fathers. In all, seven instances of parent/children links and five marital ties occurred. Forty-six possible kinship ties existed in weavers bearing common last names.

After 1790, a core group of artisans worked for the company. Unlike the earlier era of textile manufacture, these weavers retained employment for over three years. Although transient labor still plagued the firm, some weavers, especially the apprentices, maintained employment. The Brownell brothers, for instance, began in 1789 and left in 1797. Anthony Shaw, indentured in 1790, discontinued his employ in 1796. The transience of labor proved expensive for Almy and Brown. Their problems in elevating production levels stemmed from the short duration of employment, and the high percentage of apprentices in the workshop. The company found replacement of craftsmen both time consuming and costly as looms went unattended. The student weavers required instruction in all the aspects of weaving and specific directions for each new fabric type introduced. Master and journeymen lost valuable time by showing the apprentices how to put the correct warp onto the loom and how to thread the harnesses. Toward the final phase of the workshop, apprentices and trained weavers all wove about 1,000 yards or more per year, which increased annual totals to a more profitable level.

By that time, however, Almy and Brown deemed the workshop unprofitable and began expanding their sale of warps by consignment. In 1793, the partnership made a concerted effort to increase sales of both cloth and yarn to shops throughout Rhode Island and the remainder of the country. Between 1791 and 1798, Almy and Brown advertised domestic fabrics for sale in their store on South Main Street in Providence. One such notice stated "have for sale 1,000 pieces of cotton goods among which are a variety of Nankeens both twilled and plain and various other kinds suitable for the present and approaching season."[63] Lack of enthusiasm for commercially made domestic goods led Almy and Brown to send samples of their fabrics to New York, Boston and other cities.[64]

The weavers who found themselves unemployed as a result of Almy and Brown's decision to discontinue cloth fabrication, adjusted to the change but with a variety of success. Isaac and Moses Brownell formed a partnership with their brother Peter and opened a cloth store.[65] Though initially successful, by 1816 when Moses died, the firm went into receivership.[66] Isaac Brownell then turned to operating a boarding house in Providence.[67]

Benjamin Cornell probably represents the most pliable of former employees. He worked as a teamster, truckman and huxter in addition to weaving for the Blackstone Manufacturing Company.[68] Walter Cornell, however, removed to Tiverton where he found employment as a night watchman for a textile firm in Newport.[69] In about 1848 Cornell left the state and moved west. Gideon Smith reported the following to the Rhode Island Society for the Encouragement of Domestic Industry in 1861:

> I should think about 12 years past, an old man, very respectable in appearance called on me at the old mill as it is termed in Pawtucket, wishing to look around before he took his departure for the western country where his children had gone saying he was formerly employed by Almy and Brown (Slater's Partners) and stated he brought out cotton for the mill in a pillow case: his name was Walter Cornell.[70]

Although not found in company records, Cornell must have continued to work for the firm when he did not guard the mill in Newport.

Samuel Cross had become involved in trade as a mariner by 1826.[71] His employment proved none too lucrative as when he described his property on Planet Street for taxation in 1814, he wrote: "This estate is very much in debt and in direct taxes to pay. I should be willing to sell the estate for $1,000.00" [72] Thomas Healy and Anthony Shaw also found little profit in their new positions. Thomas Healy declared bankruptcy in 1810 as an unsuccessful trader. Anthony Shaw, Jr. of Warwick, a mariner, died insolvent in June of 1815.[73]

Some of the workshop alumni found success in other businesses. Alexander Shaw became an agent for the Fiskeville Manufacturing Company.[74] James McKerris invested in the Warwick Spinning Mill with his father-in-law. Ichabod Tabor continued providing Almy and Brown with services through 1801. By 1835, when he died, he left only $41.34 in moveables, but his estate also included a house and property accumulated through his success as a spinner, weaver and tailor.[75]

Several of the workshop weavers found life after working for Almy and Brown difficult. The cause for their insolvency or low economic level does not correlate directly with their loss of hand weaving employment. The Brownells declared themselves insolvent in 1816, which was sixteen years after Almy and Brown discontinued their workshop operation. Peter Brownell credited the lack of protective tariffs against the flood of British goods after the War of 1812 with their financial problems. The year, 1816, marked a sharp decline in Rhode Island's textile industry. Since the Brownells relied on American manufactures, they too experienced hard times. Samuel

Cross blamed direct and indirect taxes for his desire to rid himself of his property on Planet Street in 1814. He suffered the effects of the embargo against British manufactures. As a mariner, the conflict with England made sea travel dangerous and the limits on trade inhibited his profits.

For some insolvency or indebtedness at death presents a deceptive image. Ichabod Tabor's estate shrank as a result of gifts to his children before death. As in Anthony Shaw's case the desire to aid family by offering property as early inheritance led to posthumous bankruptcy. Several former company weavers, who had obtained success as mill owners or other petty entrepreneurs, died in debt because of their generosity to their sons and daughters. The financial shape of the estate, however, did not reflect lowered living conditions as relative guaranteed comfort and care until death.

Of the Almy and Brown weavers unemployed in 1800 less than half left the textile profession. Several altered their career within the field becoming spinners, merchants, factory agents or textile entrepreneurs. Others shifted to less skilled and less easily identifiable positions including yeoman and laborer. Other than Alexander and Oliver Shaw who worked at farming for Almy and Brown, little connection between the two trades existed among these company weavers.

In 1806, Almy, Brown and Slater reinstituted cloth manufacture. Slater's involvement in the weaving process increased during the period as Pawtucket accounts maintained records of cloth yardages and spinning tallies.[76] Aside from managerial changes, fabrics manufactured differed from the earlier attempt. Rather than nankeen, velvet, satin, corduroy, baronette and other fancy cloth, the textiles woven between 1806 and 1809 reflected the owners' desire to compete with the domestic manufacturer. The firm's artisans wove ticking, shirting, sheeting, check, plaid, stripe, chambray, gingham and jean. These nine fabrics encompass the typical sorts of goods produced in most Rhode Island cotton mills from this period onward. In turning to utilitarian cloth, entrepreneurs recognized their inability to compete with less expensive imports without the assistance of duties.

When Almy and Brown resumed textile manufacture in 1806, Edward W. Lawton oversaw the operation. The record books listed yardages produced beside amounts of yarn spun. E.W. Lawton wrote to Almy and Brown requesting supplies for the Looms. He stated:

> The weavers are using borrowed slaies which are called for by the owners. Would thank you to procure two or three number forty and send out today if possible. Without them the weavers must stop. We cannot possibly get one here. Probably James Thurber, sign of the lion

has them. If he has only 48 or upwards, we would like two or three of them.[77]

According to Gras and Larson between 1816 and 1820, the company employed 566 weavers in the region to whom they put out webs. None of the weavers appeared to work solely at textile production, however the artisans took from three to six weeks to return the finished goods.[78] One memo E.W. Lawton wrote in July 1808 indicates that the company did put out some of their warps to domestic weavers. "By J. Bucklin, we send a bundle of yarn for Betsy Graham which she is to weave, or will please give her the enclosed pattern and direct her to weave it three quarter wide—should she not call for it you will please send her word."[79] Since there are references to weaving on site as well as in the home, the firm probably maintained both systems simultaneously between 1806 and 1809 only later discontinuing workshop manufacture entirely.

The second phase of cloth manufacture, however, was not without frustration. In a letter to John Withingham of Poughkeepsie, Almy and Brown expressed their dissatisfaction with fabric production.

> We are glad to hear thou art extending thy business by setting up more looms as we are desirous to encourage the manufactures of yarn into cloth by others rather than ourselves wishing to promote the industrious mechanic and manufacturer of cloth. We wish thee to increase thy sales to the full extent of sales of cloth in the part of the country where thou lives having been obliged ourselves to get our yarn wove into blue stripes etc. in certain of our pay we shall prefer doing that to manufacturing it ourselves.[80]

Due to the length of time between issue of warp and receipt of the finished product, loss of yarn through embezzlement, or poor quality weaving, Almy and Brown found cloth manufacture costly and of small profit. The necessity of providing equipment to those in their shop or slay and loom accessories for rent to domestic company weavers added even more expense to the weaving process. Personnel problems, though overseen by an agent, increased irritations and frustration as putting out required employment of large numbers. Thus, by 1809, the partners still preferred direct sale of cotton yarn and thread rather than involving themselves with cloth manufacture.

The production of large quantities of cotton yarn by Almy, Brown and Slater and other mills provided local weavers with a consistent source of high quality warp. By the end of the 1790s two spinning factories operated within a thirty-mile radius of Providence including Almy Brown and Slater and the Warwick Spinning Mill. Both businesses received major financial support from William Almy and Smith Brown. By 1809, seventeen factories spun cotton within thirty miles of Providence working 13,296 spindles and yielding 510,000 pounds of yarn per annum. The companies employed about 1000 looms in weaving fabrics.[81] Of the firms operating in 1809, Almy and Brown owned shares in four mills, and Samuel Slater invested in five factories. Almost two decades after mechanical experimentation, William Almy, Smith Brown and Samuel Slater retained domination in yarn manufacture in the state. The mills increased yarn production within the state dramatically resulted in either a proliferation of weaving in workshops and putting out or the companies experienced difficulty in marketing their goods. The firms accounted for an additional 1000 looms, which by themselves encouraged commercial weaving.

Almy and Brown distributed their warp, knitting yarn and sewing thread to states throughout the country including Massachusetts, Connecticut, New York, Pennsylvania and Maryland. Thus the sale of manufactured cotton yarns increased throughout the United States supplied by the new water powered mills. Almy and Brown sought to broaden the market for cotton yarn by making it readily avasilable to farm wives for the first time. They based some of their advertising on the idea that farmers and their families devoted unnecessary time and effort in fiber preparation. In a letter to Elisha Boardman, they wrote: "We have likewise sent some to Giles Meigs who has before sold of it and found it salable and even find it so where even any kind of thy vicinity do as much of this business as others."[82] By selling their warps to local dry goods stores, Almy and Brown encouraged domestic weavers to adopt the use of machine-spun yarn in their homes.

The history of textile manufacture and technology centers primarily on the three partners William Almy, Smith Brown and Samuel Slater. Due to their profound involvement in textile manufacture within the state, numerous mills were founded and designed to conform to the management structure of their early mill. Many were founded with their money. The management, organization and marketing techniques of the firm influenced the character of weaving throughout the state and country. During the following decades the number of spinning mills increased dramatically. The introduction of more efficient technology including the invention of the power loom had a massive impact on weaving and weavers. From 1789 through 1830, the rapid production of yarn required the employment of vast numbers of weavers.

Chapter Five

"I will thank you to put yarn out to good weavers only"[1]

Between 1810 and 1821, outwork weaving became the predominant method of commercial hand-woven fabric manufacture. Outwork networks grew during an era of technological and organizational experimentation in the textile industry. Technological change centered on reproducing British textile machinery and improving textile equipment already in use. Organizational innovation focused on establishing efficient and productive work environments. Textile mill owners drew on several systems to produce fabric by hand prior to the development of a marketable power loom. They duplicated craft workshop conditions within the factory setting, they contracted with craftsmen to weave in independent enterprises, hired weavers to work in mill owned housing and they issued webs to individuals to produce fabric in their homes. By comparing successful and failed commercial hand cloth manufacturing efforts, this chapter offers insights into outwork weaving as a system of manufacturing cloth between 1810 and 1821.

Outwork resulted not only from experimentation in factory production but also from changes in communities and families.[2] By the first quarter of the 19th century, inheritance patterns, over-population, and limited local land resources threatened communities and family unity. Exchange networks enabled rural communities to attain self-sufficiency; farm families bartered goods and services. While such bartering provided rural families with the necessities of life, what was available locally limited the scope of exchanges. A growing dependence on non-agricultural pursuits and the tension of cooperative networks set the stage for new sources of income made available by textile mills. With industrialization, factory labor and outwork offered new opportunities. They provided a cash-based as opposed to a commodities- and services-based system. They enabled women to contribute to the family's cash income. Finally, outwork presented families with a means of going beyond the community by purchasing commodities produced elsewhere.[3]

Changes in rural economy and family life coincided with a generalized reclassification of work. The disintegration of an artisan-based labor system allowed for the rise of semi-skilled outwork weavers. Domestic manufacturing had operated alongside professional handloom weaving and resulted in two types: semi-skilled home weavers and craft trained handloom weavers. The rejection of factory-labor by professional handloom weavers increased the opportunities for semi-skilled outworkers and marked the ultimate demise of craft-dependent fabric production.

Textile manufacture was one of the first mechanized industries to incorporate outwork production into its manufacturing procedures. The era is significant in that it constituted a time of trial and adjustment for a labor system that provided women, and young adults, with an acceptable means of earning supplementary income. Social, economic and technological factors encouraged women in disproportionate numbers to participate in outwork weaving. Improvements to textile machinery diminished or changed the skills required to produce yarn, thread or cloth. As a result, managers redefined jobs to suit the requirements of increasingly mechanized factories.[4] Both Daryl Hafter and Mary Blewett indicate that women willingly worked at newly created positions rejected by men with craft skills. Gender divisions in work denied women places in already-defined work situations, particularly those involving labor outside the home. Yet, outwork weaving was both timely and fortuitous for women; it positioned them at the vanguard of change and innovation.[5] As a result, forces that kept trained male artisans from participating in company-owned weave shed work also made part-time outwork performed in the home attractive to semi-skilled female workers.[6] The popularity of putting-out and the demand for hand weaving by textile mills during this era provided rural Rhode Island families with an important source of supplementary income for over thirty years.

THE RELATIONSHIP BETWEEN MECHANIZATION AND HAND PRODUCTION

One of the forces behind work reclassification was the development of equipment to replicate tasks formally performed by hand. The reproduction of British textile technology, and improvements to it after 1790 did not eliminate the involvement of skilled craftsmen in textile manufacture. During the early phases of mechanization, cotton textile mills continued to incorporate handwork into factory production. Subsequent technological innovations limited, and ultimately excluded, hand processes from textile manufacturing.[7]

Initially, inventive genius focused on fiber preparing and spinning processes. Spinning and fiber preparing machines required differing skills and abilities than those needed for hand processes. The new machinery effectively cast hand spinners out of cotton mill employment. Each improvement broadened the market for machine-spun cotton thread and further reduced the need for commercial hand spinning. The displacement of hand spinners from cotton mill workforces occurred rapidly after 1790 when Samuel Slater introduced spinning frames that could produce both cotton warp and weft. As mechanisms suitable for processing wool and flax came into use, hand spinners found little need for their skills but the displacement of hand spinners, like the displacement of hand weavers occurred gradually because of the later introduction of woolen or linen technologies.

The displacement of hand weaving from the cotton textile industry occurred at a much slower rate than that of hand spinning. First, a marketable power loom and complementary equipment including warpers and dressers were not developed until 1814, about twenty-four years after the elimination of hand spinning from the factory environment. Second, in Rhode Island, economic conditions, power shortages, ineffective protective tariffs and technological limitations hampered the diffusion of power loom technology. As a result, power looms were not generally used in the state until about 1826. Third, in Rhode Island, outwork weaving continued until at least 1840 because the nature of the woolen fiber forced technological innovation in the woolen industry to lag behind mechanization in cotton textile manufacturing.[8]

Since about twenty-four years elapsed between the elimination of hand spinning from mill work and the introduction of a marketable power loom, textile manufacturers had either to restrict their production to thread, warp and yarn, or to find a good way of incorporating hand weaving into their production procedures. Some Rhode Island mills did confine their output to the manufacture of thread, warp and yarn. By 1820, 21 out of 82 mills restricted their manufacture to thread alone and 31 sold textiles as both thread and fabric.[9] As more spinning mills competed with one another for the sale of warp, yarn and thread, mill owners found their options limited and their decisions clear. Their survival required bringing other, perhaps less competitive, products to market. The manufacture and sale of simple utilitarian fabrics proved profitable and less competitive, particularly prior to 1816, when the Napoleonic War and the War of 1812 disrupted foreign trade.[10]

EARLY CLOTH MANUFACTURE

At first, textile mills used a variety of means to produce cloth. Before out-work came to predominate, in Rhode Island, Almy and Brown of Providence tried to duplicate craft workshop conditions within the factory setting. As described earlier, the firm initiated mill-owned weave sheds in the cellars of houses in Providence. Almy and Brown were not alone in establishing weave sheds to produce fabric. Union Manufacturing Company, Colombian Manufacturing Company and the Stone Mill in Warwick among other early Rhode Island cotton mills also implemented the factory weave shed system for cloth manufacture.[11]

By reproducing craft workshop conditions in company-owned weave sheds, textile mill owners attracted a small number of British immigrant weavers to enter into contracts. Mill owners hoped that immigrant textile workers might impart their knowledge of mechanized spinning to them. Yet, immigrants brought with them strong craft ideals and memories of negative experiences in British textile factories. The desire to adhere to craft traditions and to prevent either close supervision or displacement, made the factory weave shed environment unattractive.

The artisan-based labor system was on the brink of obsolescence. Yet, the weave shed craftsmen endeavored to set their own standards and reestablish the craft. They showed their dissatisfaction with the mill system by avoiding it, by shifting from job to job or by investing in independent ventures.[12] Gary Nash and Cynthia Shelton suggest that the weave shed environment failed to attract sufficient artisans to insure success of the early weaving and spinning factories. Both the environment and the association of the work with poorhouse labor repelled prospective employees from the enterprises.[13]

As a result of these problems, many early Rhode Island factory-weaving businesses failed. Mill owners reacted to the situation by instituting other forms of fabric manufacture: they contracted with weavers to produce fabric in independent weave sheds, issued warps to individual part-time weavers and commissioned cloth agents to issue warps to weavers.[14]

For Almy and Brown, the shift from the workshop to outwork fabric production occurred smoothly as several of their own workshop weavers instituted artisan-owned weave shed enterprises in Providence. In 1794, Almy and Brown began to hire independent master craftsmen to weave cloth from Almy and Brown's machine-spun warps. John Maguire, Ichabod Tabor and James McKerris wove goods for the firm in independent weave sheds after leaving Almy and Brown's workshop. In addition, the company records indicate that David Buffum, Peter Stowell, James Wheaton and

John Reynolds, none of whom had worked in the weave shed, agreed to produce fabric for Almy and Brown between 1789 and 1791.[15] This system of cloth manufacture suffered the same fate, as the mill owned workshops because there were not enough independent weavers in Providence to manufacture the fabric needed by the firm.

As early as 1794, Almy and Brown had sold warps to Benjamin Shepard, an entrepreneur who owned a small jenny spinning shop. By 1802 Almy and Brown contracted with Silas and Benjamin Shepard, Benjamin's sons, to weave, dye and bleach about 1900 yards of ticking in their weaving shop in Taunton, Massachusetts. The agreement between Almy and Brown and the Shepards accounts for all of Almy and Brown's cloth manufacturing in 1802. The method of contracting all their weaving with a single independent workshop continued until 1806. By that time the Shepards had produced well over 14,000 yards of ticking for Almy and Brown.[16]

The conditions of the agreement regulated production by requiring that the Shepards convert one third of the yarn they took from Almy and Brown into fabric for the firm. In addition, Almy and Brown did not demand that they weave exclusively for the firm. The system eliminated may of the problems associated with company-owned workshop management for the partners. Almy and Brown supplied yarn and received the finished product. In addition, Almy and Brown no longer had to tie up capital in looms, associated equipment or in space to house the weave shed enterprise. The Shepards had to battle transient labor, damaged warps, broken equipment or illness among workers. The brothers insured quality and quantity in a timely manner or suffered the loss themselves.[17]

After 1806, the Shepard brothers severed their contract with Almy and Brown and turned to individual private investments. Silas Shepard became Superintendent of the Taunton Manufacturing Company. His interests also centered on technological innovation. Between 1816 and 1824, Silas developed several textile mechanisms including a filling frame, an upright power loom and a bobbin winder. By 1810, Benjamin Shepard left his father's textile mill and moved to Middleborough, where he operated a cotton textile business until about 1837. Almy and Brown neither expanded the system nor found individuals to contract to fabricate their cloth. For a time, they focused on marketing the yarn and thread produced in their Pawtucket and Warwick mills.[18]

In contrast to Almy and Brown's initial efforts, the Blackstone Manufacturing Company of Mendon (now Blackstone), Massachusetts contracted with artisans to weave in the kitchens of the firm's tenement housing. In 1811, the company records indicate that at least three weavers contracted to manufacture fabric for the firm in mill housing. Thomas Brand, James

Cupples and Leonard Dobbins rented mill tenements and wove in the kitchens of their rented dwellings. The firm appears to have treated the resident artisans with deference; several other mill employees moved from place to place in the tenements to make sure that Dobbins and Cupples would live in the same house. Their accommodations were located in the building best suited to weaving.[19]

Textile firms recruited immigrant craftsmen, because they knew that foreign artisans were likely to have some knowledge of textile technology. It may be that all three of these resident weavers were foreign and that the firm did not plan to manufacture all their fabric by hiring professional weavers to work in factory-owned facilities. Leonard Dobbins had recently arrived from Ireland just prior to working for the Blackstone Manufacturing Company.[20]

One resident weaver's contract has survived. On September 17, 1811, Cyrus Butler and Seth Wheaton, investors in the company, corresponded regarding an agreement with Thomas Brand. "Sir, we have engaged Thomas Brand to go to Blackstone to weave 9/8 checks at nine cents full yard of full width number twelve warp and find him our looms and use of warping tools. He finding reed and harness, brushes and sizing and doing all the work of spooling, quilling, warping, etc."[21] The document is specific in describing the kind of cloth, the equipment, and the services Brand must supply. It does not specify the amount of cloth or the tenure of the contract. In addition, Blackstone weaving ledgers do not list Brand among the weavers.

Brand's contract differs from those issued by Almy and Brown to their workshop weavers in several respects. First, the Blackstone Manufacturing Company provided fewer materials than did Almy and Brown. Although both Brand and the Almy and Brown weavers had to quill and spool their weft, Almy and Brown provided their weavers with reeds, harnesses and brushes. Second, the Blackstone Manufacturing Company did not stipulate the rate or quantity of production, whereas Almy and Brown required that their artisans weave at the rate of five yards per day moreover the firm required the total yardage to be manufactured by a specific date. On the basis of this evidence, it would seem that the textile mill did not rely as heavily on the fabric production of these three resident weavers as did Almy and Brown on their workshop artisans. Since the Blackstone Manufacturing Company established their outwork network simultaneously with this form of textile manufacture, they did not rely heavily on the skills and productivity of resident weavers alone. The firm probably hired foreign textile workers as consultants who could provide them with information about the organization, management, and machinery of successful British textile mills.[22] In the cases of Cupples and Dobbins no contracts exist but rental rolls indicate that they resided at the Blackstone Manufacturing Company for about one year. During that time Cupples produced 423 yards of chambray, and stripe and Dobbins wove 391 yards of chambray, gingham and stripe. The low yardage total indicates that the weavers did not live and work at the mill for long. Records of the settlement of accounts buttress this assessment by showing that Cupples remained in Mendon from about August 1811 through October 1812. Dobbins continued weaving for the mill until December 1812. Like other native or immigrant handloom artisans, neither Dobbins, Brand nor Cupples continued weaving for the textile mill for extended periods. The short duration of their employment related either to the work environment, management controls or to the firm's changing needs.[23]

OUTWORK WEAVING

Since neither native-born nor immigrant skilled male weavers were willing to work in factory-owned weave shed settings, and since the number of artisan weavers inclined to contract for factory labor was insufficient, mill owners had to find other ways to manufacture fabric. No letter or journal describes the strategies involved or identifies individuals who recognized where available workers might be found. Business accounts, however, provide evidence that agents and mill owners came to resolve their fabric production problems with outwork. During the jenny workshop era, workshop owners put out linen, wool and cotton for spinning by hand by women in nearby homes. Dyeing, and finishing procedures might also be put out to individuals. The application of the same methodology to outwork weaving did not take a tremendous leap in thought or in organization. Adrienne Hood has shown that during the 18th century that gradual gender shift from male to female weaving occurred during the 18th century. Spinning mills took advantage of the local domestic weaving workforce.[24]

Textile company store accounts indicate that, from the outset, that individuals exchanged domestic textile production for store goods. Many of these accounts refer to payment in woven handkerchiefs, tow cloth, fustian, aprons or other textile goods produced at home by women. The numerous and widespread examples of this activity indicate that mill owners discovered a resource of part-time semi-skilled female weavers residing on farms and in homes throughout the state.[25]

Textile manufacturers did not invent outwork. Entrepreneurs adapted the system from a well-established custom of supplementing agricultural income by taking in raw materials to process in the home. Studies of industry in the English countryside suggest that outwork existed in England from as early as the fourteenth century.[26]

In Rhode Island and elsewhere in New England, few farmers could increase income by expanding their acreage. As the smallest state in area, Rhode Island had limited free land. Moreover, the state, composed primarily of glacial moraine, had a rocky landscape and thin soil. From the outset some families supplemented agricultural income with day labor, mining and trades. By the mid eighteenth century, non-agricultural income was essential to most Rhode Island families. By the early nineteenth century, New England as a whole suffered from localized over-population.

Initially rural populations pursued trades to retain self-sufficiency. Local networks allowed individuals to exchange commodities and services for what they needed but could not buy with cash or produce. At first these cooperative networks assured the self-sufficiency of rural communities. As the populations grew, however, the availability of local fertile land diminished. Inheritance traditions had led farmers to acquire tracts of land sufficient for all their sons to support each of their son's nuclear families. With the growth of the resident population, this custom rapidly ate up fertile agricultural resources. As a result there was local land shortage, despite vast untamed lands to the west. Farmers were faced with several options: see the family disperse by having some members acquire properties elsewhere, move away to less densely populated regions with plentiful fertile acreage, encourage offspring to develop interests in non-agricultural pursuits through apprenticeship training or find some way to survive with limited land holdings.[27]

Fortuitously the local land shortages occurred at a time when mill owners sought a dispensable and cheap source of labor, particularly a workforce unfettered by troublesome craft traditions. Though committed to earning money or exchanging labor for goods, the rural weaving labor force was not composed of individuals trained in the weaver's art. Joseph France, a Rhode Island master weaver, quoted James Butterworth's British weaving book, which reported that few outworkers knew how to read a pattern or draft a design. Although France published Butterworth's guide verbatim altering only a few words, his retention of the complaint about outworkers suggests that lack of skill was a problem in both the United States and Britain.[28] Outwork weavers were not entrepreneurs, few started independent weaving enterprises or established their own textile mill. Rather, this group of predominantly female part-time artisans saw weaving as a way to pay for goods not produced on the farm, to earn cash to purchase additional lands or to attain financial independence. Weaving was a means not an end; to outworkers weaving remained attractive only as long as some other form of outwork did not pay better. Women could pursue weaving outwork without disrupting their sphere of domestic work because the labor was performed at home.[29]

In addition, though the market for domestic fabrics influenced the manufacturer's choice of product line, the skills of the available extra-factory workforce also determined the kinds of cloth to manufacture. Most textile mills hired outworkers to produce utilitarian fabrics requiring very little skill or knowledge of weaving beyond the basics. Almy and Brown altered the kinds of fabric they produced between 1790 and 1804. Weave shed artisans wove a wide variety of goods from plain weave to velveret between 1789 and 1796 but Almy and Brown could not keep the firms' looms busy, because, in large part, skilled weavers were unwilling to work for the mill. Their attempt to increase the number of weavers capable of producing at least some fabrics resulted in the production of simple bedticking. Merchant weavers put out webs to local part-time weavers or hired some weavers to work in their weave shed. Work on less complex fabrics enlarged the pool of employees available for textile work and resolved the labor scarcity problem for a time.[30]

Other factors also influenced the decision to switch from complex fancy fabrics to plain cloth production. Correspondence with cloth merchants indicates that Almy and Brown's line of fancy fabrics was not generally popular with the rural population. On the contrary, foreign complex weave fabrics held far more appeal than domestically manufactured specialty goods in both price and distinction. Evidently American firms lagged behind British and French textile manufactures in setting fashion and in providing stylish goods. As a result, provincial fabrics found a limited market for their velvets, weaverettes and baronettes. American manufactures were suitable for household needs such as work shirts, bedclothes, toweling and mattress covers as long as the prices were competitive.

By 1810, textile mills commonly manufactured simple utilitarian goods such as check, stripe, shirting and sheeting. All the fabrics were simply constructed, and the materials had a wide appeal. The availability of semi-skilled labor, the demand for simple and inexpensive goods, the lack of foreign competition with the passage of the Embargo Act and the complementary needs of the rural population and textile mill owners determined fabric choices.[31]

Outwork became the predominant method of hand-woven fabric manufacture between 1810 and 1821. The textile mills organized almost identical putting-out systems. There is some evidence to indicate that textile mill owners shared information on establishing outwork weaving networks. The Blackstone Manufacturing Company, for instance, contacted Caleb

Greene and the Coventry Manufacturing Company of Coventry, Rhode Island regarding methods of issuing work and paying for labor. Each firm's outwork employment and compensation systems were so similar that the prices of the goods and rates of compensation were within pennies of each other.[32]

Most of Rhode Island's spinning mills followed the same general outwork scheme. The number of individuals involved and the amount of warp risked at one time required keeping complex and detailed records documenting outwork and outworkers. These account books also provide ample details of fabric quality, quantity and cost.[33] A certain percentage of machine-spun warp and weft was made into or organized into webs. Webs consist of warp put into weaver's chains for warping on the loom, and of weft prepared for quills. The yarn was pre-measured for each kind of fabric and each specific width and length.

Each web received a ticket and a number. The ticket indicated the weight, coarseness of the goods, the pattern and payment. The ticket number and information on the ticket were recorded in a ledger. When the materials were issued to weavers, the weaver's name, and the date that the webs were issued were added to the account book. The weavers took the ticket with them and would return it with the completed fabric. Manufacturers might issue as many as 270 webs to over one hundred outwork weavers each year. Once woven, each web produced between 25 and 75 yards of fabric. Consequently a large amount of capital was at risk at one time.

Once these webs were prepared, the mill had to find ways to distribute efficiently the work to weavers and to maintain records. Mills dispersed the webs to weavers in three ways: local weavers might pick up webs and receive weaving instructions at the company store; family members who worked in the mill might sign for warps to be woven by someone else in their home; or agents might arrange to have materials delivered to the weavers who lived far from the store.[34]

Although the putting-out system provided the textile industry with a plentiful and previously untapped labor force, outwork was a mixed blessing. Issuing warps to great numbers of local outworkers directly from the mill or factory store created problems that textile mill owners found insurmountable. To put-out warps directly from the factory, the mill owner or agent hired and oversaw hundreds of part-time transient employees. Manufacturers maintained little control over these laborers, as the weavers did not work on company property, but away from the mill site.

The productivity levels of outworkers in comparison to those of the factory weave shed artisans demonstrate the effects of fabric manufacture without oversight and without a strong commitment of outworkers

to weaving. Almy and Brown required their workshop weavers to produce five yards of fabric per day. Even so, John Reynolds, an independent master weaver associated with the firm, suggested that the requirement was not challenging. Nonetheless outworkers did not achieve the expected level of production. Outworkers, as part time workers, averaged just 25 yards at thirteen-week intervals and a total of 200 yards per year. To counteract low productivity rates, firms had to risk more warps to more part time workers.[35]

As more and more factories began to manufacture fabric by issuing warps to outworkers, their networks extended over further distances from the mills. Distance also affected the rate of completion. Those who lived far from the mill or store relied on agents to deliver warps to them. Hence, they and their neighbors would receive webs on the same day and would also return the completed fabric at the same time. Blackstone Manufacturing Company outworkers resided in almost every city and town in Rhode Island. Although the textile mill was built in Massachusetts near the Rhode Island border, only 188 out of 760 outworkers lived in Massachusetts.[36]

Mills issued large quantities of yarn for about three month's time, risking embezzlement and suffering losses due to shoddy workmanship. The quality of the finished fabric varied widely. As a result, it is not surprising that some fabrics were returned in an unsaleable condition. These pieces of cloth, classed as "gauzy," "shoddy" or "poor," resulted in loss to the mill and fines to outwork weavers.

Although the term "shoddy" probably reflects lack of skill, "gauzy" is more suggestive of embezzlement. Embezzlement of yarn or cloth was not uncommon among British outworkers. Weavers sought to fend off pauperism by lightening the fabric and retaining unused threads. To a great extent, embezzlement was a symptom of the decline of the trade. Under similar circumstances, American outworkers also resorted to theft of either completed fabric or yarn.

Part-time weavers sought to receive the most from their efforts. This resulted in the development of several forms of defalcation. Gauzy fabrics resulted from using insufficient weft or filling. The weaver might keep unused weft and possibly warp to make additional yardage. It was like getting paid twice for the same web. Others would not necessarily return completed cloth to the factory that issued the web but would sell their fabric to the highest bidder. The broad geographic area facilitated fabric sales over which webs were distributed and the span of time between delivery and pick up. Outworkers opted to be paid now rather than await the proper mill's agent.[37]

Embezzlement was enough of a problem that firms encouraged other employees or trusted neighbors to help guard against theft. The agents of Blackstone Manufacturing Company, for instance, requested that one neighbor spy on the activities of an outworker. In a letter to Duty Smith, Stephen Tripp wrote:

> Phoebe Finch who lives in your neighborhood took some yarn of us last spring to weave into coverlets. She has returned about half of them and the remainder about 35 pounds of yarn she has now and I suppose it is not wove. I have understood that her husband has lately returned to Burrilville intends or says he intends to carry her away with him and fearing that she may be influenced by him to carry away or to sell our yarn, I should be obliged to you if you will have an eye to her conduct.[38]

Whether Duty Smith was successful in performing this task or willing to do it is not known. Since Phoebe Finch continued to work for the firm until 1820, she must have satisfied her employers by completing the coverlets or returning the warps. It is also apparent from this exchange that agents had to maintain an awareness of personal problems affecting outworkers as well as an understanding of the financial records.

The use of part-time semi-skilled artisans to weave fabrics was also plagued by transience. Blackstone Manufacturing Company records indicate that few employees continued to weave for the firm for more than two years. Between 1810 and 1820, the factory hired a total of 760 artisans to take in warps, yet their annual workforce never exceeded 150 outworkers. About fifty-three weavers wove for the mill for over six years. About 66 percent of the labor force changed each year. Several factors led to the short tenure of worker employment including the use of weaving as a supplement to family income, death, marriage, geographic mobility, weaving as a part time occupation and perhaps dissatisfaction with the terms of employment. Equally important, outworkers displayed little loyalty; they switched employers or changed from one kind of outwork to another whenever they could earn more.[39]

A related development resolved some of the problems of outwork for the mills: the system of contracting out large amounts of warp to commission agents began around 1807. Some textile manufacturers solved the inequities of outwork by delegating the risks and annoyances of the system to the commission agent. As a result, middlemen hired the large labor force, maintained copious records, arranged to deliver yarn and collected the finished product. The merchant also absorbed the risks as manufacturers penalized the agent for shoddy workmanship, dirty cloth, wasted

warps, theft and any other losses except acts of God. The use of commission agents redirected many outwork problems but did not make outwork issued from mills obsolete. Rhode Island mills used these systems side by side until about 1826. Cloth agents removed the paperwork, tedium and risk from factory management but did not improve the efficiency.[40]

OUTWORK WEAVERS

The pitfalls and risks of the putting-out system led to record keeping detailing fabric manufacture but not offering a clear image of the weaving population. Cloth records emphasize production; cloth quality, cost and other aspects of manufacture yet provide little information about the weavers themselves aside from earnings, productivity and sometimes residence. The scant surviving correspondence between weavers and the mill agents rarely mentions the specifics of life and livelihood. Unlike surviving literary efforts generated by Lowell Mill "girls," Rhode Island's outwork weavers have left us few written insights.

Business and cloth accounts reflect a male bias that obscures the female weaving population. Typically ledgers name the male head of household rather than the artisan. In other instances the ledger clearly indicates the relationship between the household head and the actual outworker as in the cases of "Mercy Brightman of Martin," "Perry Edwards' wife," or "Colonel Stephen Abbott's widow." The use of the head of household's name to represent the work of family members suggests families were the basic unit of production. Further ledger accounts link a single name to a variety of work performed by family members. A single account might list outwork weaving, factory work such as carding, and spinning, and other forms of extra-factory labor such as picking. The work of many individuals is grouped and attributed to a single household unit under one name. This accounting method diminishes the significance of individual earnings but maintains the importance of family contributions to the economic well being of the household.

Because of the system of crediting the household head for outwork weaving, only thirty percent of the 1248 names obtained from five textile mills records are female. Occupations of the people listed in the accounts suggest that many of them were not the individuals doing the weaving. Fifteen percent of the Blackstone Manufacturing Company weavers were listed elsewhere in company records as pickers, day laborers, dye-housemen, or teamsters. Picking and waste picking constitute outwork requiring little skill. These tasks might have been performed by very young children or, by other family members than the outwork weaver. Day laborers and teamsters hired for occasional labor worked the slack seasons of their regular trades. Since the records contain such a variety of tasks under individual names, it is likely that the records represent the collective work of families.

Civil records identified over one half of the names recorded in cloth ledgers as farmers, husbandmen or yeomen. None of the weaver's names were the same as those listed in full-time in-house factory labor such as spinners, carders or machinists. Less than 1 percent of the Blackstone outworkers resided in company housing indicating that the remainder either owned or rented property outside the factory village. As a result, a much greater percentage of the 1248 names listed in cloth ledgers are those of farmers than suggested by textile accounts. Despite the seasonal nature of agricultural employment, it is unlikely that the farmers themselves took in outwork, as records indicate a consistent level of fabric production throughout the year. These factors all contribute to the assumption that the names listed in the cloth accounts are not necessarily the names of the people who actually wove and that the names in the weaving ledgers often hide the work of women.

That women rather than men were weavers is suggested by both contemporary accounts and mill advertisements. For instance, in 1817, Henry Bradshaw Fearon described the outwork system as he saw it during his travels in Providence, Rhode Island.

> A considerable portion of weaving is done by women who have or live in farm houses. They receive 3 1/2 d. per yard for 3/4 wide stout dark gingham, an article, which is sold at 13 1/2 d. wholesale and 15 d. retail. These female weavers do not in general follow the occupation regularly. It is done during their leisure hours and at the dull time of the year.[41]

Want advertisements for weavers corroborate Fearon's description. Earlier, during the late 18th century, advertisements for apprentice weavers either for factory or master-owned workshops requested applications from boys.[42] Indeed, Almy and Brown only hired one woman to work in their eighteenth century weaving workshops.[43] By 1810, however, advertisements solicited female weavers.[44] John Arnold hired "ten experienced young women to work spring shuttle looms" but also wanted twelve "native lads" as apprentices in the cotton mill industry.[45] In 1815 the Rutenberg Factory advertised for eight or ten unmarried women to weave plain weave.[46] In each case, textile firms recruited women to work on an outwork basis, whereas in-house workshop weavers were men or boys.

Land and probate records as well as local histories and advertisements offer insights into the composition of the outwork weaving population.

In large part the population of weavers mobilized by the outwork system resided in the rural areas of the state; all but about 140 out of the 1248 handloom outworkers resided in Rhode Island's less densely populated rural areas such as Burrilville, Glocester, Smithfield, and Hopkinton. To some degree, the location of the five textile factories determined who worked for them as weavers. The mills were located in Mendon, Massachusetts, and Cranston, Hopkinton, Providence and Warwick, Rhode Island. A large percentage of each mill's weavers lived close to the factory. Yet each mill also employed workers in outlying areas, and, as a result, the outworkers for the five mills studied here lived in every city and town in the state.

As suggested earlier, the circumstances that caused individuals to supplement their income with outwork weaving were felt most strongly in the rural areas of Rhode Island. As outwork developed, it supported both the economy of the traditional farm family and the self-sufficiency of the farm community. Outwork solidified rather than eroded the solidarity and independence of the family unit. Women and children supplemented family income without leaving home, and young adults aided the family without moving to the city. The rise of factory outwork occurred at an opportune time both for farming families in need for supplementary income and for mills in need of a large labor force of workers to produce fabric.[47]

Based on these conclusions and on some specific examples from the data collected, the weaving population may be described. The outworkers fall into four distinct categories depending on common economic conditions, age distribution and family structure: a.) Young adults between the ages of 15 and 25 who continued to reside with their parents, b.) young newly married women with no or few children, c.) widows and single women acting as household heads and d.) professional weavers.

The largest group of outwork weavers includes women from ages fifteen to twenty-five. Almost 80 percent of the 1248 names represent heads of households whose daughter or young wife took in outwork to supplement the family income. Parents with unmarried young adult children often took in warps. The propensity to become involved with outwork depended on the necessities of life and stages of the life cycle. Families supplemented their income to purchase land to help male children establish themselves on their own farms, or to purchase those things the family could not otherwise acquire. During this period in a family's history, the father's or the household head's name appears in the ledger as well as an occasional child's name. Almost 10 percent of the outworkers named were men over forty with large families consisting of children in their late teens or early twenties.[48]

One graphic example of this is the case of Peleg Cranston. In 1814, his family included twelve children, five males and seven females, ranging in age from 13 to 29. Several of Peleg Cranston's children wove for the Blackstone Manufacturing Company during 1814 and contributed their earnings to the family. In 1811 and 1812 Amy and Mary Cranston, two of Peleg's daughters, married two brothers, Clark and Gorton Howard. As soon as the sisters married the Howard brothers, Clark and Gorton's names are listed on the mill roster. The wives continued to take in warps during the early years of their marriage. Though their names never actually appear in the ledger; clearly their earnings supplemented the family incomes.[49]

Weaving records suggest that neither the Cranstons nor the Howards relied heavily on weaving for their subsistence. During 1813 and 1814 the families never produced more than 800 yards of fabric, and averaged three hundred yards annually. In each case, the income probably contributed to the Cranstons and the Howards move westward to New York in 1819.[50]

That 70 percent of the names listed in the weaving ledgers are linked by marriage suggests that the Howard families and Peleg Cranston's family were typical. As young couples began to establish financial independence from their parents, supplementary non-agricultural income played an important role.

Another category of outwork weaver consisted of single or widowed women who headed a household. Over 50 percent of the 365 female names listed in cloth accounts were female household heads. This factor in part reflects the male bias in the account books, but more importantly it suggests that the mill entrepreneur treated the family's earnings as those of an individual, the household head. Clearly the income earned in outwork provided family support.

For Ruth Mowry, widowed in 1818 with six young children, weaving allowed her to support her family without public assistance. In 1818, Ruth Mowry's husband, Jonathan, died leaving his wife and children thirty acres of "mostly unimproved land destitute of any kind of shelter for man or beast." Ruth petitioned the court to allow her to retain some items from her husband's estate that would allow her to earn an income. The court allowed her to have one loom, one lot of harnesses, four shuttles, a pair of temples, a 23 dent reed, quill wheels, swifts, a 34 dent reed, spools and warping bars as well as bed and furnishings. These tools enabled Ruth Mowry to continue weaving for the Blackstone Manufacturing Company through 1822 when the mill discontinued outwork. Ruth Mowry depended greatly on her earnings from weaving. She produced almost 2,000 yards of fabric each year making her earnings almost equivalent to a spinner's annual wage from factory work.[51]

Like Ruth Mowry, widows Ann Tucker and Catherine Saunders contributed to the support of their families by weaving over 200 yards annually. Saunders averaged 600 yards of cloth per year between 1811 and 1815. Her household consisted of one female child between the ages of 26 and 35 in 1820. Ann Tucker produced 640 yards of cloth from 1811 and 1822. Tucker became a seamstress between 1822 and 1825 when she died. Though neither woman produced sufficient amounts of fabric to support their families, their earnings through outwork, supplemented agricultural income.[52]

Other widows increased their earnings by taking in less-skilled outwork tasks such as picking and waste picking. Hannah Babcock and Mary Streeter both took in waste picking. Several widows maintained their husband's farming interests but the widow's ability to succeed in agriculture depended upon the age of her children.[53]

Outwork weaving attracted female household heads and young married women with small children for several significant reasons. Outwork provided women with young children with a way to support themselves while caring for their children at home. Weaving was an activity that might be interrupted at anytime without damaging the cloth and as such would conform to the daily routines of a household. Although the handloom was both large and cumbersome, it was not hazardous to the worker or other family members. The handloom did not remove fingers, or otherwise maim either the operator or the curious young observer. Finally, though weaving did require some training, the skill required to produce simple utilitarian fabrics such as denim or sheeting was minimal and could be learned in a short time.

Eighteen names from the cloth ledgers identified artisans who supported themselves solely by weaving. These craftsmen were categorized as professional weavers in two ways. Either they produced over 2,000 yards of fabric in a year for textile firms or they were listed elsewhere in civil records as weavers. Probate inventories of some artisans indicated that they owned weaving workshops and employed two to five other artisans by taking in warps from textile firms. Outwork weaving played an important role in a full time weaver's life, as it might constitute the difference between solvency and bankruptcy in a changing market for textile products.

Though master craftsmen clung tenaciously to hand weaving for their sole source of income, by 1820 many were forced to file bankruptcy or to seek alternate forms of employment due to technological change and economic conditions. The numerous artisans who might successfully compete with outwork cloth manufacturing no longer wove profitably in a market flooded with power loom goods. As textile mills incorporated power looms into their production procedures, full-time hand weavers lost their toe hold on solvency.

Of the eighteen professional or full time artisans recorded in weaving ledgers, at least half petitioned the Rhode Island General Assembly for relief from insolvency between 1816 and 1830. Alexander McMurray's life experiences indicate how professional hand weavers might change careers and become successful in an alternate form of employment. McMurray arrived in New York from Scotland in 1811 at age 26. By 1817 he had moved to Rhode Island and lived in Burrilville, weaving for the Blackstone Manufacturing Company. He produced enough shirting, denim, stripe and gingham to support his family. By 1820 he moved to Coventry and suffered losses. That year he petitioned for aid for insolvent debtors as a weaver. McMurray's reason for bankruptcy was attributed to his "failure to perform his trade for three years." His estate valued at $73.90 listed no cloth making equipment. His debts and losses amounted to $1567.00. However, by the time he died in 1852, McMurray had entered into a partnership with his daughter's husband as a merchant and had achieved affluence and status in the community. He contributed to the building of a school and supported the Congregational church in Coventry.[54]

Like McMurray, Pardon Case also declared himself insolvent in 1820. Pardon Case was born in 1790 in West Greenwich and by 1813 he had married Priscilla Westgate of Cranston and lived in Warwick where he pursued the weaving trade. Case took in warps from a variety of cotton spinning mills as his name appears in an A. and W. Sprague ledger for 1812, and his petition for relief indicates that he also worked for Lippitt Manufacturing Company and the Providence Manufacturing Company.

Case's 1820 petition to the General Assembly of the state of Rhode Island reveals the small distance between success and destitution. His petition read,

> Pardon Case of Warwick by a variety of misfortunes was rendered unable to pay his just debts that he has been obliged to witness his hard earnings stripped from him and support of his family by the failure of others and in particular his loss of one year's service in the same way . . . unless he is relieved by your honors his family must be reduced to want and himself drawn from useful business to spend his days in prison.[55]

The failure of others referred to in the petition is the failure of Edmund Hool [sic] to honor his offer to employ Case for one year and pay him $675.00 for that year. The loss of salary in 1820 resulted in bankruptcy at age 30 and the destitution of his wife and children.

In addition to McMurray and Case, Eden Russell, Edward Howard, Joseph France, Christopher Young, Stephen Greenhalgh, Thomas Slack,

John Shearman and Anthony Shaw all declared bankruptcy before 1826. Most of the bankruptcies occurred during the post-Napoleonic War and post-War of 1812 depression when foreign textiles flooded the market with inexpensive goods. These goods had not been exported to the United States during the embargo and disrupted trade of the war years. The era coincides with the period when cotton mills struggled with economic, and energy problems while trying to implement power weaving equipment in textile mills.[56]

Obviously professional weavers were not the only ones affected by the introduction of power weaving equipment in textile mills. By 1821, technological change began to color the face of outwork weaving with the impact of Paul Moody's 1814 power loom and of William Gilmore's 1817 duplication of the scotch crank loom in Rhode Island. Despite the early introduction of power looms, outwork weaving networks continued mostly unaffected by these technological changes until about 1821.[57]

CLOSING THE BOOK ON OUTWORK WEAVING OF COTTON FABRICS

The Blackstone Manufacturing Company discontinued outwork weaving entirely by 1822. As early as 1817 company had introduced power loom weaving for shirting and sheeting and later added power loom stripe to their list of machine manufactured fabrics. They continued to produce stripe, ticking and check by hand but discontinued their use of cloth agents or commission merchants and relied on local outworkers to manufacture the handloom cloths until 1822.

Between 1817 and 1821, the textile industry in Rhode Island suffered a crippling depression. Along with deficiencies of the 1816 tariff, technological limitations of the newly developed power looms, waterpower shortages and a variety of other developments, the depression inhibited the introduction of power loom technology. Rhode Island cotton textile mills continued to put out warps locally and also used commission merchants between 1817 and 1826. By 1830 cotton cloth manufacture was performed only by machines. Between 1817 and 1826, firms manufactured four-harness multi-shuttle fabrics by hand as power loom mills cornered the market on two-harness, single shuttle cloth. Although outwork continued, less people could perform the tasks because the complexity of fabric manufacture increased. Mill correspondence indicates that mill-agents and commission merchants found it difficult to attract sufficient numbers of outworkers to do the increasingly complex weaving patterns. Some weavers sought outwork in other fiber types such as wool and flax where technology lagged behind cotton textile production technology. Rowse Babcock of Westerly, for instance, continued to hire local outworkers to produce woolen plaids until 1840 when he died.[58] By 1826 thousands of individuals had stopped hand weaving cotton cloth, yet there is no evidence of hardship. Outwork weaving of cotton fabric did not immediately disappear. It gradually disappeared over the course of four to nine years. During those years, outwork weaving became a less attractive source of supplementary employment. Before discontinuing cotton weaving outwork, firms gradually decreased the price paid per yard. In 1813, the price paid for gingham was 11 cents per yard, but by 1826, the price for the same cloth was 3 cents per yard.[59]

As a result, other forms of outwork or part-time income-producing tasks became more attractive. Some weavers switched to other work even if it was merely weaving another fiber type. Benjamin and John D. Langworthy for instance appear both in the 1813–15 records of George Thurston and Company producing cotton textiles and later in the records of Rowse Babcock weaving woolen plaids.[60] Obviously, the Langworthys discovered that weaving woolens could prove satisfactory as a supplementary source of income. Unlike professional craftsmen outworkers were not limited by training or tradition to a single form of income but followed market demand. For instance, Joseph France shifted from weaving to bleaching. Others might take in waste picking, perform day labor or take in other kinds of outwork.

As the leaves of cotton factories weaving ledgers turned and power loom accounts replaced individual accounts, outwork weavers sought and found other forms of outwork. The putting-out system could take many shapes including palm leaf hat making, broommaking, shoemaking and other semi-skilled and unskilled activities. As a result of the shifting demands for labor as well as the continuing need for cash, farm-based workers performed whatever work they could find. It is clear that displaced cotton weavers participated in many kinds of outwork, there is little evidence to show what kind of outwork they preferred or found more lucrative after the demise of cotton outwork hand weaving. We know very little of what became of those individuals who found there were no more cotton warps to take home.

Between 1810 and 1820, textile outwork's success depended upon the rejection of factory labor by artisans, the availability of semi-skilled workers and the needs of the agricultural population. Weaving artisans' refusal to work in the factory setting accelerated the breakdown of artisan-based fabric production. It opened the door for employment of domestic cloth manufacturers who had woven simple utilitarian goods for home use or barter. Male rejection of technologically redefined jobs created opportunities for women who were not craft or tradition bound. The availability of piece work for married and unmarried women within the home proved attractive because home fabric manufacture for textile mills provided much needed supplementary income without disrupting the household unit. Women could complete orders and continue to ensure the smooth operation of the home. Despite the continued tie of outwork to home production, putting out might be viewed as one of the first efforts to incorporate women into the general labor force.

The rise of outwork during the early nineteenth century and the development of the factory labor system marked the process of transforming gender roles, family and work. Initially technological change solidified the family. Subsequent developments, however, took work out of the home and placed it in the factory, removing female family members from the home and putting them in factory-owned housing. In addition, the shift in workplace, deprived married women with children from participation in the workforce. The process that initially saved rural families later facilitated the destruction of the unit and dispersal of family members.

Chapter Six
"All other Inventions were Thrown into the Shade"[1]

American experimentation in power loom technology commenced about twenty years after Almy, Brown and Slater's successful mechanization of spinning in 1790. Production levels limited by unwieldy, inefficient and costly outwork created the great impetus for entrepreneurs' financial encouragement of attempts to mechanize weaving. Inventors clamored to develop the first marketable automatic looms. Efforts peaked during the decade between 1810 and 1820 when the United States Patent Office recorded thirty-eight power loom designs. The first power loom patent registered in the United States' patent office credited Philo Clinton Curtis of Oneida, New York with the invention in 1810. Although Curtis's 1810 patent received approval, the design was not generally adopted. His wooden machine relied on the handloom for inspiration, as did most contemporary power looms. Crude mechanical motions enacted by levers and ropes rendered the design imperfect.[2]

The invention of the power loom offers an important and rare opportunity to evaluate both the innovative process and the innovator. No early power looms may be dismissed as irrelevant to the development of a successful and marketable product. The thirty-eight recorded patents are only a fraction of contemporary mechanized loom designs. Of them, Rhode Islanders claim only six designs. However, other sources increase the number of Rhode Island power looms to over ten models. Additionally, Rhode Island mechanics in concert with southeastern Massachusetts and some eastern Connecticut machinists worked to develop an array of power loom improvements and warper and dresser designs.[3]

The history of power loom development between 1810 and 1830 is also one of emulation. During this period, it is consistent with the nature of education, whether academic or technical, which encouraged emulation, imitation or memorization. As David Jeremy has demonstrated, American entrepreneurs and artisans did not reinvent power loom technology functioning well elsewhere. They imitated existing foreign machinery. By copying it, and using it they soon discovered ways to improve it. American mechanics and manufacturers gained access to European designs in three ways: a.) Americans visited England to study machines in operation in English factories; b.) Entrepreneurs and artisans acquired designs, saw patents and specifications published in the *Repertory of Arts, Manufactures and Agriculture,* a British publication, or saw examples of the machinery; c.) Immigrants who had worked in British cotton textile mills brought experience and information with them to the United States. They offered their skills and experience to the highest bidder. As a result, British technology was neither unknown nor unfamiliar to Americans and immigrants disposed to copy and patent the designs.[4]

The challenge of developing something better out of already existing foreign technologies spurred mechanics on to create many innovations. The history of textile technology offers numerous examples of imitation leading to innovation. Samuel Slater emulated the Arkwright designs in Pawtucket and introduced mechanized textile manufacture to the United States. Paul Moody imitated the British power loom designs studied by Frances Cabot Lowell, and developed what is acclaimed as the first commercially successful power loom in the United States. Emulation encompasses more than copying successful designs. When writers of pedagogy described the learning process, copying implied improvement upon the original. Compatibly, by improving on old designs, Americans established the two way flow of information described by David Jeremy. Once British technology had been transported to the United States, American mechanics found ways to upgrade the machinery. They introduced better designs at home. Some American mechanics emigrated to Britain to offer their new technologies abroad. Loom designs developed independently in the United States also resulted from emulation. Independent designers drew on ideas and formulations learned in acquiring skills for other trades as well as information from abroad. The designs incorporated gears or cams in ways familiar to the inventor from previous experiences. For example, John Bailey, a clockmaker of Hanover Massachusetts, built clockwork geared spinning devices for Moses Brown.[5]

AMERICAN POWER LOOM DESIGNS: 1810–1820

The work of independent local mechanics illustrates the relationship between training and innovative ideas. Job Manchester's life and work offers the best example of the interplay of experience, knowledge of foreign designs, and mechanical outcome among Rhode Island power loom inventors. Job Manchester, a mechanic who lived in Coventry Rhode Island, recorded his ideas, conceptualizations, machine designs and results in reminiscences published by the Rhode Island Society for the Encouragement of Domestic Industry in 1864. Manchester's detailed letter provides an honest appraisal of his work. His experiences raise several allied points applicable to any of several Rhode Island power loom designers. Manchester resided and worked in a sparsely populated section of Rhode Island. Initially, Job Manchester toiled in isolation in his father's attic drawing on his personal understanding of handloom weaving for inspiration. Only later did he relocate nearer to the mainstream of textile machine production. Manchester's later power looms benefit from experience and training received while employed in a textile mill machine shop and working to install and repair Gilmore's scotch power loom. In addition to these strong influences, Manchester's work reflects gradual technological innovation. One improvement rests upon what he had learned from previous efforts. Manchester's insights and detailed descriptions document the contriving mind of a mechanic/inventor. Few of Rhode Island's power loom inventors have left such detailed accounts of their work.

Manchester's first textile-related innovation was an attachment to a handloom, which could increase daily fabric production. His interest in handloom improvement derived from his family's involvement in domestic textile production. Enchanted by the family loom and by the skills and time required to fabricate cloth, he considered the problem of making machinery to improve or simplify the weaving process. As a child, he had wound quills for domestic weaving. He retained that vision as he wrote: " . . . I have before my mind a graphic vision of the old family handloom with its "slam-slam" as when I sat winding quills."[6] In 1812, he sought to improve the fly shuttle loom by developing a system to push the shuttle across the warp with each beater stroke. He discovered that he could not successfully sell his invention because the beater of an ordinary handloom could not support the weight of the additional equipment and still produce good fabric.

Manchester's concern for simplifying the hand weaving process while increasing productivity conformed to a trend in handloom improvements. In 1788, David Buffum operated a small weave shed in Newport Rhode Island using fly shuttle looms. He developed a drop box system for shuttles, which enabled the weaver to produce checks with ease. His son, Darius, recalled: "My father invented an improvement on the loom by introducing a sliding box at each end of the lathe for weaving checks; the box so fixed as to raise and fall first throwing one shuttle and weaving a stripe and then the other."[7] In addition to Buffum's unpatented improvement were those of Amos Wittemore and David Greive of Massachusetts. At the Beverly mill, weavers used an improved shuttle mechanism to increase productivity but the design of the shuttle is unknown. Concern for increasing fabric output was not limited to the United States. According to the *Repertory of Arts, Manufactures and Agriculture*, in 1806 Sieur Despeau registered a patent, which made the shuttle work more or less automatically. Despeau's loom used the treadle to separate the warp and to actuate two springs on either side of the warp. The springs forced the shuttle across the loom's expanse once the shed was opened to its most extreme point. The attachment reduced fatigue, allowing the weaver to produce more cloth per day. The device was affordable for the artisans costing only 48 francs.[8]

Efforts to increase fabric production prior to a viable power loom design sought to achieve the goal by adding mechanisms to the handloom while retaining a skilled artisan as operative. Like the spinning jenny, which could be incorporated into a workshop or domestic environment, fly shuttles and drop boxes did not disrupt the traditional work organization or encourage the development of a factory-work environment. Initial shuttle and drop box improvements may have responded to the need for increased productivity while recognizing the distaste for factory work conditions associated with the British textile industry. Additionally weaving mechanization like that of the spinning process replaced both artisan and hand tool with several machines. In order to mechanize the weaving process fully, the handloom and the weaver had to be replaced by a warper, a dresser, power looms and operatives to run them.

As British mechanics before him had realized, Manchester recognized that mechanizing the entire weaving process might offer greater compensation than would fly shuttle improvements. Factory owners, not individual artisans would purchase many of the looms rather than one or two fly shuttle attachments. By 1814, the machine shop of Cromwell Peck and Company was the site of Manchester's next inventive efforts. Manchester's first power loom model produced a single four harness pattern called "Large M's and O's" which is a form of diaper weave. According to Perez Peck, a full-scale model of the simply constructed loom was evidently capable of weaving quality fabric perfectly. Manchester reported that he altered the basic structure of the handloom by eliminating some of the superstructure in the rear portion of the loom near the warp beam. But from the center of the loom to the cloth beam, he retained the original structure "not yet being able entirely to shake off the imposing vision of the old family loom."[9]

Cams regulated the beater and harness motions. The beater, like beaters on handlooms, was suspended from the top castle or superstructure of the loom. Pins or tappets set on the surface of a cylinder, like those on a music box or as Manchester states a "hand organ," set the levers regulating harness, beater and shuttle in their requisite motion to form the single weave pattern. Manchester may have known of Edmund Cartwright's 1786 British patent for a horizontal loom, which also incorporated "tappits" to work the treadles. The treadles enacted the harnesses, which variously raised or rested to form a pattern. However, Manchester's use of tappets extended further than pattern determination. The shuttle was set into motion by two picker sticks. A break or lever actuated by tappets on the cylinder drew back the flat steel spring, which moved the beater. The design attracted some notice but the loom's limited application doomed it to failure. Manchester rationalized the lack of interest in his invention as follows: "But as there was no power loom in use, or even heard of, among us in Coventry, at that period, the idea was generally deemed rather chimerical than practical."[10]

In the spring of 1816, Job Manchester developed a twill loom. This four-harness loom produced a simple construction weave pattern and a fabric generally produced by outworkers for local textile mills. The number of harnesses that could be set into motion in a commonly produced pattern—bed tick might have increased interest in the loom. Other early power looms had only two harnesses limiting the cloth produced to plain weave. These two factors made Manchester's second power loom more attractive to mill owners.

Manchester offers a clear image of the paths he took to develop mechanical parts for the loom. A series of cause and effect studies led to the design of the machine's gears and cams. He tested the parts by installing them in the frame of a handloom in his father's garret. He writes: "I had, however, lost some of my veneration for this relic of the past even daring to think that I could build a loom without regard to its gigantic and lofty proportions."[11]

Manchester's power loom design was much less cumbersome than the family handloom. The design relied on a series of six cams constructed on a single pulley, which raised and lowered the harnesses to duplicate the twill pattern. A lever or brake acting on a pin with a projection on the side caused the cams to initiate motion. The brake made the beater move. The beater was actuated from underneath the warp rather than above, as had his previous power loom. This feature allowed for a more compact loom framework. The mechanisms for moving harnesses, and beater were located underneath the warp. The beater was of sufficient length to allow for a shuttle box at each end and one-yard wide cloth to be produced between the boxes. The loom could be operated by hand crank.[12]

Unfortunately, Manchester's descriptions leave many details unspecified. Manchester fails to describe how the power loom improved on the diaper loom of 1814 or why he shifted from pins on a cylinder to sliding cams. The pattern of the diaper loom probably could not be varied easily. Perhaps additional cylinders with tappets were required. In any case neither model was exceptionally marketable as Manchester neither enumerated sales nor suggested he built more than the initial prototype.

Manchester's description identified at least three deficiencies of the second loom design. The looms required strong warps to withstand the force of a shuttle jamming the warp, and were thereby limited to producing coarse fabrics. Although Manchester had conceived of the idea for letting off and taking up the cloth automatically, he did not add these features to the model. He had made no provision for stopping the loom in case the shuttle failed to reach across the entire warp or in case threads broke. Manchester notes that since the beater was not positively driven, belt slippage would occur in the event of a stalled shuttle. Instead of being smashed out, the shuttle jam stopped the loom. This feature of Manchester's loom was similar to the Waltham loom of 1814 and Miller's British wiper loom patent of 1796. Manchester, cognizant of Miller's patent, incorporated some features into his power loom. Since the patent was published in the *Repertory of Arts, Manufactures and Agriculture* in 1798, it is not unlikely that Manchester viewed the specifications.[13]

A comparison of Manchester's description to that of Miller's patent description in the 1798 edition of the *Repertory of Arts, Manufactures and Agriculture* suggests that Manchester was not so isolated in Coventry. Manchester's loom, like Miller's, incorporated a series of wipers or cams. Miller's cams were all connected to a spindle, which in turn was the axis of a single ratchet pulley enacted, by a lever and pinion. A sheave two inches thick having a groove two inches deep and 1/2 inch wide regulated the movement of the lever and by that motion caused the lever to act upon the ratchet wheel once every revolution of the sheeve or axis. Miller's patent incorporated eight cams to Manchester's six. Miller used one cam for the warp beam regulation, the sheeve, itself a cam, two for moving the beater, two for moving the treadles and two for moving the shuttle. Although similarities to Miller's patent incorporated into Manchester's design are significant, design differences are also substantial. Manchester's design used a pinion rather than a ratchet wheel in a much more compact mechanical design for establishing movement. The loom had four rather than two harnesses. The beater moved by a flat spring rather than a wiper, which accounts in part for the reduced number of cams.

Manchester discovered that the attachment of gears and cams to the old family loom did not produce an acceptable result. Accordingly, he and his brothers secured sufficient lumber to build a new frame. However, he did not complete the project. He wrote:

> I well remember that the day was quite warm when we got the log to the mill and am strongly impressed that it was the month of June and just before mowing. The foregoing points being gained and having no knowledge of a rival in my enterprise, being young and without capital and the machine business on which I relied being well-nigh at a standstill after aiding my brothers through the hurry of the season, I sought and engaged in such mechanical business as I could obtain for the time being, looking to the completion of my loom as circumstances would permit.[14]

During the winter of 1816–17, circumstances permitted Manchester to work as a mechanic at Arnold's bridge, Pontiac in Warwick. In 1818, Cromwell Peck and Company of Coventry hired him. He installed some of William Gilmore's looms for the firm. Between 1817 and 1818, he worked with the scotch looms. After two years of working with the two-harness, plain weave power looms, Manchester realized that he could improve some of the loom characteristics to great advantage. Cromwell Peck and Company agent, William Anthony, encouraged Manchester to design an "improved" bed tick or twill weave loom during 1818 based on Manchester's 1816 four-harness twill weave model and his understanding of Gilmore's loom. The resulting machine incorporated sliding cams of his earlier design. The round, rather than square, camshaft was like that of the scotch loom. The new design had separate cams for throwing the shuttle. The harness action was enacted by a combination of cams and levers connected to treadles. In 1863, Manchester, now of Providence and a minister, donated a model of the sliding cam loom to the Rhode Island Society for the Encouragement of Domestic Industry. Their description of the loom provides us with a more detailed image. The design evidenced elements of the fly shuttle improvement of 1812 as well as innovative uses of cams, which had characterized all of Manchester's earlier designs. "The shuttle was thrown and the vibration of the lathe produced by means of a spiral and vertical spring and wedged shaped cam, the harness being operated by a triangular cam acting upon a treadle as ordinarily arranged." The loom was displayed in the Society's rooms at Railroad Hall in Providence in 1863. Its final resting place or disposal is unknown.[15]

Although the loom produced a good quality and quantity of cloth, certain deficiencies inhibited diffusion. Manchester built the loom but no warper or dresser. Most warper and dresser designs serviced plain weave looms. In order to make twill or bed tick, Manchester's looms required hand warping and dressing in sections. This greatly increased the time necessary to prepare the loom for weaving and made the design less attractive to mills.

Aside from time considerations, mechanized warpers and dressers ensured power loom design success for other reasons. All power loom warps required sizing. The proper dressing of new power looms presented a challenge. Newly sized warps might mildew or stick together while drying if sizing were not applied evenly, not brushed while drying or not allowed to dry completely. Sizing was necessary for power loom weaving due to added stress placed on thread by the mechanical beating action. As a result the appropriate warper and dresser made the power loom. This simple axiom was all too clear to Manchester. He recalled that a mill in Warwick purchased some of his looms but used them for plain weave rather than twill to allow mechanical warping and dressing. Simultaneous production of warpers, dressers and looms was significant. Of all the early power looms, the two most successful and marketable in New England were the scotch and Waltham looms. These two designs were marketed with all necessary supportive equipment when first put on the market.[16]

Timing of the innovation was vital. Manchester attributed sluggish sales to the following:

> Manufacturers were in the midst of the perplexity attendant on getting the power loom into operation for making plain cloth. When they had succeeded in getting a good article of shirting and sheeting woven in their own mills at a reasonable cost and with much greater dispatch than by their previous system of sending their yarns about the country to be woven by hand, they seemed disposed to pause and take a breath before attempting to make further advances. During this period the slide cam loom was measurably lost sight of.[17]

Although he submitted the description of the loom to the U.S. Patent Office in 1819, he did not receive encouragement to take out a patent and in fact, never took out a patent on this power loom design. Other factors made timing important and inhibited diffusion. Slow recovery from the depressions after the War of 1812 and Napoleonic War, failure of the tariff of 1816 to protect textile manufacturers in Rhode Island, low capitalization, and limited waterpower resources all contributed to inhibiting power loom diffusion in Rhode Island and Southeastern Massachusetts in general. Undoubtedly the poor environment for change affected the success of the design.[18]

Despite the absence of warpers and dressers and poor economic conditions, which initially inhibited diffusion, Manchester's design succeeded both technologically and commercially. By 1825, Manchester had sold 42 looms and patterns. In addition over 100 unauthorized copies of his sliding cam loom operated in Pawtucket factories. Had Manchester devoted time and energy to marketing the device and overseeing its sale, he might have benefited financially from his efforts. Distressed at discovering unauthorized copies, Manchester contacted firms to receive compensation at the rate of $3.00 per loom. After receiving $300 for his trouble, Manchester closed the door on the design, manufacture and sale of the improved bed tick loom and moved to Connecticut. In Connecticut, textile firms hired him to alter Waltham power looms with cam driven beater action to the Gilmore-type crank. By 1864, when Manchester wrote his reminiscences, he had long ago left the mechanics' trade. Whether due to his inability to profit from his inventions or a strong calling, Manchester entered the ministry.[19]

Thomas Robinson Williams' story parallels Manchester's in many ways, though his training as a watchmaker and his emigration to England offer significant variations on the theme of independent native artisan-inventor. In 1809 Williams of Newport Rhode Island experimented in designing a girth width power loom in the attic of his father's house. Like Manchester, Williams undertook his initial efforts in solitary circumstances. Limited interaction with others working toward similar goals inhibited or restricted his progress. Williams' efforts came to the attention of Rowland Hazard of the Peacedale Manufacturing Company in Peacedale, a village in South Kingstown Rhode Island. For the next three years, Williams worked for the firm building four saddle web, girth width or tape power looms. An entry in "Nailer Tom" Hazard's diary indicates that Nailer Tom's son wove on the Peacedale water looms in 1813. The looms were limited in application to specialized fabric and their sale restricted by an agreement between Williams and Hazard executed on January 18, 1814. In the agreement, Williams licensed Rowland Hazard the rights to his looms for weaving webbing and he also agreed not to sell any looms of that design to anyone other than Hazard. In return Williams received the sum of $1,500.[20]

Like Manchester's diaper loom, Williams' initial loom pattern, though capable of manufacturing webbing successfully, would not have been successful if generally marketed among textile mills, because the fabric was not of a kind made by a broad spectrum of Rhode Island manufacturers. Though narrow-width mechanical looms for tape manufacture were invented very early in Europe, Williams' loom model was for a kind not generally of interest to local mechanics and textile manufacturers. Like Manchester's diaper loom, Williams webbing loom was outside of

the general demand for power looms and as a result was not successful outside of the Peacedale Mill. Williams may have known of European efforts
or have been encouraged in that direction by Hazard who supported his
efforts. Since so little is known of Williams' machine, however, it is impossible to describe gearing or to suggest ancestry of the design.[21]

Shortly before executing his agreement with Hazard, Williams began
to experiment with other power loom designs and set his sights on a full-
width cotton power loom suitable for making all sorts of coarse and plain
fabrics. Though aided financially in building and designing a working loom
at the mill in South Kingstown, Williams was isolated from the mainstream
of the textile industry and, as a result, from the mechanical developments
of others. In July 1813, Williams moved to Pawtucket and initiated his
association with Aza Arnold, inventor, mechanic and mill owner. Arnold
supported Williams' efforts to develop equipment. Once again, Williams
benefited from the support of a textile mill owner. Undoubtedly, Arnold's
experience and creativity aided Williams in the design of a marketable
power loom.[22]

According to a patent registered in July, William's power loom with
shuttle motion controlled by cam and springs produced full-width fabric by
hand crank or waterpower. Once the machine was patented, Arnold and
Williams sought buyers for it. Arnold contracted with Williams to manufacture full-width looms. Later, Williams contracted with David Wilkinson and Company to build them. The product was purchased by Timothy
Greene's, Abraham Wilkinson's, and Aza Arnold's mills.[23]

In August of 1813, Williams wrote to local firms advertising the mechanism and expressing his desire to take warps to be woven on his machines
in South Kingstown: "I hereby take the liberty to inform you that I have
just established some of my water looms in South Kingstown where I intend
to keep a constant supply of cotton handy and should like to furnish you
with any quantity."[24] Williams' advertisement suggests that he tried to offer
mill owners an alternative to handloom outwork by providing them with
power loom outwork as an alternative. Perhaps he offered this service as
a teaser to mill owners to put out warps to him now and purchase power
looms once they had seen the results of their operation. Williams set up his
looms in South Kingstown, but it is apparent that Hazard was not inter-
ested enough in the machinery to keep them in constant use. The looms' use
in South Kingstown and other mills suggests that Williams' loom produced
saleable fabric. In 1861, Arnold wrote that he had several of the early looms
made on T.R. Williams' patent as well as looms made by three other Rhode
Island mechanics. By the mid-1820s, Williams, now an engineer in London,
had moved to England to share technological information with the British

for profit. By 1824, Williams had returned to Newport Rhode Island to develop a lancet for the medical profession. In 1830, a final T.R. Williams patent appears for manufacturing felt for the bottoms of vessels.[25]

The first Rhode Island inventor to patent a power loom design was John Thorp, a mechanic most famous for the ring spindle. Thorp, born in 1784 in Rehoboth Massachusetts, was the son of coach-maker, Rufus Thorp. John Thorp trained for the mechanics' trade in Pawtucket. He probably worked for William and Thomas Fletcher as did his brothers Comfort and David. The Fletchers maintained a textile machine manufacturing business at Mill Bridge in North Providence. Thorp also maintained a separate shop at his residence at 168 High Street and was listed as a machine maker in the 1836 Providence directory. At that time he had a shop on Federal Hill.

On March 28th 1812 at age 28, he had developed a power loom, which could also be operated by hand. The large wooden-framed cranked loom had harnesses enacted by ratchet wheels, and overhead levers with suspended weights. The pickers, placed horizontally, incorporated let-off and take-up motions using pulleys connected by a rope fed off of the warp-beam pulley.

By 1812, British artisans had created three basic power loom designs, the wiper loom, the crank loom and the vertical loom. Edmund Cartwright's vertical loom design used tappets as described earlier. But in 1811, Robert Shirreff produced an advertisement entitled "A Short Account of the Principle and Operation of the Patent Vertical Power Double Loom invented by Mr. Thomas Johnson and now the Property of Mr. Robert Shirreff of Glasgow and made by James Watts." The Johnson loom used a series of cranks and wipers as follows. The heddles were enacted by the vibration of a crank as it was forced by an eccentric wheel or wiper driven by a pinion. The beater also operated in a reciprocating motion given by a crankshaft, which connected to the lay by two rods or swords. The shuttle set into motion by a lever fixed on top of a rod or spindle driven by a rack. Although both the looms were crank looms, it is obvious there are some differences in their organization and operation. The Johnson loom uses gravity to ensure that the shuttle never deviates from its normal course, whereas the Thorp loom did not. Johnson's loom allowed for two warps to be placed back to back to conserve space, manpower, and belts, whereas the Thorp loom did not. Since descriptions differed in vocabulary and points of reference any more detailed comparisons are difficult. [26]

In 1813, David Thorp published the following notice in the *Providence Gazette:*

> This is to inform the public that the subscriber has the agency of a new
> invented and patent weaving machine and to invite all those who are
> or wish to be concerned in that useful and laudable branch of Business
> to call at his house opposite to Mr. Cleveland's cabinet maker's shop on
> Constitution Hill where he intends keeping one or more of said looms
> in operation for those who wish to purchase as he will sell by county,
> town or single rights as will best be sent the purchaser.[27]

Thorp sold rights to build copies of his brother's looms and did not himself
manufacture the machines.

After developing his first loom design, and selling rights to the design
with little success, Thorp moved from Pawtucket Rhode Island to Taunton
Massachusetts. As with Williams and Manchester, Thorp's move to a different machine shop environment introduced new ideas, new components,
additional skills and a new enthusiasm to the development of a more successful design. With Silas and Cyrus Shepard, Thorp improved his power
loom. Cyrus Shepard and John Thorp patented a vertical loom in July
1816. Thorp devised an innovative method of moving the shuttle across
the warp called a "shuttle vibrator." A light U-shaped frame moved from
side to side to force the shuttle across the warp. The loom design included a
smash protector and take-up motion but no temples. The beater was cam-
driven and the shuttle traveled over the top of the reed. The mechanism
required the attendance of a machinist who made necessary adjustments to
the machinery. Though the ministrations of a skilled workman added to the
expense of operation and should have detracted from its appeal, the design
generated intense interest.[28]

In 1816, during a tour of Rhode Island and Massachusetts textile
mills with Francis Cabot Lowell, Nathan Appleton had an opportunity to
visit Silas Shepard's mill and saw the Thorp loom. "We saw at the factory
of Mr. Shepherd, an attempt to establish a vertical power loom, which did
not promise success."[29] Despite the negative review, John Thorp built more
than thirty of the looms for Silas Shepard's Taunton Cotton Mill. Other
Taunton manufacturers incorporated the loom into their mills. Over seventy Thorp looms operated in Pawtucket. The Pawtucket Manufacturing
Company purchased twenty of his machines. Aza Arnold bought the rights
to Thorp's loom and manufactured some for himself. Mr. Hawkins of Cumberland operated four upright looms in his mill in 1818. A Mr. Franklin
purchased several of Thorp's looms for his mill near Olneyville in Providence. He operated the looms for several years with one machine operator
to every two machines. Fabric production equaled about 275 yards of cloth
per week per employee. "The cloth was better than that woven by hand"

according to John Waterman. Great demand for the loom necessitated licensing David Wilkinson and Company to build and sell the looms. Peleg Wilbur suggests that it was the most successful design prior to Gilmore and Fales' power looms. According to Kulik, by 1817, there were as many Thorp-Shepard looms in operation as there were Waltham looms. Despite this initial success, however, the popularity of the looms did not endure. The looms operated sufficiently well to answer a need, which was shortly surpassed by Gilmore's superior loom design.[30]

Between 1816 and 1829 Thorp returned to Providence. His inventive focus shifted from weaving to improvements to fiber preparing activities such as spinning. He patented several improvements to fiber processing between 1816 and 1829. In 1829, Thorp designed a narrow fabric power tape loom, which could produce several pieces of cloth at once. He received his last patent in 1844, which was an improvement to the ring spindle. John Thorp died in Providence Rhode Island leaving a very modest estate.

Elijah Ormsbee, one of eleven children of Daniel Ormsbee, was also a native of Rehoboth Massachusetts. As a young man, Elijah went to Providence to learn the trade of house carpenter and served his apprenticeship with Abel Allen. He built a house for himself on the corner of South Main and Wickenden streets in Providence. Ormsbee developed a steamboat, which was demonstrated in Providence harbor in 1794. Oziel Wilkinson assisted in the manufacture of steamboat parts. In 1798, Ormsbee received a patent for a fire engine in March 1798. The patent described "an engine for throwing water." Prior to 1812, Ormsbee had already established himself as a carpenter and ingenious inventor who had had success in diverse fields of enterprise. Between 1812 and 1815, he turned his energies toward building a power loom. The Rutenburg Mill in the Olneyville section of Providence supported his textile experimentation. The industrial research resulted in two looms in three years. Between 1812 and 1813, Ormsbee built six more looms for the Blackstone Manufacturing Company in Mendon Massachusetts. The looms were wooden framed and operated with a crank motion but very little else is known about them.[31]

Samuel Blydenburgh developed his power loom at the Lyman Mills in North Providence. He had contacted the firm and requested that they furnish him with financial support, tools and room to experiment in loom design. Blydenburgh was not unfamiliar with mechanical design as in 1798 he patented a machine for dipping candles. Blydenburgh's looms worked with a cam and spring motion. In 1813, he finished building three water looms for the company at fifty dollars each and had three unfinished machines when the firm settled his account. H. B. Lyman reported to the Rhode Island Society for the Encouragement of Domestic Industry: "After a Full trial at a heavy expense, it proved to be a failure." After his release from the Lyman Mills, Blydenburgh moved to Worcester Massachusetts where he patented a loom powered by steam, water or other source in partnership with Hezekiah Healy in 1815. Blydenburgh moved to New York where he developed a spinning throstle in 1829 and a clock in 1833.[32]

In addition to the mechanisms described previously, patents for two additional early power looms are recorded. John Standish (1830) and David Greive (1818) each designed power looms in Rhode Island. Interestingly enough, like Ormsbee, Grieve also built a steam vessel in Providence, which was patented in 1801 and tested in Providence Harbor in 1808. Other power loom designs are attributed to Mr. Ingraham of Pawtucket and Hines, Arnold and Company. John Whitehead, the handloom weaver who aided Lyman Mills with Gilmore's scotch looms, patented early loom improvements (1819) as did Amasa Stone (1835). Finally, according to Icabod Washburn, a former employee in a Kingstown Rhode Island mill, Robert Sugden, an Englishman, was hired in 1813 to produce a loom. Sugden patented a loom in Boston in December 1813. The resulting equipment was so crude and primitive that all the cogwheels were made of wood. Unfortunately so little information exists pertaining to these power looms that significant descriptions of them are impossible.[33]

IMPORTED TECHNOLOGY 1810–1820

Power loom inventors described previously were American born mechanics from either Massachusetts or Rhode Island. The following two power loom designers brought an understanding of mechanical weaving with them from Britain. William Gilmore arrived in Boston Massachusetts from Dunbarton Scotland in September of 1815. Like many immigrants before him, Gilmore brought sufficient knowledge of British machinery with him to succeed in designing a marketable and technologically superior power loom where native Rhode Island artisans had failed. According to Samuel Batchelder, Gilmore had been employed in power weaving prior to emigration and understood the construction of power looms and dressers from that job experience. In addition, it is apparent that Gilmore emigrated with the idea of sharing technological information for great profit. Batchelder reported: "He brought to Boston certain articles of Scotch manufacture which in the state of trade at that time met a profitable market."[34] Gilmore was introduced to Roger Rogerson, commission merchant and owner of Uxbridge Cotton Mill. In turn, Rogerson introduced him to the Slaters. Gilmore presented the Slaters with a proposal similar to the one offered Moses Brown by a young Samuel Slater years before. Gilmore promised to work for the Slaters without pay while he used their machine shop, tools and other resources to construct a power loom, warper and dresser. He would work without remuneration until the power looms operated successfully. John Slater employed Gilmore in his Slatersville machine shop in Smithfield Rhode Island. Some evidence suggests that Samuel Slater supported Gilmore's experimentation in power loom design. Slater wrote the following to his brother in 1816. "Are you making any progress with water looms at Smithfield? I do think we ought to get some underway as soon as it is practicable."[35] Since the Slaters' firms were adversely affected by the economic depression occurring after the war of 1812, Samuel Slater agreed to hire Gilmore to work as a machinist until "the prospects for cotton manufacture" were not so discouraging. The Slaters probably hired Gilmore to work as a mechanic first and as a potential power loom inventor second. But the second instant never came; Gilmore left the Slaters after brief employment. H.B. Lyman reported that the Slaters wanted Gilmore to build a hydrostatic pump to water their meadows rather than to design a power loom.[36]

Hence, Gilmore was easily enticed away from the Slaters by a more attractive opportunity at the Lyman Mills of North Providence. In 1815, Daniel Lyman hired Gilmore to design not only looms but also machinery for warping and dressing, which made his three inventions more attractive for investment than other weaving mechanisms. The dresser and warper developed by Gilmore earned him success in his work. Daniel Lyman set Gilmore to work making the warper, dresser and loom in a vacant room in the Lyman Mills building number 2. Lyman asked him to draft the full-sized plans on the floor of the room. Once Gilmore had sketched each machine, mechanics took measurements gauged from the drawings. From these measurements, they made patterns, cast, turned and finished the parts out of iron and brass. Samuel Greene purported that Gilmore developed the first iron framed textile equipment in the United States.[37]

The mechanical harness, reed and beater actions of all power loom designs increased friction and stress placed on loom warp yarns. This increased thread breakage and work stoppage in power loom weaving. As a result it was necessary to develop equipment, which would protect or strengthen the yarns to reduce breakage. Sizing had been used in handloom weaving to prevent the shredding and breaking of threads. With the development of power loom weaving, all warps had to be sized. Mechanical warpers and dressers, which complimented the power looms had to be developed to reduce the amount of time it took to dress the loom and to protect, dry and separate warp yarns. Lyman realized that it was important to design a warper, dresser and loom ensemble. Designing complimentary machinery ensured the success of the mechanical loom. As Manchester indicated, his four-harness twill loom could not be warped to weave twill with standard warpers and dressers. As a result mills used his four harness looms to weave plain cloth rather than warp the twill pattern by hand. It is also important to note that few descriptions or patents remain which describe available warper and dresser technology. In recognizing their importance, Lyman left a description of the machinery in his testimony to the Rhode Island Society for the Encouragement of Domestic Industry. Lyman reported:

> They built the warper first which ran the yarn in sections on large creels, separated by iron wires in circles about six inches apart. When one section was filled the bell rung and they commenced another. These creels when full were placed at each end of the dresser. The yarn from all the sections taken through holes in a copper through lead sizing rollers then brushed and wound on the loom beam in the center and run by a diagonal shaft from the roller and the take up was governed by a suction pulley on the base.[38]

Once the yarn wound onto the warp beam, a worker threaded the heddles with the pattern desired, pulled the warp through the reed and fixed the tension of the cloth beam.

Lyman's description of the warping and dressing machine is very close to Gilroy's description of the cradle warper developed in England. The warper did not have a stop action in case the threads broke or other features characteristic of later American warper technology. The machine divided the warp threads into strips or bands called biers as in Gilroy's description. Gilmore's warper used iron wires to separate segments of the warp. It should also be noted that while the warper measured out the warp threads and dresser sized the warp, that loom operatives had to thread the heddles in the desired pattern. Hence, time-consuming human involvement was necessary to dress a loom prior to weaving the warp.[39]

Once Gilmore's machine drawings had become three-dimensional mechanisms, Gilmore encountered an unanticipated problem. He had duplicated the foreign technology but he could not get it to function without experienced weaving help. The mill hired a handloom weaver, named John Whitehead. Whitehead was asked to operate the machines in order to determine their success or failure. In short, he discovered that he could produce quality fabric on the scotch loom.[40]

By 1817, Gilmore introduced the "scotch loom" as Rhode Island textile workers and mill owners came to call the machine. The scotch loom was iron-framed, and the beater moved by a crank, which differentiated it from other loom designs. The crank reflected Gilmore's knowledge of improvements of British power loom designs. Horrocks' power loom had a variable batten speed, which enabled the mills to use the looms to weave finer warps.[41]

Mill owners found Gilmore's loom desirable because of its simple construction and low cost. Gilmore wisely developed three complementary pieces, which like the Waltham looms bolstered the desirability of the loom. The ability to buy a dresser, warper and loom proven to work well together made the outlay of substantial capital less intimidating. Rhode Island entrepreneurs adopted the scotch loom in preference to the Waltham power weaving mechanism for both technological superiority and economic reasons. The two machines differed chiefly in the beater action. The scotch loom utilized a crank to beat the thread into the web whereas the Waltham loom used a cam for the same purpose. Gilmore's power loom was superior to the Waltham machine because it was composed of steel rather than wood like the Waltham looms and therefore, had increased longevity and durability. This was significant to Rhode Island mill owners who supported altering and improving existing machinery rather than buying entirely new mechanisms. Once a basic design was adopted, the sturdy looms were updated to recognize subsequent innovations. Job Manchester suggested one way in which the scotch loom performed better than the Waltham mechanism.

> It was held at Waltham as a fixed fact that cloth should be made by an accelerated motion of the lay, whereas the crank motion as used by Gilmore made the cloth while passing the minimum point, hence Waltham was slow to adopt it. Rhode Island operatives had 'ere this learned by experience that the secret of making good cloth with ease consisted quite as much from the elevation of the yarn back of the harnesses so as to give a suitable slackness to the top shade of the web as in the manner or force of the blow from the lay so be that the filling was moved forward by it to the proper point.[42]

Manchester was hired by Connecticut firms to alter Waltham looms to the crank beater system. Both Gibb and Lincoln indicated that Gilmore's loom eventually superseded the Waltham machine due to its superior mechanical action.

Gilmore's loom also proved less expensive than the Waltham machine. Rather than patent the mechanism, Gilmore accepted a purse of $1500 on May 17, 1817 from several mill owners with the promise to patent only improvements. Since the mill owners or textile machine makers did not have to buy the rights to the design, they could produce the loom at a lower cost. Gilmore patented an improvement to the loom on October 28, 1820. David Wilkinson and Samuel Greene contracted to manufacture the equipment at David Wilkinson and Company in Pawtucket in 1817. The following advertisement appeared in the *Providence Patriot* in December of 1817: "The subscribers have entered into copartnership under the firm David Wilkinson and Company for the purpose of manufacturing machinery generally power looms together with all apparatus for weaving on the most improved plans."[43] They obtained the privilege to use measured machine drawings of the loom design for ten dollars. According to Greene, however, the designs required some alterations to make the looms saleable. As a result, Greene and Wilkinson drew revised sketches based on the Gilmore inventions. The partners erected over a hundred machines for use in New England and marketed the loom as far away as Trenton, Pittsburgh, Baltimore, Georgia and Louisiana.[44]

Although Wilkinson, Greene and Rhode Island textile mills benefited from Gilmore's scotch loom, Gilmore himself did not achieve the results he had originally intended. If as Batchelder suggests, Gilmore emigrated to profit financially from sharing British textile technology with mill owners, then he received a very small percentage of the profit to be made from the introduction of a loom, warper and dresser. Gilmore was not an inventor. The duplication of the loom, warper and dresser designs was his sole contributions to the industry. Once reproduced he did not have any other inventions to conceive or to patent.[45]

The Arkwright Manufacturing Company of Coventry Rhode Island supported the power loom experimentation of an Englishman named Fales. According to Job Manchester, Fales left England in 1818 with the express purpose of introducing power loom weaving in the United States and of obtaining a reward for doing so. He had studied loom design and operation in England prior to leaving so as to be informed as to the most recent improvements. Fales' loom design reflects some design changes developed after Gilmore left Scotland. According to Manchester, Fales was less of a mechanic than Gilmore but better versed in the operation of power looms suggesting that Fales was not a mechanic but perhaps an experienced operative. Fales arrived in Rhode Island after Gilmore had introduced his loom, warper and dresser, yet Arkwright was willing to support Fales' work. The loom that Fales replicated was similar to that of William Gilmore except in the design of the beater movement, which moved on rods instead of swords. The rods were 3/4 of an inch in diameter placed on either side of the loom on the inside of the loom frame. The beater was crank driven. The introduction of a loom with a "slide lay" as described above suggests that this development was a recent improvement introduced in England prior to Fales' departure but after Gilmore's. The Arkwright looms were the first in Rhode Island to invert the beater supports. Yet by the time Manchester reported the development in 1864, it was common practice to use this mechanical configuration. Hence Fales introduced an adaptation, which was later generally incorporated into loom designs.[45]

Although, Fales' loom produced quality fabric, and was technologically more advanced than Gilmore's, it proved less popular. Gilmore's design answered the needs of Rhode Island mills. Temporal and financial availability insured the scotch loom's success as it appeared on the market two years before Fales', and contributed to diminished sale of Fales' loom. Mills had already expended sums to purchase the Gilmore looms and time and effort to learn about their operation. Peleg Wilbur of Coventry describes the situation as follows. "I believe the perpendicular web was the most successful in its operation, however awkward it may appear. When Gilmore and Fales introduced their looms, all other inventions were thrown into the shade."[46]

CONTRIVING MINDS

The power looms and dressing machinery developed in Rhode Island between 1810 and 1830 imitated existing technology. Although looms played the dominant role in the race to fill a technological gap, compatible warpers and dressing machines proved significant factors in determining success. That so few descriptions and patents for dressing machines remain confirms their less dominant role but also suggests less importance. As indicated by various contemporary authors including Lyman and Manchester, warping and dressing machinery contributed vitally to the success of the power loom. While there were thirty-eight power loom patents during this period, only three warpers and no dressing machinery were recorded. None of the patents represent the work of New England artisans and yet Waltham and at least three textile machine manufacturers in Rhode Island and Southeastern Massachusetts produced warping and dressing machines. Finally descriptions of the warpers and dressers indicate that, like the power looms, they imitated British designs.

With the exception of Manchester, few mechanics, whether foreign or native-born, initiated innovative designs for either looms or preparatory machinery during the 1810–1830 period. Designs differed from British examples to make training, the absence of detailed information, and physical reality meet in an operable mechanism. If originality and innovation played minimal parts in early American power loom design, then it played an even smaller role among Rhode Island's immigrant contributors to power loom technology. Immigrants who transported power loom technology to Rhode Island imported knowledge of one design. They did not continue to contribute to the knowledge of textile technology or make sweeping improvements on their initial design. For example, Gilmore patented one more power loom; Fales never patented any machine design; and Sugden registered only one patent. In contrast, native mechanics offered a myriad of innovations in several fields other than textiles. As described earlier, Thorp patented a variety of spinning improvements, Blydenburgh registered candle, and clock and textile innovations, Thomas R. Williams patented the lancet, and felt patents in addition to his two power looms. In short, Rhode Island and foreign immigrants' power loom inventors approached the problem of mechanizing weaving from two different standpoints.

The two routes traveled to mechanize the weaving process required different skills, talents and goals. The native-born inventors drew on their experience in the trades of clockmaker, machinist, and house carpenter to design viable machinery. To some immeasurable degree, their manual skills influenced the resulting designs and the route taken to get there. Their work evidenced knowledge of the transfer of power and motion through gears and cams as well as experience in shaping metals to fulfill mechanical needs. But the artisans also availed themselves with as much knowledge of foreign technology as possible. The knowledge and understanding also influenced their designs. In addition, Rhode Island power loom mechanics from 1820 onward built improved textile machines and designed innovations in other fields.

Brooke Hindle, Anthony F. C. Wallace, Eugene Ferguson and others have characterized the mechanical or inventive mind. Each author stresses the visual versus the verbal nature of the inventive process. Among the Rhode Island mechanics, Manchester's reminiscences best illustrate this point. He sketched verbal as well as two-dimensional images of his work and of his thinking process. Manchester's procedures for designing the loom required experimentation with three-dimensional elements of the design rather than paper and pen. He developed a series of cause and effect experiments, which allowed him to visualize what needed to be fabricated to make a power loom. His designing process resulted in models rather than in drawings. His verbal descriptions were also vivid. He led the reader to visualize a young Manchester winding quills as another family member beat the weft into the warp "slam-slam" on the family loom. He described tappets on a cylinder like those on a hand organ. His letter to the Rhode Island Society for the Encouragement of Domestic Industry was illustrated, as words could not create the same results as sketches. For Manchester's part, it was not that language was auxiliary but that he could create vivid imagery similar to that in his mind and duplicate his inventive process with drawings, models and words.[47]

The looms themselves offer another clue to how the tradesmen thought or conceived of their designs. Although the *Repertory of Arts, Manufactures and Agriculture* published the specifications of British textile machinery from 1794–1830 and was available to Americans, unique elements of Manchester's, Thorp's and Williams' designs suggest that the publication's descriptions were too general for total design plagiarism. Manchester's original model used tappets or projections on a cylinder, which enacted upon levers to replicate the necessary motions rather than limiting himself to cams and gears. No other Rhode Island designs used this method of initiating consecutive motions. Whereas Cartwright uses the term tappets in his patent, William English assures us that British mechanics used the term "tappet" to refer to cams. Cartwright's loom used the term "tappets" to refer to cams rather than levers. Manchester may have assumed that tappets referred to levers like the ones on a cylinder of a hand organ from the descriptions of Cartwright's loom published in the *Repertory of Arts, Manufactures and Agriculture* and by John Duncan in his *Practical and Descriptive Essays on the Art of Weaving* (1808). Manchester's 1818 design reflects an awareness of Miller's and Horrocks' patents as well as Gilmore's designs. The specifications for the two British patents were available in 1798 and 1814 respectively and by 1818 Manchester had built Gilmore looms for Cromwell Peck and Company. His first power loom wove a four-harness fabric. From the outset Manchester knew that to find general acceptance the loom ought to have the flexibility of weaving four-harness weaving patterns such as bed tick or plaid.[48]

Like Manchester's original work, Thorp's vertical loom design was unique to Rhode Island power looms but not unique to power looms the world over. It is unclear from whence came his idea for vertical warp. Information about British vertical looms was not published in the *Repertory of Arts, Manufactures and Agriculture* in 1813. In 1808 and in 1811, John Duncan and Robert Shirreff respectively, published brief descriptions of vertical looms. Thorp's power loom was the only vertical loom developed in Rhode Island and it was as successful as the Waltham loom prior to the introduction of Gilmore's scotch design.[49]

Though Gilmore's loom, warper and dresser met with almost immediate success, Rhode Island mechanics quickly saw potential for improvement to let-off, take up and shuttle motions. According to Pelage Wilbur, Cromwell Peck and Company built thousands of the Gilmore looms. While duplicating the design in large part, they tested a variety of patented and unpatented improvements and design changes. Their efforts initially focused on smash protectors, drop boxes, self adjusting temples, automatic let off, increasing the harnesses, stop actions and experimenting in other fiber types. Because Gilmore did not patent the loom, Rhode Island mechanics took best advantage of the situation. They may be credited with many related inventions and improvements. In fact the greatest contributions of Rhode Island mechanics rests not in the power loom itself but in their improvements to imported power loom technology. Their continued work and consistent contributions to improving initial designs bespeaks of Rhode Island mechanics' ability, knowledge and their contriving minds [50]

On the other hand, immigrant emulators immersed themselves in operating British power loom, warper and dresser technology prior to emigration. It is the knowledge of full-sized three-dimensional examples of power looms rather than greater skill or mechanical understanding, which led to their achievements. Both Gilmore and Fales studied British technology to learn all they could about existing power loom designs prior to emigration. Gilmore and Fales each emigrated with the idea that they would profit from duplicating British technology in the United States. Each man became a specialist in one set of machines. Each man had one chance for success in the United States. Their backgrounds differed. Gilmore was credited with having worked at power loom weaving, whereas Fales was not. Once the immigrant designers or duplicators had introduced their one design or set of designs, their ability to contribute to the advancement of textile technology ended. These men did not have contriving minds. They were not inventors, but rather, memorizers. Their role was significant only because they brought successful designs to Rhode Island from which Rhode Island mechanics made better looms. That neither Gilmore nor Fales persisted in the industry by improving loom designs and components affirms this assessment.

Gilmore's method of transferring his knowledge of power looms, warpers and dressers suggests knowledge of full-sized three-dimensional machines rather than of drawings and descriptions in that his method of making mechanical drawings was unconventional and unlike a mechanic's. Gilmore reproduced full-sized plans in chalk on the floor of Lyman mill's building number 2. Manchester, Thorp, Williams, Ormsbee and Blydenburgh were all capable of creating scale-measured drawings, but Gilmore did not and perhaps he could not. Gilmore conceptualized and visualized full-sized machines but he could not build a model. Lyman had mill mechanics take measurements from Gilmore's drawing to reproduce parts. In addition, the resulting machines were problematic. When Gilmore could not make them operable, John Whitehead, a hand weaver, proved the machines serviceable, and Whitehead and Wilkinson and Greene made initial refinements to create fully operable and saleable equipment. As in the case of the Slater carding machine, Rhode Island mechanics were required to recreate the British power loom technology in Rhode Island.

With the introduction of power looms during the second decade of the nineteenth century, outwork weaving entered into a period of change. The market for simple plain weave fabrics was absorbed by the earliest power loom designs. As noted, the limitations of power loom technology, the expense of investing in the new machines and a post war of 1812 and Napoleonic War depression changed the shape of outwork but did not eliminate it.

Chapter Seven
"Sending good Money to Make Bad more Valuable if Possible"[1]

In 1816, Nathan Appleton, an investor in the Boston Manufacturing Company of Waltham, Massachusetts, suggested, "the success of the power loom at Waltham is no longer a matter of speculation or opinion. It was a settled fact."[2] The diffusion of power loom technology into Rhode Island mills occurred at a rate similar to the spread of loom mechanization into textile factories in Massachusetts as a whole. By 1820, sixteen percent of the cotton textile companies in each state owned power weaving machinery.[3] Yet, "the success of the power loom" in Rhode Island was by no means "a settled fact." As late as 1826, cotton textile firms in Pawtucket, Providence, Warwick, Central Falls, Smithfield and in almost every other Rhode Island city and town used hand methods of simple cotton cloth manufacture. Mill owners continued to put out warps over broad geographic areas encompassing cloth agents in Richmond, New Hampshire and Stonington, Connecticut.[4] The great distances over which Rhode Island cotton textile manufacturers spread their warps suggest that between 1821 and 1829 the demand for handloom weavers continued to exceed the local labor supply.[5]

What factors made outwork, for a time, more feasible and profitable than early power loom weaving for Rhode Island-style textile firms? Assessments of the industrial environment are made based on an evaluation of the economic climate, availability of necessary mechanical devices, sufficient power, management organization, capital resources, and production procedures prevailing in Rhode Island between 1821 and 1829. Mill owners relied on handloom cloth manufacture because for a span of ten years economic and technological conditions made hand weaving their only recourse.

Several historians including Peter J. Coleman, Gary Kulik and David J. Jeremy have noted the extensive outwork weaving networks maintained by

Rhode Island textile entrepreneurs between 1821 and 1829. Coleman and Jeremy focused on the economic climate to discuss why mechanized weaving did not surpass commercial hand weaving more quickly. Jeremy's more comprehensive study also linked the tariff system, fixed capital and annual growth to the degree of technological diffusion. Kulik questioned whether waterpower shortages along the Blackstone River inhibited the adoption of the power loom by Pawtucket, Rhode Island textile mills.[6] In each case the author viewed the retention of the putting-out system as anomalous and attempted to determine why outwork networks continued in light of available mechanical advancements.

Yet despite Appleton's assessment of Waltham, the rate of the diffusion of mechanized weaving into Rhode Island mills mirrored the speed with which Massachusetts textile firms began using power looms during the same period. In general Massachusetts cotton mills consisted of two managerial and organizational plans. The Waltham or boardinghouse-style mills described by Appleton were greater in the number of people employed, in size of mill structures and in capitalization. As Appleton suggests, mill owners of the larger factories readily incorporated power looms into their production procedures. Whereas, the smaller, less well capitalized Rhode Island- or family-style mills continued using outworkers to manufacture fabric until around 1826. In this chapter the Waltham-style mills of Massachusetts and Rhode Island-style factories are contrasted to determine why the smaller less well-capitalized mills retained outwork and chose to produce the multi-shuttle four-harness fabrics between 1816 and 1826. The Waltham-style mill characterized by Appleton was not typical of Massachusetts' cotton mills until the 1850s. Therefore the comparative statistics between Rhode Island and Massachusetts are not surprising.[7]

Rather than regarding Rhode Island's use of outwork from 1821 to 1829 as anomalous, it would be more appropriate to view the retention of the putting-out system as the most proper and profitable method of cloth production for the circumstances, which existed in Rhode Island. By accepting the concept that there might be multiple appropriate and beneficial answers to any industrial, economic or technological problem, Rhode Island textile industry's use of outwork could be examined as one of several alternative solutions to problems faced by the textile industry from 1816 to 1830. Nathan Rosenberg's study of technological diffusion assesses how rapidly innovations attain widespread usage. Drawing on a statistical analysis of invention and innovation by John L. Enos, Rosenberg suggests that it took an average of about 13 years for an invention to receive popular commercial acceptance during this era.[8] The diffusion of power loom technology into Rhode Island textile mills falls precisely within the thirteen-year scope. Gilmore completed the scotch loom in 1817 just thirteen years before McLane's *Report on Manufactures*, which identified 102 power loom mills out of 119 Rhode Island cotton textile firms. The rate of power loom adoption by Rhode Island mills was neither prolonged nor extended but within the average period of technological diffusion. However, discrepant rates of incorporating power loom technology into Waltham-style as opposed to Rhode Island-style mills indicate that mill owners reacted very differently to similar opportunities.

Philip Scranton used the accumulation matrix to determine how a variety of economic, financial and material conditions, existing in Philadelphia between 1800 and 1885, led the city's textile entrepreneurs to organize their factories in a particular manner.[9] Applying a similar device to Rhode Island's textile industry between 1821 and 1830 will allow for an evaluation of what factors made outwork more attractive than early power loom weaving.

Handloom outwork developed in response to the correlation of several economic, social and technological conditions, which made hiring a population of semi-skilled weavers possible and necessary for both the employer and the employee. By the early 19th-century textile manufacturers had developed the putting out system. By 1807, Rhode Island spinning mills had begun to issue warps to individual part-time weavers. The weavers would obtain warps using one of three methods. Local weavers pick up instructions and yarn from the textile company store. Mill workers might sign for warps to be woven by family members at home, or cloth agents might deliver materials to the weaver's home if they lived at a distance from the store. This form of outwork resolved the problem of employing a large labor force of individuals to produce fabrics on a part-time basis. If weavers were not willing or could not come to work in a factory-owned weaving shed setting, then mill owners found a way of getting the warps to individuals who might wish to supplement their income, or might want to work but not outside their homes.[10]

Textile mill owners found that distributing webs to such a large population of extra-factory labor the mill or factory store created intractable and uncontrollable problems. Putting out factory spun webs required the mill owner or agent to hire and oversee the work of hundreds of part-time transient employees. Manufacturers could maintain little control over these laborers as the outworkers did not weave on company property, and in some cases, lived far from the mill site. In addition, the mill agent maintained detailed accounts recording amounts of warp issued, cloth returned and remuneration. Mills issued large amounts of yarn for about three months duration risking embezzlement and suffering losses due to shoddy workmanship. Part-time weavers often sought to receive the most from their efforts and would sell their fabric to the highest bidder rather than to the firm that issued the web.[11]

By contracting the cloth manufacture with commission merchants, many of the problems associated with outwork shifted from the company to the cloth agent. Middlemen hired the large labor force, maintained records, arranged to deliver yarn and collected the finished product. Silas Jillson of Richmond, New Hampshire traveled to Pawtucket almost every month to procure new orders and deliver completed work. He also saw to the delivery of the warps, and related weaving instructions to each outworker.[12] The commission merchant absorbed the risks of the system as manufacturers penalized the commission agent for shoddy workmanship, dirty cloth, wasted warps, embezzlement and any other losses except acts of God. Stephen Tripp described the Blackstone Manufacturing Company's (a mill located in Massachusetts on the border between Massachusetts and Rhode Island) policy as follows:

> I will thank you to put yarn out to good weavers only as it is no object to us to get poor cloth and have a deduction from the weaving. It has become a custom with us that the person, who puts out the yarn to weave, risks the responsibility of the weaver. That is to say his honesty and ability to pay or return the cloth or yarn. We are willing to risk the yarn and cloth in his hand or yours against unavoidable casualties such as fire and floods etc. and no further.[13]

In this way, textile manufacturers no longer forfeited profits due to poorly made fabrics or theft. The mill agent no longer oversaw hundreds of weaving laborers. Firm employees maintained only the records of yarn sent to a limited number of merchants.

The cloth merchants or commission agents evaluated the work of their laborers and suffered the losses for shoddy or tardy pieces. The use of such agents streamlined the putting-out system, reduced the losses incurred by mills and increased profits earned. As the textile mill owners before them, commission merchants penalized their employees for the tardy completion of orders but were unable to guarantee prompter service than that achieved previously by mill agents. From 1810 to 1823, the Blackstone Manufacturing Company put out warps directly from their factory and received them in between eleven and thirteen weeks. Some of the weavers took as long as one year to return fabrics. Russell Wheeler, a commission agent from Stonington, Connecticut, did not improve the average time warps remained in the outworkers' hands as his employees also brought back orders in about thirteen weeks. Wheeler penalized his laborers for late returns and shoddy workmanship to no great improvement. In July 1825, he deducted half a cent per yard from Nancy Champlin's pay because she retained an order for ten months. Wheeler threatened to dock Matilda Burdick of Charlestown, Rhode Island's pay if she failed to return the finished cloth within seven weeks. Weavers who produced shoddy merchandise received either a lesser amount for their work or nothing. Jillson also penalized his employees for late returns or badly woven goods, by reducing the amount paid or not paying them at all.[14] The commission agents did not improve the speed with which the cloth was manufactured but did remove the paper work, tedium and risk from the hands of factory management.

Russell Wheeler's and Silas Jillson's records provide some evidence for how firms used the putting-out system between 1821 and 1829. The manuscript accounts provide a clearer image of the shape putting-out took between 1821 and 1829. Yet the existence of these records and the relative dearth of comparable factory accounts has tended to create a bias in our understanding of outwork weaving during this period. Ware and Coleman both see the use of commission agents as an attempt to rein in unruly outworkers in an effort to compete with power loom production.[15] However, the similarities between outwork before and after the invention of the power loom far outweigh the differences. Since the commission agents were unable to increase the speed of production or to ensure the manufacture of fine products anymore than the previous system, cloth agents did little to improve the putting-out system except to take on the risks. Viewing the use of commission agents as a way to develop a handloom system which would compete well with power loom weaving denies the previous existence of contracted middlemen prior to 1816 and creates the false impression that the use of commission agents occurred because of problems with outwork issued directly from the mill.

The existing records for Russell Wheeler's enterprise indicate that he operated his Stonington, Connecticut commission weaving business between the spring of 1821 and August 1828. He contracted with eleven Rhode Island-based firms including Thomas LeFavour and Sons, Timothy Greene and Sons, Stephen Jenks and Sons, Smithfield Cotton Manufacturing Company, Samuel and Daniel Greene Company, Benjamin Cozzens, Providence Manufacturing Company, Andrew Hutchinson, Barney Merry and Company, Richmond Manufacturing Company and A. Kennedy. Six of the textile mills that hired Russell Wheeler also contracted outwork with Silas Jillson of Richmond, New Hampshire. In addition Jillson received warps from William Jenckes, and the Valley Falls Manufacturing Company. The Jillson records span October 1822 to June 1829.[16]

The value of the accounts lies in the information they provide about outwork performed at a great distance from the factory, the kinds of fabrics produced, how long it took for orders to be completed, the expense of the endeavor and the quality of the material woven. In addition, since the use of these commission agents spans only a few years, it becomes clear that outwork weaving continued only as a solution to a temporary situation that existed for ten years between the invention of mechanized weaving equipment and the ability to acquire and implement the technology.

The Pawtucket or Blackstone River based firms, which contracted with Russell Wheeler and Silas Jillson, provide more clues as to why and how firms maintained hand production of cloth and weavers during the period. The level of involvement in contracted out weaving may not be assessed, as each of the textile mill owners would have used more than one cloth agent and probably continued to put out webs among local weavers. Histories of these companies drawn from census reports and the commission agent accounts are striking because of their similarities. For instance, the Valley Falls Company of Smithfield was built in 1820 on the Smithfield bank of the Blackstone River by Abraham, Isaac and David Wilkinson. The mill had 540 of its 752 spindles in operation in 1820 and employed five men, two women and fifteen boys and girls in spinning. In 1825, the mill owners contracted weaving with Silas Jillson for the first and only time purchasing 662.5 yards of unidentified two-shuttle fabrics costing between five and six and 1/2 cents per yard. Judging from the price, the company probably ordered stripe. In 1829, the Wilkinsons' businesses went bankrupt and the land, water privileges and buildings were sold to the Farmers and Merchants Bank. Subsequent owners increased the number of spindles to 3,442 and purchased seventy power looms.[17] As with many Rhode Island textile businesses, the Valley Falls Company had more capital available for investment during the early years. Once the new owners purchased the firm, they introduced additional investment capital, which enabled the company to acquire new equipment.

The Pawtucket firms, Thomas LeFavour, Benjamin Cozzens, Smithfield Manufacturing Company, S. and D. Greene, Timothy Greene and Sons and Barney Merry all have similar stories. The owners either sold the business, went bankrupt or entered into new partnerships prior to 1830. Timothy Greene and Sons burned in 1829, and in June 1829, S. and D. Greene went into receivership. Samuel and Daniel Greene owned both firms. Between 1822 and 1824, they contracted 85,008 yards of cloth to Russell Wheeler for the two firms. Wheeler sold them gingham, checks, shirting and stripes. Only fourteen webs created about 1,000 yards of two-harness single shuttle weave patterns. All of the forty-nine webs contracted to Silas Jillson consisted of two shuttle fabrics. Once Timothy Greene and Sons burned there was little chance of salvaging the operation.[18]

Although the bankruptcy and sale rate of these firms appears high, the percentage of incidences of partnership changes and receivership does not deviate from the state average. Of the firms that contracted outwork with Silas Jillson and Russell Wheeler about 44% resolved their economic and technological problems successfully between 1821 and 1829. In the state as a whole, 46% of the textile firms survived during the same time period. The cause of bankruptcy then does not rest on product lines or manufacturing methods but most probably on availability of capital, the richness of the natural resources and the economic climate. The thirteen firms contracting outwork with either Wheeler or Jillson followed plans that allowed them to weather the economic hard times.[19]

Depressed economic conditions prevailed in Rhode Island between 1814 and 1820 resulting in the relatively high level of bankruptcy during the period. The environment was not conducive to the investment of money into recent and untried innovations such as power looms, warpers and dressers. The depression of 1816 led numerous Rhode Island mills to cease operation and others to curtail production severely. Subsequent protective tariffs did little to aid Rhode Island mills. In addition, Rhode Island textile factories had an average of one third less capital available to them than larger, better, capitalized Waltham or Lowell-style textile firms. The relative lack of liquid funds for investment in textile innovations also caused Rhode Island-style firms to react to the invention or introduction of power loom technology differently than in Waltham-type mills in Massachusetts. As detailed below, these factors inhibited Rhode Island textile entrepreneurs from investing in technological developments.[20]

By 1817, when William Gilmore presented the Lyman Mills and the state of Rhode Island with his successful and marketable power loom design, many of Rhode Island's textile businesses had ceased operation in reaction to a post-Napoleonic War and post-War of 1812 depression in the textile industry. When Nathan Appleton described the state of manufactures in Waltham in 1816, he contrasted it strikingly with what he had seen in Pawtucket, Rhode Island. He viewed the village during a visit with the Wilkinsons, when he reported: "He [Wilkinson] took us into his establishment, a large one, all was silent, not a wheel in motion. He informed us that there was not a single spindle running in Pawtucket except a few in Slater's old mill making yarns."[21]

The effects of the depression endured until at least 1820, when many textile factory agents complained of low profits in the 1820 Census of Manufactures. Of the eighty-four cotton textile companies reporting in

1820, thirteen described periods of bankruptcy, inactivity, or suffering due to debts. The Census of Manufactures also included descriptions of eleven mills that remained inoperative in 1820. In 1830, sixty-four out of 119 cotton textile mills in the state reported their date of establishment. Only forty percent of these businesses were founded prior to 1820 and 53% in 1824. Of those not identifying their date of establishment, about ten appear in both the 1820 and 1830 reports. By the time McLane issued his *Report on Manufactures* in 1830 not quite half the firms from the pre- depression era had weathered the economic storm. Mill agents cited foreign competition, lack of government assistance to manufacturers, poor repair, low profits and bad debts as the cause for their particular predicaments.[22]

Mill entrepreneurs were not silent in their suffering but submitted numerous petitions to the legislature of the United States. Guided by these petitions, legislators designed the tariff of 1816 to protect cotton textile industry from the flood of foreign goods, which buffeted the United States after the cessation of hostilities between Britain and France and the United States and Britain by 1815. Though intended to levy an equal duty of twenty-five percent on all imported cotton textiles, a minimum valuation proviso actually placed heavier duties on fabrics of cheap simple construction such as sheeting and shirting. All cotton cloths costing less than twenty-five cents a yard were assessed duties as if they cost twenty-five cents or six and a quarter cents a yard. The minimum duty became proportionally heavier on less expensive coarse foreign cloths than on complex weave higher priced imports. As a result of the minimum valuation proviso, Rhode Island mills and any other mills producing four-harness or more complex weave fabrics did not benefit from the tariff as much as entrepreneurs who manufactured sheeting and shirting alone. In effect, the tariff of 1816 contributed to Rhode Island's retarded and protracted recovery from the postwar depression as Rhode Island manufacturers produced more expensive multi-shuttled and multi-harnessed fabrics. Because available power looms could produce only the simple fabrics, which also received greatest tariff protection, Rhode Island textile entrepreneurs opted to avoid direct competition with domestic machine-made fabrics. Firms produced four-harness multi-shuttle cloth though they were not as well protected by the tariff. Mill owners contented themselves with a lower percentage profit for their efforts until they were able to acquire suitable power looms. Technological limitations provided mill entrepreneurs with a market unaffected by power loom technology but also less well protected from foreign competition.[23]

In general, only the higher later duties promoted manufactures in Rhode Island. Not until the passage of the 1824 and 1828 duties did the tariffs serve to bolster Rhode Island's flagging textile industry. In 1824, the government raised the minimum valuation to thirty cents and in 1828 to thirty-five cents. The minimum duties increased to 7 1/2 cents per yard and 8 3/4 cents per yard respectively on all fabrics priced under the minimum. Subsequent protective tariffs extended minimum valuations to encompass some of the kinds of cloths manufactured in Rhode Island. By 1824 and 1828, mills still discontinued the production of many finer cloths but also varied the kinds of fabrics woven by manufacturing material suitable for printing in addition to sheeting and shirting. But by 1830, most Rhode Island mill owners limited their fabric production to simpler coarser less expensive cloth, which could be manufactured by machine.[24]

In addition, the disparate growth of textile industries in Massachusetts and Rhode Island indicates a relatively slow recovery from the depression in Rhode Island. Between 1820 and 1830, the textile industry in Massachusetts grew at a rate of 21.2% annually as opposed to 12.4% annual growth in Rhode Island. The striking growth discrepancy emphasizes the economic struggle Rhode Island entrepreneurs endured in the wake of tariffs, which aided one kind of textile manufacture over another. In addition, several agents reported to the 1820 Census of Manufactures that the poor condition of spinning, carding and other fiber preparing equipment inhibited production. One reported that the dam had all but washed away. Many agents indicated that even though they continued operation, profits remained so low as to make it hardly worth carrying on. Since firms did not have funds to effect repairs, mill owners could not spare large sums to purchase new equipment.[25]

Capital management contributed to the ability of Rhode Island firms to invest in technological innovations. In comparison to Massachusetts' Waltham-style factories, Rhode Island companies were less able to invest in technological innovation. The average amount of fixed capital invested in Rhode Island almost equaled that in Massachusetts. However, Waltham-type mills had more capital available to them to invest in innovations, improvements and expansion as they retained almost one third of their capital as liquid assets.[26]

Rhode Island's comparative limited cash resources served to shape the kinds of technological innovations, which developed and the rapidity of adoption. Rhode Island entrepreneurs invested most of their capital into fixed rather than liquid assets. The lack of capital available to purchase new innovations restricted the modernization of the factories and limited the money available for improvements to profits earned. As a consequence though Rhode Island firms purchased some advancements in textile technology, manufacturers tended to modify existing machinery rather than buy new equipment.[27]

Limited capital resources also influenced the nature of mill management. As inventors developed power looms and the looms were marketed commercially, Rhode Island textile entrepreneurs awaited the introduction of improvements prior to investing in machines, which would rapidly become out-moded. In 1827, David Wilkinson offered Gilmore's entire ensemble of warper, dresser and scotch loom for $710.00. Entrepreneurs might purchase the loom separately for $85.00 but Wilkinson sold the warper and dresser only as a pair for $625.00. Though less expensive than the Waltham loom and associated equipment, Gilmore's power loom, warper and dresser represented a substantial outlay for Rhode Island textile factories.[28]

The kinds of mechanisms that were available to textile manufacturers by 1820 provide some reasons for the pattern of power loom diffusion. The invention of weaving mechanisms and improvements to them determined what fabrics Rhode Island textile factories could produce profitably by hand. Rhode Island entrepreneurs sponsored or subsidized mechanics, who tried to develop power looms and associated equipment (warpers and dressers) beginning in about 1813. Their failure to purchase marketable machinery made by the mechanics relates primarily to financial inability. The response of entrepreneurs to economic deficiencies and their inability to purchase equipment led mill owners to produce fabrics that could not be made by machine and to use handloom outworkers as their method manufacture.

In Rhode Island, textile entrepreneurs and mechanics subsidized the research of potential power loom inventors from about 1813 onward. Daniel Lyman, Aza Arnold, Arkwright Manufacturing Company, Hines, Arnold and Company, the Coventry Company, and the Petersburg Mills all financed the mechanical experimentation of individuals who endeavored to develop power weaving mechanisms. Thus it was neither a lack of interest nor "entrepreneurial conservatism" that kept mills from adopting power loom technology.[29] Rhode Island entrepreneurs, manufacturers and inventors expressed intense interest in developing a mechanical weaving apparatus.

William Gilmore, John Thorp, Thomas Williams, Elijah Ormsbee, Samuel Blydenburgh, Job Manchester and others all introduced power weaving equipment in Rhode Island between 1812 and 1818. Noticeable effects of mechanized weaving on craftsmen occurred after 1817 in Rhode Island. Handloom weaving of four-harness and multi-shuttled fabrics remained important to many Rhode Island mills because of the limitations of the early machinery. Those who depended upon power looms were limited to producing the kinds of fabrics that the machines could manufacture.

Textile firms without the capital to invest in new equipment might and did earn profits by manufacturing fabrics that could not be made by machines.

The earliest power loom designs consisted of two-harness mechanisms, which produced only tabby weave and could not duplicate any twill fabrics such as denim, bed tick, or plaid. In addition, the shuttle or picker stick arrangements did not allow for color changes in the weft and rendered the looms unsuitable for gingham, horizontal stripe, plaids or checks. Gingham, chambray, bed tick, stripe, plaids and checks constituted the fabrics most commonly manufactured by Rhode Island textile businesses by hand prior to their investment in power loom equipment.[30] The earliest power looms could not produce the fabrics Rhode Island mill owners sold as hand woven goods. With this as a consideration the mechanisms actually encouraged the continuance of outwork for more complex weave structures or multi-colored fabrics by those firms that did not have the substantial funds needed to expend on the new mechanisms.

When Rhode Island mill owners purchased power weaving equipment, they altered their product line. Manufacturers tended to limit the variety of fabrics produced to two-harness weaves such as sheeting, shirting and printing cloth. Rhode Island businessmen continued to have more complex twill or multi-shuttle fabrics woven by hand until they acquired the optimum number of power looms for the spindles operating. With the Rhode Island economy at a low ebb, it took time for entrepreneurs to accrue sufficient funds to purchase power weaving mechanisms and their associated equipment. During the interim, manufacturers opted to earn profits before investing in power looms and awaited models with greater applicability before making their power loom purchases funded by hard earned profits.

Although the textile mills produced and sold plain weave cloths, manufacturers were probably not technologically limited to tabby weave in the 1820s. Mechanics had developed some improvements to the power loom by that date. For instance, Job Manchester designed and built a four-harness loom capable of weaving diaper in 1814. In 1816, Manchester developed a twill loom and by 1818, the Coventry Company encouraged him to develop an "improved" bed tick or twill weave loom. By that date some looms capable of weaving twill, existed, yet they had not gained popularity.[31] By 1825 there were over 100 bed tick looms in operation.[32]

The invention and adoption of a loom capable of weaving the twill pattern allowed for the manufacture of one-shuttle twill weaves and consequently most of the fabrics commonly manufactured by Rhode Island firms except gingham, plaid, checks and horizontal stripes. Rhode Island manufacturers required handloom production, limited the kinds of materials they sold and supported the experimentation of mechanics, who might develop improvements to existing machinery. To ensure profits mill owners opted to produce fabrics not offered by machine manufacture and altered the kinds of fabrics produced after they invested in power weaving equipment.

Rhode Island cotton mills that did buy power looms between 1816 and 1820 acquired fewer per factory or spindle than did Massachusetts' mills. Loom-spindle ratios are inexact measurements used here to establish the extent to which firms depended upon power loom cloth production. The optimum number of spindles necessary to supply looms with warp and weft varied by the quality and fineness of the cloth manufactured. Yet great ratio discrepancies would indicate a lesser or greater dependency on power weaving over hand manufacturing cloth. Entrepreneurs would not purchase more looms than might be kept supplied by warp and weft from the spindles operating in their mill. If the loom-spindle ratio were higher than optimum or if the spindles produced more yarn than could be woven into fabrics by the power looms, excess yarn had to be marketed in some other fashion.

Rhode Island's loom-spindle ratio (1 loom: 64 spindles) of 1820 shows that some mills chose to market their machine-spun yarn as other than machine-woven fabrics. The 1820 census report confirms this. Some firms selected to spin yarn for sale to other mills or for commercial sale, others relied solely on outwork, a few used only power looms and the remaining mills produced some cloth on the power looms and some by hand.[33] Using both the Boston Manufacturing Company's (1:30) and Rhode Island's average ratio for 1830 to estimate the optimum level of looms to spindles, a power loom wove the yarn created by between thirty and forty spindles into simple coarse fabrics.

In 1820 three hundred fifteen power looms operated in seventeen factories across Rhode Island or between 18 or 19 in each mill. Almy, Brown and Slater, one of the larger Rhode Island firms, operated 1,500 spindles and thirty power looms or one loom for every fifty spindles. In contrast, the Boston Manufacturing Company of Waltham, Massachusetts housed 175 power looms weaving the yarn spun on 5,376 spindles or owned one loom for every thirty spindles.[34] In 1820, the average loom-spindle ratio in Rhode Island was one loom for every 64 spindles or more than twice the proportion of the Boston Manufacturing Company. Massachusetts's textile mills averaged one loom for every fifty spindles. Neither of the states' textile mill owners used the power loom at the optimum level. The one loom to every forty-one spindles ratio in Rhode Island's textile industry by 1830 marks the increased use of mechanized weaving.

The importance of the loom-spindle ratio is further reflected in the patterns created by the diffusion of technology among Rhode Island cotton textile mills. Mills manufacturing fabrics of tabby or a two-harness weave such as sheeting, shirting and perhaps vertical stripe owned more power loom machinery and sold only machine-woven fabrics. These mills maintained an average of one loom for every forty-four spindles. Factories that produced a variety of tabby and twill weave fabrics owned fewer looms per spindle (1:55) and used some outworkers for their cloth production. In addition to these two categories were businesses producing a variety of fabrics, which depended solely on hand weavers.[35]

Despite the variety and availability of power weaving equipment and the enthusiasm for encouraging the development of mechanized weaving equipment, cotton textile mill owners put out warps to local weavers and to cloth agents. Several authors including Gary Kulik, and Alfred D. Chandler propose that limited waterpower served to restrict the adoption of power looms into Rhode Island mills.[36]

In his study of Pawtucket, Rhode Island, Gary Kulik noted that Pawtucket firms in particular retained handloom production because of the reliance of numerous mills on the Blackstone River to power their equipment. Charles Carroll described the numerous mill villages, which lined the river and its tributaries from Worcester "2 score miles south" to Providence, listing twenty villages supporting at least one and probably more waterpowered factories each. Kulik suggested that the density of industry along the river demanded more power than the river offered. Drought exacerbated the power deficiency during the 1820s. Competition for limited power supplies increased and by 1823 led to legal action in the form of the Sergeant's Trench Case. By 1826, the court's decision defined precise water privileges for factories located along the river in Pawtucket.[37]

Census reports and expansion of Rhode Island's textile industry between 1820 and 1830 does not support the supposition that widespread waterpower deficiencies generally inhibited the diffusion of power loom technology. About 20% of the cotton textile businesses reported only half their spindles operating in the 1820 census of manufactures. Several factors suggest that the economic depression rather than limited power sources or drought contributed to the problem. Four mill-agents commented on the availability and nature of power at their factory sites. None of them expressed concern over their power source. In fact, several described an abundance of power. The agent of Greene, Tillinghast and Company of North Kingstown stated that the streams were "durable" and a Coventry mill's manager described the factory and waterpower as "sufficient." In addition by 1830, mill owners increased the amount of operating spindles and looms well above the 1820 level. In 1820, for instance, the Hope Manufacturing Company of Scituate owned 1,800 spindles and ran only 800 of them but by 1830, they owned and operated 3,400 spindles and 84 power looms in the same location. According to Zachariah Allen's formula for calculating the amount of horsepower required to operate spindles and looms, the firm required thirty-nine more horsepower in 1820 than in 1830. By 1830, Almy, Brown and Slater's Smithfield factory operated 9,500 spindles or almost double the number owned in 1820 when they ran one seventh the number owned and working in 1830. In most cases, all the looms and spindles installed during the decade between 1820 and 1830 were operating in 1830.[38]

In 1830, McLane's report suggests that limited waterpower had become a concern. Samuel Slater provided McLane with an overall description of the state of manufactures in Rhode Island in 1830. His report described the availability of waterpower in the most complimentary terms. He suggested that Rhode Island streams could furnish the "power for propelling machinery to an almost incalculable amount." However, he tempered his praise of the natural resource by reporting how individuals endeavored to ensure the continued flow of water throughout dry spells by constructing artificial works to retain the extra waters that flowed in superabundance during the spring "freshet." Slater also recorded that during the decade four steam mills had instituted business in the state.[39]

In addition to Slater's assessment of waterpower, several mill agents reported methods used to increase the size of the business in the wake of limited power. For instance, John Andrews, agent of the Richmond Manufacturing Company located in Scituate, Rhode Island, stated: "The first factory not having power for water looms, the second factory was built in 1828 to contain looms etc.; or in other words sending good money to make bad more valuable if possible." The agent of J. Rhodes and Sons of Warwick also reported that the mill could not be expanded for want of sufficient power.[40] By 1830, then, with the generally great increase of spindles and equipment by Rhode Island textile firms, the availability of sufficient waterpower became a problem.

The account books of both Silas Jillson and Russell Wheeler buttress Kulik's waterpower argument. Ten of the thirteen firms contracting with the two agents were located in Pawtucket or on the Blackstone River or tributaries of the Blackstone River. But two of the firms, Richmond Manufacturing Company and the Providence Manufacturing Company, contracted with Jillson and Wheeler and were not on the Blackstone River.[41]

As stated earlier, the Richmond Manufacturing Company of Scituate experienced waterpower shortages, but the Providence Manufacturing Company of Warwick did not acknowledge waterpower shortages in the census materials yet issued warps for weaving. The firm's history illustrates how one Rhode Island textile mill survived the 1816 economic depression and the resulting capital scarcity. In adapting to economic adversity, a pattern developed among Rhode Island textile firms consisting of reduction of production or closure, the purchase of the firm by a new partnership with more capital, the gradual increase of production and outwork, production of four harness multi-shuttle fabrics, investment in power weaving equipment, change in the kinds of fabrics manufactured, and dependence solely on machine manufactured fabrics. The Providence Manufacturing Company's history is one example of this pattern of adaptation. The mill was initially founded in Crompton, a village in Warwick, in 1807. The joint-stock concern carried on business for nine years but closed in 1816. They leased the building for several years and in 1823 another co-partnership purchased the structure and commenced business operating 2,364 out of 3,200 spindles and other machinery to match. Between 1823 and 1824, the Providence Manufacturing Company received 39,643 yards of fabric from Russell Wheeler, a commission agent in Stonington, Connecticut, and placed a single order with Silas Jillson of Richmond, New Hampshire amounting to 3,713 yards of check or stripe.[42]

After purchasing the firm, the owners limited their subsequent investments to the profits earned each year. Benjamin Cozzens states:

> The present owners have realized an average of 7 3/4% for interest of money, insurance and all hazards. This is the rate of profit upon the capital employed from year to year. This capital consists of the amount paid in 1823 and since together with annual profits since which have been added to the fixed and floating capital.[43]

By 1830, the mill had 9,316 spindles and 263 looms in operation. Most of the equipment had been added in 1824. The firm put-out the last of its webs to commission agents in 1824 suggesting that the company had procured a sufficient number of power looms to turn all the yarn produced by their spindles into cloth.

Since the mill did not operate between 1816 and 1823, and since the entrepreneurs limited capital expenditures to what could be purchased with profits, the second group of investors did not begin to acquire power looms until well after its invention and until they realized some profit on their investment. According to Cozzens, the firm's earnings continued at an average of 7 3/4% for the years before and after mechanization. The profits reaped from hand weaving the fabrics into cloth and by contracting with commission agents did not limit the growth of the mill. On the contrary, their technological expansion was curtailed by the scarcity of liquid assets and the slow recovery from the 1816 depression.[44]

The owners of the Providence Manufacturing Company ordered a variety of fabric types from Wheeler and Jillson including plaid, check, gingham, stripe and shirting. In large part, these fabrics were not those produced by power looms and consequently the factory did not compete directly with mills relying primarily on mechanical cloth production. In addition the cloths were more expensive and though not adequately protected by the 1816 tariff, the fabrics must have been sold at less expensive prices than imported materials. By 1824 the minimum valuation was increased and reduced the amount of competition from abroad. By 1830, the subsequent power loom mill manufactured shirting, printing cloth and cambric. All the fabrics were one-shuttle simply constructed cloth, which would compete well with other domestic machine-manufactured fabrics.

Hence, it was not insufficient waterpower alone that curtailed technological diffusion but the scarcity of liquid assets, change in ownership and a slow recovery from the 1816 depression. In spite of all these factors, firms survived the decade and grew while maintaining outwork networks because of the fabrics chosen for manufacture. But the production of more complex fabrics was just one component of the means manufacturers used to weather the economic conditions and accumulate profits for the acquisition of modern equipment.

Because of mechanical deficiencies, and limited investment capital, businesses employed handloom artisans to weave many types of fabrics such as ticking, plaid, gingham and chambray. These cloth types comprised the primary multi-harness materials manufactured in Rhode Island. Power looms took over simple fabric production in many cloth manufacturing mills in both Massachusetts and Rhode Island by the early 1820s. If manufacturers desired to shift entirely from hand to power manufacture, they altered the variety and complexity of products manufactured in order to gain the most benefit from the protective tariffs. For instance, by 1820 the water looms of Blackstone Manufacturing Company of Mendon (now Blackstone), Massachusetts made sheeting, shirting and stripes but local craftsmen supplied the firm with plaid, gingham, and ticking until 1823.[45] By 1830, when McLane issued his *Report on Manufactures*, the Blackstone Manufacturing Company had shifted from the production of sheeting, shirting, check, stripe, gingham, denim, plaid and chambray to sheeting and shirting.[46] The majority of the Rhode Island firms that Silas Jillson and Russell Wheeler list in their 1821 to 1829 account books contracted the hand weaving of multi-shuttle or multi-harness materials. Most of the companies discontinued their contracts by 1824 when economic conditions had improved because of the institution of two protective tariffs and because of their investment in power weaving equipment. In each set of ledgers, only one factory continued ordering hand woven complex fabrics through the merchants after 1826. In large part, the Rhode Island textile businesses carried on outwork only two years after the Blackstone Manufacturing Company.

Like the Blackstone Manufacturing Company, Rhode Island firms altered the kinds of goods they offered for sale by 1830. Of the thirty-eight firms that responded to McLane's questionnaire in 1830 all but four mills manufactured tabby weave sheetings, shirtings, and print cloths to the exclusion of anything else. Few factories manufactured more than two kinds of fabric. Five textile mills reported product lines in both the 1820 and 1830 reports on manufactures. These firms clearly show the shift from complex to plain weaves. The Natick Mills, Randall Mills, Georgia Mills, Greene Manufacturing Company and Bellefonte Mills all switched from weaving three or more cloth patterns to producing either shirting, sheeting or printed cloth. Denton Thurber, agent for the United Manufacturing Company of Providence stated: "It would require much time and labor to go into particulars, and I will only observe that prior to 1817, we made various kinds of goods but since the introduction of the power loom, we have manufactured principally power loom stripes."[47] The majority of the thirty-six looms owned by the United Manufacturing Company must have been two-harness plain weave mechanisms as were the majority of the 5,856 looms owned by 119 cotton textile firms in the state since few produced complex machine-woven fabrics.

In general the kinds of fabrics purchased through cloth agents were more complex than those that might be manufactured by power. Though the Silas Jillson records rarely identify the kinds of fabrics manufactured, the accounts indicate the price paid for particular cloth types and the number of shuttles used in weaving the cloth. The fabrics consist primarily of four-harness weaves such as denim or tick or multiple shuttle (2-3) patterns such as gingham, check and stripe. Jillson did not note any orders for sheeting and shirting and Russell Wheeler of Stonington Connecticut, only reported taking in 97 warps of sheeting. Russell Wheeler's orders consisted of 1,953 webs supplied between 1821 and 1828. A large percentage of the 493,920 yards woven by Wheeler's weavers consisted of checks gingham, plaid and stripes. Clearly the firms that put out webs to cloth agents sent only those orders that could not be completed by the machinery they owned and would not be in competition with power loom weaving firms. The evidence from both the Wheeler and the Jillson records as well as Manchester's statement about the popularity of the twill loom indicates that businesses may have adopted two-harness looms, may have put-out complex weaving and only gradually invested in more complex looms and improvements due to a shortage of liquid capital.[48]

The pattern of reduced production and outwork followed by expansion, investment in power loom technology, and change in the kinds of fabrics produced occurs among many Rhode Island textile firms. Factors inhibiting diffusion such as economic adversity, scarcity of investment capital, the tariff of 1816, availability of marketable equipment, and scarcity of waterpower shaped technological diffusion in Rhode Island-style mills. By producing goods that could not be woven by available power loom technology Rhode Island-style mills were more than able to survive. Mills earned profits that could be invested into power weaving equipment.

By 1830, within Rosenberg's 13-year average rate for diffusion, Rhode Island textile firms used power looms. Rhode Island textile mill owners harnessed the technological limitations of the early power looms and used the limitations to their advantage, but they did put up with putting out. Putting out was the production method used skillfully to overcome the factors, which had inhibited them from purchasing power weaving equipment when it was first available.[49]

Chapter Eight

"My ram turned out to be a bore":[1] Technology, Economy and Outwork in Rhode Island after 1830

By 1830, Rhode Island cotton cloth manufacturers almost universally embraced power loom technology. By that date, machinery produced simple utilitarian fabrics and some more complex textiles. The powered mechanisms could weave cotton cheaply, rapidly, productively, consistently and excellently. Cotton textile company records detail shifts in management, product types and workforce in response to the technological and economic climate. Hand spinning and hand weaving, never completely eliminated even from cotton textile manufacture, diminished dramatically in importance with each progressive mechanical change. Technological transformations of the cotton textile industry continued with the introduction of stop actions, drop boxes, dobby chains and specialty fabric looms. To some extent, increased mechanization excluded cotton textile hand weavers. The introduction of looms capable of producing specialty fabrics such as lace and narrow braids also fabricated textiles not produced domestically on an outwork basis, and therefore, did not encroach upon the shrinking outwork weaving market.[2]

Outworkers, desiring to continue weaving, looked to woolen manufacture for continued warp supplies, and discovered opportunities to ply their trade well beyond 1830. Although Rhode Island was the sixth largest manufacturer of woolens nationally in 1836, the industry never dominated Rhode Island's economy for commercial, financial and technological reasons. Consequently woolen outwork supported only a fraction of cotton manufacture's largely displaced putting out weavers.[3]

In response to the relative professional drought, only ardent hand weavers found employment. Some hand weavers supplied neighbors with fabrics made from woolen or flaxen by-products of subsistence agriculture. Other artisans sold hand-woven machine spun cotton fabrics to local shop owners in exchange for needed goods or to neighbors as blankets, hand-kerchiefs or aprons. Hand weaving declined but never entirely vanished from Rhode Island's landscape. A handful of Rhode Island families may trace their weaving ancestors from the 17th through the 20th centuries. The kinds of fabrics produced and the ways technology influenced their work changed but hand weaving persisted and weavers' papers and textile remnants of their work document its persistence.[4]

The scope and organization of hand weaving after 1830 identify the various markets for hand woven textiles and *vice versa*. The growth of woolen manufacturing in the state and the later introduction and adoption of power technology established a short-lived and limited industrial market for hand weavers enduring well into the 1840s. Rural localities with agri-cultural or horticultural dependence encouraged the cooperative network system and sheltered domestic weavers from complete displacement. These weavers continued and passed on traditions that diminished in prevalence but did not cease.

TECHNOLOGICAL DEVELOPMENT AND THE COTTON TEXTILE INDUSTRY 1830–1840

Subsequent technological innovations in the cotton textile industry dem-onstrate that machines had reduced if not abolished hand weaving associ-ated with cotton manufacturing. By the mid 1820s, power loom patenting concentrated on increasing speed, on simplifying the warping process, on reducing employee risk, on limiting product damage, and on improving fabric or yarn quality. Many fewer improvements centered on expanding the scope of machine woven materials available beyond the introduction of machines capable of processing wool, flax or silk. In Rhode Island and elsewhere, mechanics played important roles in the development of increas-ingly automatic weaving equipment. These improvements initiated by the cotton textile industry guided the woolen industry toward the develop-ment of automatic woolen looms for both simple goods and finer woolen fabrics.[5]

By 1830, power loom patents focused on designs that might sim-plify machine oversight. Automatic let-off patents enabled mills to assign a single loom operator to additional looms. In 1835, Amasa Stone of John-ston Rhode Island developed a taking-up motion. Horace Hendrick and John Comins of Killingly Connecticut also produced patentable alterations to the take-up motion in 1836. In 1837, Welcome A. Potter of Cranston

Rhode Island made a loom with a self-regulating yarn beam that also related to moving completed fabric onto the cloth beam and releasing more warp. In 1844, William H. Brayton of Warren Rhode Island also introduced a loom patent that ameliorated the letting off motion of the yarn from the yarn beam called the "Brayton let-off motion." Early let-off and take up patents incorporated some amount of tension variance in their design. The variance of warp tension from one moment of take off until the next might result in imperfect fabric. Bigelow's 1840 carpet loom design incorporated a successful and seminal let-off and take up design adapted and improved by others.[6]

Ira Draper first patented self-acting or self-adjusting temples in 1816. At first he, and then later, his family manufactured the devices for over 50 years. The U.S. patent office issued sixteen patents to individuals developing temple improvements between 1820 and 1840 in various regions from New York, Ohio, Pennsylvania Rhode Island, Massachusetts and Connecticut. Rhode Island's inventors of loom temples included John Standish of Providence (1830) and Samuel Mason of Newport (1837). Mason's improvement used the existing action of the lathe beam to actuate release and capture of the cloth as the loom wove. In this way the temples held the fabric taut as the filling shot through the shed. The temple then released the fabric to facilitate take up and let off as the reed beat the filling into place. Hayes credits Waltham's 1825 patent as the significant improvement. Neither the Draper nor the Waltham patent found general acceptance, however, as worker resistance inhibited the introduction of the device into the factory environment.[7]

Efforts to create the best shed through which the shuttle would pass resulted in a series of harness and heddle improvements. Jeptha Wilkinson of Otsego New York and Providence Rhode Island developed a machine for making reeds; and improved reeds, heddles and harnesses for the power loom. In 1834 and 1836, John Blackmar of Killingly Connecticut developed power loom harnesses. Blackmar designed new twine heddles fashioned from a single continuous piece of twine. He also repositioned the heddle knot to the top of the loop rather than the bottom to reduce friction and thereby thread breakage. To simplify the refastening of broken warp yarns and to facilitate the rewarping process, mechanics, like John Thorpe, designed knotting machines as early as 1828. While inventors aimed their loom improvements at power loom weaving, the mechanisms were also applicable to handlooms. Heddle, reed, and knot tying improvements did little to alter the market for hand weaving but introduced more durable or additional sources of loom equipment.[8]

As stop actions, improved harnesses, and automatic knotting machines increased the speed of power looms manufacturing utilitarian fabrics, other mechanics turned their attention to the development of more complex looms to weave figured fabrics, rugs and specialty goods such as braids. Once Job Manchester had developed his 1816 twill loom, manufacturers could reproduce multi-harness single shuttle weaves mechanically. In 1821 and in 1828, John Thorpe patented braiding machine designs. Pawtucket's lace manufacturers achieved national notice when Franklin Institute honored them with a prize for a dress made from lace in 1828. John Quincy Adams, then President of the United States, purchased the garment to show the progress of finer manufactures. The failure to develop drop box mechanisms impeded the production of multi-shuttle weaves such as stripes and plaids by power. David Buffum of Newport Rhode Island had already invented the same technology for the fly shuttle handloom during the 1790s. The tardy adaptation of the technology to early power looms suggests not a lack of "know how" or fiber characteristic problems but rather a market geared toward weaving simple textiles at a high speed and in quantity. Manufacturers later dyed or printed simple fabrics woven on available power looms with figured designs, which made complex or figured weaving a less attractive advancement. By 1830, 9 Rhode Island mills produced over 90,275,000 yards of fabric for printing. The majority of fabrics produced by Rhode Island cotton mills were coarse sheetings and shirtings.[9]

Only when figured textiles, including such simple woven designs as filling stripe, plaid and crepe, had begun to be fabricated on power looms did the drop box become a significant and necessary innovation. Manufacturers needed a complex loom for weaving a variety of single colored figured weaves. Gilroy and Tompkins of North Providence promoted a complex loom for weaving cotton damask in 1835. The loom design was capable of creating a multiple harness pattern woven in a single color and demonstrates mechanical interest in complex weave looms.[10]

The drop box and multiplier motions control changes in the color of the filling or the yarn inserted into the loom warp by the shuttle. Such looms are equipped with numerous shuttle boxes each supplied with a shuttle and bobbin filled with a different color weft. The mechanisms alternated shuttles according to a mechanical pattern indicated by the multiplier, such as a cam, dobby chain or jacquard card. The shift in filling color took place after an even number of picks or passes of the shuttle crossed the loom. According to the *American Cotton Handbook,* the drop box was significant to the Crompton and Knowles loom. Yet, when Crompton patented his multi-harness figure weaving power loom in Taunton in 1837, he did not incorporate a system that would enable the loom to change weft color and create even simple multicolored weaves. William Crompton initiated work on his figure loom in 1836 in Taunton while working for a machine shop associated with Crocker and Richmond. George, William Crompton's son, improved the figured loom, already used by Crocker and Richmond. Cotton factories in both the United States and England used Crompton's design. The loom, described in the patent papers, had six harnesses. Crompton's improvements to the loom extended the number and variety of figures fashionable by the loom. The loom does not incorporate a mechanism making weft color interchange possible. In 1844, John Nield of Taunton Massachusetts patented a drop or rotating shuttle box design.[10] Among the several patented improvements was a method by which the loom could change weft colors and produce plaids or striped fabrics. His model demonstrated how to change from one color to one other. His claim was:

> the mode of operating the revolving shuttle box (represented in the drawings) or turning the same around at suitable intervals of time for the purposes set forth, namely: by means of the vertical cogged wheel *l'* having pins *m,'* extending from its sides, in combination with the dogs of the notched circular plates and with the pinion on the revolving shuttle box; the same being arranged and operated substantially set forth.[12]

He also claimed the originality of both the circular notched plates used to regulate the shuttle box, and the take up motion of the loom design. In 1845, he improved the way that the shuttles passed through the shed suggesting that his original design while ingenious operated with some difficulty.

With the exception of the figured looms and drop box mechanisms, few patented inventions aimed at cotton manufacture diminished the market for handloom weaving further than it had been by 1830. Instead, the inventive mind focused on improving the product and the operation of existing machinery. Heddle, harness, reed and shuttle improvements introduced during the era could also apply to handlooms without reducing the market for handloom weaving. When applied to industrial mechanisms, these innovations eliminated the need for additional machine operators and simplified the job of overseeing the machines. Fewer factory workers might weave better fabric and maintain more machines. When weavers added temples, drop boxes or improved heddles to handlooms, they improved the product quality or productivity but did not diminish the skill of the handloom weaver or the number of weavers needed to operate the handloom.

HOUSEHOLD MANUFACTURE OF LINEN AND WOOL AFTER 1830

As improvements to industrial weaving machines point to the continued development of mechanized cotton manufacture, similarly patents, improving hand spinning and hand weaving indicate an extension of both linen and woolen household manufactures. Linen and woolen fibers grown to support oil, seed, and commodities exports as well as subsistence had already developed avenues of by-product sales through household manufactures and community exchange networks. The flax and wool raised in support of commerce centered on seed or meat, and did not result in high quality fibers. Seed exportation required crop harvesting for optimal seed rather than fiber maturation. The resulting linen was coarse and hard. The sheep grown for meat exportation had longer hair than necessary for making some woolens, but the seven-inch staple did not compare favorably with 22 inch strands imported from Spain.[13]

Domestic clip wool quality produced ample yarn for domestic household manufacture if supplemented by imported fabrics and fibers but was not sufficient to supply fabrics for the entire colony. During the seventeenth century, Rhode Island's great supplies of wool grew on the numerous and large flocks of fat mutton, which grazed on the many Narragansett Bay islands and on plantations on the southern mainland of the colony. Sheep grew so abundantly that traders exported wool to Portugal and Spain as well as to British colonies in North America. The resource, though superabundant during the 17th century, proved insufficient to gear colonial soldiers and civilian populations during the late 18th century. By the revolutionary period, British importation of goods to supplement domestic production diminished. At their height in 1772, annual imports from England valued at £925,643, but by 1776, they had decreased in amount to value £15,657. The colonists found domestic woolen sources inadequate for the production of blankets, uniforms and stockings necessary to outfit the continental army. Rhode Island clothiers to the Continental Army found textile procurement arduous and oftentimes ineffectual due to the lack of resources. After the revolution the disruption of trade between Europe and the United States during the Napoleonic Wars further inhibited the production of wool. European countries exported neither finished textiles nor fibers to the new nation during this era due to trade embargoes. Although trade impediments protected fledgling wool manufacturers, it also limited imported fibers from Spain, Portugal and England. Along with these factors, deficient domestic woolen stores inhibited industrial growth.[14]

Flaxseed exportation initiated by the mid 18th century rose to 250,000 bushels exported from New York and Philadelphia by the late 18th century. Flaxseed, exported in quantity from Connecticut, Pennsylvania, Maryland and New York, competed with Rhode Island's exporters. Flaxseed export peaked in 1782 and a flaxseed glut in Ireland diminished the significance of the trade, which declined greatly in Rhode Island by 1792. With the quantities of flaxseed raised, local farmers harvested masses of the fibers. The fibers were spun and woven above the demand for household use. Although Almy and Brown and other manufacturers found that they could develop a market for machine-spun cotton yarns for weaving in the home, flax and wool produced domestically, for both home use and commercial sale, provided families with sources of fibers that would have been wasteful not to process or trade. Patented improvements to domestic spinning and weaving devices and woodworker accounts support this claim and suggest that hand spinning and hand weaving continued beyond 1790 when waterpowered cotton spinning began.[15]

Looms were listed in domestic probate well beyond the period prior to power loom weaving adoption by cotton manufacturers and in many instances well beyond woolen power loom weaving. Certainly the number of looms diminished but they did not disappear from probate accounts entirely. Family cloth manufacture retained importance as looms in estate assessments attest. Inventories and wills indicate most dramatically the continued use of handlooms for weaving wool and flax in Rhode Island. Cranston Probate, for example, shows the rise of domestic manufacture and the decline of home production by the appearance of cloth making equipment in probate. Cranston, located just south of Providence, had a mixed economic base incorporating agriculture and industry. For those living close to the textile mills, mechanically produced fabric proved readily available. Landless residents or agriculturists not growing fibers would also seek to purchase rather than fabricate cloth. The city clearly evidences the shift from domestic to factory made but the records also show how individuals, who raised fibers, continued to weave or to have woven household fabrics. Between 1776 and 1788, 27.1 % of all inventories included looms. Between 1809 and 1820, 30% of the records listed hand weaving machinery. Between 1820 and 1844 out of 175 records taken, 25 or 14.3% recorded the ownership of handlooms. By 1844 only 2% of all inventories noted weaving mechanisms or paraphernalia.[16]

After 1820, some of the textile equipment obviously remained in storage located in a corncrib or among assorted lumber, as did Ezra Dyer's. Waterman Burlingame stored 5 looms, 4 weaver's slays and harnesses, 2 woolen, 1 linen and 1 quill wheels, two swifts, a reel and warping bars in his barn when he died in 1836. Others or their family members still used their textile equipment. William Lippitt's inventory dated 1838 contained a woolen and linen wheel, reel and loom in the east chamber of the west part of his house. Arthur Potter's inventory shows that he kept 2 looms and tackling, 4 1/2 pounds of woolen yarn and 1 pound of flax in the west chamber of his house in 1834. In 16 other Rhode Island towns and cities, estate inventories listed domestic textile equipment as late as 1868. Fabric making paraphernalia including quill wheels, reels, warping bars, harnesses, reeds and shuttles appeared as late as 1884. Artisans often stored small items in cupboards while assessors listed the dismantled looms as "old lumber." Despite the maintenance of looms and cloth making equipment, their continued employment is perhaps still in question, as the owner may have placed machinery in closets, barns or outbuildings.[17]

The percentage of looms appearing in estate appraisals diminished radically after 1830. Even known weavers did not keep their handlooms. Joseph France died in 1849 by which time land records for Burrilville listed him as a "bleacher." His estate valued at $294.68 contained no loom or other associated equipment. In 1826, the town assessed his estate in preparation of appointing him a guardian. Movables and property valued $1,585.53 but even then the account itemized no loom.[18] Though considered a weaver in Smithfield's death records for 1849, William Howard did not own a loom. By 1818 John Slater had hired Howard as a power loom warper for his mill. Preservation of weaving equipment or lack of cloth making tools did not necessarily indicate the perseverance or cessation of handloom weaving. A more complex situation existed than reflected by the study of probate records.[19]

Less densely populated outlying agricultural regions of the state supported the craft to a later date. Estate inventories in these Rhode Island regions manifest this trend. In Smithfield, for instance, hand weaving machinery and paraphernalia appeared in 17 out of 38 post 1820 probate records. Almost 50% of the Hopkinton inventories dated after 1820 contained looms. In Burrilville, 11 out of 23 noted weaving mechanisms and cloth equipment after the introduction of the power loom. In contrast Providence estate evaluations only had 4 records of handlooms and fabric making tools out of a sample of 26 after 1820. To survive in the trade, weavers had to relocate to rural areas, offer services not available in machine-made form, move to cities where commercial handloom weaving existed or change occupations.[20]

The evidence of continued family production in the form of patented improvements to hand processing equipment buttresses estate assessments. Spinning wheel improvements and the continued fabrication of hand textile equipment by local wood workers point to domestic production. Homespun and hand woven production supported the cooperative network system of exchanges. Improvements to loom reeds, harnesses, heddles and shuttles contributed to improving the family loom. "Family" spinning wheel patents continued throughout the 1820s and 30s. The Minor's head and other similar spinning wheel adaptations speak of a persistence of hand spinning well beyond 1790. Amos Minor developed a more complex spindle head for the walking wheel. By introducing a second wheel to the spindle head, Minor increased the spindle speed and the twist added to the wool with one turn of the walking wheel. His first patent was issued in 1803 but a second one in 1810 suggests that the significance of the improvement was still felt, and that domestic spinning continued. Thomas R. Hazard also noted that the Peacedale Manufacturing Company and his own firm depended upon woolen spinners well into the first quarter of the 19th century. Improvements introduced after 1820 reflect the isolation of individuals living rural portions of the United States. William Jones of Thornville Ohio patented his family spinning machine in 1826. J. Watt, F.A. Priest and G. Freeman of Jefferson County, Ohio developed an improved domestic spinning machine the same year. Nonetheless spinning by hand continued well beyond 1790 in wool and flax.[21]

Shadrach Steere, a woodworker, was born in North Smithfield in 1779. He lived there until about 1803 when he acquired a farm in Burrilville, Rhode Island. There he established himself as a maker of hoe handles, chairs and spinning wheels. Between 1808 and 1814, an account book records the details of a lucrative business in making and repairing domestic spinning wheels, quill wheels and other textile related equipment. By 1814, the accounts document a decline in linen and woolen wheel use with the decrease of wheel orders or requests to repair linen, woolen or foot wheels. For instance, in 1808 Steere receive 68 requests for woodworking from customers. Of those requests 8 were for woolen wheels, 12 were for linen wheels, 3 for repairing wheels, one clock real, one real, one quill wheel, one spindle and one spool. In addition, Steere, made chairs, and bedsteads and repaired chairs. For each linen or foot wheel sold, Steere received $5.50 and for each woolen wheel he received $3.50. Payment was received in cash or lumber. By 1810, Steere's records evidence a shift in the kinds of wooden items he produced. That year he fashioned 21 woolen wheels, 6 linen wheels, 4 quill wheels, 2 spindle, 1 real, 18 bobbins and 69 other wooden goods, lending his horse and farm products. By 1814, wheel orders diminished to 5 woolen wheels, two linen wheels, and three quill wheels. Steere also made two-dozen bobbins but had 33 orders for farm produce, chairs and labor. The diminished orders may indicate a reduction in the use of spinning wheels or an appropriate supply of the mechanisms were available within Steere's sphere of influence. Steere shifted his activities to some extent by producing bobbins for the yarn trade and by devoting himself to providing a variety of services to his neighbors such as sharing livestock and exchanging produce.[22]

By 1836, a second record book illuminates a very different environment for Steere's services. The account book notes not a single order for repair or acquisition of spinning equipment or quill wheels. Steere's records document flexibility and willingness to change. Accounts detail plank sales, repairs to chairs, handle orders, farm good trades and a lucrative business in sharing his oxen and horse and wagon with his neighbors. Like the out-work weavers, Steere adapted his woodworking to the changing markets for his skills. While needed, he supplied household manufacturers with tools. As their demands diminished, he shifted his product line and expanded the scope of services supplied. Although Steere did not fashion spinning wheels and other textile implements between 1836 and 1853, he did receive textile goods as credit against accounts from women. There are a few examples of yarn and fabric trades during the 1830s. While illuminating about wood-working through time, the account clearly shows a shift in domestic textile production. The transformation responded to increased woolen and cotton manufacture in the state.[23]

Civil records of large and cosmopolitan Rhode Island communities like Providence continued to identify handloom weavers well after 1820. The population of urban weavers consisted of single women or widows and immigrants. Between 1820 and 1847, women identified as weavers in the directories, inventories or land records tended to be widows or single family heads. The appraisal of Celinda Harris' estate in 1827 indicated that she owned few household goods not related to cloth manufacture. Ann Axtel, a black woman, headed a Cranston family consisting of one male between 0 and 10 and seven women ranging in age from 0–45 in 1810. By 1820 she had moved to Providence and lived with two female children. Between 1826 and 1832 she resided on Pawtucket Avenue and Foster's lane supporting her family by weaving. By 1832, she had left Providence for parts unknown. Deborah Cady was born in 1774, and lived in Providence at 110 Broad Street in 1826. In 1846, she identified herself as a carpet weaver living at 116 Plain Street in Providence. In each of these cases the women were single family heads and required an income producing trade. All the women produced the textiles in their homes while fulfilling their responsibilities as mother and financial support to several individuals. Outwork weaving fit their needs well by allowing them to receive warps to weave in the home as they cared for children and the house.[24]

Male weavers during this era were largely emigrants. Louis Cathier arrived in New York from France in 1823 with his wife and three children. He is listed as a resident of Providence between 1826 and 1832. He lived on North Main Street and practiced his trade there until he died at 71 in 1847. Henry and Patrick Devlin moved to the U.S. with John Devlin who arrived in America from Ireland. Henry Devlin lived in Providence between 1824 and 1828 and resided on North Main Street and Nash's Lane address. He wove between 1824 and 1826. By 1828 he had become a molder. He died in 1866 at 74.[25] Several weavers left the Providence area without a trace. Patrick Dunlap, for instance, left his wife and young child in 1820 for some unknown location. His wife submitted the following advertisement in the *Providence Patriot:* "Whereas Anne Dunlap of Smithfield in said County, wife of Patrick Dunlap late resident of Smithfield now in parts unknown, weaver, hath filed her petition in said office praying for the reason therein stated that said court would pass a decree of divorce."[26] Immigrant weavers came to the state with their trades and notions of opportunities awaiting them in Rhode Island and elsewhere. Unfortunately those that arrived during the 1820s wanting to find weaving positions or chances to introduce technological advancements, found that in the course of 30 years, Rhode Island's textile industry had caught up with Britain's and American machinists now sent improvements to Britain with the idea of becoming rich. The Samuel Slater or William Gilmore type positions and encouragement were gone and so too was handloom weaving associated with cotton textile mills.

Although commercial handloom weaving declined after 1820, artisans adjusted to the increased mechanization of cloth manufacture. Some shifted from cotton to wool because wool technology lagged behind cotton. Others changed their occupations or relocated. A few weavers remained and altered the products and services offered to the public to suit the needs of their locality. Although no known collections of Rhode Island handloom weaver's personal papers remain for this time period, Samantha Barrett's diaries and account book for New Hartford Connecticut offer insights into how independent artisans adjusted to the altered marketplace. Located about twenty miles northwest of Hartford, New Hartford was about 70 miles distant from the Rhode Island border. The small town nestled on the Douglas Pike. Since the closest major city was twenty miles from the village by turnpike, Samantha Barrett did not suffer competition from a large source of machine made goods. A small carding mill operated nearby. Rather than ruin the market for Barrett's goods, Samantha found occasional employment fabricating cloth for the mill.[27]

The location of New Hartford most closely duplicates such Southern Rhode Island towns as North Kingstown and Hopkinton. A few independent weavers probably wove fabrics at a profit in the state in much the same way as Samantha did. Samantha Barrett was born in the 1790s, as were most of the outwork weavers described by this study. She was the daughter of William Barrett who came to Connecticut from England with his wife Susanna. Throughout her adult life, Samantha remained unmarried. She lived with her sister Zeloda on a farm. Zeloda was born in 1786 and died in 1836. Zeloda Barrett specialized in the carding and spinning processes of cloth manufacture. Sometimes she took her own wool to the local mill to card on their machinery as she did on October 24, 1820: "I went to the carding machine got twenty pound of wool carded and returned very tired"[28] Zeloda spun, carded and maintained the farm while Samantha concentrated on her weaving and helped neighbors prepare looms.

Samantha's account book spans 1811 to 1823 but her diary indicates that she wove until she died in 1830. The types of fabrics she produced changed from the manufacture of yard goods in linen and wool to more specialized weaving. Her original products included blankets, aprons, diaper cloth and figured weaves. In 1811 Samantha wove material for twelve customers including sixteen yards of linen for the local factory. Throughout the year she sold six blankets, flowered bed coverings and coverlets and 276.5 yards of plaid, linen and wool. Although she received about $170 for her labors and probably ate food grown on the farm, her earnings were not sufficient for her sole financial support. Her production levels and pay during 1812 duplicated her 1811 efforts, but she made more aprons, toweling, blankets and table linens than before. Her customers decreased to 8 for that year. By 1814, she added cotton weaving the her repertoire producing 93 yards of cotton cloth, 25 yards of woolen, kersey and blankets. By 1815, Samantha increased the amount of fabric she wove to 857 yards, 27 blankets (plain, flowered and kersey) 13 pocket handkerchiefs and socks. Her earnings swelled to about $609.46. For the most part she worked linen and wool but she did weave 274 yards of cotton. Her patrons increased to sixty-one including her sister Zeloda. She charged her sister eight dollars for weaving wool. In 1816 Samantha took in a few warps from the cotton factory as well as working for 27 other individuals. She wove eight yards of woolen cloth and one kersey blanket for her mother who paid her $5 for the task. The factory compensated her about six cents per yard for her product.[29]

The following year Samantha wove 254.75 yards of wool, cotton and tow plus aprons, towels and 17 flowered, bird's eye, kersey and diamond blankets. For each flowered blanket, she received nine dollars and one dollar for a diamond or kersey bedcover. Although her annual production of yard goods fluctuated, Barrett's specialty goods increased in demand. By the 1820s blankets, carpets, handkerchiefs and table linens composed all Samantha offered for sale. Her flowered blankets continued to be her most popular item. The price remained nine dollars per bedcover through 1823. Samantha did not reduce the prices for her wool or linen fabrics throughout the time spanned by her account book charging between five and six cents per yard.[30]

Her weaving ledger concluded in 1823. Samantha's diary began May 1828 and documented a thriving weaving business. She took in orders from many of her neighbors and worked constantly Monday through Saturday weaving, spooling, warping and picking. Zeloda carded and spun most of the fibers though Samantha assisted her from 1828 onward. Samantha Barrett wove between 15 and twenty yards a week. The average size of each piece was about twenty to twenty-five yards unless she worked on a blanket.

The diary describes wool processing, carpet weaving and a single blanket but does not offer the detailed view of manufacture provided by ledger accounts. In addition to taking in work from neighbors Samantha and Zeloda produced goods to sell in the city. October 11th 1828, for instance, she and Zeloda rode to Canton located midway between Hartford and New Hartford on the Douglas Pike. There, Samantha sold flannel at 29 cents per yard and socks. Although the Barretts seemed successful in receiving orders for their work, Samantha did reduce the price charged for flowered blankets by 1829 to $7.50 to be more competitive. Since she could weave more than half a blanket a day, Samantha wove bedcovers between warps obtained from local customers.[31]

Samantha Barrett's life and work mirrors that of some Rhode Island craftsmen chosen for study. An unmarried woman, she endeavored to support herself through agriculture and domestic manufacture. Initially she produced woolen and linen yard goods for local farmers at the rate of between five and six cents per yard. When a cotton mill operated in New Hartford she chose to weave cotton both independently and for the company. Her production for the mill was minimal totaling about 200 yards in two years. The pattern of limited company weaving is similar to Rhode Island artisans who manufactured small amounts for George Thurston and Company and Blackstone Manufacturing Company. To a great but not exclusive extent factory production furnished little of the family income. Fabrics fashioned for neighbors or for exchange contributed substantially to the family's subsistence. According to letters written to and by Almy and Brown during the late 18th and early 19th century, the firm could sell machine spun cotton yarn to independent weavers for fabrication of cloth to supplement the local cooperative network. By 1820, Samantha decreased yard goods manufactures because of the competition from local cotton textile mills. She was able to continue weaving linen and woolen fabrics. Ultimately, she limited her work to blankets, aprons and handkerchiefs. Samantha successfully found outlets for her skills until her death in 1830 because of her willingness to alter the kinds of material sold to her customers.[32]

Like Barrett, Weaver Rose attained financial success in weaving specialized goods. William Henry Harrison Rose of North Kingstown Rhode Island was the last of a family of Rhode Island handloom weavers when he died in 1913. The life of William Henry Harrison Rose and his genealogy demonstrate how one Rhode Island family passed weaving skills and patterns from one generation to the next. The craft remained a constant source of employment for the Rose/Northrup family from the 18th to the 20th century.[33] Weaver Rose's mother, Anstis Northrup Rose, followed the craft her parents Mary and Robert had practiced. Mary Northrup taught weaving in Kingstown Rhode Island while her husband Robert took in warps from local farmers. Robert had learned his trade from Martin Reed another Washington County independent weaver. In a letter to Alice Morse Earle, Rose described the life his grandmother and grandfather had led.

> My grandfather and grandmother, Robert and Mary Northrup lived at what now is Stuart Vale but then known as the Fish Pond in a little hamlet of four houses. Only one of which, my Grandfather's is now standing. He owned a store and fished in the spring and wove some and went amongst the larger farmers working at his trade of weaving whilst his wife carried on the weaving at home and had a number of apprentices.[34]

Robert's life was that of a typical itinerant weaver of the eighteenth and early 19th century. He died in 1822. Robert was born in 1766 and his wife in 1771. Both the craftsmen witnessed and adjusted to massive changes in textile manufacture during their lifetime. They and other members of their family sought to remain independent artisans rather than take in machine made warps. In addition to Robert, his two brothers Thurston and John produced fabric. Thurston Northrup taught school as well as manufacturing yard goods and coverlets. John, known as Weaver John, wove primarily coverlets.[35]

From the late 18th century, the Northrup family specialized in coverlets. The manufacture of coverlets requires great skill both in warping and treadling. The complex hand weaving patterns need from four to about 16 harnesses. A skilled weaver could manufacture bedcovers rapidly once he or she had warped the loom, as coarse fibers comprised both the filling and the warp. The low number of yarns often took as little as twenty-two threads per inch in density. By using coarse yarns in warp and weft, artisans increased the number of yards made each day and expanded the level of production. This was one way to make weaving more profitable. John Northrup and Anstis Rose and her son William all made coverlets in an effort to fabricate marketable cloth. In addition to the manufacture of coarser materials the Northrups lived and worked in a rural area several miles outside Providence off major routes. Local farmers may have retained domestic manufacture of textiles *in lieu* of access to American machine made fabrics. William Henry Harrison Rose was born in 1839 at a time when most independent weavers had either moved or changed occupation. His decision to learn the trade came from a desire to follow the family's traditional trade. He and his sister Elsie were the only ones of the Roses' six children to choose weaving as their vocation. Weaver Rose and his sister lived in their parent's house erected in 1816 until they died. They located their shop in the attic of the dwelling where they maintained three looms of varying widths and number of harnesses. One of the looms was a broad-loom capable of weaving fabric 60 inches wide allowing the weaver to produce portieres in a single width.[36]

Like other post-industrial hand weavers, Rose shaped his hand weaving to meet the needs of a modern market and to ensure financial success.

> Those craftsmen who persisted in producing in the outmoded techniques of another era no longer found a wide market for their goods and were forced to seek custom orders. The choices the artisans made tended to isolate them from the cultural mainstream. It is in this setting that Weaver Rose began his work.[37]

Rose limited his production to carpets, coverlets, mats, and portieres all of which required few ends per inch, and therefore, warped and wove quickly. He specialized in coverlets done from overshot patterns in the traditional blue and white warp and weft. Rose had inherited a certain number of patterns attributed to Martin Reed. He created other drafts and received some designs from his relatives. More notable than the graphs, however, was his method of recording and storing them. Rose wrote his patterns on boards, posters, scraps of brown paper, backs of advertisements and pieces of cardboard. As unusual as his storage of them, the design names included "Sally's Fancy," "Bonaparte's March," and the "Fig Leaf" pattern.[38]

Rose altered his products to suit the available market. He simplified his task by utilizing machine manufacture, in ways that did not infringe upon the performance of the trade. Weaver Rose purchased modern machine spun yarns that eliminated all the time consuming tedious fiber preparing tasks. He used commercially produced shuttles, spools and reeds all machine-made. Even though his work required all the skills of pre-mechanized weaving, his craft still evidenced change in the tools used. Rose effectively streamlined the trade to increase the speed of cloth manufacture.[39]

Weaver Rose and Samantha Barrett offer examples of artisans who continued working at their craft by offering services unavailable to their location. Cotton mills produced simple machine woven yard goods rapidly,

cheaply and in quantity. To compete with the factories, independent craftsmen manufactured complex multi-harness fabrics. Rather than working
fine yarn counts, weavers turned to coarser yarns that increased the number of yards woven daily. In this manner, they decreased time, effort and
complexity of warping. Despite their use of coverlet patterns, coarse fibers
allowed for minimal repeats of the design thus simplifying loom warping.
William H.H. Rose's life indicates that handloom weaving did not entirely
die out even in the twentieth century. A few individuals learned the trade
and successfully supported themselves by weaving. Of course, the numbers
involved diminished almost as dramatically as company weavers after 1820.
The demand for hand-woven articles could support only a small group of
craftsmen after 1840.

"THE VEXATIONS OF OUR TRADE:"[40] RHODE ISLAND'S WOOLEN INDUSTRY AND WOOLEN TECHNOLOGY

Insufficient domestic wool supplies and staple quality obstructed the industrialization of woolen manufacture during the late 18th century and first
quarter of the 19th century. Provisioning the troops during the American
Revolution pinpointed the problems. As a result Hamilton, Coxe and others looked to cotton, formerly a fiber imported from the Sea Islands, for the
commodity to support the industrialization of textile manufacture in ways
that united 13 disparate colonies under a single economic flag. Southern
planters had begun to turn toward commercial farming and cotton grew
well in the soils and the climate of the southern states. Although farmers
raised sheep in every state of the union, Alexander Hamilton and others
identified numerous problems inherent in employing wool to encourage
industrialization and manufacture. In his 1790 Report on Manufactures,
Hamilton cited the availability of various commodities, including cotton
and wool, which would nurture a more diversified republican economy.
Political and economic policy makers viewed cotton farming as a particularly strong impetus for the developing commerce because both Southern
and Northern states would benefit. Prior to the 18th century cotton was a
fairly exotic fiber that was not deeply entrenched in domestic production.
The fiber was not linked to traditional social or exchange networks and
was free for introduction to new business and technological systems. Hamilton's approaches to urging cotton and wool manufacture differed. While
he encouraged the growth of cotton, he merely stated that the best domestic
wool was grown in Virginia. He did urge the development of industry to
support the growth of products like wool in the southern states. Obviously
Hamilton saw the northern states as fertile ground for industrialization

while the southern states tied firmly to the north by agriculture and horticulture in clear support of the industries developed above.[41]

Without the introduction of longer staple wool growing sheep, all United States commercial woolen fabric manufacturers found it difficult to compete with imported fabrics. The failure of wool growers to breed sheep with hair of sufficiently long staple persisted inhibited by trade restrictions. The first Merino wool sheep, brought to the U.S. specifically to grow wool was in 1801 by Dupont and Delessart. Yet the introduction of one or two merino rams to the flocks did little to improve the stock until a herd of 21 rams and 73 sheep were imported to the United States. There were only somewhat over 5,000 Merino sheep in the United States by 1809. Merinos were not popular among most sheep farmers who desired to raise good meat producing animals that happened to have thick long woolen coats. The Merino sheep specialized in wool growth rather than meat. As a result, some sheep farmers, notably, George Washington improved on native stock by breeding for long staple. In general efforts to improve the domestic clip proved fruitless, and even in 1830, most of the wool produced domestically were from common or shorter staple growing sheep due to the general desire to grow sheep good for meat. By 1815, wool-growers had improved their stock substantially and the sheep of the islands of Narragansett Bay were highly prized for their wool production. [42]

Ultimately the intermittent rise of woolen industrialization as compared to cotton manufacture is inextricably intertwined with household production. Whereas cotton was not grown to produce anything other than a fiber used to create textiles, both flax and wool arose out of agricultural production directed towards other income producing activities. Flax produced seeds that traders exported to Ireland to generate British currency. Currency paid for British exports to the colonies. Linseed oil pressed from flaxseeds supported the ship building trade. The fibers inexpertly raised, harvested and processed in the household became part of a community exchange network and not part of a commercial enterprise. Rhode Island farmers who raised flax also supported their families by producing subsistence products. Likewise farmers raised sheep to support the commodities trade. Their hesitance to grow Merino sheep exclusively for their fibers and their desire to improve domestic breeds indicates the importance of the meat to the marketplace and the farmers. The fibers clipped off these sheep each spring, found their way into the market as exchanges at the local general store. Shop records show that wool was entangled in the community exchange network. During the colonial period, farmers exchanged wool for goods at the local store while others traded other sorts of farm produce for the wool. During the early 19th century, shop records evidence a broadening and an increase of such interchanges until industry created cheaper, finer woolens by machine. Farmers retained some proportion of the fibers and used them to manufacture textiles.[43]

Single process mills for fulling in the seventeenth century and, by the end of the 18th century, carding brought mechanization to woolen production without the associated factory system. Neither process required great power sources to operate the mechanisms. As a result the location of the mills could be on almost any rivulet with a dam or natural drop. Many mill owners combined fulling and carding mills on the same waterpower site. Rather than disrupt the community exchange network, challenge traditional family structure or introduce new concepts of time, these single process mills incorporated well into existing social and economic structures. The single process mill continued to support domestic woolen production well into the 19th century. As shown in Chapter One, fulling mills dotted the Rhode Island landscape by the end of the 17th century and communities provided bounties or land to encourage the introduction of fulling mills near to population clusters. Although communities obviously viewed lumber and grist milling as more vital to survival, fulling mechanization proved a significant and an appreciated addition to any locality.[44]

Carding mills did not appear on the colonial landscape until later than fulling because the technology did not transport to the new world until the end of the 18th century. By 1791, Lathrop of Norwich Connecticut built carding and spinning machines for wool. Arthur and John Scholfield of Yorkshire, England emigrated to the United States in 1793 and with them brought an understanding of mechanized woolen production based on the current state of technology in England. By 1801, Arthur Scholfield established himself in business making and selling carding machines in Pittsfield Massachusetts. He sold his carding engines for $150 in 1805. By 1802 competitive carding machine manufacturers established themselves in New England. James Standring and Richard Gookins formed a partnership with strong connections to the Scholfields both in carding design and training. Standring is probably a British immigrant who worked under the Scholfields at their Byfield Massachusetts mill. Rhode Island's first noted carding mill was located in North Kingstown at the site of an 18th century fulling mill formerly owned by Benjamin Rodman. There, John Congdon and John Warner Knowles established a carding enterprise alongside the existing fulling mill in 1804. Their carding machine was of the Scholfield patents and John Scholfield probably manufactured it out of their Stonington Connecticut mill.[45]

The introduction of these early mills in the United States did little to introduce industrialization. Carding integrated well into surviving exchange structures alongside the fulling organization with which it often coexisted. The technology was also faulty and not easily augmented by additional mechanization. Carding machines produced rolls of combed fibers approximately the width of the machine roller. The rolls had to be hand pieced to make longer slivers and no machine performed this task adequately until the 1820s. Hand piecing resulted in inconsistent texture where one roll overlapped another. Hand spinners could adjust their technique to adapt to the varying thickness of the roll and produce acceptable yarn but machinery like jennies proved unforgiving of such variance. This lack impeded but did not eliminate the introduction of the factory system in wool.[46]

With the introduction of jenny workshops at the end of the 18th century, some manufacturers produced woolen and cotton blend goods. The Hartford woolen factory was not the only jenny workshop established during the 18th century, others developed in Brookfield, Boston, Stockbridge, Watertown and Ipswich Massachusetts and Somerset Maryland.[47] These were obviously not the only jenny shops instituted during the era. Some did not receive notice and may, therefore, not appear in the records. For instance, John Reynolds of East Greenwich Rhode Island developed machines for processing fibers in his weaving shop as he tried initially to turn to cotton manufacture alongside Moses Brown. He wrote to Moses Brown in 1788 as follows: "My mind seems much inclined in wool and flax at the present. If thou should incline to purchase it [a carding machine] I will let it go at a loss from the first cash. I will make the pay agreeable to thee, I will take it in goods."[48] In 1789 Moses Brown wrote to John Bailey, Jr.: "John Reynolds wants to sell his carding machine and frame as he finds the woolen business is as much as he can manage."[49] After some trial of working with machines, Reynolds opted to sell them off and turn to hand production of woolens. For a time, he tried to process textile fibers by machine. There are probably many other instances of dabbling in mechanization that occurred within Rhode Island in Providence or in other states that never quite made it into prior industrial surveys of wool production. The late 18th century era of industrial experimentation in cotton also encompassed wool. Cotton proved to be much simpler to mechanize than wool and wise entrepreneurs focused on that industry while wool awaited more favorable technological and economic climates.

If the woolen stores and staple quality proved an impediment to industrialization, so too did technology. Some early woolen factories received substantial notice for their incorporation of machinery viewed as at the technological forefront. Most particularly, Wadsworth's Hartford factory received acclaim for the woolen fabric produced to make George Washington's inaugural suit. Washington also wore the garment to address Congress and the House for the first time. Henceforth, the fabric was dubbed "Congress Brown."[50] Despite this initial flurry of praise, Henry Wansey, a British visitor, viewed the factory during 1794, and pinpointed key technological problems that doomed the enterprise to failure:

> The carding and scribbling engines, at Hartford, were of the oldest fashion. Two large center cylinders in each with two doffers and only two working cylinders, of the breadth of bare 16 inches, said to be invented by some person there. They had no spinning jennies, the yarn being all spun by hand. They were scribbling deep blue wool of the quality of Wiltshire running fine for the making coarse broad cloth; the spinning was very bad the wool not being half worked. I saw the weaving shop, five looms, two on broad cloth, two on coarse cassimeres, with worsted chains, and one narrow or forest cloth. They gave the weavers nine-pence per yard currency for the cassimeres, i.e. sixpence three-farthings sterling, dear enough considering the largeness of the spinning. They could weave six yards of broad cloth a day. I saw there some good well-combed worsted. They sort a fleece into seven sorts. I observed some very fine wool there, which they told me, came from Georgia, but it was in bad condition. The concern is carried on by a company. Nine thousand three hundred dollars have been lent towards the undertaking by the state.[51]

Wansey noted that the jenny spun fiber created poor yarn because the wool was "not half worked." While the existing carding technology suitably processed cotton, it did not sufficiently comb or align the longer stickier woolen fibers. Machine carded wool resulted in poorly formed rolags. The mechanical cards produced rolls or laps of between 16 and 20 inches in length to be pieced by hand and the varying density of the rolls at the seam resulted in poorly machine spun yarns Many of the early woolen mills put out their wool rolls to domestic spinners who could produce higher quality yarns.

In Rhode Island, Rowland Hazard purchased the Rodman's fulling mill and water right from Knowles and Congdon. He did not attempt to spin the yarns by jenny but for upwards of twenty years put his carded rolls out to women to weave. Thirty years later he described the change in woolen manufacture:

> In 1816 and later I used to employ scores of women to spin at their homes at four cents a skein, by which they earned twelve cents a day at most. The wool was carded into rolls at Peace Dale and transported to and from on the backs of horses. Some time ago I stood in a manufactory in the same

village and took note of a stripling who tended two highly improved jennies from which he was turning off daily as much yarn as six or seven hundred women formerly spun off wheels in the same time.[52]

According to Cole, Massachusetts firms continued to put out spinning to local spinsters between 1800 and 1817. Hazard counteracted the awkwardness of the production organization by purchasing or spinning cotton warps to weave cotton based wool blend fabric designed to replace linsey-woolsey. By 1819, the firm introduced spinning jacks and initiated factory spinning in wool but continued to put out spinning until the 1820s according to Thomas Robinson Hazard, Rowland's son. Hence, early woolen carding mills mirrored cotton jenny workshops in organizational adaptation. Whereas the first cotton jenny workshops spun cotton on jennies and put out flax to spin by hand, woolen workshops put out woolen rolls and acquired machine spun cotton warps to weave with woolen wefts.[53]

Woolen hand spinning, like cotton outwork weaving required mill owners to hire a large unsupervised labor force of outside contractors. The firms had to put the raw material at risk of embezzlement, damage, or poorly executed work. The time taken to deliver, retrieve and pass on the materials to the next hand processor proved lengthy and costly and required technological advancement to cure. The remedy was not quick in coming and for years woolen manufacturers struggled and failed or barely succeeded in producing woolens at a profit.

Economic and political conditions that protected the fledgling cotton industry also served to increase and shield woolen manufacture. The Embargo Act and the War of 1812 disrupted trade, and encouraged the domestic manufacture of textiles on a larger scale. Much like the period before and during the American Revolution, the absence of competitive imports encouraged domestic manufacture. While protected from outside competition, the flow of technological information from England in the form of emigration was also inhibited. The failure to advance wool supplies and mechanization created a situation that limited the growth of wool production. In 1810, even as cotton manufacturers introduced factories and machine spun cotton yarn in great quantities, Gallatin noted that, "two thirds of the clothing worn, including hosiery, and of the house and table linen used by the inhabitants of the U.S. who do not reside in the cities is the product of family manufactures."[54] That year there were three industrial woolen manufacturers in Rhode Island producing 15,000 yards of fabric that was less than one tenth of the domestic production for the same year. The firms were located in North Kingstown, Warwick and Portsmouth. Both the Warwick and the Portsmouth firms spun wool. The capitalization of woolen factories was similar to cotton factories ranging between $9,000 and $20,000 throughout the first quarter of the 19th century. Zachariah Allen's mills were the only exception to this rule and were capitalized at $95,000. By 1819 there were 24 woolen mills in Rhode Island but they were largely single process mills centering on spinning, carding or fulling. These mills do not represent the introduction of the factory system in wool but rather the failure to introduce it.[55]

Between 1810 and 1820, three significant technological changes took place that greatly affected the rise of a factory system in wool and the continuance of an outwork weaving network. These include the introduction of carding condensers, spinning jacks and power looms. In 1813 Thomas R. Williams developed woolen power looms for the Peace Dale factory. While his looms were not designed to produce broadcloth or standard yard width fabric, his power looms worked, and were used by the firm from 1813 onward. He built four saddle web, girth width or tape power looms. In an agreement with Rowland Hazard, Williams sold the rights to his looms for weaving webbing for the sum of $1,500. Power looms designed to produce standard width woolen fabrics were not introduced into the industry until the late 1820s and by 1830 the average loom-spindle ratio for wool was only 1 loom to 25 spindles. The Enterprise Mill in Portsmouth Rhode Island had 240 spindles and no looms.[56] The low loom-spindle ratio indicates that even by 1830, many woolen manufacturers put out warps for handloom outworkers to weave. In addition the kinds of fabrics produced by power looms were simple and handloom weavers continued to produce more complex multi-shuttle multi-harness fabrics for woolen firms.

In 1816, Silas Shepard and John Thorpe of Taunton, Massachusetts patented a woolen power loom.[57] The loom was a vertical loom used in the Shepard Mill prior to the patent date. Looms introduced prior to the mid-1820s did not achieve general assimilation into woolen mills for the same reasons that inhibited cotton mills from adopting power looms. The economic conditions, insufficient protection by tariffs, low levels of liquid capital, loom design flaws and low waterpower all effected woolen manufacturers too. By the mid 1820s, William Howard of Worcester Massachusetts introduced a woolen broadloom design that is considered to be seminal. Howard worked with Samuel Slater in Warwick and later in Massachusetts as a machinist in cotton mills. From that experience, he learned enough about power looms to introduce a design appropriate for wool. Other power looms included a broadcloth loom set up in Zachariah Allen's Allendale mill in 1824 and some looms for the fabrication of kersey operated out of Peace Dale Rhode Island in 1828. The early woolen power looms were like the early cotton looms. They were two harness machines with a single shuttle allowing for the production of simple fabrics including stripes and plain cloth. Woolen outwork continued in multi-shuttle multi-harness weaves as it did among cotton outworkers.[58]

In 1826, John Goulding of Dedham Massachusetts designed and patented a condenser in both the United States and Britain. The innovation created continuous rolls from the carding machines and wound the resulting rolags on bobbins. The development facilitated the incorporation of mechanized spinning into the mill environment. Although his machine resolved the problem of piecing rolls by hand, factories did not readily absorb the machines due to economic conditions. Between 1824 and 1850, the United States tariff policies impeded the development of the woolen industry. At first the importation of raw wool was impeded by duties, which offset the benefits of the protective tariffs of 1824 and 1828. By 1830 efforts to bring tariffs into line with manufacturers' needs had begun to be successful. Goulding's and other condenser designs were introduced into Rhode Island mills that numbered 41 by that date. By 1833, the tariffs had become more complementary and Rhode Islanders had adapted to the economic environment in the same fashion as they had in cotton by producing higher quality cloth.[58]

Mechanical spinning of wool initially took place in the home. Jennies introduced for domestic use soon led to the establishment of jenny workshops for wool. Although the technology was available, the entire country only had 299 jennies recorded in the 1810 census. After 1815, household use of jennies diminished in proportion to the number of machines introduced in woolen mills. The lack of condensers by this date inhibited the broad based use of jennies in factories. Waterpowered spinning was developed first by William Humphreys of Connecticut in 1811. The twelve spindle mechanism received praised for spinning as much as a 40 spindle jenny. The Peace Dale factory did not introduce spinning jennies until 1819. Very shortly after acquiring jennies, Hazard introduced spinning jacks or mules to the operation. Both the thirty spindle jack and the jennies were waterpowered. Hitz suggests that the mule purchased by Hazard was one built by Gilbert Brewster. Brewster was building and selling his jack as early as 1813. The jack or mule operated on the principle of a walking wheel. The machine initially drew the fibers out as the carriage moved away from the body of the mechanism and then imparted a twist as the carriage returned to its original position. The Providence Woolen Manufacturing Company probably owned one of Brewster's mechanisms in 1813. By 1820 the spindles operating in woolen factories had increased appreciably. By 1830 there were 24 woolen mills listed in the McLane report. Of those about 14 were single process mills operating carding machines. It is unclear whether the operations supported outwork spinners or provided rolls to local hand spinners. For hand spinners, outwork production for the multi-process woolen and cotton factories had ended and if we are to use Shadrach Steere's records as an example of the persistence of domestic hand spinning, then few domestic spinners continued to ply their trade in wool for home use.[59]

In 1836 the state's 41 woolen mills employed only 380 workers. The economic problems that stymied cotton textile industrialization and mechanization during the 1816–1826 period also contributed to wool's slow rise to prominence. By 1836, however, Rhode Island was an important national producer of linseys, broadcloths and satinets. By 1840, Rhode Island's woolen industry had doubled its size in 1832 to 41 industries. Fulling Mills still dotted the landscape numbering 45 in 1840. Still wool represented a much smaller contributor to Rhode Island's economy than cotton and by 1860 there were only 57 firms in the state. The same year there were 176 cotton textile firms in a declining state cotton industry. The woolen firms increased the variety of fabrics made producing plaids, tweeds and carpet yarns. Hazards produced both broadcloth and woolen shawls after 1847. The production of specialized fabrics became a major form of economic diversification in some Rhode Island towns. In Burrilville, South Kingstown and Hopkinton and Westerly the woolen industry was a chief source of economic growth. Until 1840, woolen manufacture centered in Washington county and in the southwest portion of the state. The woolen industry provided outworkers with a productive niche through 1840 because early power looms could not duplicate four harness or multi-shuttle patterns. The outwork weaving workforce shifted from the dying cotton outwork market and turned to weaving woolen textiles. The shrinking market for their skills and the desire to produce income led outworkers to increase their productivity and the quantity of warps taken in.[60]

WOOLEN OUTWORK AND OUTWORK WEAVERS IN RHODE ISLAND 1835–1840

Woolen outwork mirrored cotton outwork in development and change but on a much smaller scale and a decade or so later. Simple two harness single shuttle woolen power looms operated in Rhode Island almost simultaneously with comparable cotton power looms, but the general adoption of woolen power looms was not sealed until a decade later. Power looms capable of shifting from color to color and manipulating four or more harnesses were not generally used in mills until after 1840. Outwork weaving continued to be associated with Rhode Island's 41 woolen mills in 1840.

Only two out of the 41 firms had attained a loom-spindle ratio indicative of dependence upon machine woven fabrics.[61]

Although many firms used outwork weavers to produce woolen fabrics, few records have survived to support this supposition. Rowse Babcock's accounts are examples of shopkeeper involvement in outwork weaving during the 1830s and 1840s. Rowse Babcock, son of Rowse was born in Westerly in 1773 and died in April 1841 when an outwork weaving account of warps issued from his Westerly store to country weavers ends. His accounts are associated with his father's earlier store account of mixed handloom weaving dating from 1790 to 1792 detailing cooperative network weaving associated with a country store prior to cotton textile industrialization. His father died in 1801 when Rowse Jr. took over the responsibilities of the general store. In addition to managing the mercantile business, Rowse Jr. became the president of Phenix bank and a textile manufacturer with his brother in law, Horatio Nelson Campbell. H.N. Campbell was born in 1815 in Voluntown Connecticut close to Rhode Island's western border. Sometime later he married Rowse's sister Harriet. By 1835, he ran his own company selling woolen plaids out of Westerly.[62]

Although the Babcock account books detailing the years 1792 to 1835 are missing, the two volumes contrast weaving performed on an outwork basis. The survival of the 1790–1792 and 1835–1841 records is fortuitous as each span documents different kinds of exchanges, various sorts of fabrics produced and productivity changes. Each book identifies similar and partially matching labor forces. The 19th century records of Rowse Babcock's outwork woolen weaving business acquired warps from the H. N. Campbell Co. of Westerly Rhode Island. The weavers received warps, and returned finished woolen products producing largely woolen plaids during an era when woolen manufacturers attempted to diversify by producing more complex weaves by hand. Artisans wishing to continue practicing the craft had to demonstrate flexibility and shift from one fiber type to another. Between 1790 and 1792, exchanges at the store included flaxseed, tow, flannel and "all cloth." Hand weaver's family names correlate well with the hand weavers participating in outwork forty years later for the same family. While this may suggest a greater level of inheritance of skill or more continuity of family weaving than indicated in the cotton accounts, the sample is fairly small and the area not densely populated. Many of the family names are merely common for this region of Rhode Island and nearby Connecticut.[63]

Between 1835 and 1840, Babcock's commission weaving produced almost 319,300 yards of woolen plaid. With the exception of 1837, production levels increased steadily each year. In 1840 his employees manufactured

26 percent of the total yardage for all the years. Three hundred twenty weavers worked for Rowse Babcock during the six-year period. The workforce numbered 110 members in 1836 and peaked at 220 in 1839. During 1840, when producing the most yardage, Babcock employed 199 weavers indicating that each artisan had to work at a faster pace. Yardages fabricated by each weaver per year ranged between 207.6 and 443.2 yards. Many woolen outworkers wove fabrics at a consistent and highly productive rate suggestive of full time employment at weaving. Although some textile workers wove for Babcock for only one year, most of the employees continued to work for Babcock for several years. This indicates a less transient workforce than other firms. The tendency to remain in Babcock's employment resulted from the decreased demand for handloom artisans.[64]

Babcock's weaving ledger recorded the dates of delivery and return of warps. A sample containing 106 entries spanning every year of operation contributed to the establishment of average durations. Warps remained with weavers between 8 and 12 weeks. The time the yarn spent with the weavers when delivered during a certain month fluctuated peaking in January (12.2 weeks) December (11.2 weeks), November (15.2 weeks) and May (10) During the remaining months the duration ranged between seven and nine weeks. Since yarn remained in the artisan's hand longer during the winter months, harsh weather probably limited the frequency of delivery and pick up. The average size of finished fabric delivered to Babcock was 113.75 yards. Each weaver earned about $3.00 for his or her labor or received payment at the rate of three cents per yard.

Of the 360 employees for Rowse Babcock, over twenty-four had previously worked for cotton manufacturing companies. Since the derivation of that number came from the rosters of only those firms discussed in this paper many more of the weavers probably found employment in other Rhode Island and Connecticut Mills. The twenty-four artisans hired by Babcock represented an older group than the staffs of Blackstone Manufacturing company, A and W. Sprague, Almy and Brown and George Thurston Company. Most weavers' ages fell between 41 and 67. The birth years corresponded to those working for cotton manufacturers earlier in the 19th century that implies a certain continuity of the labor force. Birth years fall between 1770 and 1790 among the 79% for whom birth information was available.

Among the weaving ledgers consulted for southern Rhode Island the same names appear over and over again. Although employment years do not correspond, I suspect, that the families took in warps for more than one company or agent simultaneously. This accounts for some yardages sold and suggests that weaving contributed more substantially to family incomes than indicated by a single business's records. Otherwise one might question the reason for an artisan's continual employment in light of minimal earnings. The Rowse Babcock ledger evidences increased productivity and continuity of labor both as Babcock's employees and company weavers. Out of 360 employees at least 24 or 15 % had worked at other mills. That included the rosters of Almy and Brown, Blackstone Manufacturing Co., A. and W. Sprague, George Thurston and Co. and Russell Wheeler. A larger proportion of weavers wove for cotton and woolen manufacturers not included in the few business records consulted. The compensation for weaving a twill fabric decreased from 12.5 cents paid by Blackstone Manufacturing Co. for bed tick in 1810 to 3 cents per yard for woolen plaid in 1840. To earn even supplementary money weavers increased their productivity, and many sold well over 1,000 yards annually to the store after 1835. The duration of time warps remained in the weaver's hands also declined to less than three months and primarily a little over two months during this period. All these factors suggest that mill handloom weaving altered to become competitive with power loom production. Since the supply of weavers out ran the demand, management required higher quality and quantity of work.

Between 1820 and 1840, handloom weaving changed radically. With the implementation of machinery, that produced massive amounts of simple fabrics, the need to put out yarn diminished. Firms employed middlemen to oversee what little textile manufacture remained outside the factory. Cloth merchants found that they had to accept lower prices per yard to manufacture inexpensive fabrics competitively with machine-made products. Reduced compensation for handloom goods reflected in the weavers' compensation and agents' commission. By 1840, the artisans received less than half of what they had in 1790. Commercial handloom weaving probably continued after 1840 when Babcock's record concludes.

Clearly outwork weaving and spinning continued well after the mechanization of spinning and weaving in the cotton industry. Woolen and flax technology lagged behind cotton mechanization by a decade or more depending upon the process and the fiber. Many cotton outworkers shifted to woolen outwork. The Richmond Manufacturing Company of Richmond, Rhode Island provides us with a transitional account spanning 1820–1829. The workers produced both cotton and woolen materials for the single firm. Many of the workers residing in Richmond had worked previously for the George Thurston Company of Hopkinton, Rhode Island performing outwork cotton weaving.[65] Domestic production of textiles served to link the production of wool and flax in particular to household manufacture and in part inhibited the transition of this type of textile manufacture out of the home. The production of fibers suitable for processing into textiles on subsistence farms enabled hand weavers and spinners to find work serving individuals in the community. Industrial production often supplemented the work of independent domestic weavers.

Like cotton outworkers, woolen outworkers experienced a transformation of the marketplace responding to both technological innovation and regional economic conditions. Woolen manufacturers acknowledged their indebtedness to cotton manufacturers in designing a tighter, more organized system of outwork production. The shrinking outwork market enabled manufacturers to command greater productivity for less return and still attract sufficient workers to fulfill their orders. As outwork diminished some weavers opted to continue producing fabrics linked directly to domestic production of textile fibers. People like the Roses and the Barretts subsisted by producing blankets, coverlets and specialty fabrics well after 1840.

Even as the outwork ledgers turned to power loom production, weavers did not experience hardship from displacement. The outwork network encouraged part-time workers to supplement their earnings with other forms of income producing activities. As outwork weaving diminished, the workers merely turned to other forms of outwork for employment. Sometimes they turned to day labor and sometimes they turned to other kinds of domestic production. Few outworkers turned to factory work for an income source but instead sought work that could be performed in the home. The fluidity of occupational attributions suggests that the kinds of work pursued was not highly skilled and was easily learned. This enabled individuals to shift from one kind of outwork to another without risk, lengthy learning period or bankruptcy.

Chapter Nine

"All ye that have Woolen Weavers for Sale":[1] Putting Handloom Weavers and Machine Production in Place

The years between 1760 and 1840 witnessed the increase and reduction of hand woven and hand spun cotton and woolen production. The era neatly encompasses the spinning and weaving mania surrounding the American Revolution, the birth of the textile industry, and the development of machinery capable of duplicating textile processing and weaving tasks previously performed by hand. This simplistic evaluation of an 80-year period pays little homage to the numerous studies of cotton and woolen industrialization. From as early as 1836, cotton and woolen manufacturers and historians have generated industrial histories, business case studies, reminiscences, accounts of textile technology, and labor narratives. While exploration initially centered on industrial and inventive heroes, later works scrutinized the average worker.[2]

One dominant issue among those who have studied the early years of industrialization focuses on elemental changes in the workplace, time devoted to labor, and behavior required at the mill. Barbara Tucker saw these factors as a source of conflict and struggle, which led either to revolt or the development of discipline. E.P. Thompson examined how the general use of clocks led to changed concepts of time. During the period of industrialization, mill owners expected their operatives to work at a constant pace, arrive and leave the mill on time, and attend their machines each day of the work week. The entrepreneurs often punctuated each segment of the day with a bell. Conversely the traditional or more natural work pattern consisted of alternate periods of intense work and relaxation. Those who had lived under the more traditional schedule railed against the comparatively rigid structure imposed on their days by industrialists. Merritt Roe Smith contrasted the Harper's Ferry Arsenal with the northern federal firearms facilities to demonstrate how gunsmiths at Harper's Ferry resisted change by refusing to alter the pace, conditions and quality of their labor. Herbert Gutman, Anthony F.C. Wallace and many others document the artisan's desire to preserve their traditional method of manufacture. Handloom weavers employed in weaving work sheds and in the putting out system experienced pressure to increase their production levels and to conform to time limitations encouraged by mills. Textile factory owners gradually enforced time and quality standards as the workforce outran available handloom weaving after 1845. Early manufacturers attempted to alter the workplace by establishing shops that facilitated oversight. The failure of these early weaving sheds suggests that artisans resisted the change and owners discovered that skilled craftsmen did not clamor to obtain contracts with firms.[3]

The textile industry has served as a backdrop for a variety of studies focusing on industrialization, and mechanization. In large part, these works examine the plights, strikes and status of mill operatives. Weaving, especially hand weaving, and the textile craftsman has not gone unnoticed. The British handloom artisans have provided great opportunity for study. The strikes and revolts at the mills amplify the weaver's changing economic status. Of American handloom craft studies; Philadelphia provided the site for several works. David Montgomery, Philip Scranton and Cynthia Shelton have all looked to explain why handloom weaving persisted beyond power loom introduction in the Philadelphia region. Authors linked immigrant labor, strong benevolent societies and the maintenance of profit margins as reasons of the continued use of hand weavers. Studies of life in rural and isolated areas of the United States and Canada have produced significant studies of craft persistence through the late 19th century. Hand weaving endured in Rhode Island through the 1840s in woolen manufacture. Two studies of Rhode Island textile industry consider the state's retention of hand weaving in cotton during the 1820s. Though conflicting in conclusion, both works looked to economy, management organization and natural resources for the persistence. In large part other studies of the industry focus on the operative's viewpoint rather than on extra factory labor.[4]

The outwork network and the significance of outworkers to the rise of textile factories and other industries had not received much notice until the 1970s and 1980s. Since then, authors have formulated three viewpoints. Historians studying industrialization have discussed outwork in terms of the role the work played in developing industries. Such studies have limited the discussion of outwork to that of stopgap. Authors perceived the putting out system as an expedient endured while awaiting further technological developments. Scholars, looking to explain the community network system, the rise of market economy and self-sufficiency, have focused on the putting out system as a supplement to subsistence agricultural income and on the development of artisanal skills to diminish the impact of limited land resources. The goal was not to look at outworkers themselves but to dispel the myth of familial self-sufficiency during the colonial era. During the 1980s and 1990s a limited number of historians have studied outwork in terms of supplementary income earned by women. Although outwork weavers comprised a predominantly female population, gender definition of outworkers inhibits interpreting outwork and the family environment as well as acknowledging the importance of male outwork weaving and the greater significance of hand weaving within the community. While this study does not seek to diminish the consequence of women's contributions to familial income, it does look at handloom weaving within the scope of individual and familial earnings. More meaningful than centering on gender or outwork in particular is looking at the various kinds of weaving available to handloom artisans and how these opportunities enabled them to support a family or supplement farming income.[5]

THE WEAVERS

The past several chapters have viewed handloom weaving in various environments. Economic, technological and social conditions drew several related populations of handloom weavers to practice their trade. Domestic textile production for family use, for neighborly exchange, or for commercial purposes predominated from the 17th through late 18th centuries. By the late 18th century another arena for handloom weaving arose connected with jenny workshops and entrepreneur-owned weave sheds. Although mill-owned weave shed environment for cotton and woolen textile manufacture proved to be short term, the use of weave sheds associated with woolen manufacture continued beyond 1800. The employment environment and contractual dictates of hand production for factories removed it from the domestic setting. A somewhat different, yet overlapping, population of weavers produced fabrics for mill owners.

With the rapid rise and ultimate dissolution of cotton handloom outwork between 1810 and 1827, a large population of handloom weavers met the massive industrial demand. The artisans were not the same as those that worked in mill weave sheds. In some instances, they were not the same as the weavers, who worked in independent weave sheds. These weavers mobilized from the community exchange network and within the domestic environment followed outwork tenaciously through its various adaptations.

With the exception of immigrant master and journeyman weavers involved in mill-owned weave sheds, native Rhode Island handloom weavers mobilized for factory outwork and for meeting community or domestic demand. As the backbone of early to mid-19th century textile production, these individuals fit into the context of the family economy; the social conditions and the technology that gave rise to outwork weaving.

The 17th century brought native textile production to colonial Rhode Island as a response to local domestic fabric needs and the growth of fibers as by-products of other agricultural or horticultural activities. By mid-century, cotton made its way from the South Sea Islands to colonial Rhode Island. From several ports there, people incorporated the fibers into domestic production. Towns and cities clamored to attract weaving artisans to their area by offering bounties and establishing fulling mills regionally. By the end of the 17th century Providence alone supported 6 weavers and three fulling mills. These figures indicate that handloom production flourished commercially. Families obviously processed fibers through labor exchange or by performing the tasks themselves. Some individuals may have woven within their own homes, but the full extent of domestic weaving remains unclear.

During the 18th century a general broadening of the weaving population incorporated women into the craft performing textile production within the home as part of the community exchange network. Even before the men left the farms to fight for independence, women had already infiltrated the weaving workforce. By the final decade of the 18th century, they poised equipped to take on the new challenges presented to them in the form of machine-spun warps. Daryl Hafter has viewed women as agents of technological change because of their willingness to take on new roles or previously undefined work. Initially women introduced themselves into textile processes as spinners supplying weavers with raw materials. Working beside weavers, spinners easily developed interest in and curiosity about handloom weaving. Many may have received training from local weavers and set up looms within their homes.[6]

Women soon integrated themselves as weavers in the community exchange network. Women wove for their own families and for those of their neighbors as they had spun, hackled, carded and scutched for them before. Shopkeepers received yardage, handkerchiefs and other textiles from women, which they attributed to husband's or father's accounts further blurring the identification of handloom artisans. Women exchanged fabric for goods at local general stores. Clearly women performed weaving supplied to the local general store because account book marginal notations indicate a wife's or daughter's work. Female weavers participating in the community network greatly expanded the population of handloom weavers. By 1810, the rise of weaving women facilitated the introduction of cotton manufacture as hundreds and thousands of women had prepared to weave simple utilitarian fabrics by the time manufacturers fashioned the warps.[7]

Although women became increasingly involved in weaving after the mid-eighteenth century, male involvement did not necessarily diminish. Weaving apparently attracted two populations to produce textiles for communities prior to industrialization. Clearly the records of Catherine Greene, Thomas B. Hazard, Carder family and Oliver Gardner indicate that men and women worked to fulfill domestic textile manufacture demands prior and after industrialization. The Greene accounts indicate that she hired male and female weavers to turn her spun yarn into fabric and Hazard also hired both men and women. While the Carder family men produced fabric, the women received account book credit for spinning yarns. There appears to be no distinction between the kinds of fabrics woven or craft skill required. Since the guild system had all but disappeared few weavers apprenticed during the latter half of the 18th century and therefore, there is no reason to presume that male weavers received any more or less instruction than the women. By drawing on Hafter's premise, the absence of guild oversight led to a lack of definition or control of the craft. Close familial working environment incorporating women as spinners and fiber processors created an atmosphere conducive to adding women to the weaving workforce. In turn the necessities of life in the New World, led many men to acquire land and devote themselves to farming rather than to a trade and the transmission of skills to children during the 18th century might have created an environment for men to teach their women to weave rather than their sons. This would allow their sons to assist the family head with the numerous horticultural and agricultural tasks.[8]

The introduction of spinning technology in the 1780s created additional opportunities for hand weavers but centered on attracting male immigrants and apprentices to staff mill-owned weaving workshops. Although this created additional employment for hand weavers, positive and negative influences of jenny workshop environments proved slight and were short term. The longer-term impact of this trend was to attract guild trained immigrant weavers to urban weaving sheds associated with jenny workshops. Since the immigrant weavers largely rejected the workshop employment, they soon opened their own independent weave sheds and competed with existing native weavers. The trend did introduce a third component to the handloom weaving population and this component reacted very differently to industrialization than did native born hand weavers involved in both outwork and domestic handwork.

The golden era of weaving associated with cotton spinning mills spanned 1810–1823. Cotton manufacturing mobilized tremendous numbers of hand weavers to produce fabrics for textile mills on a part time intermittent basis. Blackstone Manufacturing Company alone employed 760 weavers between 1811 and 1823. Other firms hired comparable numbers and the demand for weavers grew to such an extent that outwork networks bled over the borders to neighboring states. If only half of Rhode Island's 36 mills in 1810 hired comparable numbers of outworkers then the state's textile industry would have employed 13, 680 people outwork weaving. This figure is somewhat inflated because some outworkers wove for more than one firm and 760 is the number of individuals weaving for Blackstone Manufacturing for the 16 years of outwork.[9]

Clearly women comprised a large part of the workforce but the actual percentage of women in relation to male outworkers remains unclear because firms often attributed a woman's work to her husband or father. Substantial indications of this practice suggest that most workers were women. Without taking the indistinct attribution into account, approximately 25% of the weavers studied were female. Almost all of the women receiving credit under their own names were widows or single, family heads. Since 42% of the males identified in weaving ledgers listed themselves in civil records as something other than weavers, clearly the wives or children of these individuals produced the fabric. If the entire 42% of male names hid female artisans than women would compose 67% of all outworkers.[10]

The female composition of the workforce is strengthened even more by the family composition and time in the cycle of the family life that the name appears in the account books. Male names appear in ledgers at two points in their lives, when they have first married, and then, later when they have large families and might require supplementary income. In each time period, male names probably masked women's earnings. At first, a newly childless wedded woman might appear under her husband's name weaving. When she had young children to care for and could not take in webs the name disappeared from the ledger only to return when the family had grown. Teenage daughters and/or the wife took in webs to support the family.

Although the workforce probably was fluid, and ever changing because of the part-time and intermittent nature of the work, this does not seem to be the case. The bulk of outwork names represents individuals aged between 21 and 40. Though substantial numbers of young adults under 20 and over 40 found work with the firms, the interesting factor concerning age stems from the birth dates not age at employment. Most of the weavers were born between 1770 and 1800. The major group of births occurred during the 1780s and 1790s. Many of the laborers had not been born when Slater successfully mechanized spinning in Pawtucket. These people grew up during the period of increased experimentation in textile machinery. Though too young to work for Almy and Brown, most of the craftsmen initially participated in the trade during their early adulthood. Unfettered by craft considerations, the part-time artisans received limited training. The laborers represent a pragmatic group of individuals seeking ways to increase their economic independence and better family support. So successfully did the outwork system fulfill this need in families that the same families continued to work as textile outworkers, first in cotton, and then, later in wool. The average age of the workforce increased by 1841 and names that appear in southern Rhode Island cotton textile operations emerge anew in complex cotton manufacture and then in woolen weaving.[11]

By the mid 1820s the market for hand woven materials shrank with the introduction of the cotton, and later, the woolen power loom. Handloom outwork associated with factories had concluded by the mid-1840s. This fairly rapid and inexorable march of "progress" and the well-documented plight of British textile workers has given the impression that technology quickly displaced a population of artisans who could not adjust to the changing marketplace nor was flexible in adapting to new markets for their skills. This was not the case among Rhode Island's handloom weavers or spinners. Instead, Rhode Island's outwork labor force remained consistent from 1810 through 1845 barring death, or migration. The constancy of the labor pool in a changing market suggests a great ability to alter the kinds of work performed in order to continue to practice hand weaving. Natural attrition decreased the size of the workforce by 1845 and domestic outworkers dependent upon weaving as a supplement to income could continue hand weaving specialty goods, as did Samantha Barrett and the Rose family until their deaths. In addition outworkers might shift from one kind of outwork to another in order to continue to supply the family with supplementary income.[12]

Where insolvency seemed to point toward displacement other impetus may be ascribed to the fallen economic status. Those weavers that did apply for aid to insolvent debtors were all men. Possibly the state treated bankrupted women differently than men and possibly more displaced female weavers would have supplemented rather than solely supported their family. Insolvent weavers stating reasons for their need reflected the chancy nature of artisanal life than the displacement of the outworker. Pardon Case, for instance, became insolvent when a textile mill reneged on a contract. Others greeted diminished circumstances because of illness. Coleman's study of insolvency indicates that economically stable families became indebted when the major income producer became ill or other similar losses occurred.[13]

Women, working as weavers, tended to bridge both the industrial and domestic spheres with ease. Therefore, they adapted well and easily to changes in the marketplace for their skills. When faced with insolvency after her husband's untimely death, Ruth Mowry did not allow the will's stated course to go unaltered. Mowry petitioned the probate court to assist her in adjusting the will's intent and ensuring her ability to support her family. She sought aid in the form of allocating all weaving equipment to her instead of land. With those tools she continued weaving for Blackstone Manufacturing Company until the firm discontinued their outwork network.[14]

Despite the evidence that some weavers experienced hardship as technological innovations were introduced and the industry expanded, there are several factors, which buffered the negative impact of mechanization on handloom outworkers. Clearly the way that female and male outwork by-profession weavers viewed the craft differed from commercial weavers dependent upon the art for their sole support. Domestic female and male outworkers evidenced a less defined and less rigid link to the craft. They willingly adjusted to changes in the market place. As the demand for cotton outwork diminished, these weavers merely took whatever kinds of outwork were available whether multi-harness, multi-shuttle cotton weaving or plain woolen warps. Immigrant and native male weavers dependent upon weaving as their sole source of income and producing over 1,000 yards of fabric for a single firm annually, suffered from the changing markets. It is this category of weavers that evidenced insolvency and financial instability as technology integrated into the mill environment and usurped the market for hand woven textiles.

Clearly outwork and domestic weavers rejected factory work as did immigrant handloom artisans. Their reasons for doing so differed. Immigrant weavers felt strong links with the craft, craft status, independence and stature of master artisan. The putting out system allowed professional independent craftsmen to take in occasional warps without committing themselves entirely to factory labor. Native born part-time domestic and outwork weavers sought income producing by-professions to supplement income while maintaining their links to the domestic sphere and the family in traditional ways. Their failure to turn to factory work centered on the necessity of moving the workplace from the home. Moreover working full-time in a factory required the abandonment domestic responsibilities and setting. The putting-out system also attracted individuals because of the flexibility allowed the worker and the relative freedom in how to perform the task.

Although weavers found themselves buffeted by changing markets for their skills, the vast majority of outwork and domestic weavers were not displaced. They changed their product lines to fit demand. Certainly the flexibility that afforded handloom outworkers financial success throughout the forty-year period also made other forms of outwork and other means of supporting the family income attractive. Rather than view the technological changes as a threat to the craft, domestic outwork weavers viewed them as opportunities that might be ridden to the crest and then plumbed to the depths. When all handloom outwork concluded, these weavers pursued domestic production for the community in specialty fabrics or moved on to other forms of outwork like palm leaf hat making, or broom making.

THE TECHNOLOGY

Technological innovations provided handloom weavers and spinners with a variety of innovative equipment for their homes. The inventions also altered the market for their skills. In some cases the innovations aided successful competition with mechanized textile production, and in others expanded the market for outwork associated with factories. The fly shuttle, spinning jenny, and Minor's head spindle are all examples of technological innovations that incorporated well and aided the hand processing of textiles and domestic production. Millwrights introduced the technology for woolen carding and fulling to the existing social and cultural landscape without disrupting family and community networks. Single process mills integrated well into established 18th century goods and services exchanges. Rather than foreshadow industrialization, these mechanical devices supported and increased the longevity of existing social and economic structures.

The introduction of spinning jenny workshops into the commercial rather than domestic setting introduced society to what might lie ahead. This developmental process, however, indicated a change in business organization and labor structure rather than guided technological change and the integration of all textile processes into one building or set of buildings. The level of production in the weave and jenny shops was severely limited and the scope of production small. As a result, the impact of the early, mechanized jenny workshops affected few factory workers and hand spinners. Early weaving shops employed only a few weavers and introduced them to a kind of work that did not find general adoption. The associated weaving work affected neither craftsmen nor textile manufacture greatly. The hand cranked carding, roving and spinning equipment added little to the general pool of warps but offered an additional source of yarn and fiber to the market place. Faulty production limited the general employment of the yarns and diminished the impact of early spinning. Nonetheless the introduction of the equipment foreshadowed the arrival of the improved machinery that would flood the market with machine-spun yarns. Workshop operations in Providence attracted traditionally trained immigrant weavers in greater numbers than native born artisans involved in domestic manufacture. The introduction of jenny workshop spinning and associated weave shed influenced an even smaller percentage of the native weaving population.

By 1790, waterpowered spinning created a generous source of yarns for weaving, knitting and ultimately sewing. Almy and Brown sought to sell a greater percentage of their yarns to weavers as yarn. They marketed their supplies to merchants in Philadelphia, cotton sellers in the southern states in exchange for raw fibers and locally. There is some indication that merchants found a great demand for cotton yarns and encouraged the sale. By 1793, when Almy, Brown and Slater discontinued spinning while erecting a new mill building, customers wrote to acquire the yarn that had disappeared from the market almost as rapidly as it had appeared. The impact of waterpowered spinning technology, therefore was not limited to outwork weavers involved in fabricating cloth for mills but also by those who bought already spun yarns for weaving at home elsewhere in the country. Waterpowered spinning throstles extinguished the market for hand spun yarn associated with cotton manufacture but did not eliminate hand spinning altogether. Domestic hand spinning continued throughout the period and woolen spinning associated with industrializing woolen manufacture fostered the continued use of outwork spinning.[15]

As with hand spinning, the introduction of mechanized equipment and the gradual development of textile manufacture initially expanded the market for hand weaving. The rapid production of the spinning throstle gave birth to outwork weaving because not all textile mill owners could sell their entire stock of machine-spun yarn as yarn. Technology further altered he market for handloom weaving by advancing. The development of the power loom in 1814 and impetus behind not adopting it generally in Rhode Island shaped the demand for handloom weaving. Rather than continue weaving simply constructed textiles in competition with firms that had acquired and used power looms, Rhode Island textile manufacturers produced multi-shuttle and multi-harness fabrics. Ultimately the economic environment improved and Rhode Island cotton textile mills adopted power looms. Improvements to the power loom continued to decrease the market for outwork cotton weaving. The decline of cotton outwork weaving coincided with the rise of woolen manufacturing in the state after 1830. Outwork weavers once again found protection in producing fabrics for an industry that had not yet adopted power loom technology. For 10 or more years, outwork weaving persisted in woolen manufacture enabling a smaller population of workers to continue.[16]

By 1830, Rhode Island textile firms consisted of 119 cotton and 22 woolen works. McLane reported prematurely that domestic handloom manufacture had all but disappeared. The Greene Manufacturing Company of Warwick no longer employed contract agents in cloth manufacture but utilized 108 power looms. The Lippitt Manufacturing Company also operated 108 power looms and had reduced their total complement of spinning and weaving labor to 28 men, 54 women and 55 children. The owners of the Arkwright Mill in Coventry reported that their production had increased four times by using 100 power operated looms. Though spinning and cloth manufactories expanded the amount of fabrics produced, they reduced the demand for weavers and other workers by improving machinery throughout time. By 1840 technological developments severely curtailed handloom opportunities to woolen and linen fabrics produced for factories and independently in outlying areas. After 1841, no evidence of company handloom weaving exists in the state. Increased mechanization eliminated handloom cloth manufacture associated with textile firms almost entirely. Weavers desiring to continue producing fabrics on handlooms could by producing specialty fabrics and serving the community network system-using fibers produced as by-products of agriculture and horticulture as before.[17]

PUTTING THE BOOK INTO PLACE

The experience of Rhode Island handloom weavers during the late 18th and 19th centuries is not marked by tragedy, or abrupt displacement. The absence of a guild system and craft stratification enabled the artisans to be more flexible and adaptable to changing markets for goods. Unlike British handloom artisans, Rhode Island weavers had always woven flax, wool and some cotton. They had not developed exclusive specialties, nor were they eliminated from weaving in various fibers because of trade or social restrictions. This absence of craft regulation and limited restrictions from the 17th century onward opened the craft to broad sectors of the population. Flexibility in training and practice allowed for variance in experience and product quality, but it also enabled weavers from three distinct sources to co-exist and in large part thrive by weaving to meet the combined demands of the community, the domestic environment and industry. Despite the gradual loss of outwork and domestic production, this relatively anonymous labor force found continued employment to support themselves until they need not. The population remained anonymous because they did not have to petition for support or vocalize the plight of displacement, as did their British cousins. The flexibility that distinguishes American society from British at the outset also characterized hand weavers and clearly marks other trades as well. Shadrach Steere's account book indicates that a woodworker shifted from fashioning spinning wheels to supporting textile manufacture by producing bobbins for industrial use. Hand spinners also adapted to changing circumstances and adjusted in ways that enabled them to continue producing yarns by hand long after 1790. The ability to adapt to changing technological conditions enabled many tradesmen and craftsmen to ride the crest of industrialization.[18]

Notes

NOTES TO THE INTRODUCTION

1. Jonathon Prude, *The Coming of the Industrial Order: Town and Factory Life in Rural Massachusetts 1810–1860* (New York: Cambridge University Press, 1985); Phillip Scranton, *Proprietary Capitalism: The Textile Manufacture in Philadelphia 1800–1885* (New York: Cambridge University Press, 1983); Cynthia Shelton, *The Mills of Manayunk: Industrialization and Social Conflict in the Philadelphia Region 1781–1837* (Baltimore: Johns Hopkins University Press, 1986); Barbara Tucker, *Samuel Slater and the Origins of the American Textile Industry 1790–1860* (Ithaca: Cornell University Press, 1984); Gary Kulik, "The Beginnings of the Industrial Revolution in America, Pawtucket, Rhode Island 1672–1829," Ph.D. diss., Brown University, 1980; Anthony F.C. Wallace, *Rockdale: The Growth of An American Village in the Early Industrial Revolution* (New York: Alfred A. Knopf, 1978); and Thomas Dublin, *Woman at Work: The Transformation of Work and Community in Lowell, MA 1826–1860*(New York: Columbia University Press, 1979).
2. Duncan Bythell, *The Handloom Weavers: A Study in the English Cotton Industry during the Industrial Revolution* (Cambridge: Cambridge University Press, 1969); Norman Murray, *The Scottish Handloom Weavers 1790–1850: A Social History* (Edinburgh: John Donald Publishers, Ltd., 1978); and Elizabeth Baker, *The Displacement of Men by Machines: Technological Change in Commercial Printing* (New York: Columbia University Press, 1933).
3. The William F. Sullivan Fellowship funded by the Museum of American Textile History in Lowell Massachusetts provided a grant, which enabled me to pursue the research. The Essex Institute Research Fellowship funded research, which has resulted in an article entitled "Unnoticed Craftsmen Noted: Commercial Handloom Weaving prior to Industrialization in Essex County Massachusetts" currently unpublished. The research for this article led me to think about what came before industrialization and chapters 1 and 2 in this volume arose out of the realization of how significant what

came before was to industrialization and outwork weaving. The National Science Foundation Studies in Science Technology and Society Research in History and Philosophy of Science and Technology enabled me to devote myself to writing this book drawing on expanded research from what I did under the Sullivan Fellowship and subsequent maturation of thought. The value of that grant to the writing of this book cannot be measured. The months spent working on the text were some of the most joyful and yet difficult months of my life.

NOTES TO CHAPTER ONE

1. Laurence C. Wroth, *The Voyages of Giovanni da Verrazano* (New Haven: Yale University, 1970), 140.
2. Wroth. *Voyages,* 137–140.
3. Perry Miller, *Roger Williams* (Indianapolis: Bobbs-Merrill, 1953), 64; and William G. McLoughlin *Rhode Island: A Bicentennial History* (New York: W. W. Norton, 1978), 8–10; and Carl Bridenbaugh, *Fat Mutton and Liberty of Conscience Society in Rhode Island, 1636–1690,* (New York: Athenaeum, 1976), 11.
4. Glenn W. LaFantasie, "A Day in the Life of Roger Williams," *Rhode Island History* 46 (1987): 99,101; Bridenbaugh, *Fat Mutton,* 13–15. Bridenbaugh's descriptions come from an extensive study of civil records including tenancy agreements and land evidences supplemented by the words of Massachusetts' colonists.
5. Bridenbaugh, *Fat Mutton,* 14; Lynne Withey, *Urban Growth and Colonial Rhode Island: Newport and Providence in the 18th Century* (Albany: State University of New York, 1986) 1–3; and McLoughlin, *Rhode Island.*
6. Bridenbaugh, *Fat Mutton,* 9–26. Or see original writing in Child to Hartlib in *Colonial Society of Massachusetts, Publication* 38: 51.
7. Bridenbaugh, *Fat Mutton,* 9–26. Or see original writing in Edward Winslow, *Hypocrasie Unmasked* (London; R. Cotes for J. Bellamy, 1646), 79–80.
8. For references to boundary disputes see: McLoughlin, *Rhode Island,* 14,15, and 39–42; Bruce C. Daniels, *Dissent and Conformity on Narragansett Bay: the Colonial Rhode Island Towns* (Middletown, CT: Wesleyan University Press, 1983), 23–47; Lynne Withey, *Urban Growth in Colonial Rhode Island: Newport and Providence in the 18th Century* (Albany: State University of New York, 1984), 26; and Winthrop's *Journal,* II, 81.
9. Federal Writer's Project, *Rhode Island: A Guide to the Smallest State* (Boston: Houghton Mifflin Company, 1937); and Sydney B. James, *Colonial Rhode Island* (New York: Scribner's, 1975), 3–4.
10. Withey, *Urban Growth,* 3; Christian McBurney, "The South Kingstown Planters: Country Gentry in Colonial Rhode Island." *Rhode Island History* 45(1986): 81–82; and William G. McLoughlin, "Synthesizing Rhode Island History: Problems, Approaches, and Opportunities," *Rhode Island History* 42(1983): 106.

11. U.S. Bureau of Census, *Historical Statistics of the United States Colonial Times to 1957* (Washington, D.C: U.S. Department of Commerce, Bureau of Census, 1969), 21; Bridenbaugh, *Fat Mutton*, 10.

12. Bridenbaugh, *Fat Mutton*, 29; McBurney, "South Kingstown Planters,"82; Susan Ouellette. "Divine Providence and Collective Endeavor: Sheep Production in Early Massachusetts." *The New England Quarterly* 69 (1966): 355–380; and William Coddington to John Winthrop, Jr. *Winthrop Papers* vol. 5:150.

13. Thomas Budd, *Good Order Established in Pennsylvania and New Jersey, 1685*(Reprint, Ann Arbor: University Microfilms, 1966) 11; and Bridenbaugh, *Fat Mutton*, 56–57.

14. Bridenbaugh, *Fat Mutton*, 56.

15. Bridenbaugh, *Fat Mutton*, 56 for Adriaen Van Der Donck's words. Thomas Budd, *Good Order Established*, 11.

16. William B. Weeden, *Economic and Social History of New England1620–1785* (New York, 1890; Reprint, New York: Hillary House, 1963), 305 also *Early Rhode Island: A Social History* (New York: Grafton Press, 1910), 115; Howard Chapin, *Documentary History of Rhode Island,* (Providence: Preston and Rounds, 1919); and Krapf, Robert Cooper, "History of the Growth of the Woolen Worsted Industry in R.I." MA thesis 1938 Brown University, 3.

17. Rolla Milton Tryon. *Household Manufactures in the United States Chicago, 1917*(Reprint New York: A. M. Kelley, 1966), 25–26; and Adrienne Hood, *The Weaver's Craft: Cloth, Commerce and Industry in Early Pennsylvania* (Philadelphia: University of Pennsylvania, 2003) 17, 107–10,111, 134–135.

18. Rolla Milton Tryon, *Household*, 210 -211. "An old-fashioned fulling party has been described as follows: When the cloth of the season was woven, the young people were invited to the house, the kitchen floor was cleared for action and in the middle were placed stout splint bottom chairs in a circle connected by a cord to prevent recoil. On these the young men sat with shoes and stockings off and trousers rolled to the knee. In the center were placed the cloths, wetted with warm soap suds, and then the kicking commenced by measured steps, driving the bundles of goods round and round the circle, until they were shrunk to the desired size. Then the girls, bare to the elbows raised and wrung out the flannels and blankets, and hung them on the fence to dry." Krapf, "History of the Growth of the Woolen Worsted Industry in R.I." 2, 83; Florence M. Montgomery, *Textiles in America 1650–1870,* (New York: W.W. Norton, 1983), 177–178; Isabel Wingate, *Fairchild's Dictionary of Textiles* (New York: Fairchild Publishing Co., 1979), 82, 254; Beverly Gordon. *The Final Steps: Traditional Methods and contemporary applications for Finishing cloth by Hand.* (Loveland Colorado: Interweave Press, 1982); M. J. Dickison. "Fulling in the West Riding Woolen Cloth Industry 1689–1770." *Textile History* 10(1979): 127–31; and W. L. Carmichael, George E. Linton, Isaac Price, *Callaway's Textile Dictionary* (Georgia: Callaway Mills, 1947) 51, 157.

19. J. Leander Bishop, *A History of American Manufactures from 1608–1860* (Philadelphia, 1868; Reprint, New York: A. M. Kelley, 1967), 305,310; Thomas Cochran, *Frontiers of Change: Early Industrialism in America* (New York: Oxford University Press, 1981), 56. Statistics for fulling mills achieved by surveying the following sources: Oliver Payson Fuller, *The History of Warwick* (Providence: Angell, Burlingham and Company, 1875), 95; S.S. Griswold, *Historical Sketch of the town of Hopkinton 1757–1876* (Hope Valley: L.W.A. Cole Job Printers, 1877) 25; Clarence Saunders Brigham, *Early Records of the town of Portsmouth* (Providence: R.J. and E.L. Freeman, 1901), 128,217, William R. Bagnall, *The Textile Industries of the United States including sketches and notices of cotton, woolen, silk and linen manufactures in the Colonial Period, vol. I, 1639–1810,* (Boston: W.B. Clark, 1893), 213; Horatio Rogers, George Moulton Carpenter, and Edward Field, eds. *Early Records of the Town of Providence,* (Providence: Snow and Farnum, 1894), v. 4;153–4; Walter Nebiker, *Historic and Architectural Resources of South Kingstown,* (Providence: Rhode Island Historic Preservation Commission, 1984),13,17; and John G. Erdhardt, *A History of Rehoboth, Seekonk, Swansea, Attleboro, East Providence, Barrington and Pawtucket,* (Seekonk: J. G. Erdhardt, 1983) v. 1:43,71.

20. Field, Rogers, Carpenter, eds., *Early Records of Providence,* part 1, vol. 8, 36.

21. John O. Austin, *Genealogical Dictionary of Rhode Island* (Albany: J Munsell's Sons, 1887), 382.

22. Austin, *Genealogical Dictionary,* 383, 385; and Rogers, Carpenter and Field, eds., *Early Records of the Town of Providence,* v. 5: 201, 279; v. 6: 73–74, 90–94; v. 11: 164; v. 21: 398.

23. Austin, *Genealogical Dictionary,* 383–384; and Rogers, Carpenter and Field, eds., Early *Records of the Town of Providence,* v.4: 153–154.

24. Fuller, *The History of Warwick,* 95.

25. Ibid, 95.

26. Cochran, *Frontiers of Change,* 56; Fuller, *The History of Warwick,* 95, 52, 191, 247; Griswold, *Historical Sketch of the town of Hopkinton,* 25,58,64; Brigham, *Early Records of the town of Portsmouth,* 128, 157, 186–7,217; Rogers, Carpenter, and Field, eds., *Early Records of Providence* v. 2:14, 83; v. 4: 153–4; Thomas Steere, *History of the Town of Smithfield* (Providence: E.L. Freeman, 1881), 101,113,114; Massena Goodrich, *Historical Sketch of the Town of Pawtucket,* (Pawtucket: Nickerson, Sibley Company, 1876), 34,61; Franklin Stuart Coyle, "Welcome Arnold(1745–1798) Providence Merchant: The Founding of an Enterprise," Ph.d. diss. Brown University, 1972, 56; Bagnall, *The Textile Industries of the United States,* 280,284, 213; Caroline Hazard, ed., *Thomas Hazard son of Robert called College Tom* (Boston: Houghton Mifflin, 1853), 101; Nebiker, *Historic and Architectural Resources of South Kingstown,*13, 17 Walter Nebiker, *Historic and Architectural Resources of Westerly* (Providence: Rhode Island Historic Preservation Commission, 1978), 13, 3 and Erdhardt, *A History of Rehoboth, Seekonk, Swansea, Attleboro, East Providence, Barrington and Pawtucket,* 43,71.

27. As a sample of the way flax is introduced into historical studies see Bridenbaugh, *Fat Mutton,* 29; Tryon, *Household Manufactures,* 44; Laurel Thatcher Ulrich, *The Age of Homespun: Objects and Stories in the Creation of an American Myth* (New York: Alfred A Knopf: 2001); Adrienne Hood, *The Weavers Craft;* and J. Leander Bishop A *History of American,* 300. Whether the histories were written in the 19th or the 20th century flax culture is linked primarily to textile production rather than to flaxseed or oil trades.

28. Report of the Board of Trade to the British House of Commons as quoted in Rolla Milton Tryon, *Household,* 80.

29. Timothy Pitkin, *A Statistical View of the Commerce of the United States,* (New Haven, 1838: Reprint, New York: A. M. Kelley, 1967), 115.

30. George J. Lough, Jr., "The Champlins of Newport: A Commercial History," Ph.d. University of Connecticut, Storrs, 1977, 117,172–181; Thomas M. Truzes, "Connecticut in the Irish-American Flaxseed Trade 1750–1775," *Eire Ireland* 12(1977): 34–63; Hood, *The Weaver's Craft,* 40–46; J. Leander Bishop, *A History of American,* 335–337,34,378; Thomas Doerflinger. *A Vigorous Spirit of Enterprise: Merchants and Economic Development In Revolutionary Philadelphia.* (Chapel Hill: University of N. Carolina, 1986); Denis O'Hearn. *The Atlantic Economy: Britain, the United States and Ireland.* (New York: Manchester University Press, 2001); and James Henretta, "The War for Independence and American Economic Development" in *The Economy of Early America: The Revolutionary Period 1763–1790,* ed. by Ronald Hoffman et al. (Charlottesville: University Press of Virginia, 1988), 65.

31. Withey, *Urban Growth,* 122.

32. George J. Lough, Jr., "The Champlins of Newport: A Commercial History," 117,172–181; and Russ Thompson and Sons to Christopher Champlin, 26 May 1792; 14 April, 1792; Richard Mathewson to Christopher Champlin, 12 Sept., 1774, Christopher Champlin to James Wallace, 26 Aug., 1775; and Cowell and Man to Christopher Champlin 9 Nov. 1774, Christopher Champlin papers, Rhode Island Historical Society, Providence, Rhode Island.

33. Pitkin, *A Statistical View,* 115; U.S. Bureau of Census, *Historical Statistics of the United States Colonial Times to 1957,* 294; Christopher Champlin papers, Rhode Island Historical Society, Providence, Rhode Island; and Withey, *Urban Growth,* 95

34. Pitkin, *A Statistical View,* 138.

35. Bagnall, *The Textile Industries of the United States,* 284; Nebiker, *Historic and Architectural Resources of South Kingstown,* 13, 17; Kenneth L. Sokoloff and Dollar. "Agricultural Seasonality and the Organization of Manufacturing in Early Industrial Economies: The contrast between England and the U.S." *Journal of Economic History* 57 (1997): 288–321; S. D. Smith. "The Market for Manufactures in the Thirteen Continental Colonies 1698–1776." *Economic History Review* n.s. 51(1998): 676–708; and Griswold, *Historical Sketch of Hopkinton,* 25, 58, 64.

36. Griswold, *Historical Sketch of Hopkinton,* 25,58, 64; Elizabeth Johnson, and James L. Wheaton, IV, comps., *History of Pawtucket Rhode Island, Reverend David Benedict's Reminiscences and New Series,* (Pawtucket:

Spaulding House Publications, 1986), 7,11,12, 70; Erdhardt, *A History of Rehoboth, Seekonk, Swansea, Attleboro, East Providence, Barrington and Pawtucket*, v. 1:43,71; Massena Goodrich, *Historical Sketch of the Town of Pawtucket*, 34,56 and 61; and McBurney, "The South Kingstown Planters," 81–94.

37. Caroline Hazard, ed., *Nailer Tom's Diary Otherwise the Journal of Thomas B. Hazard of Kingstown Rhode Island 1778 to 1840* (Boston: Merrymount, 1930), 47–54; and Gail Putnam, "The Textile Legacy of a Narragansett Planter," in *Textiles in Early America: Design, Production and Consumption, The Dublin Seminar for New England Folklife*, Peter Benes, ed., 1997: 152–167.

38. Withey, *Urban Growth*, 38–43.

39. Withey, *Urban Growth*, 91–107; and Nancy Chudacoff, "Revolution and the Town: Providence 1775–1783" *Rhode Island History* 35(3) 1976:71–90.

40. Withey, *Urban Growth*, 125–127.

41. Bridenbaugh, *Fat Mutton*, Appendix IV, 140–143; Austin, *Genealogical Dictionary*, 385; and Rogers, Carpenter, and Field, eds., *Early Records of the Town of Providence*, v. 5:121,239; v. 13:164, 177.

42. Austin, *Genealogical Dictionary* various pages; and Rogers, Carpenter, and Field, eds., *Early Records of Providence*, v. 6: 7.

43. Bridenbaugh, *Fat Mutton*, Appendix of Weavers: Providence and Newport records Thomas Applegate, Newport weaver (1641), Robert Bennett, Newport, tailor (1646), John Swallow, Newport, cloth worker (1649), Mathew West, Newport, tailor (1666), Thomas Waterman, Aquidnessett, weaver (1673), John Wood, Portsmouth, weaver (1674), William Clarke, Newport, weaver (1674) Richard Knight, Portsmouth, weaver (1680), John Carder, Warwick, Weaver (1689), Joseph Barker, Newport, tailor (1688) Richard Cadman, Portsmouth, weaver(1688), Henry Hall, Westerly, weaver 1693 William Smith, Providence, weaver(1702), Jonathan Rue, Providence(1680) William Austin, Providence, weaver(1674), Moses Lippitt, Providence, weaver's apprentice(1674–1689) and two artisans in Providence unnamed a weaver in 1674 and a dyer.

44. Bridenbaugh, *Fat Mutton*, Appendix IV, 140–143, Record Commissioners of the City of Boston, *A Report of the Record Commission of the City of Boston containing Miscellaneous Papers*, vol. 10, Document 150, 56; Francis Little, *Early American Textiles*, (New York: Century Company, 1931), 43–55; and Carder, Account Book, 1689–1759, Rhode Island Historical Society, Providence, Rhode Island.

45. Oliver Gardner, Account Cipher book, North Kingstown, 1772–1781, Rhode Island Historical Society, Providence, Rhode Island.

46. Catherine Greene, Account book c. 1776, Rhode Island Historical Society, Providence, Rhode Island.

47. Caroline Hazard, ed., *Nailer Tom's Diary*, 106,107, 108.

48. Hazard, ed., *Nailer Tom's Diary*.

49. Caroline Hazard, ed., *Thomas Hazard son of Robert*, 101–102.

50. Daniel Mowry, Account book, 1794–1796; and Rowse Babcock, Account Book, 1790–92, Rhode Island Historical Society, Providence, Rhode Island.

51. Daniel Mowry, Account book, 1794–1796. Rowse Babcock, Account Book, 1790–92, Rhode Island Historical Society, Providence, Rhode Island.
52. Tryon, *Household Manufactures*, 55.
53. Weeden, *Economic and Social History of New England 1620–1785*, 732; and Hazard, ed., *Nailer Tom's Diary*, 5–227.
54. *Providence Gazette*, 30 Jan. 1768. vol. 4.
55. *Providence Gazette*, 26 Dec. 1767, vol. 4; and *United States Chronicle* 31 May 1787, vol. 4.
56. John R. Bartlett, ed., *Records of the Colony of Rhode Island and Providence Plantation in New England*, (Providence: Knowles Anthony Company, 1861), v. 7: 218.
57. Bartlett, ed., *Records of the Colony of Rhode Island*, v. 8: 28,60
58. Bartlett, ed., *Records of the Colony of Rhode Island*, v. 8:314,332
59. Bartlett, ed., *Records of the Colony of Rhode Island*, v. 8: 451
60. Bartlett, ed., *Records of the Colony of Rhode Island*, v. 8: 87,197 and 253.
61. Greene Papers, Rhode Island Historical Society; and Hazard, ed., *Nailer Tom's Diary.*
62. Bernard Bailyn, *New England Merchants in the Seventeenth Century* (Cambridge: Harvard University Press, 1955), 74 as quoted in Lisa R. Baumgarten, "The Textile Trade in Boston, 1650–1700" *Arts in the Anglo American Community in the 17th Century 20th Annual Winterthur Conference*, Ian M.G. Quimby, ed., Charlottesville: University of Virginia Press, 1975, 220.
63. Hazard, ed., *Nailer Tom's Diary*: James Mc Williams. "Work, Family and Economic Improvement in late 17th Century Massachusetts Bay: The Case of Joshua Buffum." *New England Quarterly* 74 (2001); 355–384; and Mohanty, "Unnoticed Craftsmen Noted."
64. Mohanty, "Unnoticed Craftsmen Noted"; Greene Papers, and Mowry Papers, Rhode Island Historical Society.
65. Baumgarten, "The Textile Trade in Boston, 1650–1700," 222.
66. Baumgarten, "The Textile Trade in Boston, 1650–1700," 222.
67. Baumgarten, "The Textile Trade in Boston, 1650–1700," 223.
68. Baumgarten, "The Textile Trade in Boston, 1650–1700," 225.
69. Baumgarten, "The Textile Trade in Boston, 1650–1700," 228.
70. Baumgarten, "The Textile Trade in Boston, 1650–1700," 228.
71. Hazard, ed., *Nailer Tom's Diary;* Greene Papers, Daniel Mowry, Account Book and Rowse Babcock, Account Book, 1790–1792, Rhode Island Historical Society; Baumgarten, "The Textile Trade in Boston, 1650–1700;" and Florence M. Montgomery, "Fortunes to be Acquired: Textiles in 18th Century Rhode Island," *Rhode Island History* v. 31(1972): 53–63.

NOTES TO CHAPTER TWO

1. Laurence F. Gross, "Wool Carding: A Study of Skills and Technology," *Technology and Culture* 28 (1987): 804–827; and Charles More, *Skill and the English Working Class, 1870–1914* (New York: St. Martin's Press, 1980). For information on the cooperative exchange network see: Christopher Clark, "Household Economy, Market Exchange and the Rise of

Capitalism in Connecticut Valley, 1800–1860," *Journal of Social History* 12(1979–1980) 169–189; "Social Structure and Manufacturing before the Factory: Rural New England 1750–1830," in *The Workplace before the Factory Artisans and Proletarians 1500–1800,* ed. Thomas Max Safley and Leonard N. Rosenband, (Ithaca, New York: Cornell University Press, 1993),11–36; Winifred Rosenberg, "The Market and Massachusetts Farmers, 1750–1855," *Journal of Economic History* 41(l981): 283–314; Carole Shammas, "How Self-Sufficient was Early America?" *Journal of Interdisciplinary History* 12(1982): 247–272; Laurel Thatcher Ulrich, *Goodwives: Image and Reality in the Lives of Women in Northern New England 1650–1750* (New York: Alfred A. Knopf, 1982); "Housewife and Gadder: Themes of Self-Sufficiency and Community in Eighteenth-Century New England." *To Toil the Livelong Day: America's Women at Work, 1780–1980,* ed. Carol Goroneman and Mary Beth Norton, (Ithaca, New York: Cornell University Press, 1987) 21–34; James Henretta, "Families and Farms, *Mentalité* in Pre-Industrial America," *William and Mary Quarterly* 35(1978) 12–14; Michael Merrill, "Cash is Good to Eat" Self Sufficiency and Exchange in Rural Economies in the United States," *Radical History Review* 4(1977)52–57; Vivienne Pollock. "The Household Economy in Early America and Ulster: The Question of Self Sufficiency," in *Transatlantic Perspective on the Scotch Irish,* Tyler Blethem and Curtis Wood, eds., Tuskaloosa Alabama: University of Alabama Press, 1997. and Alan Kulikoff, "The Transition to Capitalism in Rural America," *William and Mary Quarterly* 2nd Ser. 46(1989): 120–144.

2. *Early Records of Providence, Rhode Island,* vol. 6, 7. See chart in Appendix.

3. *The Early Records of Providence Rhode Island,* vol. 4, p. 69.

4. Caroline Hazard, ed., *Nailer Tom's Diary otherwise the Journal of Thomas B. Hazard of Kingstown, Rhode Island 1778–1840,* (Boston: Merrymount Press, 1930) 50, 56.

5. Adrienne Dora Hood, "Organization and Extent of Textile Manufacture of 18th Century rural Pennsylvania: A Case Study of Chester County," 1988, Ph.D., diss. UCSD, 60–81; Hood, "The Material World of Cloth: Production and Use in 18th Century Rural Pennsylvania," *William and Mary Quarterly,* 3rd series, Vol. 53 (1996): 43–66; Hood, "The Gender Division of Labor in the Production of Textiles in 18th Century Rural Pennsylvania (Rethinking the New England Model)" *Journal of Interdisciplinary History* 27 (1994):537–561; Laurel Thatcher Ulrich, "Wheels, Looms and the Gender Division of Labor in 18th Century New England," *William and Mary Quarterly* 3rd. ser. 55(1)(1998): 3–38; Ulrich, "In the Garrets and Rat holes of Old Houses" in *Textiles in New England: Four Centuries of Material Life, Dublin Seminar for New England Folklife,* Peter Benes, ed., 1999: 6–12; Martha Coons and Katharine Koop, *All Sorts of Good Sufficient Cloth; Linen Making in New England 1640–1860* (N. Andover: Merrimack Valley Textile Museum, 1980); and John Wiley, *A Treatise on the Propagation of Sheep, Manufacture of Wool and the Cultivation and Manufacture of Flax* (Williamsburg, R. Royale, 1765).

6. David Tilton Account Book 1718–1801, Ipswich, MA; and John Gould Account Book, Topsfield, MA 1697–1723, Essex Institute, Salem, MA.

7. David Mowry, Store Acct, 1794–1808, Rhode Island Historical Society, Providence, Rhode Island.

8. Hood, "Organization and Extent," 60–81; Coons and Koop, *All Sorts of Good Sufficient Cloth* and Wiley, *A Treatise on the Propagation of Sheep.*

9. Benjamin Wait Probate, Providence, 1734 in John O. Austin *Genealogical Dictionary of Rhode Island comprising Three generations of settlers who came before 1690 with many families carried to the fourth Generation. (Albany: J. Munsell's Sons, 1887)* 405; David Mowry Store Account, 1794–1808;

10. Catharine Greene, Papers, 1768–1780, Rhode Island Historical Society, Providence, Rhode Island and Hazard, *Nailer Tom's Diary,* p.55, 386,385;

11. Hazard, *Nailer Tom's Diary,* 55, 386,385.

12. Hazard, *Nailer Tom's Diary,* 55, 386,385.

13. Hood, "Organization and Extent of Textile Manufacture," 81–96; Wiley, *A Treatise on the Propagation of Sheep;* and Museum of American Textile History, *Homespun to Factory Made: Woolen Textiles in America 1776–1876,* (N. Andover: Museum of American Textile History, 1977) 8.

14. Rolla Milton Tryon, *Household Manufactures in the United States, 1640–1860* (Chicago, 1917; Reprint New York: A. M. Kelley, 1966) 77,218; J. Leander Bishop, *A History of American Manufactures from 1608 to 1860,* (Philadelphia: E Young Company,1868; Reprint, New York: A.M. Kelley, 1967), 389; William B. Weeden, *Economic and Social History of New England 1620–1789* (1890; Reprint, New York, 1963) 791; Hood, "Organization and Extent," 88; Hazard, ed., *Nailer Tom,* 55, 304; Alice Morse Earle, *Homelife in Colonial Days* (New York: Macmillan Co., 1964, 224; and *Providence Gazette,* 13 June, 1789, vol. 26.

15. William R. Bagnall, *Textile Industries of the United States including sketches and notices of Cotton, Woolen, Silk and Linen Manufactures in the Colonial Period* (Cambridge: Riverside Press, 1893, Reprint, New York: August M. Kelley, 1971) 154–156; and Tryon, *Household Manufactures,* 218

16. *Providence Gazette,* June 13, 1789.

17. For example, Hazard, ed., *Nailer Tom's Diary,* "Made a linen Wheel Cruk for Hennery Hupper," 8th Month 1786, 100; "Fixed Mary Wormley's linen Wheel . . . " 10th Month 1786, 102; "Joseph Knowles carried Robert Browning the Hatchel. I made him—and brought me two bushels of corn for the same." 34d month 1790, 107 and "Newport pair of combs for Judith Hazard and she began to coom wool for me." 7th month 1790, 111.

18. Horatio Rogers, George Moulton Carpenter, and Edward Field, eds., *Early Records of the Town of Providence,* (Providence: Record Commissioners, 1894), vol. 6: 221–226.

19. For example, Hazard, ed., *Nailer Tom's Diary,* "Brought some flax to Daniel Stidmans," 107; "Went to Daniel Stidman's and got some linen yearn." 3rd month 1790, 108; 109 "Went to robe congdon's to geet some toe yearn but she had not done it."4th month 1790, 109; "Mary Enees coum to live with me to spin." 7th mo 1790, 111; and "Sarah Carter brought home some linen yearn and I paid her for the spinning of same." 7th month 1790, 111.

20. Hood, "Organization and Extent of Textile Manufacture;" Mohanty, "Unnoticed Craftsmen Noted: Commercial Handloom Weavers and Weaving in Essex County Massachusetts 1690–1790" unpublished.

21. Henry Wansey, *The Journal of an Excursion to the United States of North America in the summer of 1794*, (Salisbury, England, 1796; Reprint, New York: Johnson Reprint Company, 1969) 47.

22. For discussion and characteristics of weaver's skills see Norman Murray, *The Scottish Handloom Weavers 1790–1850: A Social History* (Edinburgh: John Donald Publishers, Ltd., 1978) 26,29,31; Duncan Bythell, *The Handloom Weavers: A Study in the English Cotton Industry during the Industrial Revolution*, (Cambridge: Cambridge University Press, 1969) 42: Paul Gilje, "Introduction," in *American Artisans: Crafting Social Identity 1750–1850*, Howard Rock, Paul A. Gilje and Robert Asher, eds., (Baltimore: Johns Hopkins University Press), 1995, xi–xiv.

23. For some examples of notational styles see: John Hargrove, *The Weaver's Draft Book and Clothier's Assistant*, (1792 Reprint; Worcester: American Antiquarian Society, 1979); Philo Blakeman, *The Weaver's Assistant explaining in a familiar manner the first principles of the Art of Weaving* (Bridgeport, N.L. Skinner, 1818); and Joseph France, *The Weaver's Complete Guide or the Web Analyzed*, (Providence: The Author, 1814).

24. Mary E. Black, *The Key to Weaving: A Textbook of Hand Weaving for the Beginning Weaver* (New York: Macmillan Company, 1980).

25. Black, *The Key to Weaving*, 535–39.

26. Hazard, ed., *Nailer Tom*, 302, 306.

27. Mohanty, "Unnoticed Craftsmen Noted."

28. William B. Weeden, *Economic and Social History of New England 1620–1785* (New York, 1890 Reprint, New York: Hilary House, 1963) 305 also *Early Rhode Island: A Social History* (New York: Grafton Press, 1910) 115; Howard Chapin, *Documentary History of Rhode Island* (Providence: H Gregory Publishers, 1919); Robert Cooper Krapf, "History of the Growth of the Woolen Worsted Industry in R.I." MA thesis 1938, Brown University, 3.

29. Gail Fowler Mohanty, "From Craft to Industry: Textile production in the United States," *Material History Bulletin* Spring 1990: 25–26.

30. Mohanty, "Unnoticed Craftsmen Noted," David Mowry, Store Account, Smithfield, Rhode Island, Rhode Island Historical Society, Providence, Rhode Island; Rowse Babcock, Accounts, Westerly Rhode Island, Rhode Island Historical Society, Providence, Rhode Island.

31. Sharon V. Salinger, "Artisans, Journeymen and the Transformation of Labor in Late Eighteenth Century Philadelphia," *William and Mary Quarterly*, 3d ser., 40(1983): 62–84; and Cynthia Shelton, "The Role of Labor in Early Industrialization: Philadelphia 1787–1837," *Journal of the Early Republic* 4(Winter 1984): 365–94.

32. John Rule, *The Experience of Labour in Eighteenth Century English Industry* (New York: St. Martins, 1981) p. 108.

33. A survey of British apprenticeships, in Winifred M. Rising and Percy Millean comps. *An Index of Indentures of Norwich Apprentices Enrolled with the Norwich Assembly Henry VII to George II* (Norfolk: Norfolk Record

Society, 1959) and Christabel Dale, ed., *Wiltshire Apprentices and their Masters 1710–1760* (Devizes: Wiltshire Archeological and Natural History Society, Records Office, 1961) xiii—xiv, indicates that weaving apprentices normally contracted for seven years. For changes in the apprenticeship system, see Rule, *Experience of Labour,* 95–98.

34. Paul H. Douglas, *American Apprenticeship and Industrial Education,* vol. 95, no. 216, of Columbia University Studies in History of Economy and Public Law (New York: Columbia University Press, 1968), 15. Also see Gail B. Fowler, "Rhode Island Handloom Weavers and the Effects of Technological Change 1780–1840," Ph.D., diss., University of Pennsylvania 1984, 25–26 for a study of Rhode Island apprenticeship.

35. Rule, *Experience of Labour,* 95–119.

36. Rising and Milliean, *Norwich Indentures,* xii; Alfred Plummer, *The London Weavers' Company 1600–1970* (New York: Routledge and K. Paul, 1972), 17 and Rule, *Experience of Labour,* 22, 100–101, 200–202.

37. Isaac Peckham to Moses Brown, September 15, 1789, Moses Brown Papers. Rhode Island Historical Society, Providence, Rhode Island.

38. *Providence Gazette,* October 17, 1789.

39. Daniel Mowry, Store Acct.; Rowse Babcock, Store Acct, Rhode Island Historical Society, Providence, R.I. Other store accounts buttress the idea of domestic production for commercial exchange for more evidence see: Anthony Holden, Warwick, Rhode Island, Ledger 1771–1773; and Richard Greene, Warwick, Account Book, 1713–1720; Rhode Island Historical Society, Providence, Rhode Island.

40. *Early Records of Providence,* vol. 7 48–53; Austin, *Genealogical Dictionary,* 114,223.

41. Ella Shannon Bowles, *Homespun Handicrafts* (New York: Benjamin Blom, Inc., 1972), 76; Marion L. Channing, *Textile Tools of Colonial Homes* (Marion Massachusetts: Channing, 1971), 45.

42. Rufus Smith, Jr. vs Sally Smith, Records of the Supreme Court of Rhode Island, March 1816, vol. 8: 63.

43. Jonathon Knowles Estate, Probate Records vol. 2: 313, Cranston Rhode Island.

44. Hazard, ed., *Nailer Tom's Diary.*

45. Ella Shannon Bowles, *Homespun Handicrafts,* 72.

46. Susan Gunn, "Tramp as Writ or Weaving in Deerfield prior to 1800" Historic Deerfield Summer Fellowship Program, 11 August, 1974, Typescript; 2. Gunn refers to Samuel Clark from Leicester an itinerant weaver and some weavers from Colrain. There is no description of how the itinerant plied his trade whether by bringing the loom with him or using looms in situ. See also Mohanty, "Unnoted Craftsmen Noted" for mention of John Hovey Accounts in Essex County Massachusetts. Hovey practiced weaving as an itinerant and also made slays or harnesses for individuals but there is no mention that he brought his loom with him to new locations.

47. Robert Grieve and John P. Ferald, *The Cotton Centennial 1790–1890* (Providence: J.A. and F.A. Reid Publishers and Printers, 1891) 10–11; William Bagnall, *Samuel Slater and the Early Development of Cotton*

Manufacturing, (Middletown, CT: J.S. Stewart, 1890) 12–25; and Paul E. Rivard, *The Home Manufacture of Cloth 1790–1840* (Pawtucket, 1974), n.p.; George S. White, *Memoirs of Samuel Slater,* (Philadelphia: Printed at #46 Carpenter Street, 1836) 63.

48. Darius Buffum to Elisha Dyer, 6/9/1861, *Rhode Island Society for the Encouragement of Domestic Industry Transactions for 1862,* 97; and David Buffum to Elisha Dyer, 1/1/1862, ibid., 93, 94.

49. Darius Buffum to Elisha Dyer, 6/9/1861, *Rhode Island Society for the Encouragement of Domestic Industry Transactions for 1862,* 97; and David Buffum to Elisha Dyer, 1/1/1862, ibid., 93, 94.

50. *Repertory of Arts, Manufactures and Agriculture,* 2nd series, vol.7: 455–458; David J. Jeremy, *Transatlantic Industrial Revolution: The Diffusion of Textile Technology Between Britain and America, 1790–1830s* (Cambridge, MIT Press, 1981), 47,48,49,70, 246, 264–267.

51. Hazard, ed., *Nailer Tom's Diary;* Marjorie J. Vogel, *Brief History of the Peace Dale Mill and Hazard Family Legacy* (Narragansett, Rhode Island: Narragansett Historical Society, 1988).

52. Oliver Gardner, Weaving Acct. North Kingstown, Rhode Island, Rhode Island Historical Society, Providence, Rhode Island.

53. Carder Family, Accounts, Warwick, Rhode Island, Rhode Island Historical Society, Providence, Rhode Island; and *Early Records of Providence Rhode Island,* vol. 6: 107–108.

54. Gross, "Wool Carding," 805–806; 826–827; Tryon, *Household Manufacture,* 251; Hood, "Organization and Extent" 88–90; and Bishop, *History of American Manufactures,* 160. In Rhode Island there were 23 carding machine mills in 1810. *American State Papers,* "Finance," vol. II: 693.

55. Zeloda Barrett, Diary 1804–1831, New Hartford, CT, Connecticut Historical Society, Hartford, CT.

56. Gross, "Wool Carding," 805–806; 826–827; Tryon, *Household Manufacture,* 251; Bishop, *History of American Manufactures,* 160; and Hood, "Organization and Extent" 88–90.

57. Laurel Thatcher Ulrich, *A Midwife's Tale The Life of Martha Ballard, Based on Her Diary, 1785–1812* (New York: Alfred A. Knopf, 1990) 77, 79, 382; Hood, "Organization and Extent," 136–139; Christopher Clark, *The Roots of Rural Capitalism Western Massachusetts, 1780–1860* (Ithaca, New York: 1990), 72–73; 96–98, 132–133; and Jeanne Boydston, *Home and Work, Household Wages and the Ideology of Labor in the Early Republic* (New York: 1990) 12 -29.

NOTES TO CHAPTER THREE

1. Isaac Peckham to Moses Brown, September 15, 1789, Moses Brown Papers, Rhode Island Historical Society, Providence, Rhode Island. This chapter is adapted and expanded from a previous publication: "Experimentation in Textile Technology: Rhode Island Handloom Weavers and Technological Change," *Technology and Culture* 29 (1989): 1–30.

2. For a more detailed description of the economic changes that occurred during this period in Rhode Island, see Peter J. Coleman, *The Transformation of Rhode Island 1790–1860* (Providence: Brown University, 1963), 71–74; Adrienne Hood, "Industrial Opportunism: From Factory Hand weaving to Mill Production 1700–1830," in *Textiles in Early America: Design, Production and Consumption The Dublin Seminar for New England Folklife,* Peter Benes, ed., 1997: 135–151; Daniel P. Jones, *The Economic and Social Transformation of Rural Rhode Island, 1780–1850* (Boston, Northeastern University Press, 1992); Bruce C. Daniels, *Dissent and Conformity on Narragansett Bay: The Colonial Rhode Island Town* (Middletown, CT: Wesleyan University Press, 1983); James Hedges, *The Browns of Providence Plantations* (Providence: Brown University Press, 1968); and Mack Thompson, *Moses Brown, Reluctant Reformer* (Chapel Hill, N.C.: University of North Carolina Press, 1962, 220–232.

3. Only two advertisements placed by weavers appeared in the *Providence Gazette* prior to the 1780s, one for Thomas Hill in vol. 11, No. 565, November 4, 1774, and one for William and James Wheaton in vol. 16, no. 803, May 15, 1779; and Barbara Tucker, *Samuel Slater and the Origins of the American Textile Industry 1790–1860* (Ithaca, NY: Cornell University Press, 1984) 48. Advertisements may not be a good indicator of the prevalence of commercial handloom weaving. Weaver's names appear in civil records and also family papers not yet collected by manuscript repositories. Both the Carder accounts and the Gardner accounts cited previously only recently came to the Rhode Island Historical Society. Other collections remain in the hands of private families and are not available to researchers.

4. The precise number of handloom artisans supported by the inhabitants of Providence is unavailable because city directories were not published until 1824, and other enumerations of residents did not indicate occupation until much later. In the course of this study, I discovered information on fifteen weavers, and four merchant-owned shops, these constituting all known weaving artisans who worked in Providence during the period. Eight handloom weavers operated independent shops and contracted to produce fabrics for spinning mills. These eight weavers never worked in company-owned sheds. Four weavers wove in factory-owned workshops. After varied amounts of time, each of these four artisans discontinued factory employment to begin independent enterprises. Three artisans worked for Almy and Brown and subsequently left the state; for these, we have no records of later employment.

5. Account Book, Worcester Cotton and Woolen Manufacturing Company, Baker Library, Harvard University, Cambridge, Mass. (Hereinafter Worcester Cotton and Woolen Manufacturing Co.); Robert W. Lovett, "The Beverly Cotton Manufacturing Company, or Some New Light on an Early Mill," *Bulletin of the Business Historical Society* 26(1962): 218–242; William R. Bagnall, *Textile Industries of the United States* (Boston: W.B. Clarke and Company, 1893), vol. 1:84–86, 122–131; David R. Meyer. *The*

Roots of American Industrialization. (Baltimore: Johns Hopkins, 2003); Arthur H. Cole, ed., *Industrial and Commercial Correspondence of Alexander Hamilton Anticipating his Report on Manufactures* (Chicago: A.W. Shaw, 1928; Reprint New York: Augustus Kelley, 1968), 7–11, 16, 61–65; Doron Ben-Ater. "Alexander Hamilton's Alternative: Technological Piracy and the Report on Manufactures." *William and Mary Quarterly* ser. 3, 52 (1995): 389–414; Doron Ben-Ater. *Trade Secrets: Intellectual piracy and the Origins of American Industrial Power.* (New Haven: Yale University Press, 2004); James L. Conrad, Jr., "Entrepreneurial Objectives, Organizational Design, Technology, and Cotton Manufacturing of Almy and Brown 1789–1797," *Business and Economic History,* 2d ser., 13 (1984): 7–19; Robert S. Rantoul, "The First Cotton Mill in America," *Historical Collections of the Essex Institute* 33 (1897): 1–28; Minutes of the Manufacturing Committee, Pennsylvania Society for the Encouragement of Manufactures and the Useful Arts, Historical Society of Pennsylvania, Philadelphia; Shelton, "Textile Production and the Urban Laborer: The Proto-Industrial Experience of Philadelphia 1787–1820," *Working Papers from the Regional Economic History Research Center* 5 (1982): 46–80; John Smail, "Manufacturer or Artisan? The Relationship between Economics and Cultural Change in the Early stages of 18th Century Industrialization," *Journal of Social History* 25 (1992): 791–815; Jan de Vries, "The Industrial Revolution and the Industrious Revolution," *Journal of Economic History* 54 (1994): 249–276; and David Jeremy, "British Textile Technology Transmission to the United States: The Philadelphia Region Experience," *Business History Review* 47 (1973): 24–52.

6. For more information about jenny workshops in other parts of the country see Bagnall, *Textile Industries,* 89–165; William B. Weeden, *Economic and Social History of New England 1620–1789* (New York: Hillary House, 1963), 848–856; Cole, *Industrial and Commercial Correspondence of Alexander Hamilton,* 76–11,15–17, 54–65, 71–88, 109–128; J. Leander Bishop, *A History of American Manufactures from 1608–1860* (Philadelphia: E. Young Company, 1868), 418–423; Robert Rantoul, "The First Cotton Mill in America," *Historical Collections of the Essex Institute,* 33 (1897): 1–28; Robert Lovett, "The Beverly Cotton Manufacturing Company or some new Light on an early Cotton Mill," *Business History Society Bulletin* 26 (1952): 218–243; Cynthia Shelton, "Textile Production and the Urban Laborer," 46–89; and Caroline Ware, *The Early New England Cotton Manufacture: A study of Industrial Beginnings* (Boston: 1931; Reprint New York: Russell and Russell, 1966), 1–121.

7. Cole, *Industrial and Commercial Correspondence of Alexander Hamilton,* 7–10, 39, 62–63; Bagnall, *Textile Industries,* 89–111.

8. Hugh Orr, a Scottish gunsmith who emigrated to America in 1740, brought Robert and Alexander Barr from Scotland to Bridgewater, Mass. In 1786, they built cotton carding, roving and spinning machinery. Orr, a Massachusetts state senator, exhibited the equipment publicly in his house. The mechanisms became known as the "state models." For more information, see

David J. Jeremy, *Transatlantic Industrial Revolution: The Diffusion of Textile Technologies between Britain and America 1790–1830s* (Cambridge, MA: MIT Press, 1981), 17; and Henry Nourse, "Some Notes on the Genesis of the Power Loom in Worcester County," American *Antiquarian Society Proceedings* 16 (1903): 27–28. See the following for a different picture of technological change: Angela Lakwete. *Inventing the Cotton Gin: Machine and Myth in Antebellum America.* (Baltimore: Johns Hopkins, 2003).

9. J. D. Van Slyck, *Representatives of New England Manufactures* (Boston, 1879) 563; Robert Grieve and John P. Ferald, *The Cotton Centennial 1790–1890* (Providence: J.A and R.A. Reid Publishers and Printers, 1891), 25; William R. Bagnall, *Samuel Slater and the Early Development of Cotton Manufacture in the United States* (Middletown, CT: J.S. Stewart, 1890), 37; Moses Brown to John Bailey, Jr., February 8, 1789, Moses Brown Papers, Rhode Island Historical Society, Providence, Rhode Island; and Lewis Peck and Andrew Dexter with Moses Brown, May 18, 1789, Agreements, Almy and Brown Papers. Rhode Island Historical Society, Providence, Rhode Island.

10. Paul E. Rivard, "Textile Experiments in Rhode Island 1788–1789," *Rhode Island History* 33 (1974): 39; and Thompson, *Moses Brown,* 220.

11. Paul E. Rivard, "Textile Experiments in Rhode Island 1788–1789," 39; Thompson, *Moses Brown,* 220; and John Reynolds to Moses Brown, November 25, 1788, and John Reynolds to Moses Brown, August 11, 1788, Moses Brown Papers. In August, Reynolds wrote: "My card will be ready next week and the spinning frame by the middle of the week will be fit to work with." Also see John Reynolds to Moses Brown, December 1788, Moses Brown Papers. In this letter he wrote: "when I was at thy house, I spoke to thee about buying my spinning mills but thou did not seem determined on that matter. I have never tried since I was at thy house. My mind seems much inclined in wool and flax at the present. If thou should incline to purchase it I will let it go at a loss from the first cash. I will make the pay agreeable to thee, I will take it in goods." Finally, Moses Brown to John Bailey, Jr., February 8, 1789, Moses Brown Papers, "John Reynolds wants to sell his carding machine and frame as he finds the woolen business is as much as he can manage."

12. Cole, *Industrial and Commercial Correspondence of Alexander Hamilton,* 10; Bagnall, *Textile Industries,* 105–106,107,124–125; Lovett, "The Beverly Cotton Manufactory," 226–229.

13. Lewis Peck and Andrew Dexter to Moses Brown, May 18, 1789, Agreements, and Corporate Accounts. 1789 to 1790, Almy and Brown Papers; Rivard, "Textile Experiments,"38; and Moses Brown to John Dexter, July 22, 1791, as quoted in Cole, *Industrial Correspondence,* 73.

14. Cole, *Industrial and Commercial Correspondence of Alexander Hamilton,* 73; Rantoul, "The First Cotton Mill," 16; Bagnall, *Textile Industries,* 107, 124–125, 130–131; Lovett, "The Beverly Cotton Manufactory,"224.

15. Shelton, "Textile Production," 50.

16. *Providence Gazette,* October 10, 1789, vol.26, no. 1345; *United States Chronicle,* December 27, 1792, vol. 9, no. 468; and August 27, 1789, vol. 6, no. 296.

17. *Providence Gazette,* December 26, 1767, vol. 4, no. 207.

18. Shelton, "Textile Production," 50–53.

19. Thomas Kenworthy and Moses Brown and William Almy, 1789, Almy and Brown to William McClure, Accounts of Webs Out, 1790, Almy and Brown to William McClure, Artisan Accounts, 1789–90, Almy and Brown Papers; and William McClure to Moses Brown, April 22, 1790, Moses Brown Papers.

20. William McClure to Moses Brown, April 22, 1790, Moses Brown Papers.

21. Double jean back corduroy is corduroy woven in a twill weave. It is sometimes called Genoa back corduroy. Corduroy itself is woven in any type of warp with cotton filling. The pile filling weaves with one or more warp ends over three or more. The floats are made over the same warp yarns throughout. The resulting loops are sheared and brushed up to form the wales or ridges characteristic of corduroy. For velvet and double jean back corduroy patterns, see Joseph France, *The Weaver's Guide or Web Analyzed* (Burrillville, R.I.: The Author, 1814) 17; John Hargrove, *The Weaver's Draft Book and Clothier's Assistant* (Baltimore, 1792; Reprint, Worcester Mass.: American Antiquarian Society, 1979), 11, 13, 14, 19.

22. Moses Brown to John Dexter, July 22, 1791, as quoted in Cole, *Industrial Correspondence,* 73.

23. *Providence Gazette,* October 10, 1789, vol. 26, no. 1345: "Wanted to purchase a quantity of good linen yarn, well spun from 90–140 lees to the pound for which the same price will be given as the Beverly and Worcester Factories."

24. Rita Adrosko to Gail Fowler Mohanty, March 13, 1986.

25. George S. White, *Memoirs of Samuel Slater* (Philadelphia: #46 Carpenter Street, 1836), 89; David Buffum to Almy and Brown, October 24, 1793; and Lewis Peck and William Almy and Smith Brown, 1791, Agreement, Almy and Brown papers.

26. Record of Reynolds's long involvement in textile manufacture appears first in newspaper advertisements requesting cloth for the Continental Army, as Reynolds was the agent clothier. See *Providence Gazette,* February 28, 1778. Also see letters suggesting Fulham and McKerris as weavers for Brown and Almy; John Reynolds to Moses Brown, October 1788, and July 17, 1789, Moses Brown Papers; and investment in the factory, John Reynolds to Moses Brown, March 30, 1789, Moses Brown Papers.

27. By 1791, with Slater's improvements, both warp and weft could be spun mechanically, Earlier records of yarn sale do not exist, but Reynolds probably bought cotton yarn from Brown and Almy from the outset, Cotton Manufacturing Co., Accounts, 1791, Almy and Brown Papers. Moses Brown left the partnership of Brown and Almy in 1789 but retained financial interest. Smith Brown entered into an agreement with William in the joint venture with Samuel Slater and later the merchandising firm named Almy and Brown.

28. John Reynolds to Almy and Brown, April 15, 1791, Almy and Brown Papers.

29. David Buffum to Elisha Dyer, January 6, 1862, *Rhode Island Society for the Encouragement of Domestic Industry Transactions for 1862*, 94; Darius Buffum to Elisha Dyer, June 9, 1861, *ibid.*, p. 97; Gideon C. Smith to Elisha Dyer, n.d. *ibid.*, 91; David Buffum to Almy and Brown, October 24, 1793, and Weaving Accounts, vol. 97, Almy and Brown Papers; *Newport Mercury*, June 28, 1796, and Bagnall, *Textile Industries*, 169.

30. Cotton Manufacturing Co., Accounts, 1791, and Jonathan Whiting to Almy and Brown, Artisan Accounts, 1789, Almy and Brown Papers; *Providence Gazette*, May 15, 1779; Gary Kulik, "The Beginnings of the Industrial Revolution in America: Pawtucket, Rhode Island 1672–1829," (Ph.D. diss., Brown University, 1980) 226; and Account Book, Worcester Cotton and Woolen Manufacturing Co.

31. Report of the Committee on Manufactures of Providence, as quoted in Cole, *Industrial Correspondence*, 83, 87; *United States Chronicle*, August 27, 1789; Lewis Peck and William Almy and Smith Brown, Agreement. February 4, 1791, Almy and Brown Papers; and Bagnall, *Textile Industries*, 25.

32. For one example of weave shop management prior to mechanization, see Benno Forman, "The Account Book of John Gould, Weaver of Topsfield, Massachusetts: 1697–1724," *Essex Institute Historical Collections* 105 (1969): 36–49.

33. John Rule, *Experience of Labour in the 18th Century English Industry* (New York: St. Martins, 1981), 200–202.

34. E.P. Thompson, *The Making of the English Working Class* (New York: Pantheon Press, 1963); Herbert Gutman, "Work, Culture and Society in Industrializing America 1815–1919," *American Historical Review* 78(1973): 531–588; Paul B. Hensley, "Time, Work and Social Context in New Engalnd." *New England Quarterly* 65 (1992): 531–559; David Montgomery, "The Working Class of the Pre-Industrial American City 1780–1830," *Labor History* 9 (1968): 1–22; Thomas Dublin, *Women at Work*, 66–74; Paul Rivard, *A New Order of Things: How the Textile Industry Transformed New England* (Hanover: University Press of New England, 2002) and Anthony F.C. Wallace, *Rockdale: The Growth of an American Village in the Early Industrial Revolution* (New York: Alfred A. Knopf, 1978) 177–182.

35. Rule, *Experience of Labour*, 16; Manasseh Minor, *The Diary of Manasseh Minor 1696–1720*, ed. Frank Denison Minor (New London, CT: Frank D. Minor with the assistance of Hannah Minor, 1915); Thomas Minor, *The Diary of Thomas Minor of Stonington, Connecticut 1653–1684*, ed. Sidney Minor and George Stanton, Jr., (New London, CT: The Day Publishing Company, 1889) and Gutman, "Work, Culture and Society," 538.

36. Sidney Pollard, *Genesis of Modern Management*. (Cambridge: Harvard University Press, 1965), 160–208.

37. Keith Thomas, "Work and Leisure," *Past and Present* 29(1964): 52 and Prude *The Coming of the Industrial Order: Town and Factory Life in Rural Massachusetts 1810–1860* (New York: Cambridge University Press, 1983), 36.

38. Joseph Alexander and Moses Brown and William Almy, Agreement, May 20, 1789, Almy and Brown Papers. For more information on Joseph Alexander, see Jeremy, *Transatlantic Industrial Revolution,* 18, 87; Bagnall, *Textile Industries,* vol. 1: 150–151; and Account Book, Worcester Cotton and Woolen Manufacturing Company.

39. Thomas Somers and James Leonard to Moses Brown, June 1, 1789, Moses Brown Papers.

40. Robert Francis Seybolt, *Apprenticeship and Apprenticeship Education in Colonial New England and New York* (New York: Arno Press, 1969); S.R. Epstein, "Craft Guilds, Apprenticeship and Technological Change in Pre Industrial Europe." *Journal of Economic History* 58 (1998): 684–713; Rising and Milliean, *An Index of Indentures of Norwich Apprentices Enrolled with the Norwich Assembly Henry VII to George II* (Norfolk: Norfolk Record Society, 1959) and H. J. Smith, ed., *Warwickshire Apprentices and Their Masters 1710–1760* (Oxford: Dugdale Society at the University Press, 1975).

41. Isaac Peckham to Moses Brown, September 15, 1789, Moses Brown Papers.

42. Christopher Leffingwell, Account Book 1690–1714, Connecticut Historical Society, Hartford, Connecticut.

43. Greive and Ferald, *The Cotton Centennial,* 10–11; and Bagnall, *Samuel Slater,* 13.

44. Almy and Brown to Seril (Cyril) Dodge, Artisan Accounts. 1789. Almy and Brown Papers.

45. John Reynolds to Moses Brown, June 22, 1789, Moses Brown Papers.

46. Ample correspondence indicates that both ineffective implementation of labor and faulty machinery led to lost time and lack of supplies. The most comprehensive of the documents describes both personnel and mechanical problems. "Understanding, since I came home, that MacLure and Daniel are both waiting, one for roving and the other for the head of the cylinder to season. On enquiring, finding but one roper of worth nor a probability of the other girls going at it this week induces me to think attention is more wanting to thy object. You will hereafter have machines out of loss time." Moses Brown to William Almy, November 1789; and n.d., ca. 1790, Moses Brown Papers. See also Barbara Tucker, *Samuel Slater and the Origins of the American Textile Industry 1790–1860* (Ithaca, New York: Cornell University Press, 1984), 44–47; and Kulik, "The Beginnings of the Industrial Revolution," 129.

47. Based on a six-day work week.

48. Joseph Alexander with Moses Brown, Artisan Account, September 1789, Almy and Brown Papers.

49. Joseph Bradburn to Almy and Brown, Artisan Accounts, November 11, 1789, Almy and Brown Papers, Moses Brown to William Almy, November 1789, Almy and Brown Papers. For an interpretation of the same material focusing on the role of immigrant labor and charging for time kept idle, see Kulik, "The Beginnings of the Industrial Revolution," 129; and Tucker, *Samuel Slater and the Origins,* 44–47.

50. Thomas Somers and James Leonard to Moses Brown, June 1, 1789, Moses Brown papers.

51. Thomas Kenworthy and Moses Brown and William Almy, Agreement 1789, Almy and Brown papers.

52. Thomas Kenworthy and Moses Brown and William Almy, Agreement, 1789, Almy and Brown Papers.

53. Weaver's Agreement, 1825, Peacedale Manufacturing Co., Box 3, F. 2, Baker Library, Harvard University, Cambridge, MA; Thomas Moore and Blackstone Manufacturing Co., February 17, 1812; Ayers Swansey and Blackstone Manufacturing Co., February 17, 1812, Blackstone Manufacturing Co., Mss 9, Subgroup 1, Box 9, F. 24, Rhode Island Historical Society, Providence; Christopher Leffingwell, Account Book 1690–1714, Connecticut Historical Society, Hartford, and Lydia Seamens, Indenture, 1815, Howard Papers, Rhode Island Historical Society, Providence.

54. A letter between Almy and Brown and Barnabas Allen, the father of an apprentice, identifies the proprietor's role in indenturing student weavers. See Almy and Brown to Barnabas Allen, May 25, 1791, Almy and Brown Papers.

55. Philip Scranton, *Proprietary Capitalism: The Textile Manufacture at Philadelphia 1800–1885* (New York: Cambridge University Press, 1983), 112. Scranton mentions that hand weavers spoke in terms of a price for loom work to differentiate themselves from wage labor. This continued an 18th century custom. Also Rule, *Experience of Labour*, 22.

56. Christopher Leffingwell, Account Book 1690–1714, Connecticut Historical Society, Hartford.

57. Rule, *Experience of Labour*, 22.

58. Thomas Somers and James Leonard to Moses Brown, May 15, 1789, Moses Brown Papers.

59. John Maguire to Moses Brown, September 26, 1789, Almy and Brown Papers.

60. John Maguire and Brown and Almy, Artisan Accounts, May 7, 1790, Almy and Brown Papers.

61. *United States Chronicle*, February 3, 1791.

62. Weaving Accounts, vol. 97, Almy and Brown papers.

63. Joseph Alexander and Moses Brown and William Almy, Agreements, May 20, 1789, Almy and Brown Papers.

64. The term "encouragement" is used here as it was in many contemporary newspaper advertisements instead of indicating specific wages or salary.

65. John Reynolds to Moses Brown, July 17, 1789, Moses Brown Papers.

66. Report of the Committee on Manufactures of Providence as quoted in Cole, *Industrial Correspondence*, 83, 87; and Oliver Payson Fuller, *The History of Warwick* (Providence: Angell, Burlingham and Company, 1875), 90.

67. Kulik, "The Beginnings of the Industrial Revolution," 231; Land Evidence 3:104, Pawtucket City Hall, Pawtucket, R.I., and Weaving Accounts, vols. 80, 97, Almy and Brown Papers.

68. John Reynolds to Moses Brown, October 1788, Moses Brown papers.

69. A typical entry in the Stocking Account Book reads: "July 19, 1790, John Fulham was gone from home all this week and three days last week." Stocking account, vol. 104, Almy and Brown Papers; John Fulham and Almy and Brown, Artisan Accounts, 1791, and Stocking Account, vol. 104, Almy and Brown Papers and Probate Records 4:260, East Greenwich Town Hall, East Greenwich, R.I.

70. Seybolt, *Apprenticeship Education*, 6.

71. Almy and Brown to Barnabas Allen, May 25, 1791, and Pawtucket Accounts, 1810, Almy and Brown Papers.

72. Joseph Alexander and Moses Brown and William Almy, Agreement, May 20, 1789; and Thomas Kenworthy and Moses Brown and William Almy, Agreement, 1789, Almy and Brown Papers. Also see Almy and Brown to Moses Brown, November 1789, Moses Brown Papers, where they arrange for Ichabod Tabor's housing. The following account records living arrangements for John Fulham, Joseph Allen and Alexander Shaw: Cotton Manufacturing Co. to Smith Brown, October 1789 to 1790, Miscellaneous Accounts, Almy and Brown Papers.

73. Seybolt, *Apprenticeship Education*, 14. Also see Scranton's discussion of boarding among Philadelphia weavers as a source of unity and bonding: *Proprietary Capitalism*, 201–205.

74. Cotton Manufacturing Co. to Smith Brown, November 1789 to 1790, and Almy and Brown to John Lawton, Miscellaneous Accounts, December 1790, Almy and Brown Papers.

75. Moses Brown to John Dexter, July 22, 1791, as quoted in Cole, *Industrial Correspondence*, 73.

76. John Reynolds to Moses Brown, July 17, 1789, Moses Brown Papers.

77. John Walsh to Moses Brown, June 21, 1790, and John Ashton to Moses Brown, April 30, 1789, Almy and Brown Papers; and John Reynolds to Moses Brown, November 8, 1788, Moses Brown Papers.

78. E.P. Thompson, "Time, Work-Discipline, and Industrial Capitalism," *Past and Present* 38 (1967): 56–97.

NOTES TO CHAPTER FOUR

1. When Slater met with President Andrew Jackson in Webster Massachusetts near the end of his life, the president said "I understand you taught us how to spin, so as to rival Great Britain in her manufactures; you set all these thousand spindles at work, which I have been delighted in viewing, and which have made so many happy by a lucrative employment." Slater responded "Yes sir, I suppose that I gave out the psalm and they have been singing to the tune ever since." George S. White, *Memoirs of Samuel Slater* (Philadelphia, Printed at #46 Carpenter St., 1836) 264.

2. Arthur Harrison Cole, ed., *Industrial and Commercial Correspondence of Alexander Hamilton Anticipating hit Report on Manufactures* (New York; Augustus M. Kelley Publishers, 1968; Reprint Chicago: A.W. Shaw, 1928) 9–10: Doron Ben-Ater. *Trade Secrets: Intellectual Piracy and the Origins of American Industrial Power* (New Haven: Yale University Press, 2004).

3. Ibid.
4. Cole, *Industrial and Commercial Correspondence*, 62.
5. Cole, *Industrial and Commercial Correspondence*, 72–73.
6. Cole, *Industrial and Commercial Correspondence*, 72–73; William R. Bagnall, *Textile Industries of the United States Including Sketches and Notices of Cotton, Woolen, Silk and Linen Manufactures in the Colonial Period (1639–1810)* (Boston: W.B. Clarke, 1893), 150–152; and George S. White, *Memoirs of Samuel Slater* (Philadelphia: Printed at #46 Carpenter St., 1836), 72–73.
7. Cole, *Industrial and Commercial Correspondence*, 10.
8. Bagnall, *Textile Industries of the United States*, 70.
9. Quoted from "Early Manufactures," from *Providence Journal*, April 3, 1875 in Thomas Robinson Hazard, *Miscellaneous Essays and Letters* (Philadelphia: Collins Printers, 1883), 187; and Edward Mayhew Bacon, *Narragansett Bay, Its Historic and Romantic Associations and Picturesque Setting* (New York and London: G.P. Putnam Sons, The Knickerbocker Press, 1904) 259. For information about the relationship between hand spinning and textile mechanization in England see Ivy Pinchbeck, *Women Workers and the Industrial Revolution 1750–1850* (New York: Augustus M. Kelley Publishers) 111–149.
10. Bagnall, *Textile Industries of the United States*, 98–99; 107; 123; and Cole, *Industrial and Commercial Correspondence*, 71–89; 61–64; and 7–11.
11. Cole, *Industrial and Commercial Correspondence*, 73.
12. Moses Brown to William Almy, November 1789; and n.d. ca. 1790 in Moses Brown Papers, Rhode Island Historical Society, Providence, Rhode Island
13. Coxe, "Address to an Assembly Convened to Establish a Society for the Encouragement of Manufactures and the Useful Arts (1787)" reprinted in Michael Brewster Folsom and Steven D. Lubar, ed., *The Philosophy of Manufactures Early Debates over Industrialization in the United States* (Cambridge: MIT Press, 1982) 48. See also Carole Shammas. "The Decline of Textile Prices in England and British America Prior to Industrialization." *Economic History Review* n.s. v. 47 (1994): 483–507.
14. Coxe, "Address to an Assembly Convened to Establish a Society for the Encouragement of Manufactures and the Useful Arts (1787)" reprinted in Michael Brewster Folsom and Steven D. Lubar, ed., *The Philosophy of Manufactures Early Debates over Industrialization in the United States* (Cambridge: MIT Press, 1982) 52–53.
15. Thomas Jefferson "Letters (1785–1816)" reprinted in Michael Brewster Folsom and Steven D. Lubar, ed., *The Philosophy of Manufactures Early Debates over Industrialization in the United States* (Cambridge: MIT Press, 1982), 23.
16. Cole, *Industrial and Commercial Correspondence*, 310.
17. Folsom and Lubar, ed., *The Philosophy of Manufactures*, 48, 53; Cole, *Industrial and Commercial Correspondence*, 64–65; 75–77, 94–95, 287, 311–312, and Bagnall, *Textile Industries*, 76–77.
18. Hazard, *Miscellaneous*, 187.

19. Gail Fowler Mohanty, "Unnoticed Craftsmen Noted: Handloom Weaving in Essex County Massachusetts prior to 1790," unpublished paper.
20. Katharine Paddock Hess, *Textile Fibers and their Use* (New York: J.B. Lippincott, 1958), 249–274.
21. Cole, *Industrial and Commercial Correspondence*, 64–65.
22. Cole, *Industrial and Commercial Correspondence*, 75–76. According to H.N. Slater's "Reminiscences of Samuel Slater, His Father," quoted in William B. Weeden, *Economic and Social History of New England 1620–1789* (Williamstown, MA: Corner House Publishers, 1978), 912–913, Slater got the cotton from Surinam because of its long staple length. The high quality of the staple enabled him to produce high quality yarns from the early spinning throstles.
23. Jackson and Nightingale, Savannah Georgia to Almy and Brown, February 20,1794, Almy and Brown Papers, Rhode Island Historical Society, Providence Rhode Island.
24. Fustian is a term used to denote a broad spectrum of linen and cotton and later all cotton blends. By the 19th century fustian referred to thick twilled cotton generally dyed olive, grey or other dark color. Dimity—refers to a variety of thin-corded muslin goods such as seersucker. Jean—originally made of linen and cotton twill cloth. Often dyed brown for men's clothing and dark colors. For more information see: Florence M. Montgomery *Textiles in America 1650–1870* (New York: W.W. Norton and Company, 1984) or Isabel B. Wingate, *Fairchild's Dictionary of Textiles* (New York: Fairchild Publications, 1979).
25. Catharine Haines, New York, New York to Almy and Brown, October 16, 1797, Almy and Brown Papers, Rhode Island Historical Society, Providence, Rhode Island.
26. Cole, *Industrial and Commercial Correspondence*, 70–73.
27. Cole, *Industrial and Commercial Correspondence*, 72–73.
28. White, *Memoirs of Samuel Slater*, 72.
29. White, *Memoirs of Samuel Slater*, 73.
30. James B. Hedges, *The Browns of Providence Plantations: the 19th Century* (Providence: Brown University Press, 1968) 164; James Conrad, "The Making of a Hero: Samuel Slater and the Arkwright Frames," *Rhode Island History* 45 (1986): 1–13 and White, *Memoirs of Samuel Slater*, 76.
31. White, *Memoirs of Samuel Slater*, 76.
32. White, *Memoirs of Samuel Slater*, 75.
33. White, *Memoirs of Samuel* Slater, 74.
34. Cole, *Industrial and Commercial Correspondence*, 72–74; and Bagnall, *Textile Industries of the United States* 48–155.
35. White, *Memoirs of Samuel Slater*, 96–97 for description of carding machinery; and Hazard, *Miscellaneous*, 187.
36. Paul E. Rivard, "Textile Experiments in Rhode Island 1788–1789," *Rhode Island History* 33 (1974): 43–45; and Conrad, "The Making of a Hero."
37. White, *Memoirs of Samuel Slater*, 76.
38. Moses Brown left the partnership of Brown and Almy in 1789 but retained financial interest. Smith Brown entered into an agreement with William

Almy in the joint venture with Samuel Slater, and later the merchandizing firm.

39. George S. White, *Memoirs of Samuel Slater,* 76.

40. *Cottons* (Lonsdale, Massachusetts: Lonsdale Company, n.d., c. 1948), 8. See also Gary Kulik, "Factory Discipline in the New Nation: Almy, Brown and Slater and the First Cotton Mill Workers, 1790–1808," *The Massachusetts Review* 28 (1987): 164–181; White, *Memoirs of Samuel* Slater, 73–74; Gregory Clark, "Factory Discipline," *Journal of Economic History* 54 (1994): 128–133; and Barbara Tucker, "The Family and Industrial Discipline in Ante Bellum New England," *Labor History* 2 (1979): 61–63.

41. Samuel Slater to Almy and Brown, Pawtucket Accounts, 1791. Almy and Brown Papers, Rhode Island Historical Society, Providence, Rhode Island.

42. *U.S. Chronicle,* June 2, 1791.

43. Almy and Brown to Rebecca Dean, June 6, 1796, Almy and Brown Papers. Similar letters addressed to John Sherman (June 17, 1796); Nathan Spencer (June 17, 1796); Hannah and Ann Orick (June 24, 1796); Andrew Taylor (July 29, 1796); and many others.

44. *Newport Mercury,* June 28, 1796.

45. Elijah Waring to Almy and Brown, May 22, 1797 as quoted in Barbara M. Tucker, *Samuel Slater and the Origins of the American Textile Industry 1790–1860* (Ithaca, Cornell University Press, 1984), 62.

46. *Providence Gazette,* April 16, 1796.

47. "Account of Cotton received, sold taken to our use and on Hand," Corporate Accounts, 1791. Almy and Brown Papers.

48. White, *Memoirs of Samuel Slater,* 65.

49. Weaving Account, v. 78, Almy and Brown Papers.

50. Weaving Account, v. 78, Almy and Brown Papers.

51. Weaving Account, v. 78 and 79, Almy and Brown Papers.

52. Weaving Accounts, v. 97, Almy and Brown papers.

53. Tucker, *Samuel Slater and the Origins,* 72; Bagnall, *Textile Industries,* 159–60; Louis P. Hutchins and Emma J.H. Dyson, "Draft Historical Report of the Historic American Engineering Register Survey of Old Slater Mill, August 1991," 15–16; Sarah Gleason, "An Architectural History of Slater Mill, Pawtucket, Rhode Island," Student Paper, Brown University, 1980, Dana McCleary and Ann McCleary, "No Worse for the Wear," Student Paper, Brown University, 1978; Almy and Brown's Account with Spinning Mill, v. 1, Slater Papers, Baker Library, Harvard University Abisha Washburn, bill dated April 8, 1793, Accounts Miscellaneous, Almy and Brown Papers, Rhode Island Historical Society; David Martin, Entry, March 11, 1793, Miscellaneous Accounts, Almy and Brown Papers; and David Jenckes, Almy and Brown Account with Spinning Mills, v.1, Slater Papers, Baker Library.

54. Almy and Brown to Elisha Gott, March 9, 1793, Correspondence, 1793, Almy and Brown Papers.

55. *Providence Gazette,* October 1794.

56. James Horton to Almy and Brown, 11/25/1799.

57. Weaving Account vol. 97, Almy and Brown Papers.
58. Gary Kulik, "The Beginnings of the Industrial Revolution in America: Pawtucket, Rhode Island 1672–1829," Ph.D. diss., Brown University, Providence, Rhode Island, 1980, 163.
59. U.S. Custom House, Records, Port of Providence. Rhode Island Historical Society, Providence, Rhode Island.
60. Weaving Account, vol. 97, Almy and Brown Papers.
61. Almy and Brown to Alexander T. Shaw, Artisan Account 1798–1800. Almy and Brown Papers.
62. Birth information was available for thirty-six out of seventy-six weavers. Three weavers were between nine and ten, nine between eleven and twenty, eleven between twenty-one and thirty, seven between thirty-one and forty, three between forty-one and fifty, and three over fifty.
63. *Providence Gazette*, April 16, 1796, vol. 33.
64. Almy and Brown to William Macy, May 8, 1793, Almy and Brown Papers.
65. *Providence Gazette*, November 5, 1814, vol. 50; February 24, 1810, vol. 46; May 30, 1807, vol. 43.
66. *Rhode Island American*, June 11, 1816, vol. 8; Rhode Island General Assembly, Petitions, vol. 44, doc. 24; vol. 47, doc. 32, Rhode Island State Archives, Providence Rhode Island.
67. Carlisle and Brown, *The Providence Directory containing names of the inhabitants, their occupations places of business and dwelling houses* (Providence: Carlisle and Brown, 1826).
68. Series E. Cloth Books, vol. 4–6, Blackstone Manufacturing Company, Rhode Island Historical Society, Providence, Rhode Island.
69. Walter Cornell to Almy and Brown, September 17, 1799, Almy and Brown Papers.
70. Gideon Smith to Elisha Dyer, n.d. *The Rhode Island Society for the Encouragement of Domestic Industry Transactions for 1861:* 92.
71. Carlisle and Brown, *The Providence Directory containing names of the inhabitants, their occupations places of business and dwelling houses* (Providence: Carlisle and Brown, 1826).
72. U.S. Direct Tax Evaluation, 1814, Providence, Rhode Island, Rhode Island Historical Society, Providence, Rhode Island.
73. *Providence Phoenix*, October 5, 1810, vol. 8; and August 15, 1815, vol. 13.
74. John Cady, "Providence Hose Directory containing a list of names of Residents, business firms arranged by home and business address in 1824," typescript, 1960, Rhode Island Historical Society, Providence, Rhode Island.
75. Probate vol. A7, 15, Estate No. 991, Pawtucket City Hall, Pawtucket, Rhode Island; Land Evidence vol. 22:3 and 104, Pawtucket City Hall, Pawtucket Rhode Island.
76. Pawtucket accounts, 1806–1808, Almy and Brown Papers.
77. E.W. Lawton to Almy and Brown, September 4, 1809, Pawtucket Accounts, Almy and Brown Papers.
78. N.S. B. Gras and Henrietta Larson, *Casebook in American Business History* (New York: Crofts, 1939), 226.

79. E.W. Lawton to Almy and Brown, Pawtucket Accounts, July 23, 1808, Almy and Brown Papers.
80. N.S. B. Gras and Henrietta M. Larson, *Casebook in American Business History* (New York, Crofts, 1939), 221.
81. White, *Memoirs of Samuel Slater,* 258; and "Cotton Manufacturing within a thirty mile radius of Providence, 11/14/1809," Zachariah Allen Papers, Rhode Island Historical Society, Providence, Rhode Island.
82. Almy and Brown to Elisha Boardman in Stocking Book, vol. 104, Almy and Brown Papers.

NOTES TO CHAPTER FIVE

1. The quote is from a letter written by Stephen Tripp to Norman B. Brown, May 11, 1818, Series F, Box 1 Folder 10, Blackstone Manufacturing Company, Brown and Ives Business Records, Rhode Island Historical Society, Providence, Rhode Island. This chapter is adapted and expanded from a previous publication "Outwork and Outwork Weavers in Rural Rhode Island 1810–1821" *american studies* 30 (1989): 41–68.
2. This study, along with Thomas Dublin's study of palm leaf hatmaking, Gregory Noble's research on broom making and Mary Blewett's papers on shoemaking is representative of a growing body of literature on outwork and outworkers in New England. These studies place outwork within the context of rural life and family economy during the last three-quarters of the nineteenth century. Gregory Nobles, "Commerce and Community: A Case Study of Rural Broom making Business in Antebellum Massachusetts," *Journal of the Early American Republic,* 4 (Fall, 1984): 287–308; Mary H. Blewett, *Men, Women and Work: Class, Gender and the Protest in the New England Shoe Industry 1780–1910 (*Urbana, Illinois: University of Illinois Press, 1988); "Women Shoeworkers and Domestic Ideology: Rural Outwork in Early 19th Century Essex County," *New England Quarterly,* 60 (1987): 403–428; "I am Doom to Disappointment: The Diaries of a Beverly, Massachusetts Shoebinder, Sarah E. Trask 1849–1851," *Essex Institute Historical Collections,* 117 (1981): 192–212; "Work, Gender and the Artisan Tradition in New England Shoemaking 1780–1860," *Journal of Social History* 17 (1983): 221–248; "Shared but Different: The Experience of Women in the 19th Century Workforce of the New England Shoe Industry," in *Essays from the Lowell Conference on Industrial History 1980–1981,* Robert Weible, Oliver Ford and Paul Marion, eds., (Lowell: The Conference, 1981), 77–86; Thomas Dublin, "Women's Work and the Family Economy: Textiles and Palm Leaf Hatmaking in New England 1830–50," *Tocqueville Review* 5 (Fall and Winter 1983): 297–316; "Women and Outwork in 19th Century New England Town: Fitzwilliam, New Hampshire," in Jonathan Prude and Steven H. Hahn, eds, *The Countryside in the Age of Capitalist Transformation: Essays in the Social History of Rural America* (Chapel Hill: University of North Carolina Press, 1985), 51–70; *Transforming Women's Work New England Lives in the Industrial*

Revolution, (Ithaca, New York, Cornell University Press, 1994), Chapter 2, 29–76; Christopher Clark, "Household Economy, Market Exchange and the Rise of Capitalism in the Connecticut Valley, 1800–1860," *Journal of Social History* 13 (1979–80):169–189; Daniel P. Jones, *The Economic and Social Transformation of Rural Rhode Island,* (Boston: Northeastern University Press, 1992); Lucy Simler, "The Landless Worker: An Index of Economy and Social Change in Chester County Pennsylvania 1750–1820," *The Pennsylvania Magazine of History and Biography* 114 (April 1990) 163–199 and Jonathan Prude, *The Coming of Industrial Order: Town and Factory Life in Rural Massachusetts 1810–1860* (New York: Cambridge University Press, 1985), 73–78.

3. Phillip Greven, *Four Generations: Population, Land and Family in Colonial Andover, Massachusetts* (Ithaca, New York: Cornell University Press, 1970), 25–172; Carole Shammas, "How Self-Sufficient was Early America?" *Journal of Interdisciplinary History,* 13 (1982): 247–272; Michael Merrill, "Cash is Good to Eat: Self Sufficiency and Exchange in Rural Economy in the United States," *Radical History Review* 4 (1977): 52–57; James Henretta, "Families and Farms: *Mentalité* in Pre-Industrial America," *William and Mary Quarterly* 35 (1978): 12–14; and Clark, "Household Economy"173.

4. Herbert Gutman, "Work, Culture and Society in Industrializing America 1815–1919" *American Historical Review* 73 (1973): 559–561; E.P. Thompson, *The Making of the English Working Class* (New York: Pantheon Press, 1968), 248, 360; Cynthia Shelton, *The Mills of Manyunk: Industrialization and Social Conflict in the Philadelphia Region, 1787–1837* (Baltimore: Johns Hopkins University Press, 1986), 29, 63–65; Barbara Tucker, *Samuel Slater and the Origins of the American Textile Industry 1780–1860* (Ithaca, New York: Cornell University Press, 1984), 16; and Mary Blewett, "Work, Gender," 224.

5. Daryl Hafter, "Agents of Technological Change: Women in the Pre- and Post-Industrial Workplace," *Women's Lives, New Theory, Research and Policy,* ed., Dorothy G. McGuigan (Michigan: University of Michigan Press, 1980) 159–168; Daryl Hafter, "Introduction: A Theoretical Framework for Women's Work in forming the Industrial Revolution" in Daryl Hafter, ed., *European Women and the Industrialization of Craft.* (Bloomington: Indiana University Press, 1995) and Mary Blewett, "Work, Gender," 224.

6. Nancy Cott, *The Bonds of Womanhood, Woman's Sphere in New England 1790–1835* (New Haven: Yale University Press, 1977), 70.

7. Gail B. Fowler, "Rhode Island Handloom Weavers and the Effects of Technological Change 1790–1860," Ph.D., diss., University of Pennsylvania, 1984; and E.P. Thompson, *The English Working Class,* 248–368.

8. Gail Fowler Mohanty, "Putting Up with Putting-Out: Technological Diffusion and Outwork Weaving in Rhode Island Textile Mills 1821–1829," *Journal of the Early Republic* 9 (1989): 191–216.

9. "List of Cotton Mills in Rhode Island, October 31,1811, and "Cotton Mills in Rhode Island in the year 1815," Zachariah Allen Papers, Rhode Island Historical Society, Providence, Rhode Island; United States Census, Schedules of Manufacturers for Rhode Island and Massachusetts, 1820. In

1811, 36 mills operating 31,602 spindles were located within the borders of Rhode Island. One year later, the number of mills increased to 38 and the spindlage had grown to 48,034. Gary Kulik, "The Beginnings of the Industrial Revolution in America, Pawtucket, Rhode Island 1672–1829," Ph.D., diss., Brown University, 1980, 265.

10. Peter J. Coleman, *The Transformation of Rhode Island 1790–1860* (Providence: Brown University Press, 1969), 84–85,88.

11. *Providence Gazette,* August 11, 1810; Rhode *Island American,* January 7, 1812; *United States Chronicle,* February 4, 1796; *Providence Phoenix,* January 23, 1813; and Blackstone Manufacturing Company, Brown and Ives Manufacturing Records, Mss 9, Rhode Island Historical Society, Providence, Rhode Island.

12. Tucker, *Samuel Slater,* 16; Kulik, "The Beginnings of the Industrial Revolution,"227; Gary B. Nash, " The Failure of Female Factory Labor in Colonial Boston," *Labor History* 20 (Spring 1979): 165–88; and Mohanty, "Experimentation in Textile Technology and its Impact on Rhode Island Handloom Weavers and Weaving," *Technology and Culture* 29 (1988): 1–31.

13. Mohanty, "Experimentation," and Kulik, "The Beginnings of the Industrial Revolution," 162.

14. Cloth Account, 98:8, Almy and Brown; and Cloth Book Series D, Vols. 379A, 382, 417, 713, 731; Series E, Vols. 3, 6–7, Series B, Vol. 53, Blackstone Manufacturing Company, Rhode Island Historical Society, Providence, Rhode Island.

15. Kulik, "The Beginnings of the Industrial Revolution," 226, 231; *United States Chronicle,* February 2, 1791; Cotton Manufacturing Accounts, 1791, Jonathan Whiting to William Almy and Smith Brown, October 24, 1793; Weaving Accounts, volume 80, 97; Lewis Peck and William Almy and Smith Brown, February 4, 1791, Almy and Brown Papers.

16. Benjamin Shepard to Almy and Brown, 10 May 1794, Almy and Brown Papers.

17. Cloth Account, 98:8, Almy and Brown Papers.

18. David Jeremy, *Transatlantic Industrial Revolution: The Diffusion of Textile Technology between Britain and America 1790–1830s* (Cambridge: MIT Press, 1981), 99,196,209; Margaret D. Leggett, *Subject Matter Index of Patents for Inventions issued by the United States Patent Office from 1790 to 1873 inclusive* (Washington, D. C.: Government Printing Office, 1874), 887; Samuel Hopkins Emory, *History of Taunton Massachusetts from its settlement to Present* (Syracuse: D. Mason, 1893) 660, 661, 646–647; Thomas Weston, *History of the Town of Middleboro* (Boston: Houghton Mifflin, 1906), 287; William Bagnall, *Textile Industries of the United States* Vol. I (Boston: W.B. Clarke and Company, 1893), 171–175.

19. Cyrus Butler and Seth Wheaton to Stephen Tripp, August 17; and August 24, 1811, Blackstone Manufacturing Company.

20. William P. Filby and Mary K. Meyer, *Passenger and Immigration Lists Index* (Detroit: Gale Research Company, 1981), 476; and Jeremy, *Transatlantic Industrial Revolution,* 78–83.

21. Cyrus Butler and Seth Wheaton to Stephen Tripp, September 17, 1811, Series F, Box 9, Folder 3, Blackstone Manufacturing Company.

22. Joseph Alexander to Moses Brown and William Almy, Agreement, May 20, 1789; and Thomas Kenworthy and Moses Brown and William Almy, Agreement, 1789, Almy and Brown Papers.

23. Leonard Dobbins, and James Cupples, Artisan Accounts, 1812, Series B, Box 3, Blackstone Manufacturing Company.

24. Adrienne Dora Hood, "Organization and extent of textile manufacture in eighteenth-Century rural Pennsylvania: A case study of Chester County, " PhD. diss., UCSD, 1988, 7 also see Alice Kessler-Harris, *Out to Work: A History of Wage-Earning Women in the United States* (New York: Oxford University Press, 1982), 18–19, 21.

25. See also Clark, "Household Economy," p. 173; Bettye Hobbs Pruitt, "Self-Sufficiency and the Agricultural Economy of Eighteenth Century Massachusetts," *William and Mary Quarterly* ser. 3, 4 (1984): 349–50; Laurel Thatcher Ulrich, *Goodwives: Image and Reality in the Lives of Women in Northern New England 1650–1750*, (New York: Alfred A. Knopf, 1982) 51–68 for more information about cooperative networks and trading commodities. Examples of accounts exchanging goods to pay for bills incurred to textile mills, see: Seabury Lawton, Account 1798, Joseph Waldron, Account, 1798, Timothy Sheldon, Jr., Artisan Account, 1790, Walter Allen, Artisan Account, 1790, John Croad, Accounts, 1791.1–6, Almy and Brown Papers.

26. Joan Thirsk, "Industries in the Countryside," *Essays in the Economic and Social History of Tudor and Stuart England* (Cambridge: Cambridge University Press, 1961), 72–73; E.L. Jones, "Agricultural Origins of Industry," *Past and Present* 40 (1968): 58–71. In the United States the use of outwork prior to the rise of industry is cited in Nancy F. Cott, *The Bonds of Womanhood: Woman's Sphere in New England 1780–1835* (New Haven: Yale University Press, 1977), 25.

27. Peter J. Coleman, *The Transformation of Rhode Island 1790–1860* (Providence: Brown University Press, 1963), 3–25; James Henretta, "Families and Farms: *Mentalité* in Pre-Industrial America," 8–9; Phillip Greven, *Four Generations*, 125–72; Clark, "Household Economy," 175–176; Michael Merrill, "Cash is Good to Eat," 54–55, 57–59. According to Greven, an apparent land shortage occurred due to inheritance patterns of the first two generations of settlers in the region. By the third generation, the plentiful land allotments had been overly subdivided and the resulting plots were no longer sufficient to support a family. In addition, the rise in land prices makes the accumulation of acreage more difficult. As a result parents are not able to accumulate enough acreage to provide their sons with sufficient land to support their families.

28. Joseph France, *The Weaver's Complete Guide or Web Analyzed,* (Providence: The Author, 1814), iv; Shelton, *Mills of Manayunk*, 28; Kulik, "The Beginnings of the Industrial Revolution,"163; Cloth Account Book, vol. 98:8; and Weaving Books 80,97, Almy and Brown; and David S. Landes, *The Unbound Prometheus: Technological Change and Industrial Development in Western*

Europe from 1750 to the Present (London: Cambridge University Press, 1969), 56; see also Isadora Mancoll Safner, "Joseph France: The Admirable Pirate," An *Interweave Press White Paper* (1981): 1 and 2 for proof of France's plagiarism of a British publication.

29. Blewett, "Women Shoe workers," 403; and Dublin, "Women and Outwork, 62–64.

30. "Simple utilitarian fabrics" refers to those kinds of cloth usually produced by textile firms including check, shirting, stripe, sheeting, plain cloth, chambray, plaid and bedticking. These are two or four harness weave patterns and the most elementary designs used in fabric. Plain weave is the simplest of all weaving pattern consisting of a two-harness under one and over the next one type weave. Velveret is a cotton pile fabric often ribbed like corduroy and made from extra weft woven-pile structure.

31. Cyrus Butler and Seth Wheaton to Stephen Tripp, September 17, 1811, Correspondence, Box 9, folder 3, Blackstone Manufacturing Company; Almy and Brown to James Burnham, July 15, 1795; Jackson T. Nightingale to Almy and Brown, February 20, 1794; Caleb Congdon to Almy and Brown, June 1798; and Catharine Haines to Almy and Brown, October 16, 1797, Almy and Brown Papers. Nightingale of Savannah, Georgia describes what goods might sell best. Catherine Haines states: "the coarsest whitened cotton was very saleable and perhaps when our citizens return, the fine may prove so too, but the unwhitened remains unsold and neither do I think it will sell . . . " James Burnham attributes few sales to high prices: " We have as yet made little progress in selling ticks, their prices being too high if that difficulty could be removed, we think it probable that we could dispose of them among our people and send other of our goods in return."

32. "Prices Paid for Cloth," Coventry Manufacturing Company, Series G, Box 1, Folder 1, Blackstone Manufacturing Company; and "Caleb Greene's Prices for Weaving," Series D, Box 7, Folder 3, Blackstone Manufacturing Company.

33. Weaving Accounts, vol. 97; Lewis Peck and William Almy and Smith Brown, 1791, Agreement; and Cloth Account, vol. 98:8, Almy and Brown Papers; Cloth Book Series D, Vol. 379A, 382, 417, 713, 731; Series E, Vol. 3, 6–7, Series B, Vol. 53, Blackstone Manufacturing Company; Lippitt Manufacturing Company, Weaving Book, Connecticut Historical Society, A. and W. Sprague Company, Ledger for Mill 1, Rhode Island Historical Society, and White and Robinson, Weaving Book, Connecticut Historical Society.

34. Fowler, "Rhode Island Handloom Weavers and the Effects of Technological Change," pp. 131–184; Mohanty, "Putting Up with Putting Out."

35. John Reynolds to Moses Brown, June 22, 1789, Moses Brown Papers, Rhode Island Historical Society, Providence, Rhode Island; and Joseph Alexander with Moses Brown and William Almy, Agreement, May 20, 1789, Almy and Brown Papers.

36. Some examples of evidence of issuing warps at a great distance from the factory include the Lippitt Manufacturing Company, Weaving Book; and the White and Robinson, Weaving Book which list outwork for Rhode Island companies in Connecticut; Russell Wheeler, Store Account Books,

Connecticut State Archives and Silas Jillson, Weaving Ledger, Museum of
American Textile History, Lowell Massachusetts. See also Peter J. Coleman, "Rhode Island Cotton Manufacturing: A Study in Economic Conservatism," *Rhode Island History* 23 (1964), 65–80.

37. "I have sent most of the cloth I set last Saturday for webs to come in. But a
number of webs piled which was almost out if I had waited a week longer.
But I had engaged my team and a number were waiting for webs which if
they could not have, would take them to other places," Noah Curtis to Stephen Tripp, November 13, 1818, Correspondence, Box 15, Series F, File 11,
Blackstone Manufacturing Company; Duncan Bythell, *The Sweated Trades:
Outwork in Nineteenth Century Britain* (New York: St. Martin's Press,
1978), 18, 155; and Cynthia Shelton, *The Mills of Manayunk*, 29, 45–46.

38. Stephen Tripp to Dutee Smith, October 13, 1819, series F, Box 15, Folder
12, Blackstone Manufacturing Company.

39. Dublin, "Women and Outwork," p. 57.

40. Stephen Tripp to Norman B. Brown, May 11, 1818, Series F, Box 1 Folder
10, Blackstone Manufacturing Company; and Mohanty, "Putting Up with
Putting Out."

41. Henry Bradshaw Fearon as quoted in Gertrude S. Kimball, *Pictures of
Rhode Island in the Past 1642–1833 by Travelers, and Observers*, (Providence: Preston and Rounds, 1900) 166.

42. *United States Chronicle* February 4, 1796.

43. Weaving Accounts, vol. 78,79, and 97, Almy and Brown Papers.

44. *Providence Phoenix* August 26, 1809.

45. *Rhode Island American* March 6, 1810.

46. *Rhode Island American*, May 2, 1815.

47. Dublin, "Women and Outwork,"65

48. Tamara K. Hareven, "Introduction: The Historical Study of the Live Course,"
and Glen H. Elder, Jr., "Family History and the Life Course," Tamara K.
Hareven, ed., *Transitions: The Family and the Life Course in Historical Perspective* (New York: Academic Press, 1978)1–56; Phillip Greven, *Four Generations*, 222–258; Frank F. Furstenberg, Jr. "Industrialization and the American
Family: A Look Backward," *American Social Review* 31 (1966): 326–336;
Henretta, "Families and Farms: *Mentalité* in Pre-Industrial America,"6–8.

49. Howard Papers, Rhode Island Historical Society, Providence, Rhode Island;
James Newell Arnold, *Vital Records of Rhode Island 1636–1850* (Provi-
dence: Narragansett Historical Society, 1892), vol. 12: 468, vol. 21:18,367;
United States Census 1790 and 1810.

50. Arnold, *Vital Records*, v. 2:18; v. 3:17; Howard Papers, #8, #100, #104,
Rhode Island Historical Society, Providence, Rhode Island.

51. "Prices for Labor" c. 1812, Series D, V. 713, Blackstone Manufacturing
Company; Probate Records, 3:514,728,732, Smithfield, Rhode Island; and
Arnold, Vital Records, v.2: 52, v. 7: 193; and United States Census 1810.

52. Probate v. 8: 382, 640; and Deed Book 13: 480, Smithfield, Rhode Island;
and United States Census 1820.

53. Weaving Book 1815–18, Blackstone Manufacturing Company; and United
States Census 1810.

54. Filby and Meyer, *Passenger Immigration List Index*, 1408; Cloth Book, Series D, vol. 379A, Blackstone Manufacturing Company; *Providence Gazette*, January 31, 1820; Rhode Island General Assembly, Petitions, 52, doc. 56, State Archives, Providence, Rhode Island; Land Evidence, 19:520, 21: 270, 574 and Wills, 6: 535, Coventry Town Hall, Coventry, Rhode Island.

55. Rhode Island General Assembly, Petitions 49; Arnold, Vital Records, 1:66, 17: 172; and Ledger for Mill 1, A. and W. Sprague Company, Rhode Island Historical Society, Providence, Rhode Island.

56. *Providence Gazette* May 25, 1812; *Rhode Island American* May 20, 1817; *Rhode Island American* April 9, 1816; *Providence Patriot* June 12, 1815; *Providence Phoenix* February 2, 1811; and *Providence Patriot* February 24, 1818.

57. Stephen Tripp to Jabez Averill, September 12, 1815, Box 1, F. 8, Zabdiel Rogers, Mystic to Stephen Trip, October 8, 1814, Box 1 F. 19, Blackstone Manufacturing Company; United States Census of Manufactures 1820, and Mohanty, "Putting Up with Putting Out."

58. Weaving Ledger, Rowse Babcock, Rhode Island Historical Society, Providence, Rhode Island.

59. Peter J. Coleman, "Rhode Island Cotton Manufacturing: A Study in Economic Conservatism," *Rhode Island History* 23 (1964), 76; see also Christopher Clark, *The Roots of Rural Capitalism Western Massachusetts, 1780–1860* (Ithaca, New York: Cornell University Press, 1990), 176–184.

60. Weaving Ledger, Rowse Babcock; and Weaver's Book, George Thurston and Company, Rhode Island Historical Society, Providence, Rhode Island.

NOTES TO CHAPTER SIX

1. Previously published in a somewhat altered version "All Other inventions were Thrown in the Shade: The Power Loom in Rhode Island 1810–1830" *Working in the Blackstone River Valley: Exploring the Heritage of Industrialization*, Douglas M. Reynolds and Marjory Myers, Eds., Blackstone River Valley National Heritage Corridor Commission and Rhode Island Labor Research Center, 1990, 69–88. The quote is from Peleg Wilbur to Elisha Dyer in *Rhode Island Society for the Encouragement of Domestic Industry Transactions for 1861*, 99.

2. David Jeremy, *Transatlantic Industrial Revolution: the Diffusion of Textile Technologies between Britain and America 1790–1830s* (Cambridge: MIT Press, 1981), 93–95 and Henry L. Ellsworth, *A Digest of Patents issued by the United States from 1790–1/1/1839*. Washington, D.C.: Peter Force, 1839).

3. Nathan Appleton, *Introduction of the Power Loom and the Origin of Lowell* (1858 Reprint, New York: J.J. Harper, 1969); George S. White, *Memoirs of Samuel Slater* (Philadelphia: Printed at #46 Carpenter Street, 1836); Samuel Batchelder, *Introduction and Early Progress of Cotton Manufacture in the United States* (Boston, 1863); John L. Hayes, *American Textile Machinery: Its Early History, Characteristics, contributions to the Industry of the World, Relation to other Industries and Claims for National Recognition* (Cambridge, MA: University Press, J. Wilson and Sons, 1879);

Henry Stedman Nourse, "Some Notes on the Genesis of the Power loom in Worcester County, Massachusetts *American Antiquarian Society Proceedings* 16 (1903):22–46; A. M. Goodale, *The Early History of the Power Loom,* (Boston: n.p., 1898); M. D. Leggett, *Subject Matter Index of Patents for Inventions issued by the United States Patent Office from 1790 to 1873 inclusive* (Washington, D.C.: Government Printing Office, 1874); *Rhode Island Society for the Encouragement of Domestic Industries Transactions for 1850,* pp. 51–53; for 1861, pp. 76–126; Samuel Batchelder, *Introduction and Early Progress of Cotton Manufacturing in the United States* (Boston: Little and Brown Company, 1863); Samuel Greene, "The History of the Power loom," Zachariah Allen Papers, Rhode Island Historical Society, Providence, Rhode Island and Thomas Allen Jenckes, 'Two lectures on Rhode Island Inventions," Lectures given at the Rhode Island Historical Society, November 20, 1946, Jenckes Papers, John Hay Library, Brown University, Providence, Rhode Island.

4. Since Rhode Island initiated textile industrialization in the United States with the successful mechanization of spinning and fiber preparing processes in 1790 and led other states in the growth of the cotton textile industry until about 1815, power loom innovation and implementation in the state was chosen as the focus of the study. Brook Hindle, *Emulation and Invention* (New York: New York University Press, 1981), 1–24; 127–142; and Hindle; Steven Lubar, *Engines of Change: The American Industrial Revolution 1790–1860* (Washington, D.C.: Smithsonian Institution, 1986), 74–93; *Repertory of Arts, Manufactures and Agriculture* ser. 2 vol. 2–8, 1803–1807; and Jeremy *Transatlantic Industrial Revolution.*

5. Jeremy, *Transatlantic Industrial Revolution;* Moses Brown to John Bailey, Jr., February 8, 1789, Moses Brown Papers, Rhode Island Historical Society, Providence.

6. Job Manchester to Elisha Dyer, *Rhode Island Society for the Encouragement of Domestic Industries Transactions for 1864,* 62.

7. David Jeremy, *Transatlantic Industrial Revolution;* Darius Buffum to Elisha Dyer, 6/9/1861,*Rhode Island Society for the Encouragement of Domestic Industry Transactions for 1862,* 97; and David Buffum to Elisha Dyer, 1/1/1862, 93.

8. *Repertory of Arts, Manufactures and Agriculture* 1813

9. Job Manchester to Elisha Dyer, p. 64; Perez Peck to Elisha Dyer, p. 82.

10. Job Manchester to Elisha Dyer, p. 65; William English, *The Textile Industry: An Account of the Early Inventions of Spinning, Weaving and Knitting Machines* (London: Harlow Longmans, 1969), 91; and A.M. Goodale, *The History of the Power Loom,* 20–25.

11. Job Manchester to Elisha Dyer, 64–5.

12. Job Manchester to Elisha Dyer, 65.

13. Jeremy, *Transatlantic Industrial Revolution,* 9 and 99; and Greene, "History of the Power loom," n.p.

14. Job Manchester to Elisha Dyer,, 68.

15. Job Manchester to Elisha Dyer, 45, 68–69, 72–74; and Greene, "History of the Power loom," n.p.

16. Job Manchester to Elisha Dyer, 74; John W. Lozier, *Taunton and Mason: Cotton Machinery and Locomotive Manufacture in Taunton Massachusetts 1811–1861* (New York: Garland, 1986), 63; and Perez Peck to Elisha Dyer, 82–83.

17. Job Manchester to Elisha Dyer, 75.

18. Gail Fowler Mohanty, "Putting Up with Putting Out: Power Loom Diffusion and Outwork for Rhode Island Mills, 1816–1830," *Journal of the Early Republic* 9 (1989) 191–216.

19. Job Manchester to Elisha Dyer, 75; and Greene, "History of the Power Loom." n.p.

20. "Know all men by these presents that Thomas R. Williams of Newport, in the County of Newport, State of Rhode Island, sole patentee for Williams' patent water looms for the United States of America in consideration of $1,500 received of Rowland Hazard of S. Kingstown, County of Washington state aforesaid (the receipt where of I hereby acknowledge), have licensed and by these patents do license and permit the said Rowland Hazard, his heirs and assignees four of said water looms to use and enjoy the same in all places of fully and absolutely as I could do myself, before granting these presents. And I do further covenant and agree with the said Rowland Hazard his heirs, and assignees, that I am the sole patentee and that I will not sell or convey any loom or looms for weaving webbings to any other person or persons except the aforesaid Rowland Hazard, his heirs and assignees nor suffer any person claiming under me so to do. And I do further grant to the aforesaid Rowland Hazard the privilege of making use of every and all improvements which I may hereafter make in said looms and to apply the same to his." William Bagnall *Textile Industries in the United States including Sketches and Notes of Cotton, Woolen, Silk and Linen Manufacture in the Colonial Period (1639–1810)* (Boston: W.B. Clarke and Co., 1893) 1:289–290.

21. Jeremy, *Transatlantic Industrial Revolution,* 93; Gary Kulik, "The Beginnings of the Industrial Revolution in America, Pawtucket Rhode Island 1672–1829" PhD. diss., Brown University, 1980, 317; Thomas B. Hazard, *"Nailer Tom's Diary" Otherwise the Journal of Thomas B. Hazard of Kingstown, Rhode Island 1778–1840,* ed., Caroline Hazard (Boston: Merrymount Press, 1930), xvii, 435; and Greene, "History of the Power Loom," n.p.

22. M. D. Leggett, *Subject Matter Index,* vol. 2: 879; Samuel Greene, "The History of the Power Loom," n.p.; and Aza Arnold to Edward Harris, 12 July 1861, *Rhode Island Society for the Encouragement of Domestic Industry Transactions for 1861,* 80.

23. M. D. Leggett, *Subject Matter Index,* 2:879; Zachariah Allen, "Historical, Theoretical and Practical Account of Textile Fabrics," Zachariah Allen Papers, Rhode Island Historical Society, Providence, Rhode Island, and Aza Arnold to Edward Harris, 80; and Kulik, "The Beginnings of the Industrial Revolution," 317.

24. T.R. Williams to Blackstone Manufacturing Company, August 1813, Blackstone Manufacturing Company, Rhode Island Historical Society, Providence, Rhode Island.

25. Jeremy, *Transatlantic Industrial Revolution,* 246; and William Bagnall, Textile Industries, 1:280–295.

26. Leggett, *Subject Matter Index;* Samuel Greene, "History of the Power Loom," n.p.; Bagnall, *Textile Industries,* 1:548–549; *Providence Gazette* December 4, 1813, v. 49; Lozier, *Taunton and Mason,* p65–66; and Robert Shirreff, *A Short Account of the Principle and Operation of the Patent Vertical Power Double Loom by Thomas Johnson,* (Edinburgh: Oliver and Boyd, 1811).

27. Greene, "History of the Power Loom," n.p.; *Providence Gazette,* December 4, 1813, v. 39; John Waterman Statement, Zachariah Allen Papers, Rhode Island Historical Society; and Peleg Wilbur to Elisha Dyer, p. 99.

28. Kulik, "The Beginnings of the Industrial Revolution,"319; Charles H. Clark, "John Thorp, Inventor of the Ring Spindle," *National Association of Cotton Manufacturers Transactions* 124–125 (1928): 72–95; and Greene "History of the Power Loom."

29. Appleton, *Introduction of the Power Loom,* 14; Kulik, "The Beginnings of the Industrial Revolution," 319; Greene, "History of the Power Loom," n.p.; and Aza Arnold to Elisha Dyer, 80.

30. Bagnall, *Textile Industries,* 1:77–78.

31. Greene, "History of the Power Loom," n.p.; Kulik, "The Beginnings of the Industrial Revolution," 317; Allen, "Practical, Historical and Theoretical;" and *Rhode Island Society for the Encouragement of Domestic Industries Transactions for 1861,* Appendix E.

32. H.B. Lyman to Elisha Dyer, *Rhode Island Society for the Encouragement of Domestic Industries Transactions for 1864,* 77; Batchelder, *Introduction and Early Progress,* 70–71 and Greene, "History of the Power Loom," n.p.

33. M.D. Leggett, *Subject Matter Index;* and Peleg Wilbur to Elisha Dyer, 99.

34. Batchelder, *Introduction and Early Progress,* 70.

35. Samuel Slater to John Slater, November 4, 1816, Slater Papers, Rhode Island School of Design, Providence, Rhode Island.

36. Batchelder, *Introduction and Early Progress,* 70; and H. B. Lyman to Elisha Dyer, 77; Goodale, *The Early History of the Power Loom,* 50; James L. Conrad, Jr., "Drive that Branch: Samuel Slater, the Power loom and the writing of America's Textile History," in *Technology and American History: A Historical Anthology from Technology and Culture.* Stephen Cutcliffe and Terry Reynolds, eds., (Chicago: University of Chicago Press), 1997, 45–72.

37. H.B. Lyman to Elisha Dyer, 77.

38. H.B. Lyman to Elisha Dyer, 77–78.

39. Clinton Gilroy, *The Art of Weaving by Hand and Power* (New York: G. D. Baldwin, 1844), 332–345.

40. Notes, Zachariah Allen Papers, Rhode Island Historical Society, Providence, Rhode Island.

41. Jeremy, *Transatlantic Industrial Revolution,* 93,99.

42. Job Manchester to Elisha Dyer, 67–68.

43. M. D. Leggett, *Subject Matter Index;* H. B. Lyman to Elisha Dyer, 78; Greene, "History of the Power Loom; Batchelder, *Introduction and Early Progress,* 71; and *Providence Patriot,* December 1817.

44. Jeremy, *Transatlantic Industrial Revolution,* 102–102.

45. Batchelder, *Introduction and Early Progress,* 71.
46. Peleg Wilbur to Elisha Dyer, 99.
47. Eugene S. Ferguson, "The Mind's Eye: Nonverbal Thought in Technology," *Science* 197 (1977): 827; Anthony F. C. Wallace, *Rockdale: The Growth of an American Village in the Early Industrial Revolution,* (New York: Alfred A. Knopf, 1978), 237–238; and Brooke Hindle, *Emulation and Innovation* (New York: New York University Press, 1981), 133–138.
48. *Repertory of Arts, Manufactures and Agriculture* 1813; John Duncan, *Practical and Descriptive Essays on the Art of Weaving* (Glasgow: J. and A. Duncan, 1808); and William English, *The Textile Industry,* 20–25.
49. *Repertory of Arts, Manufactures and Agriculture* 1813; John Duncan, *Practical and Descriptive Essays on the Art of Weaving* (Glasgow: J. and A. Duncan, 1808).
50. Peleg Wilbur to Elisha Dyer, 99.

NOTES TO CHAPTER SEVEN

1. Somewhat altered from article previously published as: "Putting Up with Putting Out: Technological Diffusion and Outwork Weaving in Rhode Island 1821–1829," *Journal of the Early Republic* 9 (1989): 191–216.
2. Nathan Appleton, "Introduction of the Power loom and the Origin of Lowell." *The Early Development of the American Cotton Textile Industry* (1858 Reprint; New York: J. and J. Harper Editions, 1969), 13.
3. David J. Jeremy, *Transatlantic Industrial Revolution: The Diffusion of Textile Technology between Britain and America 1790–1830s* (Cambridge, Massachusetts: MIT Press, 1981), 98, 276–278; and Gary Kulik, "The Beginning of the Industrial Revolution in America: Pawtucket, Rhode Island 1672–1829" (Ph.D. diss., Brown University 1980), 336.
4. Russell Wheeler, Store Account Books, Connecticut State Archives, Hartford Connecticut; and Silas Jillson, Weaving Ledgers, Museum of American Textile History Lowell, Massachusetts. The following firms mention using outworkers in the 1820 Census of Manufactures: Hope Manufacturing Company, Scituate, Rhode Island; Bellefonte Manufacturing Company, Cranston, Rhode Island; Henry Bliven, Newport, Rhode Island; and two unnamed factories one in Cranston and the other in Westerly, Rhode Island. The Lippitt Manufacturing Company in Warwick, Rhode Island put out weaving to the Vermont State Prison because of labor scarcity and between 1819 and 1820 issued warps throughout Pomfret and Putnam. For more information see Oliver Payson Fuller, *The History of Warwick* (Providence Rhode Island: Angell, Burlingham Company, 1875), 229; and Weaving Book Two, Lippitt Manufacturing Company, Connecticut Historical Society, Hartford Connecticut. Cloth agents, commission agents or merchant weavers received warps from spinning factories and hired outwork weavers to produce the requisite fabric. For other analyses of the Wheeler accounts see Peter J. Coleman, "Rhode Island Cotton Manufacturing, A Study of Economic Conservatism," *Rhode Island History* 23 (July 1964): 65–80; and Thomas Dublin, "Women's Work and the Family Economy:

Textiles and Palm Leaf Hat making in New England 1830–50," *Toqueville Review,* 5 (Fall and Winter 1983): 297–316; "Women and Outwork in 19th Century New England Town: Fitzwilliam, New Hampshire," in Jonathan Prude and Steven H. Hahn, eds., *The Countryside in the Age of Capitalist Transformation: Essays in the Social History of Rural America* (Chapel Hill: University of North Carolina Press, 1985), 51–70; and *Transforming Women's Work New England Lives in the Industrial Revolution,* (Ithaca, New York, Cornell University Press, 1994), Chapter 2, 29–76.

5. N.S.B. Gras and Henrietta M. Larson, *Casebook in American Business History* (New York: Crofts, 1939), 276–277. Gras and Larson indicate that Samuel Slater did not begin using mechanized looms until 1823. His use of outwork peaked between 1820 and 1825. Slater's Massachusetts mills and other Southern Massachusetts textile firms bordering Rhode Island competed with Rhode Island cotton businesses for the same local outwork labor. Cotton textile mill owners were not alone in their tenacity to hand methods of cloth production, wool manufacturers in the state issued yarn for hand weaving into woolen plaids until 1840. Rowse Babcock, Weaving Ledgers, Rhode Island Historical Society, Providence Rhode Island. See Jonathan Prude, *The Coming of the Industrial Order: Town and Factory Life in Rural Massachusetts, 1810- 1860* (New York: Cambridge University Press, 1985), 73–75.

6. Peter J. Coleman, "Rhode Island Cotton Manufacturing: A Study in Economic Conservatism," *Rhode Island History* 23(1964), 65–81; Jeremy, *Transatlantic Industrial Revolution,* 208–210; Kulik, "The Beginning of the Industrial Revolution," 336–360; Caroline F. Ware, *Early New England Cotton Manufacture: A Study of Industrial Beginnings* (New York: Russell and Russell, 1966), 78; Alfred D. Chandler, Jr., ed., *The New American State Papers* (Wilmington, Del.: Scholarly Resources, 1972), 17; Gras and Larson, *Casebook,* 225–226; and Barbara M. Tucker, *Samuel Slater and the Origins of the American Textile Industry 1790–1860* (Ithaca: Cornell University Press, 1984), 100–101. Irwin Feller describes a similar response to the introduction of the Draper loom in New England between 1894 and 1914 in "The Draper Loom in New England Textiles 1894–1914: A Study of Diffusion of an Innovation," *Journal of Economic* History 26(1966), 320–347.

7. Prude, *The Coming of the Industrial Order,* xiv-xvi, 51.

8. Nathan Rosenberg, "Factors Affecting the Diffusion of Technology," *Explorations in Economic History* 10 (1972–73) 9; and John L. Enos, "Invention and Innovation in the Petroleum Refining Industry," in *Rate and Direction of Inventive Activity* (New York: Arno Press, 1962), 309.

9. Philip Scranton, *Proprietary Capitalism: Textile Manufacturing in Philadelphia 1800—1885* (New York: Cambridge University Press, 1983), 3–11.

10. Weaving Accounts, vol. 97; Lewis Peck and William Almy and Smith Brown, 1791, Agreement; and Cloth Account, Vol. 98:8, Almy and Brown Papers, Rhode Island Historical Society, Providence Rhode Island; and Noah Curtis to Stephen Tripp, November 3, 1818, Correspondence, Box 15, Series F, File 11; Noyes Barber to Stephen Tripp, June 15, 1815, Cor-

respondence, Box 1, File 9, Blackstone Manufacturing Company, Rhode Island Historical Society, Providence, Rhode Island.

11. Fowler, "Rhode Island Handloom Weavers," 336–337, 345–352.

12. Jillson Ledgers.

13. Stephen Tripp to Norman B. Brown, May 11, 1818 Series F, Box 1 F 10. Blackstone Manufacturing Company, Rhode Island Historical Society, Providence Rhode Island.

14. Fowler, "Rhode Island Handloom Weavers," 207- 208, 263–264; Coleman, "Rhode Island Cotton Manufacturing," 75; and Jillson Ledgers.

15. Ware, Early *New England Cotton Manufacture,* 73; and Coleman, "Rhode Island Cotton Manufacturing," 71.

16. Jillson Ledgers; and Wheeler Accounts.

17. Jillson Ledgers; Wheeler Accounts; 1820 U.S. Census of Manufactures, Schedules for Rhode Island; and *McLane Report.*

18. Jillson Ledgers; Wheeler Accounts; 1820 U.S. Census of Manufactures, Schedules for Rhode Island; *McLane Report;* and William Bagnall, *Sketches of Manufacturing Establishments in New York City and of Textiles Established in the United States,* ed., Victor Clark (North Andover: Merrimack Valley Textile Museum, 1977), 255–256.

19. 1820 U.S. Census of Manufactures, Manufacturing Schedules for Rhode Island; and *McLane Report.*

20. Robert F. Dalzell, Jr., *Enterprising Elite: The Boston Associates and the World They Made (*Cambridge: Harvard University Press, 1987), 40–44, 53.

21. Nathan Appleton, "Introduction of the Power loom," 13.

22. Although the 1820 Census of Manufactures is incomplete, the census returns provide ample indications of what mill agents saw as the problems faced by the textile industry, the size, value, and property of cotton textile mills. 1820 U.S. Census of Manufactures, Manufacturing Schedules for Rhode Island. See also Dalzell's description of how Lowell-style mills reacted to falling earnings in *Enterprising Elite,* 54. U.S. Congress. Documents Relative to the Manufacturing of the United States. 21st Congress, 1st Session, Executive Document 308, 22:1(222–223), *The American State Papers, Manufactures* 3(Hereafter *McLane Report*); Jeremy, *Transatlantic Industrial Revolution,* 208–209; Ware, *New England Cotton Manufacture,* 139; and Kurt B. Mayer, *Economic Development and Population Growth in Rhode Island* (Providence, Rhode Island: Brown University, 1953), 32.

23. F.W. Taussig, *The Tariff History of the United States* (New York: G.P. Putnam's Sons, 1931), 16- 36, 77–84; and Dalzell, *Enterprising Elite,* 36. See also John Brennan, *Social Conditions in Industrial Rhode Island* (Washington, D.C.: Catholic University, 1940), 10–24.

24. For a more detailed description of the effects of the minimum valuation proviso see David J. Jeremy, *Transatlantic Industrial Revolution,* 205 and F.W. Taussig, *The Tariff History,* 29–36. Sixty-five percent of the factories produced sheeting, shirting and print cloth in 1830. The remainder manufactured fine goods, cambric, and power loom stripes.

25. Jeremy, *Transatlantic Industrial Revolution,* 18. In particular the reports of Benefit Cotton Manufacturing Company, Glocester, Rhode Island,

Keech's Cotton Manufacturing Company, Glocester, Rhode Island, Chepa-
chet Manufacturing Company, Glocester, Rhode Island, Thomas Greene's
Mill of North Providence Rhode Island, and Samuel and Daniel Greene
of North Providence, Rhode Island. Also see reports of Samuel Newell of
Providence, Rhode Island, Union Cotton Manufacturing Company of Burrilville, Rhode Island and Whitman Thurston of Foster, Rhode Island in the
1820 U.S. Census of Manufactures, Manufacturing Schedules for Rhode
Island.

26. In contrast the Waltham loom could be purchased for $125 in 1823
   though only $80 in 1830. Warpers and dressers were available for $1,600
   in 1823 and $693.75 in 1830. David Jeremy notes that over fifty percent
   of the Rhode Island firms in 1820 manufactured four or more varieties
   of cloth including bed ticks, plaids, checks, ginghams, and chambray;
   Jeremy, *Transatlantic Industrial Revolution,* 93, 204–205, 209; and
   David Wilkinson to John Slater, 11 Nov. 1823. Slater Papers, Rhode
   Island School of Design, Providence, Rhode Island. "We received a line
   from your brother Samuel Slater this morning stating the looms would
   come too high priced for a dresser at the price named. In the first place,
   we offered the whole at a produced price in order to obtain your custom with expectancy of having the building of other looms and dressing
   machines fully convinced that we should be able to give you satisfaction
   and as much worth for your money as any other establishment whatever.
   The dressing machine was not offered to him at a price separate from the
   looms." Thus, the looms, dressers and warpers were often offered in a
   group in an attempt to sell in bulk and further reduce the price. The ten
   companies located on the Blackstone River and contracting with Jillson
   and Wheeler were Valley Falls Manufacturing Company(Cumberland),
   Barney Merry(Pawtucket), Archibald Kennedy for the Seekonk Manufacturing Company in Pawtucket, Stephen Jenks and Sons(Central Falls)
   Samuel and Daniel Greene Company(Pawtucket), Timothy Greene and
   Sons(Pawtucket), Thomas Le Favour(Pawtucket) and the Smithfield Cotton Manufacturing Company(Smithfield).

27. Jeremy, *Transatlantic Industrial Revolution,* 208–209. For an alternate
   view of capitalization and accounting methods, which encourage investment in new technologies, see Judith McGaw, *Most Wonderful Machine:
   Mechanization and Social Change in Berkshire Paper Making 1801–1885*
   (Princeton: Princeton University Press, 1987), 151–154.

28. Jeremy, *Transatlantic Industrial Revolution,* 208; and 1820 U.S. Census
   of Manufactures, Manufacturing Schedules for Massachusetts and Rhode
   Island. In 1820, the fixed capital investment in Rhode Island was $24,378
   whereas it was $26,120 in Massachusetts.

29. Kulik, "The Beginning of the Industrial Revolution," 317; H.B. Lyman to
   Elisha Dyer, 18 May 1861, *Rhode Island Society for the Encouragement of
   Domestic Industry Transactions for 1861,* 77; Peleg Wilbur of Coventry to
   Elisha Dyer, n.d., *Rhode Island Society for the Encouragement of Domestic
   Industry Transactions for 1861,* 99; and Coleman, "Rhode Island Cotton
   Manufacturing," 65–81.

30. Jeremy, *Transatlantic Industrial Revolution,* 204–205, 93; and Fowler, "Rhode Island Handloom Weavers," Appendix, 368–383.
31. Job Manchester to Elisha Dyer, 19 Nov. 1864, *Rhode Island Society for the Encouragement of Domestic Industries Transactions for 1864,* 75.
32. Ibid. In a letter describing his inventions, Manchester suggests the reason for many cotton mill owners' hesitation to purchase the twill looms. "Manufacturers were in the midst of the perplexity attendant on getting the power loom into operation for making plain cloth, when they succeeded in getting a good article of shirting and sheeting woven in their own mills at a reasonable cost and with much greater dispatch than by their previous system of sending their yarns about the country, they seemed disposed to pause and take a breath before attempting further advances." More complex figured patterns such as the Damask loom (patented in 1835) were not patented until much later. H. Burt and O.D. and A. H. Boyd of Manchester, Connecticut patented an early check and plaid power loom in August 19, 1828. The earliest patent for a figured loom is one registered in 1829. Leggett, *Subject Matter Index of Patents for Inventions issued by U.S. Patent Office from 1790 to 1873 inclusive* (Washington, D.C.: Government Printing Office, 1874), II, 879.
33. Of 85 factories reporting to the Census Bureau, eleven were closed, nineteen firms produced yarn alone, seventeen factories manufactured cloth on power looms, ten businesses utilized power looms and hired outworkers to manufacture cloth and thirty-one mills continue to use the putting out system to produce their fabrics. Of the factories producing yarn alone, five mills operated on a skein by skein basis taking cotton from other mills or individuals. 1820 U.S. Census of Manufactures, Manufacturing Schedules for Rhode Island; Jeremy, *Transatlantic Industrial Revolution,* 208–209; and Ware, *New England Cotton Manufacture,* 139.
34. Jeremy, *Transatlantic Industrial Revolution,* 278; and 1820 U.S. Census of Manufactures, Manufacturing Schedules for Massachusetts.
35. 1820 U.S. Census of Manufactures, Manufacturing Schedules for Rhode Island.
36. Kulik, "The Beginning of the Industrial Revolution," 340; and Alfred D. Chandler, ed., *The New American State Papers,* 17–18.
37. Kulik, The Beginning of the Industrial Revolution," 340- 342 and 360–369; and Charles Carroll, *Rhode Island: Three Centuries of Democracy* (New York: Lewis Historical Publishing Company, 1932) 522. Legal conflict arose over rights to control waterpower. The Sergeant's Trench Case led to the fragmentation of water rights and to the estrangement of the village's textile elite. Kulik suggested that this evidence and the adoption of the power loom after the drought ended indicates the important role waterpower played in limiting the diffusion of power loom technology in the state. See also Mayer, *Economic Development and Population Growth in Rhode Island,* 32. Mayer indicates that in 1826, one third of Rhode Island's textile manufacturers still relied on handloom cloth production and one third produced yarn and twist but did not make fabric from it.
38. 1820 U.S. Census of Manufactures, Manufacturing Schedules for Rhode Island; Zachariah Allen, "Memoranda of Calculations and Rules of

Practical Mechanics," Zachariah Allen Papers, Rhode Island Historical Society, Providence Rhode Island, 24.

39. *McLane Report* (Letter from Samuel Slater). Between 1820 and 1830, the number of cotton textile businesses in the state increased from eighty-four to one hundred nineteen placing an even greater burden on the rivers and streams in the state. From census material alone it is impossible to assess when waterpower became scarce. The manufacturing censuses are issued every ten years. Shortages may have plagued factories throughout the decade following the 1820 Report of Manufactures or began to threaten expansion towards the end of the ten-year span.

40. *McLane Report* (Reports of J. Rhodes and Sons, Richmond Manufacturing Company). Richmond Manufacturing Company records indicate that the continued to put out webs from their store through 1829 producing not only cotton but woolen fabrics including flannel and kersey. See Richmond Manufacturing Company, Store Ledger, MS 360, Museum of American Textile History, Lowell, MA.

41. Jillson Ledgers; and Wheeler Accounts.

42. Jillson Ledgers; Wheeler Accounts; 1820 U.S. Census of Manufactures, Manufacturing Schedules for Rhode Island; and *McLane Report.*

43. *McLane Report.*

44. Dalzell, *Enterprising Elite,* 53–54.

45. 1820 U.S. Census of Manufactures, Manufacturing Schedules for Rhode Island; and *McLane Report.*

46. Cloth Book, Series D, vol. 382, 379A, 417, Series E, vol. 6 and 7. Blackstone Manufacturing Company, Rhode Island Historical Society, Providence Rhode Island.

47. *McLane Report.*

48. *McLane Report.*

49. Coleman, "Rhode Island Cotton Manufacturing," 65–81. Finally, a more modern example of power loom diffusion reveals that given similar economic and technological conditions that New England entrepreneurs will react similarly to Rhode Island mill owners between 1821 and 1829. Irwin Feller studied the diffusion of the Draper loom into textile mills in New England and in the South between 1894 and 1914. He suggested that the reasons for retarded diffusion could not be attributed to economic conservatism or the entrepreneurs would not have been successful in business. He concluded as I suggest in the beginning of this paper, that the firms did not invest in the innovation initially because of prevailing economic conditions and because of their need to make "rational adjustments to the changing technology." Feller, "The Draper Loom," 346–7.

NOTES TO CHAPTER EIGHT

1.   "One Hundred eagles was the price
            I paid the shiners in a trice
            I'll risque my fame and fortune too,

Quoth I on what a ram can do
Scarce did my hobby 'gin to thrive
'Ere thousand Spanish rams arrive
And what I dream'd not of before
My ram turned out to be a bore"

From the *Hampshire Federalist* by American Watchman (Wilmington, Delaware) November 3,1810 quoted by Arthur Harrison Cole, in *The American Wool Manufacture* (Cambridge, Harvard University Press, 1926), 77. The poem commemorates DuPont's and Delessert's efforts to develop a flock of Merino sheep from the importation of a single Merino ram named Don Pedro in 1801 only to have a flock of 21 Merino rams and 73 ewes brought to the United States a scant six years later. The full quote is "The vexations of our trade and the subsequent war chiefly originated or at least established, them [the household manufactures] as part of our rural economy, and they have become as much a business with the female part of our family as the raising of grain, tobacco and cotton is of the male part." Chester Whitney Wright, *Wool Growing and The Tariff A Study in the Economic History of The United States* (Cambridge: Harvard University, 1910), 20.

2. For more information about textile management and workforce changes see: Thomas Dublin, *Women at Work: The Transformation of Work and Community in Lowell Massachusetts 1826–1860* (New York, Columbia University Press, 1979); Jonathon Prude, *The Coming of Industrial Order: Town and Factory Life in Rural Massachusetts 1810–1860* (New York, 1985); Barbara Tucker, *Samuel Slater and the Origins of the American Textile Industry 1780–1860* (Ithaca: Cornell University Press, 1984); and textile firm records like those of Blackstone Manufacturing Company, Almy and Brown, Greene Manufacturing Company, A. and W. Sprague Company, all in the collection of the Rhode Island Historical Society, Providence Rhode Island. U.S. Congress. Documents Relative to the Manufactures of the United States. 21st Congress. 1st Session. Executive Document 308, 22:1(222–223) and Alfred Chandler, Jr., *The New American State Papers: Manufactures* (Wilmington, Del.: Scholarly Resources, 1972), vol. 3 (Hereafter *McLane Report*). The report provides specific information about textile mill technology and fabric manufacture in the responses to survey questions. Samuel Slater also wrote a descriptive overview essay.

3. Peter J. Coleman, *The Transformation of Rhode Island 1790–1860* (Providence, Brown University Press, 1969), 133, 135; and McLane Report see 970–975.

4. Isadora M. Safner, *The Weaving Roses of Rhode Island* (Loveland, Colorado: Interweave Press, 1985); George E. Pariseau, "Weaver Rose of Rhode Island 1839–1913," *Handweaver and Craftsman*, Winter 1954–55: 4–7, 55; and Alda Granze Kaye, "Weaver Rose: a New Perspective," *Shuttle Spindle and Dyepot* 30 (Spring 1977): 9–17.

5. Henry L. Ellsworth, *A Digest of Patents issued by the United States from 1790–1/1/1839.* (Washington, D.C.: Peter Force, 1839); and David J. Jeremy, *Transatlantic Industrial Revolution: The Diffusion of Textile Technologies*

between Britain and America, 1790—1830s (Cambridge, MA: MIT Press, 1981), 241; 252–262; and "Innovation in American Textile Technology during the Early 19th Century," *Technology and Culture* 14 (1973): 40–76.

6. Ellsworth, *A Digest of Patents;* Horace Hendrick of Killingly Connecticut, Invention Graduating Take-Up Motion for Power loom, patented September 22, 1836, # 30, William H. Brayton of Warren Rhode Island, Invention for regulating the delivery of warp from the warp beams, patented January 6, 1844, patent # 3,397; U.S. Patent Office, Washington, D.C

7. "Temple—A device on a loom located near the fell of the cloth, one on each side, the function of which is to hold the cloth out as wide as possible during the process of weaving, and prevent it from being drawn in too much by the filling. Made in various ways but the trough and roller type is most common." quoted from W.L. Carmichael, George E. Linton and Isaac Price, *Callaway Textile Dictionary* (La Grange, Georgia: Callaway Mills, 1947) 347; John L. Hayes, "American Textile Machinery," *National Association of Wool Manufacturers Bulletin* 9 (1879): 39; Ellsworth, *A Digest of Patents;* and Samuel P. Mason, Self adjusting Temples, patented March 27, 1837, patent # 291, United States Patent Office, Washington D.C.

8. Jeremy, *Transatlantic Industrial Revolution,* 48, 242, 247; Ellsworth, *A Digest of Patents;* Comfort B. Thorpe, of Smithfield Rhode Island, Power loom Shuttle, patented December 27, 1837, patent # 162; John Blackmar, of Brooklyn Connecticut, Construction of a Weaver's Harness, October 20th 1836, patent # 64; United States Patent Office, Washington, D.C.

9. Darius Buffum to Elisha Dyer, 6/9/1861, *Rhode Island Society for the Encouragement of Domestic Industry Transactions for* 1862, pp. 97,and David Buffum to Elisha Dyer, 1/1/1862: 93; and Job Manchester to Elisha Dyer, *Rhode Island Society for the Encouragement for Domestic Industries Transactions for* 1864: 45–74; McLane Report; and J. Leander Bishop, *A History of American Manufactures from 1608–1860* (1868, Reprint New York: Johnson Reprint Corporation, 1967), 312, 341.

10. M.D. Leggett, *Subject Matter Index to Patents for Inventions Issued by the United States Patent Office from 1790 to 1873 inclusive* (Washington, D.C.: Government Printing Office, 1874) 2: 888.

11. William Crompton, Power loom Patent, patented September 28, 1837, patent # 491; James Nield of Taunton Massachusetts; Loom, patented April 12, 1843; patent # 3599, 3954, 3955. Bishop, *A History of American Manufactures,* 488; Arthur Harrison Cole, *The American Wool Manufacture* (Cambridge, MA: Harvard University Press, 1926) vol. 1: 307–309; Chester Whitney Wright, *Wool-Growing and The Tariff A Study in the Economic History of the United States* (Cambridge, MA: Harvard University Press, 1910), 108; and Gilbert R. Merrill, Alfred R. Macormac, and Herbert R. Mauersberger, *American Cotton Handbook A Practical Text and Reference Book for the Entire Cotton Industry* (New York: Textile Book Publishers, Inc., 1949), 451–452.

12. James Nield of Taunton, Massachusetts, Improvement in Looms, patented September 21, 1844, patent # 3954, U.S. Patent Office, Washington, D.C.

13. For a more detailed discussion see Chapter 2. Also Adrienne Dora Hood, "Organization and Extent of Textile Manufacture in 18th Century, rural Pennsylvania: A Case Study of Chester County," Ph.D. diss., UCSD, 1988.

14. Katharine Coman, *The Industrial History of the United States* (New York: Macmillan, 1918), 186; Wright, *Wool-Growing and The Tariff,* John R. Bartlett, ed., *Records of the Colony of Rhode Island and Providence Plantation in New England,* Providence: Knowles Anthony and Company, 1859, 7: 218; 8: 28,60,314,332,451, 87, 197,253.

15. George J. Lough, Jr., "The Champlins of Newport: A Commercial History," PhD. University of Connecticut, Storrs, 1977, 17,172–181; and Russ Thompson and Sons to Christopher Champlin, 26 May 1792; 14 April, 1792; Richard Mathewson to Christopher Champlin, 12 Sept., 1774, Christopher Champlin to James Wallace, 26 Aug., 1775; and Cowell and Man to Christopher Champlin 9 Nov. 1774, Christopher Champlin papers, Rhode Island Historical Society, Providence, Rhode Island; Thomas M. Truxes, "Connecticut in the Irish-American Flaxseed Trade 1750–1775," *Eire Ireland* 12 (1977): 34–63; and Victor S. Clark, *History of Manufactures in the United States,* (Reprint 1929; New York, Peter Smith, 1949) 1: 82.

16. Council Records, vol. 1–2, Probate Books 1–6, Cranston City Hall, Cranston Rhode Island.

17. Probate Book, vol. 3: 610; vol. 5: 106–110; 227–229; 490–498; vol. 6: 420–421, Cranston City Hall; and Susan Gunn, "Tramp as Writ' Weaving in Deerfield prior to 1800," Historic Deerfield Summer Fellowship Program, August 11, 1974, typescript, 4.

18. Will book, 3: 305, Burrilville Town Hall, Burrilville, Rhode Island.

19. Will book, 2,:5, Burrilville Town Hall, Burrilville, Rhode Island; Smithfield Deaths, vol. 3; and Probate 7: 517, Central Falls City Hall, Central Falls Rhode Island; Smithfield Land Evidence, 12: 445, Central Falls City Hall, Central Falls Rhode Island.

20. Smithfield Wills, Central Falls City Hall, Central Falls, Rhode Island; Probate Books, Hopkinton Town Hall, Hopkinton, Rhode Island; and Probate Books, Burrilville Town Hall, Burrilville, Rhode Island.

21. Ellsworth, *A Digest of Patents;* and Jeremy, *Transatlantic Industrial Revolution,* 26, 34, 42, 218–219, 220; and "Early Manufactures," from *Providence Journal,* April 3, 1875 in Thomas Robinson Hazard, *Miscellaneous Essays and Letters* (Philadelphia: Collins Printers, 1883), 187.

22. Shadrach Steere, Account Books, 1808–1816; 1836–1845, Slater Mill Historic Site, Pawtucket, Rhode Island.

23. Shadrach Steere, Account Books, 1808–1816; 1836–1845, Slater Mill Historic Site, Pawtucket, Rhode Island; Carolyn Cooper, and Patrick M. Malone, "The Mechanical Woodworker in Early 19th Century New England as a Spin-off from Textile Industrialization" paper delivered at Old Sturbridge Village, March 17, 1990; and James Cauley, "Nineteenth Century Production Woodturning, A Specialty Lathe," student paper, Brown University, 1977 in the collections of Slater Mill Historic Site, Pawtucket, Rhode Island.

24. John Cady, "Providence House Directory containing a list of Names of Residents, Business firms, Arranged by Home and Business Address." Typescript, Rhode Island Historical Society, Providence, Rhode Island; Carlisle and Brown, *The Providence Directory Containing Names of Inhabitants, their Occupations, Places of Business and Dwelling Houses* (Providence, Carlisle and Brown, 1826); H.H. Brown, *The Providence Directory containing Names of Inhabitants, their Occupation, Places of Business and Dwelling Houses* (Providence: H. H. Brown, 1828, 1830, 1847); and Edwin M. Snow, ed., *Alphabetical Index of Births, Marriages and Deaths recorded in Providence,* (Providence: S.S. Rider, 1867) vol. 20.

25. William P. Filby and Mary K. Meyer, *Passenger and Immigration Lists Index* (Detroit: Gale Research Co., 1981) 310; Snow, *Alphabetical Index;* Robert Grieve, *An Illustrated History of Pawtucket and Central Falls* (Pawtucket: Pawtucket Gazette and Chronicle, 1897) 296; Carlisle and Brown, *The Providence Directory* (1824, 1826); H.H. Brown, *The Providence Directory* (1828); and Charles V. Chapin, *Alphabetical Index of Births Marriages and Deaths recorded in Providence* (Providence: H. Gregory Publisher, 1872), v. 5.

26. *Providence Patriot*, 30 August 1820, v. 2.

27. Samantha Barrett, Account Book and Diary, Connecticut Historical Society, Hartford, CT.

28. Zeloda Barrett, Diary, Connecticut Historical Society, Hartford, CT.

29. Samantha Barrett, Account Book.

30. Samantha Barrett, Account Book.

31. Samantha Barrett, Diary, 3, 11 Oct, 1828; 2,21 July, 1828; 13 May, 1829.

32. Samantha Barrett, Account Book and Diary; George Thurston and Company, Weaving Accounts; and Blackstone Manufacturing Company, Weaving Accounts, Rhode Island Historical Society, Providence Rhode Island.

33. Alda Granze Kaye, "Weaver Rose: A New Perspective," *Shuttle, Spindle and Dyepot* 30 (1977): 9–17; George E. Pariseau, "Weaver Rose of Rhode Island, 1839–1913," *Handweaver and Craftsman,* Winter 1954–55: 4–7, 55; Mrs. John W. Torbet, "Rose Genealogy," Mimeograph, Rhode Island Historical Society, Providence Rhode Island, 1978, 2c, 6, 39A.

34. Alice Morse Earle, "Narragansett Weavers," *In Old Narragansett* (New York, Charles Scribners, 1898), 36.

35. Ibid.

36. Kaye, "Weaver Rose,"10; and Pariseau, "Weaver Rose," 4.

37. Ibid. Kaye

38. Kaye, "Weaver Rose," 10, 13; Pariseau, "Weaver Rose," 4–5; Marguerite P. Davison, *A Handweaver's Pattern Book* (Swarthmore, PA: Marguerite P. Davison Publisher, 1944) and Mary Meigs Atwater, *The Shuttlecraft Book of American Handweaving* (New York: The MacMillan Co., 1937).

39. Alice Morse Earle, *Homelife in Colonial Days* (1898 Reprint: New York: MacMillan Co., 1964) 19, 60, 87, 246, 253, 314, 332, 451.

40. The full quote is "The vexations of our trade and the subsequent war chiefly originated or at least established, them [the household manufactures] as part of our rural economy, and they have become as much a business with

the female part of our family as the raising of grain, tobacco and cotton is of the male part." Chester Whitney Wright, *Wool Growing and The Tariff A Study in the Economic History of The United States* (Cambridge: Harvard University, 1910), 20.

41. Alexander Hamilton, "Report on the Subject of Manufactures," reprinted in *The Philosophy of Manufactures Early Debates over Industrialization in the United States*, Michael Brewster Folsom and Steven D. Lubar, editors, (Cambridge, MA: MIT Press, 1982), 81–95; and John R. Bartlett, ed., *Records of the Colony of Rhode Island and Providence Plantation in New England* (Providence: Knowles Anthony and Company, 1859), vol. 7: 218; v. 8: 28,

42. Cole, *The American Wool Manufacture*, 2,74–75, 78–80, 82; Coman, *The Industrial History*, 186; and Wright, *Wool Growing and the Tariff*, 12–16. 129

43. Cole, *The American Wool Manufacture*, 75–80, 83; and Wright *Wool Growing and the Tariff*, 61–63.

44. Rolla Milton Tryon, *Household Manufactures in the United States 1640–1860*, (Chicago, Illinois: University of Chicago Press, 1917), 250–251.

45. Jeremy, *Transatlantic Industrial Revolution*, 20, 119–128; and S.N.D. North, "The New England Wool Manufacture," in *The New England States Their constitutional, Judicial, Educational, Commercial, Professional and Industrial History*, (Boston, D.H. Hurd, Co., 1897) vol. 3: 197–198. In 1826 Joseph Haigh wrote to Mr. William Rawcliff from Pittsburgh PA: "I could wish your Opinion respecting Mr. Parks Mills whether they have water enough in the Summer Season, also whether an of the Mills could at a small expence be converted into our business. I could like as I cannot get my Family Work for Wages to get a small Carding Fulling and Finishing establishment to be employed by the Country Farmers, as I understand it is the custom in America to Manufacture a part at least of there own wool for there Domestic uses." Quoted from *The Hollingworth Letters: Technical Change in the Textile Industry, 1826–1837*, Thomas W. Leavitt, ed., (Cambridge, MA: MIT Press, 1969), 85–86. Carding continued to function separately from the factory system because of the domestic demand from wool-growers.

46. Elizabeth Hitz, *A Technical and Business Revolution: American Woolens to 1832* (New York: Garland Publishing, Inc., 1986), 228–229; Cole, *American wool Manufacture*, 86; Wright, *Wool-Growing and The Tariff*, 44; J.S. Iredale, "The last two Piecing Machines," *Industrial Archeology* 4 (1967): 51–53; and Hayes, "American Textile Machinery," 15–17.

47. Cole, The American Wool Manufacture, 69.

48. John Reynolds to Moses Brown, November 25, 1788, and John Reynolds to Moses Brown, August 11, 1788, Moses Brown Papers. In August, Reynolds wrote: "My card will be ready next week and the spinning frame by the middle of the week will be fit to work with." Also see John Reynolds to Moses Brown, December 1788, Moses Brown Papers. In this letter he wrote: "when I was at thy house, I spoke to thee about buying my spinning mills but thou did not seem determined on that matter. I have never tried since I was at thy house."

49. Moses Brown to John Bailey, Jr, February 8, 1789, Moses Brown Papers, Rhode Island Historical Society, Providence, Rhode Island.

50. P. Henry Woodward, "The Manufacturing Interests of Hartford," *The New England States: Their Constitutional, Judicial, Educational, Commercial, Professional and Industrial History,* William T. Davis, ed., (Boston, D.H. Hurd and Co., 1897) vol. 2: 815. Woodward also points out that Washington wore the "crow colored suit" when addressing Congress and the House of Representatives on January 8, 1790. As a result the fabric was called "Congress Brown," and sometimes "Hartford Gray."

51. David John Jeremy, *Henry Wansey and His American Journal 1794,* (Philadelphia: American Philosophical Society, 1970) 149.

52. North, "The New England Wool Manufacture," 204

53. Cole, *The American Wool Manufacture,* 96; Coleman, *Transformation of Rhode Island,* 95; and Thomas R. Hazard, "Early Manufactures,"189;

54. Wright, *Wool-Growing and the Tariff,* 20.

55. Coleman, *Transformation of Rhode Island,* 96, 105, 154.

56. Job Manchester to Elisha Dyer, *Rhode Island Society for the Encouragement of Domestic Industry Transactions for 1864:* 65; William English, *The Textile Industry: An Account of the Early Inventions of Spinning, Weaving and Knitting Machines* (London, 1969), 91; *McLane Report*; and A. M. Goodale, *The History of the Power Loom,* (Boston, 1898), 20–25.

57. Bishop, *A History of American Manufactures from 1608–1860,* vol. 2: 233; Cole, *The American Wool Manufacture,* 123; and Hitz, *A Technical and Business Revolution,* 253–267.

58. Coleman, *Transformation of Rhode Island,* 129, 135, 140; Hitz, *A Technical and Business Revolution,* 226–235; Iredale, "The last two Piecing Machines," 52–53; and Wright, Wool-*Growing and the Tariff,* 67–76.

59. Cole, *The American Wool Manufacture,* 111–112; Hitz, *A Technical and Business Revolution,* 235–249; and North, "The New England Wool Manufacture," 204.

60. Coleman, *Transformation of Rhode Island,* 135, 129, 135–140.

61. Coleman, *Transformation of Rhode Island,* 135,137, 140.

62. Frederic Denison, *Westerly and Its Witnesses* (Providence: J.A. and R.A. Reid, 1878), 179; and Stephen Babcock, Comp. *Babcock Genealogy* (New York: Eaton and Mains, 1903), 88–89, 145–146, 252.

63. Store Accounts, 1790–1792, and Weaving Book, 1835–1841, Rowse Babcock Papers, Rhode Island Historical Society, Providence, Rhode Island.

64. Weaving Book, Rowse Babcock Papers, Rhode Island Historical Society, Providence, Rhode Island. Sample consists of 57 entries in 1835, 24 in 1836, 8 in 1837, 7 in 1838, 10 in 1839, and 6 in 1840.

65. Richmond Manufacturing Company, Richmond, Rhode Island, Store Account, MS 360, Museum of American Textile History, North Andover, MA; and George Thurston and Company, Hopkinton, Rhode Island, Store Account, Rhode Island Historical Society, Providence, Rhode Island.

NOTES TO CHAPTER NINE

1. A. Rambler. "The Price of Weavers in Greenville," in the William A. Mowry Letter Books, MSS 571, Rhode Island Historical Society. Reprinted with permission. The complete quote is:

> All ye that have got Woolen Weavers For Sale,
> Can sell them in Greenville Wholesale or Retail;
> That Great Man of Traffic that Deals in the Fleece,
> Will Richly buy them at Nine pence a Piece.
> A Famed Speculator is this Mr. Steere,
> When Wool is so Cheap and Cloth is so Dear,
> And Knowing that Laborers Always were Geese,
> He thinks He can Buy them at Nine Cents a Piece.
> He gave a Commission 'tis Plain to be Seen,
> To a Great Man of Mutton,
> They call Mr. Greene,
> He told him bid Nine pence, and not be Afraid,
> To add something more if they'd take it in Trade.
> But Those who have got Woolen Weavers to Sell,
> Won't sell them in Greenville,
> I'm sorry to Tell,
> Wher'er Ladies must Wear their Hoops very Narrow,
> Since Bay of the Privy was Closed by Cock Sparrow.
> But Now this Rambler is Sorry to Tell,
> That Some of Our Weavers,
> Don't Like the Big Hoops Well,
> To go through a Small Pass They were not Afraid.
> They said it Could ne'er hurt a Wrinkled Old Maid.
> A man they call Fred, Who has long been a Slave,
> Has now of his Wills and his Master's took Leave,
> He got up his Horse just to Tell Him the News,
> He offered Him Nine pence if he would enlist,
> To Weave a few cuts of Cobbler's Twist.

2. Several manufacturers organizations gathered reminiscences in their organizational publications including *Rhode Island Society for the Encouragement of Domestic Industries Transactions, National Association of Wool Manufacturers;* and even earlier are Zachariah Allen, *The Practical Tourist Sketches of the State of the Useful Arts and of Society, Scenery, etc. in Great Britain, France and Holland* (Providence: A.S. Beckwith, 1832); Nathan Appleton, "Introduction of the Power Loom and the Origin of Lowell," in *The Early Development of the American Cotton Textile Industry* (1856 Reprint., New York, J. and J. Harper Editions, 1969); James Montgomery, *A Practical Detail of Cloth Manufacture in the United States* (1840 Reprint, New York: Johnson Reprint Co., 1968); and George S. White, *Memoir of Samuel Slater* (Philadelphia: Printed at #46 Carpenter's St., 1836); Samuel

Bachelder, *Introduction and Early Progress of Cotton Manufacturing in the United States* (Boston: Little Brown and Co., 1863); William R. Bagnall, *Samuel Slater and the Early Development of Cotton Manufacture in the United States* (Middletown, Connecticut: J.S. Stewart, 1890); *Sketches of Manufacturing Established in New York City and of Textiles Established in the United States* ed., Victor Clarke (N.Andover, Massachusetts: Merrimack Valley Textile Museum, 1977) Microfiche; *The Textile Industries of the United States Including Sketches and Notices of Cotton, Woolen, Silk and Linen Manufacture in the Colonial Period (1639-1810)* (Boston: W.B. Clarke and Co., 1893); J. Leander Bishop, *A History of American Manufactures from 1608 to 1860,* (Reprint Philadelphia, 1864, New York: A. M. Kelley, 1967); Arthur Harrison Cole, *The American Wool Manufacture* (Cambridge, MA: Harvard University Press, 1926) Victor S. Clark, *History of Manufactures in the United States,* (Reprint 1929; New York, Peter Smith, 1949); and Michael Brewster Folsom and Steven D. Lubar, ed., *The Philosophy of Manufactures Early Debates over Industrialization in the United States* (Cambridge: MIT Press, 1982)

3. Barbara Tucker, "The Family and Industrial Discipline in Ante Bellum New England," *Labor History* 21 (1979): 55-74; *Samuel Slater and the Origins of the American Textile Industry 1780-1860* (Ithaca: Cornell University Press, 1984); E.P. Thompson, "Time, Work-Discipline and Industrial Capitalism," *Past and Present* 38(1967): 58-97; Merritt Roe Smith, *Harper's Ferry Arsenal and the New Technology: the Challenge of Change* (Ithaca, NY: Cornell University Press, 1977); Herbert Gutman, "Work Culture and Society in Industrializing America, 1815-1919," *American Historical Review* 78(1973): 531-588; Anthony F.C. Wallace, *Rockdale: The Growth of An American Village in the Early Industrial Revolution* (New York: Alfred A Knopf, 1978); and William Sisson, "From Farm to Factory: Work Values and Discipline in Two Early Textile Mills," *Working Papers from the Regional Economic History Research Center* 4(1981):1-27.

4. David Montgomery, "The Shuttle and the Cross: Weavers and Artisans in the Kensington Riots of 1844," in *Workers in the Industrial Revolution: Recent Studies of Labor in the United States and Europe,* ed. Peter N. Stearns (New Brunswick, N.J.: Transaction Books, 1974) pp. 44-74; Philip Scranton, *Proprietary Capitalism: Textile Manufacturing in Philadelphia 1800—1885* (New York: Cambridge University Press, 1983); Gary Kulik, "The Beginnings of the Industrial Revolution in America: Pawtucket Rhode Island 1672-1829," Ph.D. diss., Brown University, Providence Rhode Island; and Peter Coleman, "Rhode Island Cotton Manufacturing: A Study of Economic Conservatism," *Rhode Island History* 23 (1964): 65-80; Gail Fowler Mohanty, "Putting Up with Putting-Out: Technological Diffusion and Outwork Weaving in Rhode Island Textile Mills 1821-1829," *Journal of the Early Republic* 9 (1989): 191-216; Cynthia Shelton, *The Mills of Manyunk: Industrialization and Social Conflict in the Philadelphia Region, 1787-1837* (Baltimore,: Johns Hopkins University Press, 1986); Frank G. White, "Heads were Spinning: The Significance of Patent Accelerating Spinning Wheel Heads." *Textiles in Early America: Design Production and*

Consumption The Dublin Seminar for New England Folklife, Peter Benes, ed., 1997: 64–81; and Kris Inwood and Phyllis Wagg, "The Survival of Handloom Weaving in Rural Canada Circa 1870," *Journal of Economic History* 53 (June 1993): 346–358.

5. Gregory Nobles, "Commerce and Community: A Case Study of Rural Broommaking Business in Antebellum Massachusetts," *Journal of the Early American Republic,* 4 (Fall, 1984): 287–308; Mary H. Blewett, *Men, Women and Work: Class, Gender and the Protest in the New England Shoe Industry 1780–1910* (Urbana, Illinois: University of Illinois Press, 1988); "Women Shoe workers and Domestic Ideology: Rural Outwork in Early 19th Century Essex County," New *England Quarterly,* 60 (1987): 403–428; "I am Doom to Disappointment: The Diaries of a Beverly, Massachusetts Shoe binder, Sarah E. Trask 1849–1851," *Essex Institute Historical Collections,* 117 (1981): 192–212; "Work, Gender and the Artisan Tradition in New England Shoemaking 1780–1860," *Journal of Social History,* 17 (1983): 221–248; "Shared but Different: The Experience of Women in the 19th Century Workforce of the New England Shoe Industry," in *Essays from the Lowell Conference on Industrial History 1980–1981,* Robert Weible, Oliver Ford and Paul Marion, eds., (Lowell: The Conference, 1981) pp. 77–86; Thomas Dublin, "Women's Work and the Family Economy: Textiles and Palm Leaf Hat making in New England 1830–50," *Toqueville Review* 5 (Fall and Winter 1983): 297–316; "Women and Outwork in 19th Century New England Town: Fitzwilliam, New Hampshire," in Jonathan Prude and Steven H. Hahn, eds, *The Countryside in the Age of Capitalist Transformation: Essays in the Social History of Rural America* (Chapel Hill: University of North Carolina Press, 1985) 51–70; Christopher Clark, "Household Economy, Market Exchange and the Rise of Capitalism in the Connecticut Valley, 1800–1860," *Journal of Social History* 13 (1979–80):169–189; Daniel P. Jones, *The Economic and Social Transformation of Rural Rhode Island,* (Boston: Northeastern University Press, 1992); Carole Shammas, "How Self-Sufficient was Early America?" *Journal of Interdisciplinary History,* 13 (1982): 247–272; Michael Merrill, "Cash is Good to Eat: Self Sufficiency and Exchange in Rural Economy in the United States," *Radical History Review,* 4 (1977): 52–57; James Henretta, "Families and Farms: Mentalite in Pre-Industrial America," *William and Mary Quarterly,* 35 (1978): 12–14; and Clark, "Household Economy,"173; and Jonathan Prude, *The Coming of Industrial Order: Town and Factory Life in Rural Massachusetts 1810–1860* (New York: Cambridge University Press, 1985) 73–78.

6. Daryl Hafter, "Agents of Technological Change: Women in the Pre- and Post-Industrial Workplace," *Women's Lives, New Theory, Research and Policy,* ed., Dorothy G. McGuigan (Michigan: University of Michigan Press, 1980) 159–168; Mary Blewitt, "Women Shoe workers and Domestic Ideology: Rural Outwork in Early 19th Century Essex County," New *England Quarterly,* 60 (1987): 403–428; Adrienne Dora Hood, "Organization and extent of textile manufacture in eighteenth-Century rural Pennsylvania: A case study of Chester County," PhD. diss., UCSD, 1988; *Nailer Tom's*

Diary otherwise the Journal of Thomas B. Hazard of Kingstown, Rhode Island 1778–1840, (Boston: Merrymount Press, 1930); Anthony Holden, Ledger 1771–1773, Warwick Rhode Island, Richard Greene, Account Book 1713–1720 and Daniel Mowry, Store Account; Warwick, Rhode Island, Rhode Island Historical Society, Providence, Rhode Island.

7. Daniel Mowry, Store Acct.; Rowse Babcock, Store Acct, Rhode Island Historical Society, Providence, R.I.

8. Daryl Hafter, "Agents of Technological Change: Women in the Pre- and Post-Industrial Workplace," *Women's Lives, New Theory, Research and Policy*, ed., Dorothy G. McGuigan (Michigan: University of Michigan Press, 1980) 159–168; Catherine Greene, Household Accounts, Rhode Island Historical Society, Providence, Rhode Island; Hazard, *Nailer Tom's Diary*; Daniel Mowry, Store Account, Rhode Island Historical Society, Providence, Rhode Island and Oliver Gardner, Weaving Account, Rhode Island Historical Society, Providence, Rhode Island.

9. Gail Barbara Fowler, "Rhode Island Handloom Weavers and the Effects of Technological Change," PhD. diss., University of Pennsylvania, 1984, 184–244, as study of the handloom weavers employed by the firm throughout time from the Weaving ledgers determined the figures used here.

10. See Chapter 7 of Fowler "Rhode Island Handloom Weavers" for the source of the figures and how the figures were derived.

11. Many of the weavers that worked for George Thurston Company later worked for Rowse Babcock. The chances of correlating the workforce between the two firms was heightened by their close proximity. The Langworthy's and Brownings appear in the two ledgers as well as others. Workers for the Richmond Manufacturing Company of Richmond Rhode Island between 1820 and 1829 also correlate to the workers for Thurston and Babcock. Waity Longworthy, for instance, appears in all three accounts. Maxon Johnson appears in both the Thurston and Richmond accounts. C.A. Whitman's Weaving book of 1819–1823 contains the names of several workers that wove for A. and W. Sprague during an earlier period such as Harding Knight, and Esther Realph. In addition Pardon Case's petition to the Rhode Island General Assembly indicated that he worked for additional firms. A small number of the A and W Sprague employees appeared on the Blackstone Manufacturing Company ledger. See George Thurston and Company, Weaving Ledger, 1813–1814; Rowse Babcock, Store Account, 1835–1841; Blackstone Manufacturing Company, Rhode Island Historical Society, Providence, Rhode Island and Richmond Manufacturing Company, Richmond, Rhode Island, Museum of American Textile History, Lowell, MA.

12. Duncan Bythell, *The Handloom Weavers: A Study in the English Cotton Industry during the Industrial Revolution*, (Cambridge: Cambridge University Press, 1969); Norman Murray, *The Scottish Handloom Weavers 1790–1850: A Social History* (Edinburgh: John Donald Publishers, 1978); Thomas W. Leavitt, editor, *The Hollingworth Letters: Technical Change in the Textile Industry, 1826–1837* (Cambridge: MIT Press and The Society for the History of Technology, 1969); and John Rule, *Experience of Labour*

in the 18th Century English Industry (New York: St. Martins, 1981) 200–202.

13. Peter J. Coleman, "The Insolvent Debtor in Rhode Island: 1745–1828," William *and Mary Quarterly,* ser. 3, 32 (1965): 413–434; Elizabeth Baker, *Displacement of men by Machines: Technological Change in Commercial Printing* (New York: Columbia University Press, 1969); *Providence Patriot,* February 5, 1820; Rhode Island General Assembly, Petitions, vol.45, doc. 25; vol. 49, doc. 36; vol. 52, doc. 56; Rhode Island State Archives, Providence, Rhode Island.

14. Probate Records, 3:514,728,732, Smithfield, Rhode Island; and Arnold, *Vital Records,* vol. 2: 52, v. 7: 193.

15. Louis P. Hutchins and Emma J. H. Dyson, "Draft Historical Report of the Historic American Engineering Register Survey of Old Slater Mill," August 1991, 15–16; Sarah Gleason, "An Architectural History of Slater Mill, Pawtucket, Rhode Island," Student Paper, Brown University, 1980, Almy and Brown's Account with Spinning Mill, v. 1, Slater Papers, Baker Library, Harvard University.

16. Mohanty, "Putting Up with Putting-Out" 191–216; Gary Kulik, "The Beginnings of the Industrial Revolution in America, Pawtucket Rhode Island 1672–1829," Brown University, Ph.D. diss, 1981, 340–342; and Peter J. Coleman, "Rhode Island Cotton Manufacturing: A Study in Economic Conservatism," *Rhode Island History* 23 (1964), 65–80.

17. Reports of Greene Manufacturing Company, Lippitt Manufacturing Company, Arkwright Company in U.S. Congress. Documents Relative to the Manufactures of the United States. 22nd Congress, 1st Session. Executive Document 308, Alfred Chandler, Jr., *The New American State* Papers (Wilmington, Del.: Scholarly Resources, 1972) v. 3:270–275, (*The McLane Report*); Greene, Lippitt Arkwright in McLane Report.

18. Shadrach Steere, Account Books, Slater Mill Historic Site, Pawtucket, Rhode Island.

Bibliography

MANUSCRIPTS AND MUSEUM COLLECTIONS

A. *Private Papers*

American Textile History Museum, Lowell, Massachusetts.
 Richmond Manufacturing Company, Richmond Rhode Island, Store Account.
Baker Library, Harvard University, Cambridge, Massachusetts.
 Peacedale Manufacturing Company, Business Accounts.
 Slater Companies, Papers.
 Worcester Cotton Manufacturing Company, Account Book.
Connecticut Historical Society, Hartford, Connecticut.
 Barrett, Samantha. Diary 1815–1820, 1828–1830.
 Barrett, Zeloda. Diary 1804–1831.
 Leffingwell, Christopher. Account Book 1690–1714.
 Lippitt Manufacturing Company. Weaving Book.
 White and Robinson. Weaving Book.
Connecticut States Archives, Hartford, Connecticut.
 Wheeler, Russell. Store Account Books.
Historical Society of Pennsylvania, Philadelphia, Pennsylvania.
 Society for the Encouragement of Manufactures and Useful Arts, Minutes of the Manufacturing Committee.
John Hay Library, Brown University, Providence, Rhode Island.
 Jenckes, Thomas Allen. "Two Lectures on Rhode Island Inventors." Paper Presented at the Rhode Island Historical Society, 20 Nov. 1946. Jenckes Papers.
Peabody Essex Institute, Salem, Massachusetts.
 John Gould, Account Book, Topsfield Massachusetts, 1697–1723.
Rhode Island Historical Society, Providence, Rhode Island.
 Allen, Zachariah. Papers.
 Almy and Brown. Business Records.
 Arkwright Corporation. Weaver's Book.
 Arnold, Aza. Papers and Correspondence.
 Babcock, Rowse. Account Books 1790–1792.

Blackstone Manufacturing Company, Brown and Ives Manufacturing Records.

Brown, Moses. Papers.

Cady, John. "Providence House Directory containing a list of names of Residents, business firms arranged by home and business address in 1824." Typescript. 1960.

Carder Papers, Carder Account Book, 1689–1759. Warwick, Rhode Island.

Champlin, Christopher, Champlin Papers, Correspondence and Business Records.

"Cotton Manufacturing within a thirty mile Radius of Providence, 14 Nov. 1809,"Miscellaneous Manuscripts.

Gardner, Oliver, Account Cipher Book, North Kingstown 1772–1781.

Greene Manufacturing Company. Correspondence.

Greene, Catherine. Account Book, c. 1776.

Howard Family Papers. Foster Papers. Peck Manuscript. Box 14.

Mowry, Daniel. Account Book, 1794–1796.

A Rambler, "The Price of Weavers in Greenville." William A. Mowry Letter Books.

Sprague Company, A. and W., Ledger for Mill 1.

Steere, Syria and Family. Papers.

Thurston and Company, George. Weaver's Book.

Torbet, Mrs. John W. "Rose Genealogy." 1978. Mimeograph.

Rhode Island School of Design, Library, Providence, Rhode Island.

Slater, Samuel. Papers. Rhode Island School of Design Library, Providence, Rhode Island.

Slater Mill Historic Site, Pawtucket, Rhode Island.

Gleason, Sarah. "An Architectural History of Slater Mill," Pawtucket, Rhode Island, Student Paper, Brown University. 1980.

Hutchins, Louis P. and Emma J. H. Dyson, "Draft Historical Report of the Historic American Engineering Register Survey of Old Slater Mill," August 1991.

McLeary, Ann and Dana. "No Worse for the Wear." Student Paper, Brown University, 1978.

Steere, Shadrach. Account Books.

B. Civil Records

Birth, Death, Marriages, Land Evidence, Wills and Probate. Burrilville Town Hall. Burrilville, Rhode Island.

Birth, Death, Marriages, Land Evidence, Wills and Probate, Central Falls City Hall, Central Falls, Rhode Island.

Birth, Death, Marriages, Land Evidence, Wills and Probate. Charlestown Town Hall. Charlestown, Rhode Island.

Birth, Death, Marriages, Land Evidence, Wills and Probate. Coventry Town Hall, Coventry, Rhode Island.

Birth, Death, Marriages, Land Evidence, Wills and Probate, Cranston City Hall, Cranston, Rhode Island.

Birth, Death, Marriages, Land Evidence, Wills and Probate. Foster Town Hall. Foster, Rhode Island.

Birth, Death, Marriages, Land Evidence, Wills and Probate. Gloucester Town Hall, Gloucester, Rhode Island.

Birth, Death, Marriages, Land Evidence, Wills and Probate. Hopkinton Town Hall, Hopkinton, Rhode Island.

Birth, Death, Marriages, Land Evidence, Wills and Probate. Pawtucket City Hall, Pawtucket, Rhode Island.

Land Evidence, Wills and Probate, Providence City Hall, Providence Rhode Island.

Providence Direct Tax 1798, Lists A, B, D and E; Rate Valuation, 1790–1830, Providence City Records, Rhode Island Historical Society, Providence, Rhode Island.

Birth, Death, Marriages, Land Evidence, Wills and Probate, Richmond Town Hall, Richmond, Rhode Island.

Birth, Death, Marriages, Land Evidence, Wills and Probate, Scituate Town Hall, Scituate Rhode Island.

Birth, Death, Marriages, Land Evidence, Wills and Probate, Smithfield Town Records, Smithfield, Rhode Island.

Birth, Death, Marriages, Land Evidence, Wills and Probate, South Kingstown Town Hall, South Kingstown, Rhode Island.

Birth, Death, Marriages, Land Evidence, Wills and Probate, Westerly Town Hall, Westerly, Rhode Island.

Record Commissioners of the City of Boston. *A Report of the Record Commission of the City of Boston containing Miscellaneous Papers.* Vol.10, Document 150.

Rogers, Horatio, George Moulton Carpenter and Edward Fields, eds., *Early Records of the Tow of Providence.* Providence: Snow and Farnum, 1894.

C. State Records

Rhode Island. General Assembly. Petitions. Vols. 32–35, Box 33–39. Rhode Island State Archives. Providence, Rhode Island.

D. Federal Records

Hamilton, Alexander. "Report on the Subject of Manufactures." Reprinted in *The Philosophy of Manufactures Early Debates over Industrialization in the United States.* Michael B. Folsom and Steven D. Lubar, eds. Cambridge, Massachusetts: MIT Press, 1982.

U.S. Bureau of Census. 1790–1830. Rhode Island Federal Census, National Archives RG29, M637 (10), M32 (45,46), M252 (58,59), M33 (115,116,117); M19 (167, 168), microfilm.

U.S. Bureau of Census, *Historical Statistics of the United States Colonial Times to 1957* Washington, D.C.: U.S. Department of Commerce, Bureau of Census, 1960.

U.S. Congress. Documents Relative to the Manufactures of the United States. 21st Congress. 1st Session. Executive Document 308, 22:1(222–223). *The New American State Papers: Manufactures, 3.*

———, Manufactures. 11th Congress. 2nd Session. *The New American State Papers: Manufactures.* 1:124–42.

———, Report on Manufactures. 2nd Congress. 1st Session. *The New American State Papers: Manufactures* 1:43–70.

U.S. Customs House. Alien Reports or Passenger Lists 1798–1807. Port of Providence, East Greenwich, and Pawtucket. Rhode Island Historical Society, Providence, Rhode Island

U. S. District Tax. Tax Evaluation. 1816. Rhode Island Historical Society, Providence, Rhode Island.

E. Museum Collections

Costume and Textile Collection. Rhode Island Historical Society, Providence, Rhode Island

Costume and Textile Collection. Rhode Island School of Design Museum, Providence, Rhode Island.

Costume and Textile Collection, Department of Textiles, Fashion Merchandizing and Design, University of Rhode Island, Kingstown, Rhode Island.

Textile Collection, Slater Mill Historic Site, Pawtucket, Rhode Island.

PUBLICATIONS

A. Contemporary Sources

Allen, Zachariah, *The Practical Tourist Sketches of the State of the Useful Arts and of Society and Scenery, etc. in Great Britain, France and Holland.* Providence: A.S. Beckwith, 1832.

Appleton, Nathan, "Introduction of the Power Loom and the Origin of Lowell." in *The Early Development of the American Cotton Industry.* 1858 Reprint. New York: J and J. Harper Editions, 1969.

Arnold, Asa to Edward Harris, 12 Jul. 1861. *Rhode Island Society for the Encouragement of Domestic Industry Transactions for 1861:* 80.

Bishop, J. Leander *A History of American Manufactures 1608–1860.* Philadelphia: E. Young Co., 1864 Reprint, New York: A. M. Kelley, 1967.

Blakeman, Philo. *The Weaver's Assistant explaining in a familiar manner the first Principles of the Art of Weaving.* Bridgeport: N.L. Skinner, 1818.

Brown, H.H. *Providence Directory containing the Names of Inhabitants, their Occupations, Places of business and Dwelling Houses.* Providence: H.H. Brown, 1828,1830,1832, 1847.

Budd, Thomas. *Good Order Established in Pennsylvania and New Jersey,* 1685, Reprint, Ann Arbor: University Microfilms, 1966.

Buffum, Darius to Elisha Dyer, 9 June 1861. *Rhode Island Society for the Encouragement of Domestic Industry, Transactions for 1862:* 97.

Buffum, David to Elisha Dyer, 6 Jan.1862. *Rhode Island Society for the Encouragement of Domestic Industry Transactions for 1862:*94.

Carlisle and Brown. *Providence Directory containing the Names of Inhabitants, their Occupations, Places of Business and Dwelling Houses.* Providence: Carlisle and Brown, 1824, 1826.

Clinton, Gilroy. *The Art of Weaving by Hand or Power.* New York: G.D. Baldwin, 1844.

Corwin, Edward T., comp. *Ecclesiastical Records of the State of New York* Albany, 1901. Vol. I: 399–400.

Coxe, Tench. "Address to an Assembly Convened to Establish a Society for the Encouragement of Manufactures and Useful Arts (1787)." Reprinted in Michael Brewster Folsom and Steven D. Lubar, eds. *The Philosophy of Manufactures: Early Debates over Industrialization in the United States*. Cambridge: MIT Press, 1982.

Duncan, John. *Practical and Descriptive Essays on the Art of Weaving*. Glascow: J. and A. Duncan, 1808.

France, Joseph. *The Weaver's Complete Guide or the Web Analyzed*. Providence: The Author. 1814.

Hargrove, John. *Weaver's Draft Book and Clothier's Assistant*. 1792 Reprint.; Worcester: American Antiquarian Society, 1979.

Hazard, Thomas B., *"Nailer Tom's Diary" Otherwise the Journal of Thomas B. Hazard 1778–1840*. ed., Caroline Hazard. Boston: Merrymount Press, 1930.

Jefferson, Thomas. "Letters (1785–1816)" reprinted in Michael Brewster Folsom and Steven D. Lubar, eds., *The Philosophy of Manufactures: Early Debates over Industrialization in the United States*. Cambridge, MIT Press, 1982.

Knight, Perry G., *A Guide for the Home Domestic Manufacturer*. Providence: Miller and Hutchins, 1821.

Lyman, Henry B. to Elisha Dyer. 28 May 1861. *Rhode Island Society for the Encouragement of Domestic Industry, Transactions for 1861*: 76–78.

Manchester, Job to Elisha Dyer. *Rhode Island Society for the Encouragement of Domestic Industry, Transactions for 1864*: 45–74.

Mann, Thomas. *Picture of a Factory Village*. Providence: 1833.

Maverick, Samuel *Massachusetts Historical Society Proceedings*, 2nd ser. I 243; *Massachusetts Historical Society Collections* 3rd ser., III, 316.

Minor, Manasseh. *The Diary of Manasseh Minor 1696–1720*. ed., Frank Denison Minor. New London: Frank D. Minor with the assistance of Hannah Minor, 1915.

Minor, Thomas. *The Diary of Thomas Minor of Stonington Connecticut 1683–1684*, ed., Sidney Minor and George Stanton, Jr. New London: The Day Publishing Company, 1899.

Montgomery, James. *A Practical Detail of Cloth Manufacture in the United States*. 1840 Reprint. New York: The Johnson Reprint Company. 1968.

More, Charles. *Skill and the English Working Class, 1870–1914*. New York: St. Martins Press, 1980.

Newport Mercury, January 1, 1760–1820. Newport: James Franklin, Printer.

Ogden, Samuel. *Thoughts What Probable Effect Peace with Great Britain will have on Cotton Manufacturing of this Country Intersperse with Remarks on Bad Management in Business and the Way to Improvement so as to meet Imported Goods in Cheapness at Our Home Market, Pointed Out*. Providence: Goddard and Mann. 1815.

Pitkin, Timothy. *A Statistical View of the Commerce of the United States*. New Haven, 1838 Reprint. New York: A. M. Kelley, 1967.

Providence Gazette, 1762–1820. Providence: William Goddard (1762–1769), John Carter (1769–1820).

Providence Patriot, 1814–1820. Providence: Jones and Wheeler.

Providence Phoenix, May 11, 1802–1820. Providence: William W. Durham, Printer.

Repertory of Arts, Manufactures and Agriculture, 1794–1802. London: G. and T. Wilkie and G.G. Robinson, 1794–1803.

Rhode Island American and Gazette 1808–1820. Providence: Dunham and Hawkins(1808–1814), Miller and Mann(1814–1813), Miller, Goddard and Mann (1815–1820).

Shirreff, Robert. *A Short Account of the Principle and Operation of the Patent Vertical Power Double Loom by Thomas Johnson*. Edinburgh: Oliver and Boyd, 1811.

Smith, Gideon C. to Elisha Dyer n.d., *Rhode Island Society for the Encouragement of Domestic Industry Transactions for 1861*: 91–92.

Wansey, Henry. *The Journal of an Excursion to the United States of North America in the Summer of 1794*. Salisbury England, 1796 Reprint; New York: Johnson Reprint Company, 1969.

White, George S. *Memoirs of Samuel Slater*. Philadelphia: Printed at #46 Carpenter's Street. 1836.

Wiley, John *A Treatise on the Propagation of Sheep, Manufacture of Wool and the Cultivation and Manufacture of Flax*. Williamsburg: R.Royale, 1765.

William Coddington to John Winthrop, Jr. *Winthrop Papers*. Boston: Massachusetts Historical Society, 1929. vol. 5:150 *United States Chronicle 1786–1800*. Providence: Bennett Wheeler, 1786–1800.

Wilkinson, Edward S. to Elisha Dyer, 16 December 1861. *Rhode Island Society for the Encouragement of Domestic Industry Transactions for 1861*: 87–88.

B. Journals and Articles

Baumgarten, Lisa R., "The Textile Trade in Boston, 1650–1700." *Arts in the Anglo American Community in the 17th Century 20th Annual Winterthur Conference*. Ian M.G. Quimby, ed., Charlottesville: University of Virginia Press, 1975, 220–228.

Ben Ater, Doran. "Alexander Hamilton's Alternative: Technological Piracy and the Report on Manufactures." *William and Mary Quarterly* 3rd ser. 52 (1995) 389–414.

Blewett, Mary H. "Women Shoeworkers and Domestic Ideology: Rural Outwork in Early 19th Century Essex County." *New England Quarterly* 50(1987): 403–428.

———. "I am Doom to Disappointment: The Diaries of a Beverly, Massachusetts Shoebinder, Sarah E. Trask 1849–1851." *Essex Institute Historical Collections* 117(1981): 192–212.

———. "Work, Gender and the Artisan Tradition in New England Shoemaking 1780–1860." *Journal of Social History* 17 (1983) 221–248.

———. "Shared but Different: The Experience of Women in the 19th Century Workforce of the New England Shoe Industry." eds., Robert Weible, Oliver Ford and Paul Marion. *Essays from the Lowell Conference on Industrial History 1980–1981*. Lowell: The Conference 1981, 51–70.

Chudacoff, Nancy. "Revolution and the Town: Providence 1775–1783," *Rhode Island History* 35 no. 3 (1976): 71–90.

Clark, Charles. "John Thorp, Inventor of the Ring Spindle." *National Association of Cotton Manufactures Transactions*. 124–125 (1928): 72–95.

Clark, Christopher. "Household Economy, Market Exchange and the Rise of Capitalism in Connecticut Valley, 1800–1860." *Journal of Social History* 12 (1979–1980): 169–189.

———. "Social Structure and Manufacturing before the Factory: Rural New England, 1750–1830." Thomas Max Safley and Leonard N. Rosenband, eds., *The Workplace before the Factory: Artisans and Proletarians 1500–1800*. Ithaca, New York: Cornell University Press, 1993, 11–36.

Coleman, Peter J. "Rhode Island Cotton Manufacturing: A Study in Economic Conservatism." *Rhode Island History* 23 (1964) 65–80.

———. "The Insolvent Debtor in Rhode Island 1745–1828." *William and Mary Quarterly,* ser.3. 32 (1965): 413–434.

Conrad, James L. Jr., "Entrepreneurial Objectives, Organizational Design, Technology and Cotton Manufacturing of Almy and Brown, 1789–1797." *Business and Economic History* 2nd ser. 13 (1984): 7–19.

———. "The Making of a Hero: Samuel Slater and the Arkwright Frames." *Rhode Island History* 45 (1986): 1–13.

———. "Drive that Branch: Samuel Slater, the Power loom and the writing of America's textile history." *Technology and American History A Historical Anthology from Technology and Culture,* Stephen Cutcliffe and Terry Reynolds, eds., Chicago: University of Chicago Press, 1997, 45–72.

Cummings, Abbott Lowell. "Connecticut Homespun." *Antiques* 66 (1954): 206–209.

deVries, Jan. "The Industrial Revolution and the Industrious Revolution." *Journal of Economic History* 54 (1994): 249–276.

Dublin, Thomas. "Women's Work and the Family Economy: Textiles and Palm Leaf Hatmaking in New England 1830–1850." *Tocqueville Review* 5 (Fall and Winter 1983):297–316.

———. "Women and Outwork in 19th Century New England Town: Fitzwilliam, New Hampshire." in Jonathan Prude and Steven H. Hahn, eds. *The Countryside in the Age of Capitalist Transformation: Essays in the Social History or Rural America*. Chapel Hill: University of North Carolina Press, 1985, 51–70.

Earle, Alice Morse. "Narragansett Weavers." *In Old Narragansett*. New York: Charles Scribner's, 1898.

"Early Manufactures." *Providence Journal*. April 3, 1875.

Elder, Glen H. Jr. . "Family History and the Life Course." in Tamara K. Haraven, ed. *Transitions: The Family and the Life Course in Historical Perspective* New York: Academic Press, 1978.

Enos, John L. "Invention and Innovation in the Petroleum Refining Industry." *The Rate and Direction of Inventive Activity, Economic and Social Factors: a conference of the Universities-National Bureau Committee for Economic Research and the Committee on Economic Growth of the Social Science Research Council*. New York: Arno Press. 1961.

Epstein, S.R. "Craft Guilds, Apprenticeship and Technological Change in Preindustrial Europe." *Journal of Economic History 58 (1988): 684–713.*

Feller, Irwin. "The Draper Loom in New England Textiles 1894–1914: A Study of Diffusion of an Innovation." *Journal of Economic History* 26 (1966): 320–347.

Ferguson, Eugene S. "The Mind's Eye: Nonverbal Thought in Technology." *Science* 197 (1977): 827.

Forman, Benno. "The Account Book of John Gould, Weaver of Topsfield, Massachusetts: 1697–1724." *Essex Institute Historical Collections* 105 (1969): 36–49.

Furstenberg, Frank F. Jr. "Industrialization and the American Family: A Look Backward." *American Social Review* 31 (1966): 326–336.

Gilje, Paul. "Introduction." In *American Artisans: Crafting Social Identity 1750–1850*. Howard B. Rock, Paul A. Gilje and Robert Asher, eds., Baltimore: Johns Hopkins University Press, 1995, xi-xvi.

Gross, Laurence F. "Wool Carding: A Study of Skills and Technology." *Technology and Culture* 28(1987): 804–827.

Gutman, Herbert, "Work, Culture and Society in Industrializing America 1815–1919." *American Historical Review* 78 (1973):331–388.

Hafter, Daryl. "Agents of Technological Change: Women in the Pre- and Post Industrial Workplace." in Dorothy G. McGuigan, ed., *Women's Lives, New Theory, Research and Policy*, Michigan: University of Michigan, 1980, 159–168.

Haraven, Tamara K. "Introduction: The Historical Study of the Life course." In Tamara K. Haraven, ed. *Transitions: The Family and the Life Course in Historical Perspective*, New York: Academic Press, 1978.

Hayes, John L. "American Textile Machinery." *National Association of Wool Manufacturers Bulletin* 9(1879):39.

Henretta, James. "The War for Independence and American Economic Development." in Ronald Hoffman, et al. eds., *The Economy of Early America: The Revolutionary Period 1763–1790*. Charlottesville: University Press of Virginia, 1988.

———. "Family, Farms, *Mentalité* in Pre-Industrial America." *William and Mary Quarterly* 359 (1978) 12–14.

Hensley, Paul B. "Time, Work and Social Context in New England." *New England Quarterly* 65 (1992): 531–559.

Hobswam, E.J. "The Tramping Artisan." *Economic History Review* 2nd ser. 3(1950–51): 299–320.

Hood, Adrienne. "The Gender Division of Labor in the Production of Textiles in 18th Century Rural Pennsylvania (Rethinking the New England Model)" *Journal of Interdisciplinary History* 27 (1994): 537–561.

———. "The Material World of Cloth: Production and Use in 18th Century Rural Pennsylvania." *William and Mary Quarterly* 3rd Ser. 53 (1996): 43–66.

———. "Industrial Opportunism: From Handweaving to Mill Production 1700–1830." In *Textiles in Early America: Design, Production and Consumption, The Dublin Seminar for New England Folklife*, Peter Benes, ed., Boston: Boston University, 1997, 64–81.

Iredale, J. S. "The last two Piecing Machines," *Industrial Archeology* 4 (1967): 51–56.

Jeremy, David. "British Textile Technology Transmission to the United States: The Philadelphia Region Experience." *Business History Review* 47 (1973): 24–52.

———. "Innovation in the American Textile Industry during the Early 19th Century." *Technology and Culture* 14 (1973): 40–76.

Jones, E.L. "Agricultural Origins of Industry." *Past and Present* 40 (968):58–71.

Inwood, Kris and Phyllis Wagg. "The Survival of Handloom Weaving in Rural Canada Circa 1870." *Journal of Economic History* 53 (June 1993): 346–358.

LaFantasie, Glenn W. "A Day in the Life of Roger Williams." *Rhode Island History* 46 (1987):

Kaye, Alda Granze. "Weaver Rose: A New Perspective." *Shuttle, Spindle and Dyepot* 30 (Spring 1977): 9–17.

Kulik, Gary. "Factory Discipline in the New Nation: Almy, Brown and Slater and the First Cotton Mill Workers, 1790–1808." *The Massachusetts Review* 28 (1987) 164–181.

Kulikoff, Alan. "The Transition to Capitalism in Rural America." *William and Mary Quarterly* 2nd ser. 46 (1989): 120–144.

Lewton, Frederick L. "Samuel Slater and the Oldest Cotton Machinery in America." *Smithsonian Institution Annual Report* 1926: 505–511.

Lincoln, Jonathan Thayer. "The Beginnings of the Machine Age in New England, David Wilkinson of Pawtucket." *New England Quarterly* 6 (1933): 716–732.

Lovett, Robert W. "The Beverly Cotton Manufacturing Company, or some New Light on an Early Mill." *Bulletin of the Business Historical Society* 26 (1962): 218–242.

Main, Gloria. "Gender, Work and Wages in Colonial New England." *William and Mary Quarterly* 3rd ser. 51 (1994): 39–69.

McBurney, Christian. "The South Kingstown Planters: Country Gentry in Colonial Rhode Island." *Rhode Island History* 45(1986): 81–82.

McLoughlin, William G. "Synthesizing Rhode Island History: Problems, Approaches, and Opportunities," *Rhode Island History* 42(1983): 106.

McWilliams, James E. "Work, Family and Economic Improvement in Late 17th Century Massachusetts Bay: The Case of Joshua Buffum." *New England Quarterly* 74 (2001): 373.

Merrill, Michael. "Cash is Good to Eat' Self-Sufficiency and Exchange in Rural Economies in the United States." *Radical History Review* 4 (1977): 52–57.

Mohanty, Gail Fowler. "Experimentation in Textile Technology and its Impact on Rhode Island Handloom Weavers and Weaving." *Technology and Culture* 29 (1988): 1–31.

———. "Putting Up with Putting-Out: Technological Diffusion and Outwork Weaving in Rhode Island Textile Mills 1821–1829." *Journal of the Early Republic* 9 (1989): 191–216.

———. Outwork and Outwork Weaving in Rural Rhode Island: 1810–1821." *american studies* 30 (1989): 41–68.

———. "All Other Inventions were Thrown into the Shade: The Power Loom in Rhode Island 1810–1830." Blackstone River Valley National Heritage

Corridor Commission in conjunction with the University of Rhode Island's Labor Research Center, 1990, 69–88.

———. From Craft to Industry: Textile Industrialization and Production in the United States 1760–1840: A Brief Review." *Material History Bulletin* 31 (Spring Printemps 1990): 15–22

———."Industrialization and Production of Textiles in the United States: A Bibliography," *Material History Bulletin* 31 (Spring/Printemps 1990): 23–32.

———. "Woven Documents: Technological and Economic Factors Influencing Rhode Island Textile Production to 1840." in Linda Welters and Margaret T. Ordoñez, eds., *Down by the Old Mill Stream*. Kent Ohio: Kent State University Press, 2000, pages 51–82.

Montgomery, David "The Working Class of the Pre-Industrial American City 1780–1830." *Labor History* 9 (1968): 1–22.

———. "The Shuttle and the Cross: Weavers and Artisans in the Kensington Riots of 1844," in Peter N. Stearns, ed., *Workers in the Industrial Revolution: Recent Studies of Labor in the United States and Europe*. New Brunswick New Jersey: Transaction Books, 1974, 44–74.

Montgomery, Florence. "Fortunes to be Acquired: Textiles in 18th Century Rhode Island." *Rhode Island History* 31 (1972): 53–63.

Myers, R.J. "Occupational Readjustment of Displaced Skilled Workmen." *Journal of Political Economy* 37(1929): 473–89.

Nash, Gary B. "The Failure of Female Factory Labor in Colonial Boston." *Labor History* 20 (Spring 1979): 165–188.

Nobles, Gregory. "Commerce and Community: A Case Study of Rural Broommaking Business in Antebellum Massachusetts." *Journal of the Early American Republic* 4 (Fall, 1984): 287–308.

North, S.N.D. "The New England Wool Manufacture." In William T. Davis, ed., *The New England States, Their Constitutional, Judicial, Educational, Commercial, Professional and Industrial History*. Boston: D.H. Hurd, Co.,1897.

Norton, Mary P. "Labor in the Early New England Carpet Industry." *Business History Review* 26 (1952):19–26.

Nourse, Henry. "Some Notes on the Genesis of the Power loom in Worcester County." *American Antiquarian Society Proceedings* 16 (1903): 22–46.

Ouellette, Susan. "Divine Providence and Collective Endeavor: Sheep Production in Early Massachusetts." *The New England Quarterly* 69 (1966): 355–380.

Pariseau, George E. "Weaver Rose of Rhode Island 1839–1913." *Handweaver and Craftsman* Winter 1954–55:4–7,55.

Pollard, Vivienne. "The Household Economy in Early Rural America and Ulster: The Question of Self Sufficiency." In *Ulster and North America Trans Atlantic Perspectives on the Scotch Irish*. Tyler Blethen and Curtis Wood, eds. Tuscaloosa Alabama: University of Alabama, 1997.

Pruit, Bettye Hobbs. "Self-Sufficiency and the Agricultural Economy of Eighteenth Century Massachusetts." *William and Mary Quarterly* ser. 3,4 (1984): 349–50.

Putnam, Gail. "The Textile Legacy of a Narragansett Planter." *Textiles in Early America: Design, Production and consumption The Dublin Seminar for New*

England Folklife, Peter Benes, ed., Boston: Boston University, 1997, 152–167.

Rantoul, Robert S. "The First Cotton Mill in America." *Historical Collections of the Essex Institute* 33 (1897): 1–28.

Rivard, Paul E. "Textile Experiments in Rhode Island 1788–1789." *Rhode Island History* 33 (1974): 33–47.

Rosenberg, Nathan. "Factors Affecting the Diffusion of Technology." *Explorations in Economic History* 10 (1972–73): 9.

Rosenberg, Winifred. "The Market and Massachusetts Farmers 1750–1855." *Journal of Economic History* 4 (1981): 283–314.

Safner, Isadora Mancoll. "Joseph France: The Admirable Pirate." *An Interweave Press White Paper* 1981:1 and 2.

Salinger, Sharon V. "Artisans, Journeymen and the Transformation of Labor in Late 18th Century Philadelphia." *William and Mary Quarterly* 3d ser. 40 (1983): 62–84.

Shammas, Carole. "How Self-Sufficient was Early America?" *Journal of Interdisciplinary History* 12(1982): 247–272.

———. "The Decline of Textile Prices in England and British America Prior to Industrialization." *Economic History Review* 47 (1994): 483–507.

Shelton, Cynthia. "The Role of Labor in Early Industrialization: Philadelphia 1787–1837." *Journal of the Early Republic* 4 (winter 1984): 365–94.

———. "Textile Production and the Urban Laborer: The Proto-Industrial Experience of Philadelphia 1787–1820." *Working Papers from the Regional Economic History Research Center* 5 (1982):46–80.

Simler, Lucy. "The Landless Worker: An Index of Economic and Social Change in Chester County Pennsylvania." *The Pennsylvania Magazine of History and Biography* 114 (April 1990): 163–199.

Sisson, William. "From Farm to Factory: Work Values and Discipline in two early Textile Mills." *Working Papers from the Regional Economic History Research* 4 (1981): 1–27.

Smail, John. "Manufacturer or Artisan? The Relationship between Economics and Cultural Change in the Early Stages of Eighteenth Century Industrialization." *Journal of Social History* 25 (1992): 791–815.

Smith, S.D. "The Market for Manufactures in the Thirteen Continental Colonies 1668–1776." *Economic History Review* 51 (1998): 676–708

Sokoloff, Kenneth L. and David Dollar. "Agricultural Seasonality and the Organization of Manufacturing in Early Industrial Economies: The Contrast between England and the United States." *Journal of Economic History* 87 (1997): 288–321.

Stearns, Raymond Phineas. "Correspondence of John Woodbridge, Jr. to Richard Baxter." *The New England Quarterly* 10 (1937): 572.

Thirsk, Joan. "Industries in the Countryside." In F.J. Fisher, ed., *Essays in the Economic and Social History of Tudor and Stuart England in honour of R.H. Towney.* Cambridge: Cambridge University Press, 1961.

Thomas, Keith. "Work and Leisure," *Past and Present* 29, (1964) 50–66.

Thompson, E.P. "Time-Work Discipline and Industrial Capitalism," *Past and Present* 38(1967):56–97.

Truxes, Thomas M. "Connecticut in the Irish-American Flaxseed Trade 1750–1775." *Eire Ireland* 12 (1977): 34–63.

Tucker, Barbara. "The Family and Industrial Discipline in Antebellum New England." *Labor History* 21 (1979): 55–74.

Ulrich, Laurel Thatcher. "Wheels, Looms and the Gender Division of Labor in 18th Century New England," *William and Mary Quarterly 3rd ser.* 55 (1998): 3–38.

———. "In the Garrets and Rat holes of Old Houses," *Textiles in New England: Four Centuries of Material Life, Dublin Seminar for New England Folklife Annual Proceedings,* Peter Benes, ed., Boston: Boston University Press, 1999, 6–12.

———. "Housewife and Gadder: Themes of Self-Sufficiency and Community in Eighteenth Century New England." *To Toil the Livelong Day: America's Women at Work, 1780–1980.* eds., Carol Goroneman and Mary Beth Norton, Ithaca and London: Cornell University Press, 1987. Pages 21–34.

White, Frank G. "Heads were Spinning" The Significance of the Patent Accelerating Spinning Wheel Head." *Textiles in Early America, Design, Production and Consumption, Dublin Seminar for New England Folklife Annual Proceedings,* Peter Benes, ed., Boston: Boston University Press, 1997, 64–81.

Woodward, P. Henry. "The Manufacturing Interests of Hartford," *The New England States: Their Constitutional, Judictial, Educational, Commercial, Professional and Industrial History.* William T. Davis, ed., Boston: D.H.Hurd and Company, 1897.

C. Other Publications, Unpublished Papers and Dissertations.

Arnold, James Newell. *Vital Records of Rhode Island 1636–1850.* Providence: Narragansett Historical Society, 1892.

Atwater, Mary Meigs. *The Shuttlecraft Book of American Handweaving.* New York: Macmillan Company, 1937.

Austin, John O. *Genealogical Dictionary of Rhode Island comprising Three generations of settlers who came before 1690, with many families carried to the fourth generation.* Albany: J. Munsell's Sons, 1887.

Babcock, Stephen, comp. *Babcock Genealogy.* New York: Eaton and Mains, 1903.

Bacon, Edward Mayhew. *Narragansett Bay, Its Historic and Romantic Associations and Picturesque Setting.* New York: G.P. Putnam Sons, The Knickerbocker Press, 1904.

Bagnall, William R. *Samuel Slater and the Early Development of Cotton Manufacture in the United States.* Middletown, Connecticut: J.S. Stewart, 1890.

———. *Sketches of Manufacturing established in New York City and of Textiles Established in the United States.* ed., Victor Clark. North Andover: Merrimack Valley Textile Museum. 1977. Microfiche.

———. *The Textile Industries of the United States Including Sketches and Notices of Cotton, Woolen, Silk and Linen Manufacture in the Colonial Period(1639–1810).* Boston: W.B. Clarke and Company, 1893.

Bailyn, Bernard. *New England Merchants in the Seventeenth Century.* Cambridge: Harvard University Press, 1955.

Baker, Elizabeth. *Displacement of Men by Machines: Technological Change in Commercial Printing.* New York: Columbia University Press, 1933.

Barber, Elizabeth Wayland. *Women's Work The First 20,000 Years.* New York: W. W. Norton Company, 1994.

Bartlett, John Russell, ed. *Records of the Colony of Rhode Island and Providence Plantations in New England.* Providence: Knowles Anthony and Company, 1861.

Batchelder, Samuel. *Introduction and Early Progress of Cotton Manufacturing in the United States.* Boston: Little Brown and Company, 1863.

Ben-Atar, Doron. *Trade Secrets: Intellectual Piracy–The Origins of American Industrial Power.* New Haven: Yale University Press, 2004.

Bicknell, Thomas William. *The History of the State of Rhode Island and Providence Plantations.* New York: American Historical Society, Inc., 1920.

Black, Mary E. *The Key to Weaving: A Textbook of Handweaving for the Beginning Weaver.* New York: Macmillan, 1980.

Blake, Frances. *History of the Town of Princeton.* Princeton, Massachusetts: By the Town, 1915.

Blewett, Mary H. *Men, Women and Work: Class, Gender and Protest in the New England Shoe Industry 1780–1910. Urbana, Illinois: University of Illinois Press, 1988.*

Bogdonoff, Nancy Dick. *Handwoven Textiles of Early New England: The Legacy of a Rural People 1640–1860.* Pennsylvania: Stackpole Books. 1975.

Bowles, Ella Shannon. *Homespun Handicrafts.* New York: Benjamin Blom, Inc., 1972.

Boydston, Jeanne. *Home and Work, Household Wages and the Ideology of Labor in the Early Republic.* New York: Oxford University Press, 1990.

Bridenbaugh, Carl. *Fat Mutton and Liberty of Conscience: Society in Rhode Island 1636–1690.* New York,: Atheneum, 1976.

Brigham, Clarence Saunders. *Records of the Town of Portsmouth.* Providence: R. J. and E.L. Freeman, 1901.

Bythell, Duncan. *The Handloom Weavers: A Study in the English Cotton Industry during the Industrial Revolution.* Cambridge: Cambridge University Press, 1969.

———. *The Sweated Trades: Outwork in 19th Century Britain.* New York: St. Martin's Press, 1978.

Cady, John. "Providence House Directory containing a List of Names of Residents, and Business Firms arranged by Home and Business address in 1824." 1960. Typescript.

Cameron, E.H. *Samuel Slater: The Father of American Manufacture.* Maine: Fred L. Tower Company, 1960.

Carmichael, W.L., George E. Linton, and Isaac Price. *Callaway's Textile Dictionary.* Georgia: Callaway Mills, 1947.

Carroll, Charles. *Rhode Island: Three Centuries of Democracy.* New York: Lewis Historical Pub. Co., 1932.

Chandler, Jr., Alfred. *The New American State Papers.* Wilmington, Delaware: University of Delaware Press, 1972.

Channing, Marion L. *Textile Tools of Colonial Homes*. Marion, Massachusetts: Channing, 1971.

Chapin, Charles Value. *Alphabetical Index of Birth, Marriages and Deaths recorded in Providence*. Providence: H. Gregory Publishers, 1872.

Chapin, Howard. *Documentary History of Rhode Island*. Providence: Preston and Rounds, 1919.

Chase, J.R. *History of Washington and Kent Counties in Rhode Island*. New York: W.W. Preston Company, 1889.

Clark, Christopher. *The Roots of Rural Capitalism in Rural Massachusetts,. 1780–1860*. Ithaca, New York: Cornell University Press, 1990.

Clark, Victor S. *History of Manufactures in the United States*. Reprint 1929; New York, Peter Smith, 1949.

Cochran, Thomas. *Frontiers of Change: Early Industrialism in America*. New York: Oxford University Press, 1981.

Cole, Arthur Harrison. *The American Wool Manufacture*. Cambridge, Massachusetts: Harvard University Press, 1926.

———. ed. *Industrial and Commercial Correspondence of Alexander Hamilton anticipating his report on Manufactures*. Chicago: A.W. Shaw, 1928; Reprint New York: Augustus M. Kelley Publishers, 1968

Coleman, Peter J. *The Transformation of Rhode Island*. Providence: Brown University, 1963.

Coman, Katherine. *The Industrial History of the United States*. New York: Macmillan, 1910.

Cooke, Edwin S. Jr. "Rural Artisan Culture: The Pre-industrial Joiners of Woodbury and Newton Connecticut." Paper read before the 1983 American Studies Association Conference. Philadelphia, Pennsylvania. Mimeograph.

Coons, Martha and Katharine Koop, *All Sorts of Good Sufficient Cloth: Linen Making in New England, 1640–1860*. Andover, Massachusetts: Merrimack Valley Textile Museum, 1980.

Cooper, Grace Rogers. *Copp Family Textiles*. Washington, D.C.: Smithsonian Institution,1971.

Cott, Nancy. *The Bonds of Womanhood, "Woman's Sphere" in New England 1790–1835*. New Haven: Yale University Press, 1977.

Cottons. Lonsdale Massachusetts: Lonsdale Company, n.d.

Coyle, Stuart. "Welcome Arnold (1745–1798) Providence Merchant: The Founding of an Enterprise." Ph.d. diss. Brown University, 1972.

Dale, Christabel, ed,. *Wiltshire Apprentices and their Masters 1710–1760*. Devizes: Wiltshire Archeological and Natural History Society, Records Office, 1961.

Dalzell, Robert F., Jr. *Enterprising Elite: The Boston Associates and the World They Made*. Cambridge, Massachusetts: Harvard University Press, 1987.

Daniels, Bruce C. *Dissent and Conformity on Narragansett Bay: The Colonial Rhode Island Towns*. Middletown, CT: Wesleyan University Press, 1983.

Davison, Margurite P. *A Handweaver's Pattern Book*. Swarthmore, Pennsylvania: Margurite P. Davison Publisher, 1944.

Denison, Frederick. *Westerly and its Witnesses*. Providence: J.A. and R.A. Reid, 1878.

Doerflinger, Thomas M. *A Vigorous Spirit of Enterprise: Merchants and Economic Development in Revolutionary Philadelphia.* Chapel Hill: University of North Carolina, Press, 1986.

Douglas, Paul H. *American Apprenticeship and Industrial Education.* Vol. 95 no. 216 of Columbia University Studies in History, Economy and Public Law. New York: American Studies Press, 1968.

Dublin, Thomas. *Women at Work: The Transformation of Work and Community in Lowell, Massachusetts 1826–1860.* New York: Columbia University Press, 1979.

————. *Transforming Women's Work: New England Lives in the Industrial Revolution.* Ithaca, New York: Cornell University Press, 1992.

Earle, Alice Morse. *Homelife in Colonial Days.* 1898 Reprint. New York: Macmillan Company, 1964.

————. *In Old Narragansett.* New York: Charles Scribners, 1898.

Ellsworth, Henry L. *A Digest of Patents issued by the United States from 1790–1/1/1839.* Washington, D.C.: Peter Force, 1840.

Emory, Stephen Hopkins. *History of Taunton Massachusetts from its settlement to Present.* Syracuse: D. Mason, 1893.

Eldridge, William Henry. *Henry Genealogy.* Boston: T.R. Marvin and Son, 1915.

English, Walter. *The Textile Industry: An Account of the Early Inventions of Spinning, Weaving and Knitting Machines.* London: Harlow Longmans, 1969.

Erdhardt, John G. *History of Rehoboth, Seekonk, Swansea, Attleboro, East Providence, Barrington and Pawtucket.* Seekonk: J.G. Erdhardt, 1983.

Federal Writer's Project, *Rhode Island: A Guide to the Smallest State.* Boston, Houghton Mifflin Co, 1937.

Fields, Edward, Horatio Rogers and George Moulton Carpenter, eds., *Early Records of the Town of Providence.* Providence: Record Commissioners, 1894.

Filby, William P. and Mary K. Meyer, ed. *Passenger and Immigration Lists Index.* Detroit: Gale Research Company, 1981.

Fowler, Gail B. "Rhode Island Handloom Weavers and the Effects of Technological Change 1790–1860." Ph.d. diss. University of Pennsylvania. 1984.

Fuller, Oliver Payson, *The History of Warwick.* Providence: Angell, Burlingham and Co., 1875.

Gibb, George Sweet. *The Saco Lowell Shops: Textile Machinery Building in New England 1813–1849.* New York: Russell and Russell, 1969.

Gilkeson, Jr., John S., *Middle-Class Providence, 1820–1940.* Princeton: Princeton University Press, 1986.

Goodale, A.M. *The Early History of the Power Loom.* Boston: n.p.,1898.

Goodrich, Massena, Historical Sketch of the Town of Pawtucket. Pawtucket: Nickerson, Sibley Company, 1876.

Gordon, Beverly, *The Final Steps: Traditional Methods and Contemporary Applications for Finishing Cloth by Hand.* Loveland Colorado: Interweave Press, 1982.

Gras, N.S.B. and Henrietta Larson. *Casebook in American Business History.* New York: Crofts, 1939.

Greven, Phillip J. Jr. *Four Generations: Population, Land and Family in Colonial Andover, Massachusetts.* Ithaca, New York: Cornell University Press, 1970.

Grieve, Robert. *An Illustrated History of Pawtucket and Central Falls.* Pawtucket: Pawtucket Gazette and Chronicle, 1897.

Grieve, Robert and John P. Ferald. *The Cotton Centennial 1790–1890.* Providence: J.A. and F.A. Reid Publishers and Printers, 1891.

Griswold, S.S. *Historical Sketch of the town of Hopkinton 1757–1876.* Hope Valley: L.W. A. Cole, Job Printers, 1877.

Gunn, Susan. "Tramp as Writ or Weaving in Deerfield prior to 1800." Historic Deerfield Summer Fellowship Program. 11 Aug. 1974. Typescript.

Hafter, Daryl. "Introduction." In *A Theoretical Framework for Women's Work in Forming the Industrial Revolution in European Women and Pre Industrial Craft.* Daryl Hafter, ed., Bloomington Indiana: Indiana University Press, 1995. np.

Harrison, Arthur Cole, ed., *Industrial and Commercial Correspondence of Alexander Hamilton anticipating his Report on Manufactures.* Chicago: A.W. Shaw and Company 1928.

Hayes, John L. *American Textile Machinery: Its Early History, Characteristics, Contributions to the Industry of the World, Relation to Other Industries and Claims for National Recognition.* Cambridge, Massachusetts: University Press, J. Wilson and Sons, 1879.

Hazard, Caroline. *Thomas Hazard, son of Robert called College Tom.* Boston: Houghton Mifflin and Company, 1893.

———. ed., *Nailer Tom's Diary Otherwise the Journal of Thomas B. Hazard of Kingstown Rhode Island 1778 to 1840.* Boston: Merrymount Press, 1930,

Hazard, Thomas Robinson. *Miscellaneous Essays and Letters.* Philadelphia: Collins Printers, 1883.

Hedges, James B. *The Browns of Providence Plantations the Nineteenth Century.* Providence: Brown University Press, 1968.

Hess, Katherine Paddock. *Textile Fibers and their Use.* New York: J.B. Lippincott, 1958.

Hindle, Brook. *Emulation and Invention.* New York: New York University Press, 1981.

——— and Steven Lubar. *Engines of Change: The American Industrial Revolution 1790–1860.* Washington, D.C.: Smithsonian Institution Press, 1986.

Hitz, Elizabeth. *A Technical and Business Revolution: American Woolens to 1832.* New York: Garland Publishing, Inc., 1986.

Hood, Adrienne Dora. "Organization and Extent of Textile Manufacture in 18th Century Rural Pennsylvania: A Case Study of Chester County." Ph.d. diss., UCSD, 1988.

———. *The Weaver's Craft Cloth, Commerce, and Industry in Early Pennsylvania.* Pennsylvania: University of Pennsylvania Press, 2000.

Huntington, Ellsworth. *Civilization and Climate.* New Haven: Yale University Press, 1924.

———. *The Redman's Continent: Chronicles of America.* New Haven: Yale University Press, 1919.

Hutchinson, Thomas. *History of the Colony and Province of Massachusetts Bay.* ed., Lawrence Mayo, Cambridge: Harvard University, Press, 1936, I, 67.

James, Sydney V. *Colonial Rhode Island: A History.* New York: Scribner's, 1975

Jeremy, David J. *Transatlantic Industrial Revolution: The Diffusion of Textile Technologies between Britain and America, 1790–1830.* Cambridge: MIT Press, 1981.

———. *Henry Wansey and His American Journal, 1794.* Philadelphia: American Philosophical Society, 1970.

Johnson, Elizabeth and James L. Wheaton, IV, comps. *History of Pawtucket Rhode Island, Reverend David Benedict's Reminiscences and New Series.* Pawtucket: Spaulding House Publications, 1986.

Jones, Daniel P. *The Economic and Social Transformation of Rural Rhode Island 1780–1850.* Boston: Northeastern University Press, 1992.

Kessler-Harris, Alice. *Out to Work: A History of Wage-Earning Women in the United States.* New York: Oxford University Press, 1982.

Kimball, Gertrude B. *Pictures of Rhode Island in the Past 1642–1833 by Travelers and Observers.* Providence: Preston and Rounds, 1900.

Krapf, Robert Cooper. "History of the Growth of the Woolen Worsted Industry in Rhode Island." MA Thesis, Brown University, 1938.

Kulik, Gary. "The Beginnings of the Industrial Revolution in America: Pawtucket, Rhode Island 1672–1829." Ph.D. diss., Brown University, 1980.

Lakwete, Angela. *Inventing the Cotton Gin: Machine and Myth in Antebellum America.* Baltimore: Johns Hopkins Press, 2003.

Landes, David S. *The Unbound Prometheus: Technological Change and Industrial Development in Western Europe from 1750 to the Present.* London: Cambridge University Press, 1969.

Langworthy, William Franklin. *The Langworthy Family.* New York: William F. and Orthello S. Langworthy Publishers, 1940.

Leavitt, Thomas., ed. *The Hollingworth Letters: Technical Change in the Textile Industry 1826–1837.* Cambridge, Massachusetts: MIT Press, 1969.

Leggett, M.D. *Subject Matter Index of Patents for Inventions issued by the United States Patent Office from 1790 to 1873 inclusive.* Washington, D.C.: Government Printing Office, 1874.

Little, Francis. *Early American Textiles.* New York: Century Company, 1931.

Lough, Jr., George J., "The Champlins of Newport: A Commercial History." Ph.d. diss., University of Connecticut, Storrs, 1977.

Lozer, John W. *Taunton and Mason: Cotton Machinery and Locomotive Manufacture in Taunton Massachusetts 1811–1861.* New York: Garland, 1986.

Malone, Dumas. *Dictionary of American Biography.* New York: Charles Scribners, 1936.

Mayer, Kurt B. *Economic Development and Population Growth in Rhode Island.* Providence, Rhode Island: Brown University, 1953.

McGaw, Judith. *Most Wonderful Machine: Mechanization and Social Change in Berkshire Paper Making 1801–1885.* Princeton: Princeton University Press, 1987.

McLoughlin, William G. *Rhode Island: A Bicentennial History,* New York: W.W.Norton Company, 1978.

Merrill, Gilbert R., Alfred Macormac and Herbert R. Mauersberger. *American Cotton Handbook: A Practical Text and Reference Book for the Entire Cotton Industry.* New York: Textile Book Publishers, 1949.

Meyer, David E. *The Roots of American Industrialization*. Baltimore: Johns Hopkins, 2003.

Miller, Perry. *Roger Williams*. Indianapolis: Bobbs-Merrill, 1953.

Mitchie, Thomas S. "The Craftsmen of Roxbury Massachusetts: Clock making in the Early Nineteenth Century." Paper read before the 1983 American Studies Association Conference. Philadelphia, Pennsylvania. Mimeograph

Mohanty, Gail Fowler. "Unnoticed Craftsmen Noted: Commercial Handloom Weavers and Weaving in Essex County Massachusetts 1690–1790." In preparation.

Montgomery, Florence. *Textiles in America, 1650–1870*. New York: W.W. Norton Company, 1983.

More, Charles. *Skill and the English Working Class*. New York: St. Martin's Press, 1980.

Murray, Norman. *The Scottish Handloom Weavers 1790–1850: A Social History*. Edinburgh: John Donald Publishers, Ltd., 1978.

Museum of American Textile History, *Homespun to Factory Made: Woolen Textiles in America (1776–1816)* N. Andover: Museum of American Textile History, 1977.

Navin, Thomas R. *The Whitin Machine Works since 1831: A Textile Machinery Company in an Industrial Village*. New York: Russell and Russell, 1969.

Nebiker, Walter. *Historic and Architectural Resources of South Kingstown*. Providence: Rhode Island Historic Preservation Commission, 1984.

———. *Historic and Architectural Resources of Westerly*. Providence: Rhode Island Historic Preservation Commission: 1978.

Nye, David. *America as Second Creation: Technology and the Narrative of New Beginning*. Cambridge: MIT Press, 2003.

O'Hearn, Denis. *The Atlantic Economy: Britain: the United States and Ireland*. New York: Manchester University Press, 2001.

Pinchbeck, Ivy. *Women Workers and the Industrial Revolution 1750–1850*. New York: Augustus M. Kelley Publishers, 1969.

Plummer, Alfred. *The London Weaver's Company, 1600–1700*. New York: Routledge and K. Paul, 1972.

Pollard, Sidney. *Genesis of Modern Management*. Cambridge: Harvard University Press, 1965.

Prude, Jonathan. *The Coming of the Industrial Order: Town and Factory Life in Rural Massachusetts 1810–1860*. New York: Cambridge University Press, 1985.

Rising, Winifred and Percy Millican, comps. *An Index of Indentures of Norwich Apprentices Enrolled with the Norwich Assembly Henry VII to George II* Norfolk: Norfolk Record Society, 1959.

Rivard, Paul E. *The Home Manufacture of Cloth: 1790–1840*. Pawtucket: Slater Mill Historic Site, 1974.

———. *A New Order of Things: How the Textile Industry Transformed New England*. Hanover, NH: University Press of New England, 2002.

Rule, John. *The Experience of Labour in Eighteenth Century English Industry*. New York: St. Martins, 1981.

Safner, Isadora M. *The Weaving Roses of Rhode Island*. Loveland, Colorado: Interweave Press, 1985.

Scranton, Phillip. "Milling About: Paths to Capitalist Development in the Philadelphia Textile Industry 1840–1865." Paper read before the Social Science History Association Meetings. Nashville, Tennessee: 22–25 Oct. 1981. Mimeograph.

———. *Proprietary Capitalism: The Textile Manufacture in Philadelphia 1800–1885*. New York: Cambridge University Press, 1983.

Seybolt, Robert Francis, *Apprenticeship and Apprenticeship Education in Colonial New England and New York*. New York: Arno Press, 1969.

Shelton, Cynthia. *The Mills of Manayunk: Industrialization and Social Conflict in the Philadelphia Region 1781–1837*. Baltimore: Johns Hopkins University Press, 1986.

Smith, H.J., ed., *Warwickshire Apprentices and their Masters 1710–1760*. Oxford: Dugdale Society at the University Press, 1975.

Smith, Merritt Roe. *Harper's Ferry Arsenal and the New Technology: The Challenge of Change*. New York: Cornell University Press, 1977.

Snow, Edwin M. , ed., *Alphabetical Index of Births, Marriages and Deaths recorded in Providence*. Providence: S.S. Rider, 1867–1870.

Steere, Thomas. *History of the Town of Smithfield, Rhode Island*. Providence: R.J and E.L. Freeman, 1881.

Taussig, F.W. *The Tariff History of the United States*. New York: G. P. Putnam's Sons, 1931.

Thompson, Edward Palmer. *The Making of the English Working Class*. New York: Pantheon Press, 1963.

Thompson, Mack. *Moses Brown: Reluctant Reformer*. Chapel Hill: University of North Carolina Press, 1962.

Tryon, Rolla Milton. *Household Manufactures in the United States*. Chicago, 1917; Reprint New York: A. M. Kelley, 1966.

Tucker, Barbara. *Samuel Slater and the Origins of the Textile Industry 1790–1860*. Ithaca, New York: Cornell University Press, 1984. .

Ulrich, Laurel Thatcher. *A Midwife's Tale: The Life of Martha Ballard, Based on Her Diary, 1785–1812* . New York: Alfred A Knopf, 1990.

———. *Goodwives: Image and Reality in the Lives of Women in Northern New England 1650–1750*. New York: Alfred A. Knopf, 1982.

———. *The Age of Homespun Objects and Stories in the Creation of an American Myth*. New York: Alfred A. Knopf, 2001.

Van Slyck, J.D. *Representatives of New England Manufactures*. Boston: Van Slyck and Company, 1879.

Vogel, Marjorie J. *Brief History of the Peace Dale Mill and Hazard Family Legacy*. Narragansett: Narragansett Historical Society, 1988.

Wallace, Anthony F.C. *Rockdale: The Growth of an American Village in the Early Industrial Revolution*. New York: Alfred A. Knopf, 1978.

Ward, Barbara McLean. "Urban Craft Structure and Artisan Culture in Early 18th Century Boston: The Evidence of the Goldsmith Trade." Paper read at the 1983 American Studies Association Conference. Philadelphia, Pennsylvania. Mimeograph.

Ware, Caroline F. *Early New England Cotton Manufacture: A Study of Industrial Beginnings*. New York: Russell and Russell, 1966.

Weedon, William Babcock. *Early Rhode Island: A Social History of the People.* New York: Grafton Press, 1910; Reprint Williamstown Massachusetts: Corner house Press, 1978.

———. *Economic and Social History of New England 1620–1785*. 1890 Reprint; New York, Hillary House, 1963.

Weston, Thomas. *History of the Town of Middleboro* Boston: Houghton Mifflin, 1906.

Wingate, Isabel B. *Fairchild's Dictionary of Textiles*. New York: Fairchild Publishing Company, 1979.

Withey, Lynne. *Urban Growth and Colonial Rhode Island: Newport and Providence in the 18th Century.* Albany: State University of New York, 1984.

Wright, Chester Whitney. *Wool Growing and The Tariff: A study in the Economic History of the United States.* Cambridge, Massachusetts: Harvard University Press, 1910.

Wroth, Lawrence C. *The Voyages of Giovanni da Verrazano.* New Haven: Yale University, 1970.

Index